Patterns of the Past

Interpreting Ontario's History

A collection of historical articles published on the
occasion of the centenary of the Ontario Historical
Society

Edited by
Roger Hall, William Westfall, and Laurel Sefton MacDowell

Dundurn Press
Toronto & Oxford
1988

Co-ordinating editor: Freya Godard
Design and Production: Andy Tong
Printing and Binding: Gagné Printing Ltd., Louiseville, Quebec, Canada

The Ontario Historical Society wishes to acknowledge the generous financial assistance provided by the Ontario Ministry of Culture and Communications, Lily Oddie Munro, Minister. The publisher wishes to acknowledge the generous assistance and ongoing support of **The Canada Council, The Book Publishing Industry Development Programme** of the **Department of Communications** and **The Ontario Arts Council.**

Canadian Cataloguing in Publication Data

Main entry under title:

Patterns of the past

Includes bibliographical references.
ISBN 1-55002-035-8 (bound) ISBN 1-55002-034-X (pbk.)

1. Ontario - History. I. Hall, Roger, 1945-   .
II. Westfall, William, 1945-   . III. MacDowell,
Laurel Sefton, 1947-   .

FC3061.P38 1988   971.3   C88-093669-X
F1058.P38 1988

Dundurn Press Limited   **Dundurn Distribution Limited**
1558 Queen Street East   Athol Brose, School Hill,
Toronto, Canada   Wargrave, Reading
M4L 1E8   England
                                         RG10 8DY

Table of Contents

Foreword

A century ago Ontario society was beginning to gain a sense of itself as a distinct community. Part of this awareness was manifested in a general desire to understand and preserve both the memory and the physical aspects of Ontario's past at a time when rapid social and economic change threatened to obliterate many of the landmarks that had helped to identify the common experience of the people. Such celebrations as those that marked the hundredth anniversary of the coming of the United Empire Loyalists and the glorification of the War of 1812 were all a part of this widespread cultural movement.

To help preserve the physical aspects of Ontario's past, a number of groups were drawn together in 1888 in "The Pioneer Association of Ontario," which was reconstituted and expanded in 1898 as the Ontario Historical Society. The work of preservation began on a rather small scale but has grown remarkably over the last century to the point where the Society is now a leading advocate in the movement to preserve and propagate the history of the province. This fine collection of new essays celebrates the centenary of the Ontario Historical Society and helps to carry on the original mandate of the Society.

Over the last hundred years there have been many changes in the Society. It has grown to more than 2,000 members, it publishes a well-established scholarly journal, *Ontario History*, it conducts workshops and outreach programs that bring history to new groups and new generations, and it works closely with the Ontario government and other groups to preserve the heritage of the province.

Through this period of growth, the objectives of the Society have remained largely the same. The Society continues to be a focal point for matters related to the province's heritage, bringing together local historical societies, enthusiastic amateur students of the past, and a growing number of academic historians, as well as teachers and government officials. Heritage appreciation, which began with the preservation of historical artifacts and documents, now embraces not only a wide range of historical evidence — from buildings to bridges, from city streets to rural vistas — but also the attempt to present this evidence in a way that can convey meaning, self-knowledge, and awareness to Ontario society at large.

Such awareness is also cultivated through a program of scholarly publication. Begun as *Papers and Records* of the Ontario Historical Society, and now continued as *Ontario History*, the flagship publication of the Society is one of the oldest historical journals in Canada. Over the years the journal has expanded upon its original interest in the publication of historical documents to include articles, book reviews, bibliographies, comments, and notices as well as other matters of importance to those interested in Ontario's past. In the process, the journal has helped to make the study of Ontario a matter worthy of scholarly interest. The Society also publishes an excellent newsletter to keep members up-to-date on recent heritage issues, and practical historical booklets for teachers and students.

Another theme in the history of the Society has been the relationship that the Society has enjoyed with the Government of Ontario. From the beginning, the Society has been a strong advocate, with the government, in matters relating to Ontario's past. It was instrumental, for example, in the establishment of the provincial archives, an institution that has now grown to become, in itself, a central element of the heritage movement. The Society has also played an important part in the preservation of Fort York and the establishment of Upper Canada Village, and has inspired the creation of museums and other heritage projects in countless Ontario communities. More recently the Society has worked closely with the provincial government to establish legislation for historical sites, heritage preservation, the erection of historical plaques, and many other related issues.

Over the last century, the definition of heritage has changed markedly for the Ontario Historical Society. From Loyalist roots, the Society has expanded to hold a more comprehensive appreciation of the diversity of our province's history; indeed, the Society has led the search for a broader understanding of Ontario's past. In the next hundred years the Society will undoubtedly face new challenges as it seeks to preserve a fascinating past and to present it to the people of Ontario.

Ian E. Wilson
Archivist of Ontario

Preface

The formal occasion for the publication of *Patterns of the Past* is the centenary of the founding of the Ontario Historical Society. In that sense, the book carries on the Society's long-standing commitment to making the province's rich and varied past better known. Over the years the Society has published documents and records, instructional pamphlets, occasional papers, bibliographies, historical monographs, and of course, *Ontario History*, the quarterly journal.

This book brings together eighteen scholars from a number of disciplines. The range of interests exhibited in these fresh interpretive essays serve to remind readers that the serious pursuit of Ontario's past has grown into a substantial intellectual industry. Ontario history is now taught at all the province's major universities; the Ontario government currently sponsors a large variety of popular and scholarly historical projects and helps to preserve the built and natural environment; as well a considerable number of publishers have emerged who devote most of their time and energies to Ontario concerns. All of this activity suggests a promising future for students of the province's history.

The OHS has a strong record in advancing the heritage movement, but its senior position amongst the province's historical groups means it has a particular responsibility to ensure that interest in the province's past is sustained at all levels. The immediate goal of this collection of essays is to fulfil that responsibility in a scholarly sense. At the same time the Editors are confident that there is much of interest here for the general reader.

Ontario's historiography — the history of historical writing in this province — has undergone dramatic changes during the last 100 years. Earlier historians concentrated upon politics and the lives of prominent citizens. During the 1930s an interest emerged in economic history, a movement that was sustained after the Second World War. More recently interdisciplinary approaches have influenced much historical writing, and there has been much more emphasis on what might be called social history. In large measure this collection demonstrates — as one might expect — the current trends in historical writing. Hence, we have interpretive articles on native peoples, rural life, women, children, ethnic groups, and the working classes. As well, the volume includes innovative articles on science in society, literature and the small town, changing urban environments, and conservation. Ontario history traditionally has been concerned with politics and business (the two often being intertwined in the Ontario past), and these topics are treated here as well, but they appear more completely in their social context. Our general purpose has been to create a volume of readings that was wide-ranging and catholic in taste, one that would show the different ways in which the patterns of the Ontario historical experience differ but do fit together, and finally, one that would attract not only scholars but also the serious reading public.

Acknowledgments

The Editors would like to take this opportunity to thank all those who have given freely of their time and abilities in the production of this book. Foremost on that list, of course, are the individual authors of the articles. When the idea for this project was first conceived, a call went out for papers, and the response was large and gratifying. In fact we could have produced a book two or three times the size of the present one had time and circumstances permitted. We should also like to thank the substantial number of scholars and specialists who took the time to read and criticize the submissions at various stages. Their anonymity is part of the process of scholarly adjudication, but we would like to take this opportunity to assure them that their efforts are greatly appreciated by authors and editors alike.

We are particularly indebted to the Ontario Heritage Foundation, an agency of the Ontario Ministry of Culture and Communications (Lily Oddie Munro, Minister) for the funding that made this publication possible.

A few people deserve specific mention. Lorne Ste. Croix and Elizabeth Price of the Ministry of Culture and Communications helped us secure financial support for the project; Kirk Howard and Jeanne MacDonald at Dundurn Press helped to facilitate the work of the editors in countless ways; Grace Matthews of the OHS office devoted much of her time to the administrative side of the project; and both Kathie Hill of Erindale College, University of Toronto, and Florence Judt of Atkinson College at York University provided invaluable secretarial assistance. Many thanks to Bruce Trigger and Alice Munro for providing illustrative material. Finally, the editors are particularly grateful to Freya Godard, our Co-ordinating Editor. Freya's tasks went far beyond the editing of the manuscript; she provided sound advice at all stages of production. Moreover, not only did she co-ordinate the submissions of eighteen individual authors, but she had to deal with the varying needs and opinions of three editors. All was performed admirably.

Roger Hall, William Westfall, Laurel Sefton MacDowell

Patterns of the Past

Interpreting Ontario's History

Edited by
Roger Hall, William Westfall, and Laurel Sefton MacDowell

FROM THE PAST
1888~1988
FOR THE FUTURE

THE MYSTERY OF THE
NEUTRAL INDIANS

Abraham Rotstein

The French who first penetrated the St. Lawrence Valley were less fortunate than their Spanish confreres in Mexico and Peru, for they failed in the end to find the El Dorado that they had so ardently sought. Instead, the nomadic hunting and gathering tribes whom they encountered in the St. Lawrence Valley lived at the margin of starvation. Father Bressani wrote that they "reflect[ed] the poverty of the Soil ... and, through necessity, fasted more than half the year."[1]

It was not long, however, before the French chanced upon an extraordinary Indian enclave in the Niagara Peninsula. In startling contrast to the terrain of its northern neighbours, this land was as lush, beautiful, and overflowing with abundance as one could imagine. Although utterly different from the elaborate cities and pyramids that the Spaniards found, it was from the beginning proclaimed to be "the earthly paradise of Canada." But this paradise was hardly destined to endure more than three and a half decades after its discovery by the French. By now, it has become a largely forgotten chapter in Canadian history — as mysterious to the modern historian as it was to the early explorers.

Etienne Brûlé had first reached the land of the Neutral nation in 1615, and his stirring accounts of the country inspired Joseph de la Roche Daillon to stay the winter among the Neutrals in 1626-27. "This country," Daillon stated, "is incomparably larger, more beautiful, and better than any of these countries.... There is an incredible number of stags... and other animals.... A stay there is quite recreating and convenient; the rivers furnish much excellent fish; the earth gives good grain, more than is needed. They have squash, beans, and other vegetables in abundance."[2] Subsequent visitors such as de Galinée also commented on the abundant fish and game and declared, "There is assuredly no more beautiful region in all of Canada."[3]

But the political status of the people of this region north of Lake Erie between the Grand and the Niagara rivers was even more exceptional than the rich ecology. The very name "la Nation neutre" that underlines this status was, in fact, a strictly European designation for the Atiouan-daronk[4] and one that highlighted their exceptional role among their neighbours. It was this political configuration of the region that proved to be a complete puzzle from the very first. Champlain put his finger on the nub of the problem as follows: "It must be understood that there is not a single tribe that lives at peace except the Neutral nation."[5]

The history of the Neutral Indians antedates the coming of the white man, and most of it is now unavailable to us. On the eve of the development of the great fur-trade routes into the interior of the continent, this extraordinary Indian institution collapsed. By 1652, after the brutal Iroquois destruction of Huronia and the dispersal of the Neutrals, this chapter was over.

This early episode has languished in obscurity for three centuries because we are still stymied by the portent of these events. Yet the curious anomaly of a neutral enclave in a sea of active hostilities, which struck Champlain and his contemporaries so forcibly, is highly illumi-nating for our understanding of the dynamics of the fur trade. Within the three and a half decades of the sparsely recorded history of the Neutrals, we may see in close-up a cross section of the political forces at play among the Indians. These very forces were soon recapitulated on the larger stage of Indian-White relations that shaped the fur trade.

Who Were the Neutrals?

Champlain knew at first hand that in the St. Lawrence Valley and Great Lakes region, intertribal relations were dominated by fierce opposition between two major groups. On the one side were the Five-Nation Iroquois and on the other, the Huron Confederacy and their Susquehan-nock and Algonkian allies (see Figure 1). Within this political-military configuration, only the Neutrals remained aloof. Despite their own skirmishes and wars with the Fire Nation (Atsistaehronons) to the west, it was the Neutrals' position vis-à-vis this Huron-Iroquois rivalry that was significant. Champlain said of the Neutrals, "Between the Iroquois and our tribe [the Huron] they are at peace and remain neutral. They are welcome with either tribe, but never venture to engage in any dispute or have any quarrel with them, although they often eat and drink together as if they were good friends."[6] This remarkable paradox in early North American history has never been adequately explained.

For the Neutral Nation, a distinct set of political arrangements was necessary to maintain the appropriate balance in Iroquois-Huron rela-tions. Living as they did between the Hurons to the north and the League of the Iroquois to the southeast, the Neutrals were strategically situated to play just such a role. We know, for example, that Neutral ter-ritory served as a meeting place between Huron and Iroquois. Com-menting in 1641, when the institution of neutrality was beginning to

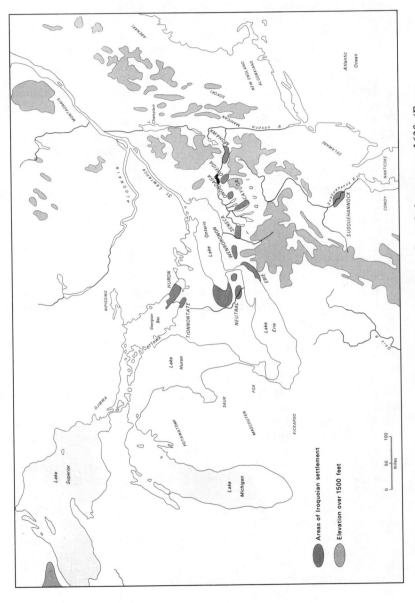

Figure 1: Distribution of Iroquoian and other tribes in the lower Great Lakes area, c. 1630. (From Bruce Trigger, The Children of Aataentsic [Kingston and Montreal: McGill-Queen's University Press, 1976, repr. 1987], Vol. I, pp. 92-93)

wane, Lalemant noted the important security setting that the Neutrals had previously provided: "Nay, even formerly, the Huron and the Iroquois, when they met in the same cabin or in the same village of this Nation, were both in security so long as they did not go out into the fields; but for some time the rage of one against the other has been so great that, in whatever place they be, there is no security for the most feeble."[7]

The Neutral Nation was a part of the larger Iroquoian language-cultural group that also included the Huron, Petun (Khiounoutatenon-non, or Tobacco Nation), Erie, Susquehannock (Andaste), and the Five-Nation Iroquois — the Seneca, Mohawk, Oneida, Onondaga, and Cayuga.[8] (The adjective "Iroquoian" as used here will refer to this larger cultural group rather than strictly to the Five-Nation Iroquois.) Although it has proved to be "notoriously difficult" to estimate the size of these aboriginal populations, the most reliable figures for the Neutrals place them in the range of 20,000 to 40,000 people before the serious epidemics of the late 1630s. They were roughly equal in size to the Huron and the Iroquois confederacies and approximately twice as large as the Petun, Susquehannock, and Erie respectively.[9] This Neutral population was distributed among some forty-odd villages and several small hamlets that were concentrated to the east of the Grand River near the Hamilton-St. Catharines district at the Western end of Lake Ontario. The territorial boundaries of this nation extended as far west as Lake St. Clair, but this western region was occupied by village settlements only in pre-historic times.[10]

Mythology and Politics

Some indication of the political significance of the Neutral Nation can be gathered from the place ascribed to them in Iroquoian mythology. According to tradition, the ten tribes of the Iroquoian language-cultural group mentioned earlier were all descended from the Neutrals. A.C. Parker noted that "[o]n both sides of the Niagara River were the villages of the Attiwanaronk or Neutral, considered an old and parent body of all the Huron- Iroquois." Among the Neutrals resided Jikonsaseh, the "Mother of Nations" or "peace queen," who ruled over the League and non-League Iroquoians alike. A lineal descendant of "the first woman born on earth," she was later succeeded by her eldest daughter.[11] It remained within her jurisdiction to preserve the neutrality of the Neutral Nation as well as maintain the military-political balance between Huron and Iroquois. In early historic times, her village of Kienuka, just to the east of the Niagara River, had a special status. It was later described as "America's first Peace Court, and the first Hague, and its location was not ill-chosen as a 'city of refuge.' " With the Seneca's dispersal of the Neutrals in 1652, Jikonsaseh was said to have been among the captives taken, thereafter to be protected by the Seneca.[12]

The common ancestry of the historic Iroquoian tribes alluded to by the "peace queen" myth is supported by both ethnographic and archaeological evidence. Lalemant writes:

> We have every reason to believe that not long ago they all made but one People, — both Huron and Iroquois, and those of the Neutral Nation.... But it is probable that, in progress of time, they have become removed and separated from one another — some more, some less — in abode, in interests, and in affection; so that some have become enemies, others Neutral, and others have remained in some more special connection and communication.[13]

Archaeological work suggests that the Ontario Iroquoian tribes descended from a common "Middleport" base centred on the Niagara Peninsula between 1300 and 1400.[14] This culture was parallelled by the Oak Hill Horizon in New York State from which the historic Iroquois tribes developed. There would also appear to be an extensive reciprocal interaction between these two cultures.[15] Despite subsequent doubts about the historical authenticity of the "peace queen" account, therefore, the myth itself illuminates both the longevity and the importance of the Neutrals' special political role.

Neutral territory for example, provided a special sanctuary to various refugees, including Brûlé, who was released from Iroquois captivity into Neutral territory in 1616.[16] Three further instances are recorded in the *Jesuit Relations*. Le Jeune recounts the story of a Huron who had escaped from an Iroquois war party, was found by some Neutral men, and brought to safety in their village. Similarly, a young Huron girl, having escaped from Iroquois captivity, was brought to a Neutral village, "in a land of peace." A right of asylum, therefore, existed for both Iroquois and Huron so long as they remained within the Neutral villages. One unfortunate Seneca, returning from an attack on a Huron village, "was hotly pursued and caught by the Hurons at the gates of the Aondironnons [a tribe of the Neutral Nation], before he had time to enter any cabin. For that reason he was considered a fair capture."[17]

Adjoining tribes went to great lengths to prevent the penetration of Neutral territory by the French, so as not to upset this delicate political balance in native relations. When wintering with the Neutrals in 1626-27, Daillon, the French Recollet, encountered hostility among them because of previous Huron propaganda:

In a word, the Hurons told them so much evil of us to prevent their going to trade; that the French were unapproachable, rude, sad, melancholy people, who lived only on snakes and poison; that we eat thunder, which they imagine to be an unparalleled chimera, relating a thousand strange stories about it; that we all had a tail like animals; that the women have only one nipple in the center of the breast; that they bear five or six children at one time, adding a thousand other absurdities to make us hated by them and prevent their trading with us.[18]

Yet to insist, as Daillon did, that the Hurons' attempts to limit contact between the French and the Neutrals was "so that they might have the trade with these nations themselves exclusively, which is very profitable to them"[19] fails to appreciate the full nature of the problem. The Hurons apparently did not object to French traders or priests visiting the Neutrals, for Brûlé and others had travelled to Neutral villages on several occasions.[20] Lalemant wrote: "Many of our Frenchmen who have been here [among the Hurons] have, in the past, made journeys in this country of the Neutral Nation for the sake of reaping profit and advantage from furs and other little wares that one might look for."[21] What the Hurons did object to, however, was the French *wintering* among the Neutrals, which would suggest the establishment of a more permanent and formal political relationship. Such an occurrence would certainly have had an impact upon the larger framework of native trade and politics in the area.

It was not only the Hurons, but other tribes such as the Ottawas (Cheveux Relevés), who also sought to prevent French intrusion.[22] More important however, the Neutrals themselves adhered strictly to these political arrangements and would hardly have done so if the sole purpose of these arrangements had been to exclude them from trading directly with the French. Thus when Brébeuf and Chaumonot subsequently visited Neutral country in 1640, they encountered hostility similar to that experienced by Daillon. Gifts of peace were refused by the Neutrals, who declared, "do you not know ... the danger in which you are and in which you are putting the country?" Lalemant wrote, "[The Neutrals] threatened the Fathers with the arrival of the Sonontwehronons [the Seneca]" and "As our presents had not been accepted, that meant there was no security for them [the French Fathers] in the country."[23]

These replies by the Neutrals to Brébeuf and Chaumonot seem in retrospect to be a reference to the mounting tensions and a curious premonition of the Iroquois invasion and their own dispersal that was to follow. But at the time, the substantial intrusion of the French into the situation would certainly have disrupted the tenuous harmony existing within this neutral enclave.

Neutral Zones in North America

But what was the underlying significance of this political arrangement? It was not unique to this area of the Great Lakes, for similar instances of political neutrality have been found in other parts of North America. Harold Hickerson, the distinguished American anthropologist, has found evidence of "debatable" or "buffer" zones between the tribal territories of the Chippewa and Sioux in Wisconsin and Minnesota, and he suggests that these zones recurred throughout the Plains and Woodland regions. These buffer zones served to reduce hostilities and to aid in the sharing of game.[24]

Neutral arrangements, moreover, were not limited merely to a defined territory but in some cases included specific people or tribes in strategic locations in early North America.[25] This feature, with several variations on the theme, is most evident in various political dealings of the Iroquois. Not only did their confederacy constitute a loose political and military alliance among the Oneida, Cayuga, Seneca, Onondaga, and Mohawk, but it later came to include several "tributary" tribes. Most notable among these were the Delaware Indians. Defeated in war by the Cayugas in 1712, the Delawares were "adopted" by the Iroquois and became politically and militarily expedient as buffers or "props" along the Cherokee war trail. The Delawares were prohibited by the Iroquois from going to war unless called upon to do so, and for this reason, as Weslager notes, the Iroquois "relegated the Delaware to a position of 'women' by applying the symbolic attributes of the female to them as a nation of women, devoid of political or military power."[26]

Arrangements of this latter kind, however, were often ad hoc, informal, or transient forms of neutrality. The formal, full-scale, institutional "neutrality" of the Neutral Indians, being of such long duration, was exceptional and as such requires further explanation.

The Flint Hypothesis

One explanation for this mysterious neutrality was offered by commentators at the turn of this century along the lines of the "flint hypothesis." W.R. Harris, for example, suggested that in their control of the chert beds (a material essential to the manufacture of flint arrowheads) along the Niagara Escarpment, the Neutrals occupied a crucial political locale. "The Iroquois were too shrewd and the Huron too far seeing to make an enemy of a people who manufactured the material of war, and controlled the source of supply."[27] The argument continues that when the Dutch began to supply the Iroquois with firearms, this role of the Neutrals was no longer of any importance, which accounts for their dispersal in 1652.

The flint hypothesis may have been inspired by the seemingly parallel case of the reddish catalinite stone used to make the Indian calumet or peace pipe. This stone could only be found in one place in the Coteau des Prairies in southwestern Minnesota. This area was regarded by the local Indians as a neutral zone, or Country of Peace.[28] Several similar cases have also been recorded. The salt deposits of the Zuñi in New Mexico and of the Pomo Indian territory in California, arrowheads in the southeastern United States, vermilion near Chibougamau in northeastern Canada, and the red ochre of the Cypress Hills in the Canadian northwest are all examples of resources that conferred a special neutral status on the places where they were found.[29]

There is an apparent similarity in the flint explanation to these latter cases, where strategic or vital goods are found only in one place. The chief problem with the flint hypothesis however, is that flint beds were not located exclusively on Neutral territory but have been found in abundance in Huronia and among the villages of the Iroquois. Hence, though the location of an essential resource might explain the special status of other areas, it is not a suitable explanation in the case of the Neutrals.[30]

Yet subsequent research into the Neutral Indians has failed to produce an alternative explanation. Some historians have in fact tended to downgrade the whole question into the realm of the "obvious." To George Hunt, for example, "the wonderment over Neutral neutrality is considerably stranger than the fact of their neutrality. If Indians are regarded as at all a rational people, it is hard to see what there is about their neutrality that is abnormal."[31] Professor Hunt may indeed have forgotten the astonishment of the early travellers over the non-combatant role of the Neutrals in relation to their neighbours, as well as the background in Iroquoian mythology.

But no other detailed hypotheses have yet been offered. The upshot of this extended mystery about the Neutral Indians has recently been summarized succinctly by Elsie M. Jury, who notes that "no firm reason has yet been advanced for their neutrality."[32]

The Port of Trade Hypothesis

Perhaps the answer may lie after all in the realm of trade institutions, but not in the way that Daillon conceived it when he imputed monopolistic purposes to the Hurons. Instead, we will have to disentangle ourselves from European preconceptions of tribal economic life and try to reconstruct, however tentatively, some picture of the economic milieu of intertribal trade in pre-contact North America around the Great Lakes region.

An extensive Indian trade network criss-crossed North America and antedated the arrival of the white man. Joseph Lafitau, a meticulous observer of Indian life who is regarded as the founder of scientific anthropology, wrote in 1724:

> The savage nations have always traded with each other. Their trade is similar to that of antiquity, since it is a straight exchange of staples against staples. They all have something which the others do not have, and the trade moves all these items from one group to the other. These consist of grain, wampum, furs, fur robes, tobacco, fish nets, canoes, clothes of moose hide, quills, meat from the hunt, cotton mats, cooking implements, calumet pipes, in short everything that is used for sustaining human life.[33]

Subsequent historians and archaeologists have offered ample confirmation of the pervasiveness of Indian long-distance trade, and some of the evidence will be referred to presently.

What comes to mind as a pertinent hypothesis to explain this exceptional neutrality of the Neutral Indians is Karl Polanyi's concept of the "port of trade."[34] This is a technical concept that applies specifically to the distinct features of a pre-modern society with its dynamic interaction of political, strategic, and economic forces.

The "port of trade," Polanyi states, is a "functional alternative" to modern market institutions in primitive and archaic societies. It provides a locale for the exchange of goods other than by the purely "economic" procedures of modern competition. Under modern conditions, we tend to take some of the vital underpinnings of commerce for granted: adequate policing to protect persons and goods against violence and strong-arm tactics and courts for enforcing contracts and settling legal disputes. None of these existed under the pristine conditions of intertribal relations.[35]

Thus, the port of trade serves a vital political function in that it provides the essential secure place within which trade can take place under uncertain military conditions. Given the volatility of intertribal relations in pre-contact North America, questions of politics and security had to be resolved before the occasion of trade. There could be no haphazard or casual trade relations between tribes, for that would have been too dangerous; an institutionalized relationship between trading partners in different tribes was required.

The port of trade was "a specific organ of foreign trade in non-market economies"; as such, it served as a meeting place where the necessary safety could be guaranteed for trade between normally or potentially hostile tribes. In order to facilitate this exchange, the typical port of trade would be situated in a readily accessible place, frequently, though not necessarily, at the head of a river, on a coast, or on the border between two ecological zones. "The function of the 'port of trade' is to offer military security to the host; civil protection to the foreign traders; facilities of anchorage, debarkation, and storage; judicial authorities, agreement on the goods to be traded; agreement concerning the 'proportions' of the different trade goods."[36] In this way, the port of trade was a pre-modern institution in which the security of the trader's person and his goods was the primary consideration.

A prominent example of the port of trade phenomenon in North America has been identified by Anne C. Chapman in the case of the Aztec and Mayan pre-conquest civilizations of Central America.[37] Trade was carried out amid continual warfare both between and within the Aztec and Maya empires. Like other ports of trade, the Aztec and Mayan ports of trade were located in politically weak spots on islands at the bottom of the Gulf of Mexico between the two empires. In these independent areas, the goods of distant trading people were stored. The actual distribution of these goods was controlled to a large extent by the host population. In this classic case, the inhabitants of the port of trade were not themselves involved in trade but acted only as neutral administrators.[38]

Similar examples can be found in other centuries and on other continents. In antiquity, Al-Mina and Ugarit on the North Syrian coast are amongst the earliest ports of trade, dating from the second millennium B.C. These two coastal cities served as a source of imports to the hinterland empires of Babylonia, the Hittites, and Egypt, maintaining their political neutrality at the behest of the large, powerful empires.[39] So too in the slave port of Whydah on West Africa's Guinea coast, administered trade with all the major European powers took place under the auspices of a politically neutral state.[40]

A port of trade, then, can assume a number of different political-economic forms. It may variously act as an independent organ of a small state or as the possession of a hinterland empire; its neutrality may be the result of an agreement between empires, consensus among overseas traders, or more rarely, by virtue of the port's own military or naval strength. Finally a port of trade may be linked with overseas exchange or equally well with long-distance overland trade. The point remains, nonetheless, that this pre-modern institution had several manifestations that varied in their precise nature, just as market institutions do today.

Examined within the context of Polanyi's global "port-of-trade" hypothesis and the general background of intertribal trade in North America, the "neutrality" of the Neutrals becomes less mysterious. Not only did the Huron and Iroquois Confederacies constitute the major opposing political alliances in the region, but each was involved in an extensive network of external trade. To the north of the Neutrals, the Huron occupied the agricultural region of the southeast shore of

Georgian Bay, on the margin of the Canadian Shield. Living on the border between two different ecological zones, the Hurons of this region had great potential for carrying trade between the northern hunting and gathering Algonkian tribes and the more southerly agriculturalists of the Iroquoian societies. Even in pre-historic times, contact between these two groups "centered around a reciprocal exchange of corn, nets, and tobacco for skins, dried fish and meat."[41] Thus the Hurons, who traded their surplus corn for skins to be used as clothing — a vital commodity in that climate — came to be referred to as the "granary of most of the Algonkians."[42]

To the east of the Neutrals, the Iroquois also carried out an extensive trade that, again, was predicated upon differences in ecology between the Iroquois and other tribes. Thus in the historic period the Iroquois traded surplus corn and vegetables for skins, meat, and the birch bark canoes of the nomadic Algonkian tribes to the north.[43] Stites believes that intertribal trade was the principal means by which the Iroquois obtained wampum and charms, as well as finer materials such as jasper and quartz.[44] Moreover, evidence of trade, both within the confederacy and outside it, is given by Morgan in his detailed description of foot trails running throughout Iroquois territory from Albany to Buffalo and beyond.[45]

Located between these two political and trade networks, the Neutrals inhabited the warmest part of Southern Ontario, a region that supported a rich variety of game and fish and was renowned for its hunting the year round. Jérôme Lalemant observed, "The people of the Neutral Nation greatly excel in hunting Stags, Cows, wild Cats, wolves, black bears, Beaver and other animals of which the skin and the flesh are valuable.... They have also multitudes of wild Turkeys, which go in flocks through the fields and woods."[46] They had an extensive horticulture as well, and this sedentary life, surplus of food, and strategic geographical location gave them an important role in intertribal trade. They traded their surplus tobacco, black squirrel skins, and the famous "Erie Stones"[47] with the Hurons, and one can surmise a similar pattern of intertribal exchange with the Iroquois and the Erie to the south and east.[48] Daillon also observed some local trade, namely, the arrival of ten men from the village Ouarononon (Onguiaahra, the village of an associated Neutral tribe to the east of the Niagara River), "coming to trade at our village."[49]

Yet the conventional trading activity on their own behalf is not enough to account for the Neutrals' exceptional status. What does suggest itself, however, as the key to the original problem, is the general strategic location of the Neutrals astride the main routes of intertribal trade. "For this country being the ordinary land route of some Iroquois Tribes and of the Hurons," the Neutrals were crucial to both as the major access route to more distant tribes. Historic maps show that the two key land routes running south from Huron country and west from Iroquois country led to Neutral Territory (see Figure 2). Father Le Jeune, situated in Huronia, spoke of the Neutrals as a "main gateway for the Southern tribes."[50] Similarly for the Iroquois, Neutral territory constituted the principal route to the Canadian interior. Morgan stated that the Iroquois trail passing from Albany in the east to Buffalo and Neutral country in the West

> not only connected the principal villages of the Iroquois, but established the route of travel into Canada on the west, and over the Hudson on the east. The pursuits of trade, and the development of the resources of the country in modern times have shown this to be one of the great natural highways of the continent.... [T]he establishment of this great route of travel furnishes evidence of a more general intercourse of the Iroquois with the east and the west, than has ever been ascribed to them.[51]

Though the importance of these land routes cannot be overstated, since the Iroquoian tribes travelled mostly overland,[52] the Neutrals were also strategically located for water transportation. This is clear, for instance, from Lalemant's description of travel throughout the Great Lakes and St. Lawrence waterways:

> This stream or River is that through which our great lake of the Hurons, or fresh-water Sea, empties; it flows first into the Lake of Erie, or of the Nation of the Cat, and at the end of that lake, it enters into the territory of the Neutral Nation, and takes the name of Ongiaahra [Niagara], until it empties into the Ontario or lake of saint Louys, whence finally emerges the river that passes before Quebek, called the St. Lawrence. So that, if once we were masters of the coast of the sea nearest to the dwelling of the Iroquois, we could ascend by the river saint Lawrence without danger, as far as the Neutral Nation, and far beyond, with considerable saving of time and trouble.[53]

It was precisely this route that the French were later able to exploit for the fur trade after the demise of the Neutrals, in order to gain access to Louisiana. From Lake Erie they proceeded to Detroit, then up the Maumee River to Wabash and from there down the Ohio to the Mississippi River. They secured this route by a number of forts, two of the more important ones on former Neutral ground at Niagara and

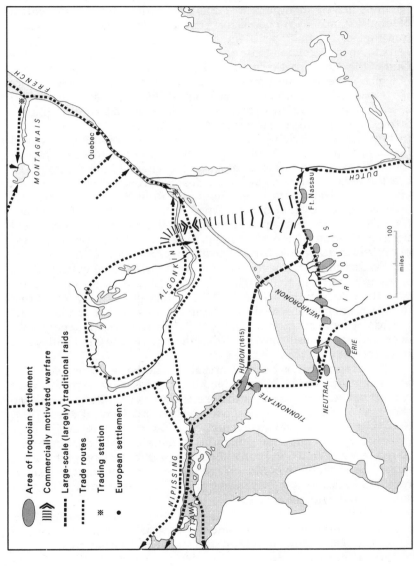

Figure 2: Intertribal relations, c. 1615. (From Bruce Trigger, The Children of Aataentsic [Kingston and Montreal: McGill-Queen's University Press, 1976, repr. 1987], Vol. I, pp. 294-295)

Detroit. This route, which was used in the later prosecution of the fur trade, was based on previous aboriginal travel.[54]

Though the evidence is by no means abundant, existing ethnohistoric accounts and archaeological studies support the view that the Neutrals played an important role as intermediaries in the movement of long-distance luxury goods from the south that were often en route to a further destination. Lalemant mentions that the Neutrals were accustomed to receiving trade goods from a distant tribe living near the Gulf of Mexico; in particular, they obtained "a kind of oyster, the shell of which serves to make porcelain beads [or wampum belts], which are the pearls of the country."[55] Archaeological work has tended to confirm such a contention. In 1920, Houghton was impressed by the quantity of Strombus (large conch shells from the Gulf of Mexico) at a Neutral site in the Niagara Peninsula. Conrad Heidenreich, William Fitzgerald, and Rosemary Prevec and William Noble have noted that the shell objects found in the Huron and Neutral villages originated from the southeast coast of the United States and were passed on by the Susquehannock and the Neutrals themselves. Similarly, Ridley's study of Neutral archaeology uncovered an abundance of shell trade beads.[56] The Neutrals also appear to have played an intermediary role in the movement north of raccoon skin robes from the Eries, and gourds for the storage of oil, which originated from further south.[57]

Furthermore, the Neutrals may have been involved in trade to the west, an occurrence that might help to explain their hostile relations with the Fire Nation of the Lake Michigan region. Ridley found that "western-oriented material motifs and artifacts verfies [sic] historical records of these contacts to the west."[58] This western influence, however, may just as easily have been derived through the Ohio Valley and from contact with the Eries.

For the post-contact period, archaeologists have discovered many European artifacts in historic Neutral villages even though direct contact between Europeans and Neutrals was slight. Ridley found no shortage of European trade goods on several Neutral sites. W.A. Kenyon's controversial excavation of a Neutral site near Grimsby revealed equally impressive amounts of material of European origin. So too Marian White's examination of Kienuka (the village of the peace queen), a probable Neutral village site east of the Niagara River, revealed indications of extensive trade in European goods.[59] On this subject Fitzgerald has concluded:

> The rapid increase in number and variety of European articles [found in Neutral sites and dated] shortly after [the Huron made] direct contact with the French in conjunction with the abundance of marine shell [also found in Neutral sites] may be interpreted as indicat-

ing the Neutral acted as middlemen between the Andaste and Huron despite the absence of ethnohistorically recorded alliances between the Andaste and Neutral until 1652. Because the Neutral were on peaceful terms with the New York Iroquois until 1647, they could have visited the Susquehannocks more easily than could the Huron.[60]

Accordingly, it is likely that the Neutrals, in their role both as traders and as intermediaries for trade between Huron and Iroquois and for goods from further points on the North American continent, saw goods from far away moving in both directions through their territory.

Parallel cases are to be found elsewhere across North America. The fishermen of the village of Wishram, at the head of the Long Narrows on the Columbia River, "acted as middlemen or factors" between tribes of the Rocky Mountains and those of the coast and plains.[61] The Mandans were to serve a similar function in exchange between a number of tribes in the American Midwest.[62] More familiar sites were Trois Rivières, Tadoussac, and Prairie du Chien, all prominent posts in the fur trade that owed their origin to previous intertribal relations.[63]

On piecing together this admittedly fragmentary evidence, we begin to find a coherent argument for the hypothesis that the region of the Neutral nation constituted a variant of Polanyi's "port of trade." Situated at the apex of a continental trade network, the Neutrals provided a place free of warfare for the flow of trade goods from the south to the Huron and Iroquois trade networks. The broad territorial domain of the Neutrals would permit reasonably safe travel to particular Neutral villages where the safety of the trader would be guaranteed. With an abundant supply of food and game, the criss-crossing of land and water routes that connected this territory with Iroquois, Huron, and Algonkian traders, Neutral villages provided an ideal place for other tribes to meet for the purposes of trade.

Though Neutrals traded actively on their own account, their other distinctive function as passive traders and as intermediaries for other trade partners made their status unique in this area. This role as purely "disengaged" hosts to trading parties from other tribes is indicated by the Neutrals' own lack of mobility on water. Daillon and other Frenchmen who visited Neutral country in the hope of establishing trade routes to Montreal were frustrated by the Neutrals' reputation as notoriously bad canoeists. In suggesting a water route from Neutral country to the St. Lawrence region, Daillon stated: "I see but one obstacle, which is that they know little about managing canoes, especially at rapids." Thus, hopes of establishing a water route to New France were frustrated from the outset. "The whole difficulty [was] that we did not know the way."[64]

Certainly this function of Neutral territory as a politically neutral meeting ground for Huron and Iroquois might well have changed over the years, and in fact there is evidence that the specifically trade-oriented functions of such an institution grew more important in the period for which we have written records.[65] And it is difficult to speculate at what point the basic configuration of political forces undergirding this unique status of the Neutrals — specifically, the Huron-Iroquois opposition — might first have come into play.[66] But at least for the period under consideration here, the port-of-trade hypothesis seems to afford a promising vantage point from which to appreciate the unique concatenation of forces that helped to keep the Neutrals neutral.

The Dispersal

If the Neutral Indians were such an important institution in early historic tribal and trade relations, the final question to be resolved is: Why were they dispersed by the Iroquois in 1652? If these neutral ports of trade were essential to the intertribal flow of trade before the extensive proliferation of the fur trade with the Europeans, why were this tribe and its institutional role so completely destroyed?

The continued neutrality of the Neutral nation clearly rested upon the maintenance of the military-political balance between the Huron and the Iroquois confederacies. Thus the dispersal of the Neutrals would have to be explained as part of the fate of this broader political-economic framework. In fact, the Neutrals were not dispersed (1652) until *after* the Five Nations' assault and their destruction of the Hurons in 1649. This suggests that the institution of neutrality was no longer of any importance after the disruption of traditional Huron-Iroquois trade and the rise of Neutral-Huron tensions in the late 1640s.[67] Archaeological evidence suggests that the Neutrals were slowly moving east toward the Iroquois in this period. Marian White's conclusion that the four Neutral villages east of the Niagara were new and temporary occupations between 1630 and 1645 supports the claim that the traditional trade patterns were taking on an increasing eastern emphasis in that period.[68]

What this suggests, therefore, is that the coming of the white man and the fur trade that ensued disrupted in certain specific ways the balance of native tribal relations and in particular the special institution of the Neutrals. Though the fur trade was still to be channelled through an extension of pre-existing native institutions and trade networks, increasing contact with the white man brought an expansion in the range and character of trade goods, particularly firearms, and a change in the source of their goods. Hence it disrupted the basic political balance that had existed among the Indians.

Yet this is quite different from the frequent assertion that European contact brought the inevitable and general destruction of native institutions. Observers have been far too hasty in concluding that the resultant new economic pressures led rapidly to the alteration or collapse of these trading institutions. For this verdict washes out prematurely the subsequent two centuries or so of the predominance of Indian institutions in the fur trade. To be sure, the fur trade brought an expansion of trade and a reordering of its direction; it displaced completely the centrality of the Neutral "ports" and created new political configurations in their place. But it did not bring about the overall destruction of basic native trade patterns.

In this regard, the striking neutrality of Albany both before and after 1652 is indeed instructive. One is tempted to conjecture as to its function from the Iroquois perspective as an alternative or complement to the Neutral port of trade. We are confronted with the extraordinary fact that in a region replete for over a century and a half with skirmishes, wars, and intrigue, Albany remained neutral and unscathed. As McIlwain points out, it was the influence of the Iroquois "that gave to Albany practical immunity from attack in all the wars between France and England, while all northern New England and even the neighbouring Connecticut valley were harried by war parties."[69] Hence, Albany remained inviolate throughout, even though it was essentially a white trading post — first in Dutch and then in British hands — and as such afforded little protection from attack. Located at the "intersection of two of the most important lines of communication on the continent," Albany offered access to Canada via Lake Champlain and the Hudson River as well as a route to the interior through the Great Lakes and the Mississippi basin. Amidst changing tides of French-English wars and shifting Indian alliances, such evidence as we have about this extraordinary phenomenon suggests that it was the Iroquois who, by general agreement, were the principal guarantors of Albany's status as a neutral enclave.[70]

After the destruction of the Neutral Indians, the Iroquois maintained and reaffirmed the important function of a neutral port of trade in a region much more closely under their supervision. The appearance of the Europeans and the introduction of firearms had altered Indian relations in the eastern Great Lakes area. The port of trade accordingly changed from a neutral area in an intermediate zone guaranteed by two strong powers (the Huron and the Iroquois) to Albany alone, a single "port" on the edge of the Iroquois sphere of influence and guaranteed solely by them.

New trade networks were reconstituted and new political links forged among Indians and Europeans. But the underlying Indian patterns that directed trade through political channels were preserved; they were merely reconstituted in a new setting.

NOTES

I am substantially indebted to Richard Kleer and to Dr. Hugh Grant for research assistance on this project. This paper will appear as a chapter in a forthcoming book on the fur trade in Canada.

1   Francesco Giuseppe Bressani was one of the missionaries at Huronia between 1645 and 1649. He had worked earlier among the Algonkians at Trois Rivières. He wrote in 1653 after returning to his native Italy. See R.G. Thwaites, ed., *Jesuit Relations and Allied Documents: Travels and Explorations*, 73 vols. (Cleveland: Burrow Brothers, 1896-1901), Vol. 38, pp. 243-45.

2   See Daillon's letter in Gabriel Sagard-Théodat's *Histoire du Canada*, 4 vols. (Paris: Librairie Tross, 1866), Vol. 3, pp. 798-811; or an English translation by H.H. Langton (manuscript, University of Toronto), pp. 106-17; or see J.G. Shea's translation, in Christian LeClercq, *First Establishment of the Faith in New France by Christian LeClercq*, 2 vols. (New York, 1881; repr. ed., New York: Ams Press, 1973), Vol. 1, pp. 269-70.

3   The explorer Galinée visited the region north of Lake Erie near Lake St. Clair in 1669 (after the dispersal of the Neutrals) and called it the "earthly Paradise of Canada":

> The woods are open, interspersed with beautiful meadows, watered by rivers and rivulets filled with fish and beaver, an abundance of fruits, and what is more important so full of game that we saw there at one time more than a hundred roebucks in a single band, herds of fifty or sixty hinds, and bears fatter and of better flavor than the most savory pigs of France. In short, we may say that we passed the winter more comfortably than we should have done in Montreal. Cited in James Coyne, ed., *Exploration of the Great Lakes, 1669-1670 by Dollier De Casson and De Bréhant De Galinée*, Ontario Historical Society, Papers and Records, Vol. 4 (Toronto: Ontario Historical Society, 1903), pp. 51-55; this series was later converted to periodical form under the title *Ontario History*.

4   The Neutrals were referred to as Atiouandaronk ("they who understood the language") by the Huron, and as Attiragenrega by the Iroquois. Although early French missionaries applied the term "nation" rather indiscriminately, recent studies have suggested that the Neutrals constituted a confederacy of distinct tribal subdivisions much like the Huron and the Iroquois. See Marian White, *Iroquois Culture History in the Niagara Frontier Area of New York State*, University of Michigan Museum of Anthropology, Paper 16 (Ann Arbor: University of Michigan, 1961); White, "Ethnic Identification and Iroquois Groups in Western New York and Ontario," *Ethnohistory*, 18 (1971), 19-38; White, "On Delineating the Neutral Iroquois of the Eastern Niagara Peninsula of Ontario," *Ontario Archaeology*, 17 (1972), 62-74; White, "Neutral and Wenro," in *Handbook of North American Indians*, Vol. 15, *Northeast*, ed. Bruce Trigger (Washington: Smithsonian Institution, 1978), pp. 407-11. For a good review of the ethnohistory of the Neutrals up to 1963, see G.K. Wright's *The Neutral Indians: A Source Book* (Rochester, N.Y.: New York State Archaeological Assoc., 1963).

5   *The Works of Samuel de Champlain*, 6 vols., ed. H.P. Biggar (Toronto: Champlain Society, 1929; repr. ed., Toronto: University of Toronto Press, 1971), Vol. 3, p. 227.

6   Ibid., pp. 99-100. Lalemant stated in 1641: "[The Neutrals] have cruel wars with other Western Nations, and especially with the Atsistaehronons, or Fire Nation — from which they took last year a hundred prisoners; and this year, having returned there for war with an army of two thousand men, they again brought away more than a hundred and seventy, towards whom they conduct themselves with almost the same cruelties as the Hurons do toward their enemies." *Jesuit Relations*, Vol. 21, p. 195.

7   *Jesuit Relations*, Vol. 21, p. 193. Sagard-Théodat gives a similar description in *The Long Journey to the Country of the Hurons*, ed., with an Introduction, by George M. Wrong, trans. H.H. Langton, Champlain Society Publications, Vol. 25 (Toronto: Champlain Society, 1939), p. 158.

8   The Wenro were also an Iroquoian tribe but generally held to be too small to merit separate consideration in this group. The Wenro are seen as "an isolated development from the same branch [of the Iroquois] which gave rise to the large Neutral and Erie tribal groups." J.V. Wright, *The Ontario Iroquois Tradition*, National Museum of Canada, Bulletin No. 210 (Ottawa: Queen's Printer, 1966), p. 84. According to Le Jeune, the Wenro were allied with the Neutral Confederacy:

> As long as this Nation of Wenrohronons was on good terms with the people of the Neutral Nation, it was sufficiently strong to withstand its Enemies, to continue its existence, and maintain itself against their raids and invasions; but the people of the Neutral Nation having, through I know not what dissatisfaction, withdrawn and severed their relations with them, these have remained a prey to their Enemies; and they could not have remained much longer without being entirely exterminated, if they had not resolved to retreat and take refuge in the protection and alliance of some other Nation. *Jesuit Relations*, Vol. 27, pp. 25-27.

Threatened by the Iroquois and neglected by the Neutrals, the Wenro migrated to Huronia and were absorbed by the various tribes of the Confederacy.

9   Bruce Trigger suggests that the Huron, Iroquois, and Neutral confederacies were of generally equal size, nearly 20,000 people each before the 1630s. See his *Children of Aataentsic*, 2 vols. (Montreal: McGill-Queen's University Press, 1976), Vol. 1, pp. 31-32, 94, 98, 443n. William Noble is willing to estimate as high as 40,000-45,000 people for the Neutrals, and as low as 12,000 for the Iroquois. See his "Iroquois Archaeology and the Development of Iroquois Social Organization (1000-1650 A.D.)" (Ph.D. dissertation, University of Calgary, 1968), pp. 43-44.

10   *Jesuit Relations*, Vol. 21, p. 189. Cf. Marian White's discussion of the location of the Neutral villages. White, *Iroquois Culture*, pp. 25-40.

11   A.C. Parker, *The History of the Seneca Indians*, Empire State Historical Publications, No. 43 (Long Island, N.Y.: Ira J. Friedman, 1926), pp. 19-20, 44. Parker was a descendant of the Cattaraugus Seneca.

12   Parker, *The Archaeological History of New York, Part I*, New York State Museum, Bulletin Nos. 235, 236 (Albany: University of the State of New York, 1922), p. 158.

13   *Jesuit Relations*, Vol. 21, pp. 193-95.

14   J.V. Wright, *Ontario Iroquois Tradition*, pp. 94-101.

15   Donald Lenig, "The Oak Hill Horizon and Its Relations to the Development of the Five Nations Iroquois Culture," *Researches and Transactions of the New York State Archaeological Association*, 15, No. 1 (1965), 3-5, 71-77.

16   Champlain, *Works*, Vol. 3, pp. 214-24. See Trigger's discussion, *Aataentsic*, Vol. 1, pp. 305-7.

17 *Jesuit Relations*, Vol. 8, p. 151; Vol. 33, pp. 97, 83. See also William C. Noble, "Neutral Iroquois Settlement Patterns," *Canadian Journal of Archaeology*, 8, No. 1 (1984), 19: "It is well documented, for instance, that the Neutral Iroquois towns, villages and hamlets represented a symbolic sanctuary to fugitives (Sagard 1939: 158; *Jesuit Relations* 21:193; *Jesuit Relations* 45:243). Once inside a Neutral settlement, the right of asylum was immediately granted. This concept of symbolic and real sanctuary was sometimes interpreted to pertain to the entire Neutral territory (*Jesuit Relations* 33:95, 97), or at least to a symbolic division at the Niagara River. Once inside a Neutral settlement, however, there was no doubt as to the interpretation of asylum. This practice of settlement sanctuary broke down when it was first violated by the Iroquois after the Huron dispersal of 1649. The Neutrals simply surrendered Huron refugees to the Iroquois (*Jesuit Relations* 45:243; Du Creux 1951 II:566), probably in the face of war threats."

18 LeClercq, *First Establishment*, p. 267. The translation should read more correctly in one part: "one breast in the middle of their chest" (cf. the French text of Sagard-Théodat, *Histoire du Canada*, Vol. 3, pp. 803-4).

19 LeClercq, *First Establishment*, pp. 267-68.

20 Trigger, *Aataentsic*, Vol. 1, pp. 374-76, 379.

21 *Jesuit Relations*, Vol. 21, p. 203.

22 Champlain stated: "I should have liked very much to visit this tribe [the Neutrals], but the people where we were [the Ottawa] dissuaded me." *Works*, Vol. 3, p. 100.

23 *Jesuit Relations*, Vol. 21, pp. 217, 221.

24 See Hickerson, *The Southwestern Chippewa: an Ethnohistorical Study*, American Anthropological Association, Memoir 92 (Menasha, Wisconsin: George Banta, 1962). Hickerson expands the scope of this discussion in "The Virginia Deer and Intertribal Buffer Zones in the Upper Mississippi Valley," in *Man, Culture, and Animals*, ed. Anthony Leeds and Andrew P. Vayda (Washington: American Association for the Advancement of Science, 1965), pp. 43-65. Hickerson also draws our attention to the two following references. Lewis H. Morgan claimed that these neutral zones were universal throughout North America. Outside of a tribe's actual territory existed "a wide margin of neutral grounds, separating them from their nearest frontagers . . . and claimed by neither." *Ancient Society* (Cambridge, Mass.: Harvard University Press, 1969), pp. 101-2. On reading this, Frederick Engels offered a comparison with many similar phenomena in early European history:

> It is the same as the boundary forest of the Germans, the waste made by Caesar's Suevi around their territory, the *isarnholt* (in Danish, *jarnved, limes Danicus*) between Danes and Germans, the Saxon forest, and the *branibor* (Slav, "protecting wood") between Germans and Slavs, from which Brandenburg takes its name. *The Origin of the Family, Private Property and the State* (New York: International Publishers, 1972), pp. 153-54.

25 Hickerson cites the example of the Neutral Menominees who were permitted access to the debatable zone between the Chippewa and Sioux upon a negotiated agreement. *Southwestern Chippewa*, Chap. 2. Radisson mentions a "nation called among themselves Neuter; they speak the Beef and Christinos' speech, being friends to both." *The Voyage of Pierre Esprit Radisson*, ed. A.T. Adams (Minnesota: Ross and Haines, 1961), p. 147.

26 C.A. Weslager, "The Delaware Indians as Women," *Journal of the Washington Academy of Science*, 34, No. 12 (1944); cited by Frank Speck, "The Delaware Indians as Women," *Pennsylvania Magazine of History and Biography*, 71-72 (1946-47):377. When this period of subjection ended in 1756, "Sir William Johnson formally 'took off the petticoat' from the Lenapé [Delaware], and 'handed them the war belt' " Cf. D.G. Brinton, *The Lenâpé and their Legends* . . . (New York: Ams Press,

1969), p. 121. Speck notes that this tribal attribution as women has also been interpreted as a prestigious titled related to the "tribal matron" or honourable, non-combatant role as peacemakers similar to the "peace queen" of the Neutral Nation.

27   W.R. Harris, "The Flint Workers — A Forgotten People," in *15th Annual Archaeological Report*, Ontario Provincial Museum (Toronto: King's Printer, 1900), p. 34. This thesis was very popular among other members of the Provincial Museum of Ontario. See, for example, Rowland B. Orr, "The Attiwandarons," in *25th Annual Archaeological Report*, Ontario Provincial Museum (Toronto: King's Printer, 1913), pp. 7-20.

28   Cf. Jonathan Carver, *Travels Through the Interior Parts of North America in the Years 1766, 1767, and 1768*, 3rd ed. (London: C. Dilly, 1781), p. 99: "I should have remarked, that whatever Indians happen to meet at La Prairie du Chien, the great mart to which all who inhabit the adjacent countries resort, though the nations to which they belong are at war with each other, yet they are obliged to restrain their enmity and to forbear all hostile acts during their stay there. This regulation has been long established among them for their mutual convenience, as without it no trade could be carried on. The same rule is observed also at the Red Mountain . . . from whence they get the stone of which they make their pipes: these being indispensable to the accommodation of every neighbouring tribe, & similar restriction becomes needful, and is of public utility."

29   Matilda C. Stevenson wrote of the Zuñi site: "The place is neutral ground, and in times of war one was safe from the attacks of the enemy so long as one remained within the recognized limits of the lake." Because of the sanctity of the area, the neighbouring Hopi, Navaho, and Apache Tribes were "accorded complete freedom in collecting the salt, although the lake is claimed as the special mother of the various tribes." "The Zuñi Indians: Their Mythology, Esoteric Fraternities, and Ceremonies," in *23rd Annual Report*, Smithsonian Institution, Bureau of American Ethnology (Washington: Government Printing Office, 1904), p. 357. With reference to the Pomo Indian territory, see A.P. Vayda, "Pomo Trade Feasts," in *Tribal and Peasant Economies*, ed. George Dalton (Garden City, New York: Natural History Press, 1967), p. 496.

The neutrality of a group in Georgia producing arrowheads is related by a Colonel Jones:

> . . . among the Indians who inhabited the mountains, there was a certain number or class who devoted their time and attention to the manufacture of these darts. That as soon as they had prepared a general supply, they left their mountain homes and visited the sea-board and intermediate localities, exchanging their spear and arrowheads for other articles not to be readily obtained in the region where they inhabited. The further fact is stated that these persons never mingled in the excitements of war; that to them a free passport was at all times granted, even among tribes actually at variance with that of which they were members; that their avocation was esteemed honorable, and they themselves treated with universal hospitality (cited in Charles Rau, "Ancient Aboriginal Trade in North America," (1872) *Annual Report*, Smithsonian Institution [Washington: Government Printing Office, 1873], pp. 387-88).

Vermilion, the much-prized red, mercuric oxide dye, is found in the territory of the southern Mistassini. The neutrality of this area is referred to by Julius Lips, "Naskapi Law," *Transactions of the American Philosophical Society*, New Series, 37 (1947), 443. Cypress Hills was the apparent location of an ochre, similar to catalinite, used in the manufacture of pipes. Isaac Cowie noted its special status in *The Company of Adventurers* . . . (Toronto: William Briggs, 1913), pp. 303-4, and Jack Elliott discussed the existence of ochre in "Tobacco Pipes among the Hivernant Hide Hunters, A.D. 1860-1882," *Western Canadian Journal of Anthropology*, 3, No. 1 (1972), 147.

30 The so-called "flint hypothesis" appears to rest on three quite separate propositions: (1) that located in Neutral territory was the best or only source of chert in the region; (2) that the Neutrals were particularly skilled in the manufacture of flint materials; and (3) that flint arrowheads (or projectile points) were a sufficiently important trade good to warrant the neutral status of its manufacturer, the Neutrals, between the Huron and the Iroquois. More recent investigations tend to discount heavily the argument that flint was the key to explaining the neutral status of this area.

In no case, however, is the evidence unambiguous. With regard to the location of the raw materials, Frank Ridley found the beaches of Huronia to have "endless quantities of chert boulders" (*Archaeology of the Neutral Indian* (Islington, Ont.: Etobicoke Historical Society, 1961), p. 6), and Charles Wray found an abundance of local sources of chert for use by the New York Iroquois. This would suggest that the Neutrals were not particularly important suppliers of this raw material. Paradoxically, however, Heidenreich suggests that much of the flint found in Huronia originated from the outcrops of the Niagara Peninsula located in the area of the Petun and Neutrals. Conrad Heidenreich, *Huronia: A History and Geography of the Huron Indians, 1600-1650*. ([Toronto]: McClelland and Stewart, 1971), p. 228; similarly for the Iroquois, Wray states that despite numerous local deposits, "a great amount of flint was brought in to New York from neighbouring states and Canada" ("Varieties and Sources of Flint Found in New York State." *Pennsylvania Archaeologist*, 18, No. 1-2 (1948), 41.

Were the Neutrals, therefore, particularly skilled flint workers? Wilfred Jury's study of the Port Franks region of Lake Huron supports such a case in pre-historic times (*Report on Prehistoric Flint Workshops at Port Franks, Ontario*, Museum of Indian Archaeology, Museum Bulletin No. 8 (London, Ont.: University of Western Ontario, 1949); and Houghton identified historic Neutral sites near the Niagara River by the presence of numerous flint scrapers and tools. Frederick Houghton, "The History of the Buffalo Creek Reservation," *Buffalo Historical Society, Publications*, 24 (1920), 34. Ridley concurs that "an unusual quantity of chipped end-scrapers are found in Neutral middens." *Archaeology*, p. 51.

Thus, while it is likely that the Neutrals did trade chert or arrowheads, it is a different matter altogether to suggest that this exchange was so essential as to secure the tribes' neutrality. Although such cases of neutral territories resulting from the possession of vital resources have been observed in other instances (see note 24 above; see also William Fenton, "Problems arising from the Historic North-eastern Position of the Iroquois," in *Essays in the Historical Anthropology of North America*, Smithsonian Miscellaneous Collections, Vol. 100 (Washington: Smithsonian Institution, 1940), p. 187), flint was hardly so scarce or restricted a resource as to explain the Neutrals' political status.

Finally, the recent archaeological work of William Fox puts the flint hypothesis to rest fairly convincingly. The Onondaga chert located on historic Neutral territory had been a favourite source for Iroquoian and pre-Iroquoian tribes for centuries; moreover, evidence suggests that the Hurons received flint products originating from Neutral territory. Nonetheless, there were many alternative sources of chert in Ontario, in particular the Collingwood outcropping located among the Petun, and tribes were quite willing to use other sources of secondary quality. William A. Fox, "Historic Neutral Lithics," a revised version of a paper presented to the 1972 Canadian Archaeological Association Meeting, 1977; "An Analysis of an Historic Huron Attignawantan Lithic Assemblage," *Ontario Archaeology*, 32 (1979), 61-88. Despite its romantic appeal, therefore, the flint hypothesis has little ethnographic or archaeological justification.

31   George T. Hunt, *The Wars of the Iroquois: A Study in Intertribal Trade Relations* (Madison: The University of Wisconsin Press, 1940), p. 52.

32   Elsie Jury, *The Neutral Indians of South-Western Ontario,* Museum of Indian Archaeology, Bulletin of the Museums No. 13 (London, Ont.: University of Western Ontario, 1977), p. 3.

33   J.F. Lafitau, *Moeurs des Sauvages Amériquains* .. , 2 vols. (Paris: Saugrain L'aîné and C.E. Hochereau, 1724), Vol. 2, p. 332; my translation. Cf. the published translation, *Customs of the American Indians,* 2 vols., Champlain Society Publications, Vols. 48-49 (Toronto: Champlain Society, 1974), Vol. 2, p. 184. In his introduction to the Champlain Society edition, William Fenton refers to Lafitau's work as "the first blaze on the path to scientific anthropology" (Vol. 1, p. xxix).

34   For an application of the related concept of a "gateway community" to the case of the Neutral Indians, see Susan Jamieson, "Economics and Ontario Iroquois Social Organization," *Canadian Journal of Archaeology,* 5 (1981), 27.

35   Karl Polanyi, "Ports of Trade in Early Societies," *Journal of Economic History,* 23 (1963), 30-32. Reprinted in *Primitive, Archaic and Modern Economies: Essays of Karl Polanyi,* ed. George Dalton (Garden City: Doubleday, 1968), pp. 238-60.

36   Polanyi, *The Livelihood of Man,* ed. H. Pearson (New York: Academic Press, 1977), p. 95. See also Polanyi, "The Economy as Instituted Process," in *Trade and Market in the Early Empires: Economies in History and Theory,* ed. Karl Polanyi, Conrad M. Arensberg and Harry W. Pearson (Glencoe, Illinois: The Free Press, 1957; reprint ed., Chicago: Henry Regnery, 1971), pp. 243-70.

37   Anne C. Chapman, "Port of Trade Enclaves in Aztec and Maya Civilizations," in Polanyi et al., eds., *Trade and Market,* pp. 144-53.

38   Ibid., pp. 114-17.

39   Robert B. Revere, "'No Man's Coast': Ports of Trade in the Eastern Mediterranean," in Polanyi et al., eds., *Trade and Market,* pp. 38-63.

40   Rosemary Arnold, "A Port of Trade: Whydah on the Guinea Coast," in Polanyi et al., eds., *Trade and Market,* pp. 154-76.

41   Trigger, *Aataentsic,* Vol. 1, p. 174. On prehistoric trade see Trigger's discussion, pp. 168-76. Much the same point was put by Trigger in a later article on the subject ("Sixteenth Century Ontario: History, Ethnohistory, and Archaeology," *Ontario History,* 71 (1979), 210): "Longterm similarities between the Iroquoian pottery of southern Ontario and that found in what appear to have been Nipissing sites farther north suggest that from early times the Iroquoians of Simcoe county had exchanged nets, tobacco, and surplus corn for furs, dried fish and meat with these and neighbouring northern Algonkian-speaking hunting peoples."

42   *Jesuit Relations,* Vol. 8, p. 115. See Elisabeth Tooker's *An Ethnography of the Huron Indians, 1615-1649,* Smithsonian Institution, Bureau of American Ethnology, Bulletin No. 190 (Washington: Government Printing Office, 1964). With regard to Huron-Northern Algonkian trade in the early historic period, see Trigger, *Aataentsic,* Vol. 1, pp. 351-55.

43   Robert Arnold Goldstein, *French-Iroquois Diplomatic and Military Relations, 1609-1701* (The Hague: Mouton, 1969), p. 31; William M. Beauchamp, *A History of the New York Iroquois* ... , University of the State of New York, Bulletin No. 329 (Albany, N.Y.: New York State Education Department, 1905), p. 159.

44   Sarah Henry Stites, *Economics of the Iroquois,* Bryn Mawr College Monograph Series, Vol. 1, No. 3 (Lancaster, Penn.: New Era Printing Co., 1905), pp. 79-80. Stites cites the following references to the *Jesuit Relations:* Vol. 12, p. 189; Vol. 50, p. 135; Vol. 39, p. 27; Vol. 10, p. 51; Vol. 19, p. 125.

45   Lewis H. Morgan, *League of the Iroquois,* with an Introduction by William N. Fenton (Rochester, 1851; reprint ed., Secaucus, New Jersey: Citadel Press, 1972), pp. 47-48; see also Book 3, Chap. 3. Recent archaeological evidence (see note 56 below) bears out the assumption that these routes existed at least as early as the seventeenth century.

46   *Jesuit Relations*, Vol. 21, p. 195-97.

47   Le Sieur François Gendron arrived as surgeon at Sainte-Marie Among the
     Hurons in 1643, from where he travelled to Niagara Falls, a district occupied by
     the Neutrals. It was here that he learned of the curative value of Erie stones, a
     lesson that was later to make him famous as a surgeon in Europe. "At the
     bottom of certain rocks a foam was forming from the bounding waters and
     becoming a stone or rather a petrified salt which has a slight yellow tinge, which
     possessed the fine virtue of curing some purulent wounds and malignant ulcers.
     In this horrible place some Indians were living ... and they were trading with the
     people 'érienne' stones (the name being derived from the name of the lake), and
     they carried and distributed these stones to the other nations." Gendron,
     Quelques Particularitez du Pays des Hurons ... (Paris: D. Bechet and L. Billaine,
     1660), pp. 7-8; cited in Wilfred Jury and Elsie Jury, *Sainte-Marie Among the
     Hurons* (Toronto: Oxford University Press, 1954), pp. 105-7. Jury and Jury
     suggest that this stone "in all probability was the *calc tuffa*, a deposit of fluffy
     calcium carbonate from lime waters exuding from the limestone rocks." Ibid., p.
     107.

48   See Frank Ridley, *Archaeology*, p. 58; William Beauchamp, "The Origins and
     Antiquity of the New York Iroquois," *American Antiquarian and Oriental Journal*,
     8 (1886), 359.

49   LeClercq, *First Establishment*, Vol. 1, p. 268.

50   *Jesuit Relations*, Vol. 21, p. 193; Vol. 16, p. 253.

51   Morgan, *League*, pp. 47-48. Again, these earlier statements are confirmed by
     more recent archaeological evidence. See, for example, William C. Noble, "The
     Neutral Indians," in *Essays in Northeastern Anthropology in Memory of Marian E.
     White*, ed. W. Englebrecht and D. Grayson, Occasional Publication in Northeas-
     tern Anthropology, No. 5 (Rindge, New Hampshire: Department of Anthropol-
     ogy, Franklin Pierce College, 1978), p. 160: "Trading obviously constituted an
     important element in historic Neutral life, and there is much accumulating
     evidence to indicate that the Neutrals stood at an important middle position at
     the ends of two major trade networks. One route of course involved the French-
     Petun-Huron exchange system to the north, while a second linked the Neutrals
     to allies south of Lake Erie (the Wenro, Andaste and Eries) who formed a
     northern extension of the aboriginal Ohio to Mississippi River exchange system.
     This situation is borne out archaeologically, for we see the historic Neutrals
     luxuriating in riches derived from the south (steatite, marine whelk shells, wam-
     pum), as well as goods from the north (particularly European items and perhaps
     Huron corn). In exchange, the Neutrals had their own resource to trade, namely:
     finished chert items, tobacco, furs, and probably meat and rendered oil . . .
     Marine shells and iron trade axes too were obviously recycled in various
     directions." See also W.A. Kenyon, *The Grimsby Site: A Historic Neutral Cemetery*
     (Toronto: Royal Ontario Museum, 1982), p. 226: "Throughout our work at
     Grimsby we were impressed with the fact that the Neutral were a prosperous
     people with trade relations which stretched from Montreal to the Gulf of Mexico
     and from Minnesota to the Atlantic. Details of their trading practices, as of the
     trade routes themselves, may never be known. But shells from the Gulf of
     Mexico and beads from Montreal attest to the richness and complexity of the
     trade." Finally, cf. Jamieson, "Iroquois Social Organization," p. 20: "There is also
     evidence that the Neutral and eastern Algonkins were engaged in direct trade
     prior to extensive European contact and that the Huron traded among the
     Andaste in historic times (Thwaites 1896-1901, 33:185-187; Trigger 1976:245)."

52   Trigger, *Aataentsic*, Vol. 1, p. 159.

53   *Jesuit Relations*, Vol. 21, p. 191.

54   W.T. Easterbrook and H.A. Aitken, *Canadian Economic History* (Toronto:
     Macmillan, 1956), pp. 128-29.

55 *Jesuit Relations*, Vol. 21, p. 201.

56 Frederick Houghton, "The History of Buffalo Creek Reservation," p. 34; Conrad Heidenreich, "Huron," in Trigger, ed., *Handbook of North American Indians*, Vol. 15, p. 384; Fitzgerald, *Lest the Beaver Run Loose: the Early 17th Century Christianson Site and Trends in Historic Neutral Archaeology*, National Museum of Man, Mercury Series, Archaeological Survey of Canada, No. 111 (Ottawa: National Museums of Canada, 1982), p. 296; Rosemary Prevec and William C. Noble, "Historic Neutral Iroquois Faunal Utilization," *Ontario Archaeology*, 39 (1983), 43, 47; Ridley, *Archaeology*, pp. 29, 52.

57 Ridley, *Archaeology*, Vol. 1, 62-63.

58 Ridley, *Archaeology*, p. 61. See also E.J. Wahla, "The Straits of Detroit: Land of Attiwandaronk," *The Totem Pole*, 27 (1951), 1-5.

59 Ridley, *Archaeology*, pp. 22, 26, 59; Walter A. Kenyon, "Some Bones of Contention," Rotunda, 10, No. 3 (1977), 4-13; Marian White, *Iroquois Culture*, pp. 54-55.

60 Fitzgerald, *Lest the Beaver Run Loose*, p. 301.

61 A discussion of the Wishram traders can be found in Charles Grenfell Nicolay, "The Oregon Territory," originally published as an appendix to Catherine Parr Traill, *Backwoods of Canada* (London: M.A. Nattali, 1846), pp. 54-55.

62 The Mandan villages, located in the present-day state of North Dakota, mediated the exchange of guns and European goods from western tribes and the skins of western nomads in the 1700s. See Edward M. Bruner, "Mandan," in *Perspectives in North American Indian Change*, ed. Edward H. Spicer (Chicago: University of Chicago Press, 1961), pp. 187-277.

63 Champlain stated, "Savages might come freely without fear or danger, inasmuch as the said Three Rivers is a place of passage" (*Works*, Vol. 1, p. 137); Tadoussac, "From earliest times a favourite rendezvous of the Montagnais and other Eastern tribes, became under the French an important fur-trade center." (*Jesuit Relations*, Vol. 2, p. 302n). Prairie du Chien in Wisconsin was a prominent area for Indian trade and was also considered neutral ground. Recall in this connection Jonathan Carver's observation in 1766 (see note 28 above) that even the members of tribes at war with one another maintained peaceful relations while trading there. Even Nuklukahyet, at the junction of the Tanah River and the Yukon, "is a neutral trading ground to which all the surrounding tribes resort in the spring for traffic." H.H. Bancroft, cited in D. Taxay, *Money of the American Indians* (New York: Nummus Press, 1970), p. 96.

64 LeClercq, *First Establishment*, p. 266n.

65 There is debate, for example, on the question to what extent the trade networks we have examined here were in existence before the arrival in North America of European traders. For a brief summary of the two sides in this debate, see Fitzgerald, *Lest the Beaver Run Loose*, pp. 288-91.

66 Trigger warns, for instance: "It is dangerous to assume that the Huron tribes as they were known in the seventeenth century already existed at this time [viz., the sixteenth century] . . . Archaeological evidence of the joining and splitting of whole communities and segments of communities prior to historic times clearly indicates that any attempt to project the historic Huron tribes as unitary entities back into the protohistoric period is doomed to failure." "Sixteenth Century Ontario," p. 210.

67 Sagard-Théodat spoke of growing Huron-Neutral hostility in 1630 which reached the point of Huron war preparations. He claims that the Neutral were a much more populous nation than the Huron, which seems unlikely, given other population estimates. Nonetheless, the Huron were confident of the support of the Fire Nation against the Neutrals, though no warfare resulted (see Sagard-Théodat, *The Long Journey*, pp. 156-66).

68 White, *Iroquois Culture*, pp. 25-37.

69 McIlwain, Introduction to Wraxall, *Abridgement of Indian Affairs*, p. xlvi.

70   Arthur H. Buffington, "The Policy of Albany and English Westward Expansion," *Mississippi Valley Historical Review*, 8 (1921-22), 327. See also Allen W. Trelease, *Indian Affairs in Colonial New York: The Seventeenth Century* (New York: Cornell University Press, 1960), pp. 115, 223-24, and Bruce Trigger, "The Mohawk-Mahican War (1624-28): The Establishment of a Pattern," *Canadian Historical Review*, 52 (1971), 276-86.

RURAL CREDIT AND RURAL DEVELOPMENT IN UPPER CANADA, 1790-1850

Douglas McCalla

In Upper Canada, as in much of the rest of colonial North America, commerce was at the centre of the financial and credit system until at least the 1850s. By then, the colony had developed from an extremely marginal economy in North America into what (with the Montreal region) was about to be the heartland of the new Dominion of Canada. Upper Canada's economic health rested on its productive farm economy, in which land ownership was widely diffused and in which there was substantial rural prosperity. If it still had much potential for development, it was evidently competitive in contemporary terms; that is, it bore comparison with the farming of adjacent regions of the United States. It was undoubtedly the premier agricultural economy in Canada.[1]

In this economy, the principal local business institution, and the one component of the business system with which ordinary Upper Canadians routinely came into contact,[2] was the town or country retailer. Contrary to the widely met view that commercial capital was a distinct, essentially short-term, form of wealth, much of the local merchant's wealth, as he accumulated it, was geographically immobile. Given the lack of liquidity of the economy, he tended to find it easier to extend his local investments, for example into grist- and sawmills, than to attempt a wider spatial diversification of his capital. In addition, population density, communications and roads, and household incomes were not developed enough to support much specialization or localization anywhere in the rural economy. Only in the embryonic urban centres did some limited retail specialization begin to be possible, and only after 1830 did wholesaling emerge as a distinct business in the province.[3] Initially, wholesale firms too were general. Behind the country retailer was a system of middlemen, focused, in the case of Upper Canada, on Montreal, the chief centre of the province's import trade. Beyond Montreal the lines of credit and trade ran from Glasgow, Liverpool, and London. This system imported textiles, groceries, and iron and hardware; handled most of the exports that Upper Canada was able to produce and sell; and was often directly involved in the exchange of local produce and in physical processing, such as sawing, grinding, carding and fulling, distilling, and potash boiling.

The country merchant was also at the centre of the financing of the system.[4] Here his function was to grant credit, usually on payment terms of a year or more, on goods purchased by the farmers, artisans, labourers, and others who made up the rural economy. Such credit might be seen essentially as consumer credit, in that only a small part of it was directly for tools, equipment, and building supplies that had an obvious function as capital. But it can also be viewed as loans in support of investment, in that it permitted farmers, and other producers, to use whatever means they possessed initially for other purposes, such as the acquisition of land or stock, or the construction of buildings, in the knowledge that they could postpone their payments for imported goods and, ideally, make them from sales of produce twelve or more months later. Because the ordinary result of a farmer's work included not merely the production and sale of crops but also the expansion and improvement of his farm, such credit helped to create capital in the province.

Although Upper Canada developed successfully under it, this business system has far more often been viewed unfavourably than favourably, especially by authors inspired by populist or Marxist interpretations of the place of lenders in a capitalist rural economy. S.D. Clark, the distinguished Canadian sociologist, expressed the critique forcefully in his analysis of the 1837 rebellion in Upper Canada:

> From his experience in dealing with the local merchants, and up through the economic hierarchy, the Upper Canadian farmer found himself in a hopelessly unprotected position. He was forced to sell at the price offered and to buy at the price demanded. Heavy capital expenditures during the first few years of settlement in the country had put him in debt, and as a result of his unequal bargaining position in buying and selling his debt mounted.
>
> A good deal of his animus was directed towards the local merchants who had him so completely in their power, but the merchants were only the visible representatives of an extensive and all-pervasive system of economic control which bound down the farmer.[5]

This opinion of rural credit has been echoed by many others. For example, Lillian Gates argued that the settlers' "need of capital to develop [land] caused them to become hopelessly indebted to the frequently denounced 'Shopkeeper Aristocracy' and eventually to lose their land."[6] Such a view of merchants has a long pedigree in the province, going all the way back to its first Lieutenant-Governor, John Graves Simcoe, who argued in 1794, "It is necessary to break through the monopoly which the merchants at present exercise over the produce of the Country."[7]

Central to the criticism of the credit system was the charge that the merchant was essentially a monopolist who manipulated the terms of exchange to his advantage. The farmer, it was implied, lacked any serious influence in his situation and, for reasons that are not clearly spelled out in the standard critique, the merchant took advantage of this helplessness to lend the farmer much more than he could repay. The long-term result was that the merchant could charge interest and eventually, if he wished, seize the farmer's land. Such views resemble those that have often been taken of the credit system in rural primary production elsewhere, such as in the fishery of Atlantic Canada. Harold Innis, for example, spoke eloquently of "the glaring evils of the truck system" there.[8]

There are many flaws in this description of the credit system, as the literature on the topic has begun to make clear.[9] The critics offered virtually no economic analysis, presenting neither evidence nor theory to explain why local prices fluctuated in a world of such monopoly power. Nor was it clear why the merchant should regard the legal rate of interest, 6 per cent in Upper Canada, as sufficient return on the capital tied up in farmers' accounts, or why he should deliberately lend so much that he could eventually take over his customer's farm. He could not farm it himself, and nowhere did tenancy become the main form of land tenure in Upper Canadian agriculture. It must be presumed, therefore, that sooner or later the merchant intended to resell the land to another unsuspecting intending farmer so as to start the cycle over again. Here, it was necessary for the merchant to realize a high enough price on the resale to compensate for his costs in carrying the previous farmer's debts.

Curiously enough, despite the critics' sympathy for those they see as victims, they have seldom recognized the implicit condescension of their view that farmers were unable to perceive what was occurring and thus to avoid at least some of the traps that were laid for them. In this respect it is important to recall that Upper Canada was an immigrant society, to which people had come and continued to come voluntarily, adjacent to the dynamic American economy, to which it was possible to move and from which came considerable information on living standards, prices, and costs.[10]

His role in the credit system was not usually something the country merchant set out to acquire. William Gilkison, launching the town of Elora, warned his storekeeper there, "This country is bad to collect debts.... I would rather keep the goods than trust foolish persons."[11]

Very quickly, the new merchant found he could not sell unless he extended credit. As Benjamin Tett, newly launched in a store at a favourable location on the Rideau Canal, reported to his principal supplier, "For the short time I have commenced business here my Sales have been considerable, nearly all however upon credit."[12] Whatever the terms the merchant might set, moreover, his debtor had some ability to control when and how he repaid the debt.

The process of credit extension is well illustrated by the firm of Barker and Stevenson in what would become the town of Picton (see Table 1). Opened during 1825, this firm doubled its yearly sales in five years, and by the early 1830s it had 250 to 300 customers on its books and annual sales of over £2,000. Such sales made it a relatively substantial country retail firm.[13] After just one year of trade, the value of debts due to it by customers was its principal asset, greatly exceeding the value of inventory (as taken at or near its annual low point). In relation to sales of the previous year, customer debts mounted rapidly, and by 1832, immediately following two excellent years in the province's wheat economy, the debts due to it exceeded its annual sales. That overdue debts were growing is indicated by the rising value of promissory notes, for these represented a later stage in a merchant's collection process, as he formalized his book debts in a way to permit lawsuits or the securing of bank credit. During 1832 no payments of any kind (even in the form of a promissory note) were made on over twenty per cent of Barker and Stevenson accounts.[14]

Not surprisingly, it soon became a main goal of the retailer to secure payment of the sums due him. Here he encountered Upper Canada's chronic liquidity problem: "cash," that is specie or bank notes, was scarce in rural Upper Canada, because of the ill-conceived currency laws[15] and the limited development of financial institutions in the province before the 1830s, and possibly because most Upper Canadians were so indebted that they tended to pay away money when they saw it. Of thirteen retail firms in the province whose records it has been possible to analyse, only two recorded as much as 20 per cent of all credits on customer accounts in cash. For Barker and Stevenson, from 1829 to 1837, just 10 per cent of all credits were in the form of cash.[16]

When the merchant sought a role in handling local exports, it was not just in search of further profit, but also as a way for both his customers and him to make payments. Here he had every incentive to look for markets for the full range of products that the local economy might produce. Thus, Benjamin Tett entered the steamboat wood business: "Several of my Customers being desirous of getting in Steam Boat wood, I would engage to supply during the present winter four hundred Cords."[17] The process is also illustrated by Barker and Stevenson's produce shipments (see Table 2). Not only wheat, usually seen as this economy's staple export, but pork, staves, and timber were shipped to Montreal for sale.

When the merchant sought a role in handling local exports, it was not just in search of further profit, but also as a way for both his customers and him to make payments. Here he had every incentive to look for markets for the full range of products that the local economy might produce. Thus, Benjamin Tett entered the steamboat wood business: "Several of my Customers being desirous of getting in Steam Boat wood, I would engage to supply during the present winter four hundred Cords."[17] The process is also illustrated by Barker and Stevenson's produce shipments (see Table 2). Not only wheat, usually seen as this economy's staple export, but pork, staves, and timber were shipped to Montreal for sale.

Table 1
Credit Extended by Barker and Stevenson
1825-1833

	A Book Debts Due £	B Due on Promissory Notes £	C Total Customer Debts £	D Sales in Calendar Year £	E C/D (prev. year) x 100 %	F Inventory £
1825				676		
May 25, 1826	273	21	294	1,213	43	119
June 13, 1827	455	72	527	1,484	43	64
June, 1828	658	113	771	1,642	52	120
May 1, 1829	1,196	177	1,373	1,801	84	228
June 5, 1830	1,300	457	1,757	1,999	98	123
June 7, 1831	1,558	522	2,080	2,448	104	239
June 1, 1832	1,723	845	2,568	2,320	105	338
June 1, 1833	1,684	968	2,652	2,326	114	358

Source: University of Guelph Archives, Goodwin-Haines Collection, William Grant Papers, XR1 MS A131002, Barker and Stevenson Inventory Book, plus memo of sales, 1825-33.

Table 2
Produce Transactions, Barker and Stevenson (Principal Items),
1826-1837
(Figures are values in £ Hfx. cy.)

	Wheat & Flour	Pork	Staves	Total Wood[a]	Potash	Total	Percentage Wheat & Flour
A. Shipped to Lower Canada[b]							
1826	206	—	92	252	—	458	45
1827	254	160	102	102	6	522	49
1828	492	200	213	241	22	955	52
1829	191	473	175	200	13	877	22
B. Credited to Customer Accounts							
1829	121	347		95	—	563	21
1830	229	384		102	13	728	31
1831	237	566		59	54	916	26
1832	386	282		8	48	724	53
1833	559	250		38	22	869	64
1834	421	250		9	24	704	60
1835	682	345		62	58	1,147	59
1836	1,813	420		8	5	2,246	81
1837	663	385		34	79	1,161	57

a Total wood includes staves.
b In year ended May. Note that the basis of the two series is different, and this explains the discrepancies in 1829, the year in which there is an overlap.

Source: A. University of Guelph Archives, Goodwin-Haines Collection, William Grant Papers, XR1 MS A131002, Barker and Stevenson Inventory Book.
B. AO, D.B. Stevenson Papers, MU 2887-8, ledgers, 1828-37

Apart from financing and handling the community's imports and exports, the merchant also participated in the often-neglected local exchange economy. For example, at least thirty local products, of which butter and cheese were the leading ones, can be found in an 1836 "barter book" kept by Barker and Stevenson.[18] These purchases by the firm were due both to the needs of the business and the Stevenson family and to the fact that some products could be resold locally. Not everyone in the rural economy farmed, nor were all who owned land primarily farmers; nor could most farmers be wholly self-sufficient even in locally producible commodities.[19] Because middlemen were often not needed in such local buying and selling, the Stevenson books offer only a glimpse of this activity. Records of artisans, merchants, and farmers all confirm, however, that locally traded goods and services, some of which might be marketed only in modest amounts, added up to a significant source of income for those who produced them. And it was in the local economy that the income of people such as innkeepers, carpenters, shoemakers, and smiths was earned.[20]

Although local exchange is often depicted essentially as a form of barter, credit was central to it. Bargains were usually expressed not solely in terms of physical commodities but in terms of prices, which appear to have been relatively standard, and time was an essential element, for the transactions between parties were not usually simultaneous or precisely equal in value. In local trade, many Upper Canadians were at once debtors and creditors, as they extended credit to their neighbours and received credit from them. Each kept whatever record of his transactions he thought necessary, and periodically people "set off" their respective claims. The process is illustrated by a settlement between Alexander McMartin, a merchant and miller at Martintown, in the Eastern District, and Donald McNaught, a carpenter. In March 1852 they reckoned their mutual dealings for the past seven years. During the period, McNaught had earned £53 by his craft and run up £47 in charges at McMartin's enterprises. As this transaction shows, in one vital respect local exchange did not resemble extra-regional trade: to the extent that transactions were local and reciprocal, promises to pay in the future could be essentially equivalent to actual payment, for the promises were cancelled out in the periodic settlements of accounts. In this example, an exchange of £6 could settle £100 worth of transactions.[21]

Even where the country merchant was not a party to the bargain, he might have a part to play in this local economy. When, as usually happened, such settlements of accounts left one party with a net obligation to the other, the account might simply be continued from the new base. If the net creditor required payment, however, both parties encountered the economy's liquidity problem. In the circumstances, it was often in the accounts of the merchant, with whom all had dealings, that balances were reconciled. Not all local trade required the participation of the merchant, but virtually all sets of merchants' accounts that survive offer much evidence of these transactions. At its simplest, the process enabled a debtor who had a credit balance with the merchant to transfer that credit to a third party who owed the merchant money. But more complex variations on the pattern were evident. Thus, a merchant might accept as payment of a debt a claim on another person who also owed him money but which, for whatever reason, he expected to be able to collect eventually (for example, through future wage labour or produce or income that the debtor expected from elsewhere).

There is no reason to think that in these transactions, merchants did not seek to sell high and buy low. But despite what is frequently asserted, accounts offer little evidence that different customers were routinely charged different retail prices.[22] It would have been a complex process to haggle with each customer over each item. The only client to whom it would have been easy to charge an exceptionally high price was one so weak and dependent that his account was liable to end up as a bad debt anyway.[23] Such customers were more likely to be cut off from further credit than to be extended more at higher prices. Similarly, merchants based their prices for produce on current market information, and the accounts strongly suggest that, though bargaining occurred on whether to buy, on quality, and on credit and payment terms, customers delivering on the same day obtained the same price for produce of the same quality.[24]

As described here, the position of the country merchant resembles in some respects the image that critics of the system have presented. Certainly, the merchant was very much at the heart of the rural economy, and it is reasonable to assume that he sought to maximize his earnings, however he defined them, within the constraints under which he operated. Foremost among his problems was probably his own reliance on credit from his suppliers and his need to meet or carry his own debts. The other principal constraint, and the one central to this paper, was competition.[25]

Almost everywhere, retailers had local competition from other merchants and millers. When W.H. Smith compiled his first *Canadian Gazetteer* in 1846, there were at least 160 communities in Upper Canada that supported two or more "stores" (see map). And even where a merchant had no immediate local competitor, a community with one or more stores or mills was seldom far away. Such local competition derived directly from competition among numerous wholesalers for

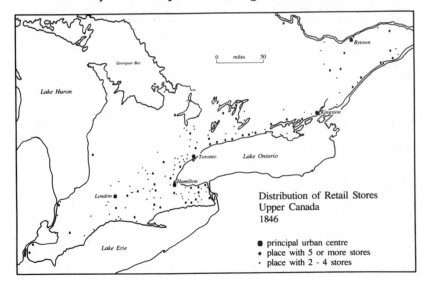

Distribution of Retail Stores
Upper Canada
1846

● principal urban centre
• place with 5 or more stores
· place with 2 - 4 stores

the trade of the province and thence from competition among British exporters, both merchants and manufacturers. That the competition was real is suggested by the substantial rate of failure among wholesalers and retailers.[26] There could, of course, be many proximate causes of failure, but however it occurred, bankruptcy shows that there were market forces that prevented the merchant from transferring his own payment problems to others.

At the local level, at least in places with only two or three stores, the merchant was partly able to predict what his rivals would do, and local projects often brought rivals together in mutual ventures such as the construction of steamboats. Sometimes, this co-operation went as far as formal agreements, for example in regard to fixing the local price of wheat.[27] But even at the purely local level there were strong pressures on such arrangements, for each party needed grain in order to collect debts and make payments and thus had an incentive to try to bend or take extra advantage of such agreements. The result was often a quick collapse of the deal.

Besides, farmers had their own ideas about prices and could stay home or take their wheat elsewhere if their usual merchant did not satisfy their expectations. A letter from Benjamin Tett to Thomas McKay, the Bytown miller for whom he acted as a buyer, illustrates the situation:

> Mr. Scott told me to pay 5/10 per bushel, but as 6/- is paid at Portland, Beverly & all other places in the neighborhood and in some instances as high as 6/3 per bushel the Farmers will Sleigh it to where they can obtain the highest price — the high price of wheat has considerably exceeded my expectation.[28]

Especially when prices were expected to rise, speculative buyers who were prepared to pay cash entered the field as well, further disrupting local patterns. In the late summer of 1836, for example, the usual supplies of wheat did not reach Yonge Mills, at the top of the St. Lawrence River, because American buyers had bought up much of what surplus the province had that year.[29] It was also possible for a producer to arrange to consign his produce through a local merchant, if the latter would not buy it or if the producer was convinced that the price offered locally was too low and was willing to bear the costs of shipment.[30]

It is common to picture the pioneer farmer as isolated, and travel conditions as impossible, but the demands on farmers' time were not so onerous and the roads were not so bad as to preclude regular off-farm travel, sometimes for considerable distances.[31] In much of Upper Canada, as we have seen, a farmer had several nearby places which he could make his prime marketing point. The records of Walter Beatty, who lived a few miles from the St. Lawrence in well-established Yonge Township, indicate the possibilities. He routinely visited eight or nine places within a ten-mile radius of his farm, including at least three mills and the large town of Brockville.[32] Because stores, mills, churches, town meetings, and bees were all sources of market news, not only the individual farmer who travelled, but his neighbours too, could form ideas about the prevalent prices and market conditions.

The travel possibilities for a farmer are well illustrated by Benjamin Crawford's diary, which records the activities on a farm (newly established in 1836) in the heart of the western peninsula of Upper Canada. The entries make it clear that news of wider market developments was often brought by a neighbour, son, or hired hand. About once a year in the early 1840s, and up to six times a year after 1845, someone from the farm undertook a longer journey to take wheat, oats, or hogs to what seemed the most suitable market, in this case usually along the road to, or as far as, the head of Lake Ontario, at Hamilton, over fifty miles away.[33]

The farmer who sold for cash in a major market might also make purchases there, and thus merchants and millers in the province's principal towns, even several days' travel away, had an influence on remoter and apparently more isolated communities. There were costs and risks in such journeys, but that they were made, or could be, must have had an effect on local prices as well. In the longer term, both merchants and farmers had to recognize that there were real costs of transport, and this sustained the price differentials between central and remoter markets. There were fluctuations in prices and imperfections in the process, but prices for the principal commodities moved in accordance with wider market trends and, for purely local trades, also in relation to local conditions.[34]

Competition was thus the prime force that prevented local merchants from exploiting their customers in the drastic and systematic manner depicted by critics. Farmers could still have found themselves entrapped in debt if the terms of trade had moved systematically against them over a protracted period, but the evidence discounts this possibility. There was no long-term downward trend in the price of most Upper Canadian farm produce after the post-war deflation, which ended in 1822, and if anything, there was some downward trend (from trough to trough) in the prices of manufactured goods and, perhaps, ocean shipping after that date.[35] In addition, unlike primary producers in some regions, Upper Canadian farmers were not fundamentally bound to a single commodity. They had numerous ways of earning money, so that even when things were unfavourable for wheat, they could earn at least enough by other means to sustain themselves, carry their debts, and await better yields or prices.[36]

As the critics have not always recognized, it took two to make a bargain. That is, it is necessary to consider why people went into debt and what determined how much debt they contracted. The staples thesis tended to assume that immigrants depended on necessities not available in the New World to sustain themselves and implied that the migrant had little choice but to buy what he did.[37] However true this may have been of the sixteenth and seventeenth centuries, it is harder to accept for the nineteenth. S.D. Clark spoke rather of "heavy capital expenditures" as the prime cause of indebtedness, but did not explain what those expenditures were, what "heavy" meant, or whether they could not be incurred incrementally as a person's income grew.

Land, presumably, was the farmer's largest immediate cost, though it was quite possible to rent land rather than buy it.[38] Because of the complexities of land policy, it is best to leave aside the question of free land grants and concentrate on the private land market. Land was scarcely homogeneous, and the would-be purchaser had many choices to make: he could, for example, minimize his immediate outlay by buying unimproved and relatively remote land, and a smaller rather than a larger acreage.[39] If he had more capital or predicted a higher return on his labour when he used it less for clearing and more for farming, he might look for a more developed farm, a more developed location, and superior soil. Whatever his choice, he could find much land available on credit, secured either by mortgage or, more often, by a contract in which title did not transfer until payment was completed. Houses, outbuildings, livestock, and tools (which in fact were usually modest in the period) all needed to be built, bred, acquired, maintained, and improved; again the farmer had to make many choices as he did so. He had to decide, for example, whether to develop his farm rapidly, perhaps by hiring labour to clear new land, or much more slowly, perhaps even hiring himself out to work for others.[40]

When the farmer went into debt, as all but the small minority with substantial capital probably did, he surely did so with a view to what he expected to be able to pay, or at least carry, in the future. Those to whom he became indebted had to share his view of his future to some degree for him thus to accumulate debts, though no creditor was necessarily in a position to know how large his other debts were. In the extent of his borrowing, he might be proved over-optimistic in many ways, for example about crop yields, prices for produce or land, or the rate at which he could expand his output. His ability to pay could also be affected by personal or family misfortunes, such as accident, illness, and death. It is thus understandable that many farmers had debt problems at times, and that some, through over-optimism, misfortune, or bad timing (for example, buying land at the height of the market), became entrapped by debt. But for any group of farmers similarly situated, there was likely to be substantial variation in both the level of indebtedness and, to a degree, in the character of the indebtedness (for example the proportion for land as opposed to that owed to merchants). Those who were forced to give up and move on were only part of the rural community. It is equally important to this paper that this happened only to some, whereas others, working in the same system, established themselves as successful commercial farmers.[41]

Far from the commercial system being the essential cause of excessive farmer indebtedness, credit actually had a further part to play in enabling the farming system to work. It is possible to distinguish analytically between debt assumed through undue optimism (or extravagance) and debt as a way of coping with potential problems whose timing could not be anticipated precisely. Rather than having to guard entirely on his own against a bad harvest, disease in his livestock, or lower prices than expected for one or more of his principal crops, the farmer could generally rely on retail credit to help sustain him. If a crop failure proved to be the beginning of a longer-term crisis of production, or if a turn in prices inaugurated a long downward slide, to rely on extra credit could be a recipe for deepening one's indebtedness rather than smoothing the fluctuations. But in Upper Canada, neither of these general conditions occurred.

Thus far the commercial relationship of retailer and farmer has been seen as one in which each side had choices and constraints. This view should not be construed as placing merchant and farmer on equal planes, nor as seeing rural society as a homogeneous community consisting solely of essentially equally placed farmers. In the case of the relationship between a leading merchant with up to several hundred customers and a farmer with but a few commercial suppliers, after all, the merchant could more readily do without that farmer than vice versa. Moreover, the merchant, through his multifarious activities, which generated a much larger flow of transactions through his hands than through the farmer's, earned a larger income and controlled more wealth. He was also much more likely to hold other positions of leadership in the community.[42] When merchant and farmer bargained, perhaps especially in regard to credit limits and payment arrangements for overdue debts, the farmer must often have felt himself in a weaker position, and this undoubtedly contributed to the rhetoric of class conflict that colours the critical view of the function of commercial credit. Because farmers sometimes felt this way does not, however, prove that the basic terms of exchange were monopolistic or even that farmers were victimized by paying or receiving unfair prices.

Class tensions were most likely to be intense during the periodic nineteenth-century commercial crises, when severe credit contractions radiating outward from England or New York brought urgent demands for payment. The resultant liquidity crisis highlighted the economy's reliance on credit for its ordinary and routine functioning by temporarily interrupting that credit. Now, if the retailer wished to

remain in favour with his suppliers, he was in greatest need of payments from his customers, but like everyone else they were pressed for
payment from all sides and were not immediately able to earn much
extra income or extra cash. If customers could not pay, the retailer might
resort to lawsuits, the taking of further security for debts due, and even
foreclosures. These steps could help him by impressing his creditors
and perhaps, at the margin, ensuring that he received more of the
community's scarce funds. But they involved lawyers and costs, and, in
the short term, lawsuits and land sales would yield no money at all,
when money was his most urgent need. The problem was clearly expressed by one hard-pressed supplier of farm implements in the 1837-
38 crisis: "There is no dependance to be put in our best men in relation
to the payment of debts. Confidence is destroyed, and but very few feel
under any obligation to pay. To sue is worse than useless."[43]

At the retail level the effect of such crises was likely to be longer-
term, by provoking a reconsideration of who should continue to receive
credit. In a process that occurred at every level of the system from
wholesaler to retailer to customer, those with debts that were excessive
in relation to the revised views of their future ability to pay might now
be driven out by creditors' claims on their assets, claims that would
make it difficult for them to get credit from another local merchant. That
is, their problem can also be viewed as an inability to secure new credit
with which to repay old debts. Lacking credit in the community, such
people had little choice but to join those who were in motion for other
reasons and to move on. Even the departure of such people from a
community, or the province, did not undo all the developmental effects
of the credit they had hitherto received, however, because they ordinarily left behind at least some of the fruits of that investment. Nor
apparently were all who left permanent losers; some at least might
succeed elsewhere if they were able again to fit themselves into a local
network of credit.

As commercial crises revealed, the relationship between the commercial system and the agricultural economy was essentially symbiotic
rather than competitive, and neither could have developed independently. It was actually in the merchant's interest for the farmer to prosper,
so he could buy more, produce more, and be able to pay his debts when
they fell due. Far from limiting agricultural wealth and development,
the credit system was integral to the circular and cumulative process by
which a new province, through external investment and local capital
creation, built up its wealth, notably by continuing to develop its farm
economy. This is not to argue that the credit system was the cause of this
development, for apparently similar systems of rural credit have also
been associated with subordination and persistent dependence. Such
may have been the case, for example, in the outport economy of parts
of Atlantic Canada.[44] Where communities lacked the agricultural base

and potential for diversification that Upper Canada possessed, were isolated from one another, and were not prosperous or large enough to sustain local retail competition, there was a greater possibility that the credit system would take on the exploitative character that critics have assumed it invariably had. Yet even in such relatively isolated communities, the system may have been unduly blamed for more complex social and economic conditions.[45]

Through the commercial system, the Upper Canadian economy derived external credit that amounted, on average, to something like the total value of its imports for the current year. The actual annual credit would vary with fluctuations in imports, exports, and other capital flows, but the credit provided through the import trade can best be seen as a long-term credit increasing incrementally as the value of imports rose. It is possible to estimate the scale of this credit from evidence on imports received at Quebec, the principal port of entry for Upper and Lower Canada. In 1831, for example, the value there of merchandise imports paying 2 $1/2$ per cent duty, the chief category of imports (including manufactures), was £1.25 million.[46] Because Upper Canada's population was approaching one-half of Lower Canada's, at least one-third of these imports were probably destined for Upper Canada. Indeed, because important items that bore specific duties, such as sugar, are not included in the above figure,[47] because per capita income and market involvement may have been higher in Upper than in Lower Canada, and because Quebec values were less than the prices paid by Upper Canadian retailers or consumers, such a figure is at the low end of the possible range. At a minimum, Upper Canada in 1831 must have benefited from a credit of £400,000 (£1.7 per capita). That this was a substantial sum is indicated by seeing it alongside the annual average of £200,000 cy that the British taxpayers spent on the construction of the Rideau Canal between 1828 and 1832, a sum that is generally considered to have had an important developmental impact; or the £260,000 in discounts provided by the province's only chartered bank, the Bank of Upper Canada, in 1831.[48]

Such external capital was provided as part of the process of British commercial expansion, and it was the Upper Canadian economy that had to pay for it, as for most other capital, external or domestic, on which it drew. Indeed, one reason for the level of retail prices in Upper Canada, which have usually been seen as high, was that they had to cover not merely the costs and risks of purchase and movement, but those of credit too, including interest for six or, probably more commonly, twelve months and the risk of bad debts. In essence, those Upper Canadians who paid their bills were paying a share of the costs of the bad debts run up by their neighbours who did not pay. The continuing provincial growth shows that the economy earned sufficient returns to carry such costs (that is, at least to pay interest on the net amount of capital invested in it) and to sustain its expansion.

During the period from 1790 to 1850, Upper Canada was rapidly becoming a "strong, flexible, and diverse economy."[49] It did so essentially through a process of immigration and the creation of local wealth, within the dynamic economy of the larger North Atlantic world. At the local level, the country store was the principal link between an immediate local economy and the network of business institutions through which that wider economy functioned. The store supplied imports, both necessities and other desired articles that the economy could afford. It marketed exports. It helped, through its contributions to exchange and liquidity, to develop the local market. The system delivered external capital to the economy amounting at least to the value of the current year's imports. And it helped bear the risks of developing a new and uncertain region, both by smoothing economic fluctuations and by bearing the risk of not being able to collect sums lent. What prevented it from being exploitative in the manner that critics have often portrayed it to be was the abundant competition for a share of the returns that were predicted, and, to a degree, realized, from this development process.

NOTES

This is a revised version of a paper prepared for the Conference on Merchant Credit and Labour Strategies in the Staple Economies of North America, held at St. John's, Nfld., August 27-29, 1987. I very much appreciated the comments there by Winnifred Rothenberg and Stephen Innes. The financial support and encouragement of the Ontario Historical Studies Series and of the Social Sciences and Humanities Research Council of Canada (in the form of a Leave Fellowship and a Research Grant) are gratefully acknowledged, as is the research assistance of Linda McIntyre Putz. I wish also to thank Robin Fisher and Jack Little for the opportunity to present a preliminary version of these ideas at a seminar at Simon Fraser University.

1   John McCallum, *Unequal Beginnings: Agriculture and Economic Development in Quebec and Ontario until 1870* (Toronto: University of Toronto Press, 1980). See also R.M. McInnis, "Marketable Surpluses in Ontario Farming, 1860," *Social Science History*, 8 (No. 4, 1984), 395-424.

2   On the provincial banking system, see Peter Baskerville, *The Bank of Upper Canada* (Toronto: Champlain Society, 1987). For a pertinent overview of the role of commercial credit in another context, see Jacob M. Price, *Capital and Credit in British Overseas Trade: The View from the Chesapeake, 1700-1776* (Cambridge, Mass.: Harvard University Press, 1980), esp. pp.121-22.

3   On the character and development of Upper Canadian wholesaling, see Douglas McCalla, *The Upper Canada Trade, 1834-1872: A Study of the Buchanans' Business* (Toronto: University of Toronto Press, 1979). See also T.W. Acheson, "The Nature and Structure of York Commerce in the 1820s," *Canadian Historical Review* [CHR], 50 (No. 4, 1969), 406-28.

4   When banks developed in the province, they used local merchants as their
     agents in some communities that were too small to support a branch, but only a
     small minority of retailers had this particular financial role.

5   S.D. Clark, *Movements of Political Protest in Canada 1640-1840* (Toronto: Univer-
     sity of Toronto Press, 1959), pp. 429-30. See also D.A. Nock, "S.D. Clark and the
     Rebellions of 1837," paper presented to The 1837 Seminar, University of
     Edinburgh, May 1987.

6   Lillian Gates, *Land Policies of Upper Canada* (Toronto: University of Toronto
     Press, 1968), p. 43. See also Gary Teeple, "Land, Labour and Capital in Pre-Con-
     federation Canada," in G. Teeple, ed., *Capitalism and the National Question in
     Canada* (Toronto: University of Toronto Press, 1972), p. 57: "The magistrate
     merchants were always at hand, ready to take advantage of a pioneer's need for
     manufactured goods and, in the absence of much money in circulation, willing
     to extend credit. The result was often disastrous for the settler." Leo Johnson has
     argued a similar case in "The Settlement of the Western District 1749-1850," in
     F.H. Armstrong et al., eds., *Aspects of Nineteenth-Century Ontario* (Toronto:
     University of Toronto Press, 1974), p. 23. For a different view, somewhat more
     in line with the view of merchants taken in this essay, see Johnson's "The
     Contradiction between Independent Commodity Production and Capitalist
     Production in Upper Canada 1820-1850," unpublished paper.

7   *The Correspondence of Lieut. Governor John Graves Simcoe*, Vol. 3, *1794-1795*
     (Toronto, 1925), pp. 138-39, Simcoe to George Rose, Oct. 21, 1794.

8   *The Cod Fisheries: The History of an International Economy* (rev. ed., Toronto:
     University of Toronto Press, 1956), p. 282. The truck system involved the domi-
     nance of a company store, to which producers were indebted and which paid
     them for produce not in money but in usually over-priced goods; to challenge
     the system exposed the debtor to the risk of having his old debts immediately
     and fully enforced.

9   Allan Greer, *Peasant, Lord, and Merchant: Rural Society in Three Quebec Parishes
     1740-1840* (Toronto: University of Toronto Press, 1985), esp. pp. 140-76. Stephen
     Innes, *Labor in a New Land: Economy and Society in Seventeenth-Century Springfield*
     (Princeton: Princeton University Press, 1983).

10   For a farmer's correspondence which makes frequent reference to news from the
     United States, see Archives of Ontario [AO], MS 199, Isaac Wilson Letters
     (copies), 1811-33.

11   University of Guelph Archives, Gilkison-Fraser Collection, XR1 MS A116,
     William Gilkison to Simon Fraser, Apr. 13, 1833.

12   Queen's University Archives [QUA], Tett Papers, vol. 1, p. 1, Tett to Macintosh
     and Co., Nov. 11, 1833.

13   National Archives of Canada, Buchanan Papers, MG 24, D 16, vol. 85, p. 60441,
     George Borthwick, "Remarks upon Analysis of Outstandings at Hamilton, 30
     June, 1856."

14   AO, D.B. Stevenson Papers, MU 2887-8, ledgers.

15   Angela Redish, "Why Was Specie Scarce in Colonial Economies? An Analysis of
     the Canadian Currency, 1796-1830," *Journal of Economic History [JEH]*, 44 (No. 3,
     1984), 713-28.

16   Douglas McCalla, "The Internal Economy of Upper Canada: New Evidence on
     Agricultural Marketing Before 1850," *Agricultural History*, 59 (No. 3, 1985), 397-
     416.

17   QUA, Tett Papers, vol. 1, p. 27, Tett to McPherson and Crane, Nov. 28, 1839.

18   AO, D.B. Stevenson Papers, MU 2886, Barter Book, July 5, 1836, to June 27, 1837.

19   David Gagan, *Hopeful Travellers: Families, Land, and Social Change in Mid-Victorian
     Peel County, Canada West* (Toronto: University of Toronto Press, 1981), p. 109;
     Bettye Hobbs Pruitt, "Self-Sufficiency and the Agricultural Economy of
     Eighteenth-Century Massachusetts," *William and Mary Quarterly*, 3rd ser., 40
     (No. 3, 1984), 333-64.

20 McCalla, "The Internal Economy of Upper Canada."
21 AO, Alexander McMartin Papers, MU 1973, file F-3-7, A. McMartin Dr. to
    Donald McNaught. Here, in fact, no money changed hands, because McNaught
    agreed to rent a lot from McMartin for 30/- per year for the next four years.
22 It has not yet been possible to conduct any systematic study on the point, but
    this is the clear impression I have formed from scanning dozens of such
    accounts. For the view that prices were not "fixed" until later in the century, see,
    e.g., William Stephenson, *The Store That Timothy Built* (Toronto: McClelland and
    Stewart, 1969), pp. 19-23.
23 For further discussion of pricing, especially at wholesale, see McCalla, *The Upper
    Canada Trade*, pp. 39-40.
24 One variation was between a cash price and a book credit price, the latter
    usually being somewhat higher. On occasion variation arose from contracts
    where the price was settled at another time from that of the actual delivery.
25 Michael Bliss, *Northern Enterprise: Five Centuries of Canadian Business* (Toronto:
    McClelland and Stewart, 1987), p. 9 and passim.
26 Michael B. Katz, *The People of Hamilton, Canada West: Family and Class in a Mid-
    Nineteenth-Century City* (Cambridge, Mass.: Harvard University Press, 1975), pp.
    176-208.
27 Metropolitan Toronto Library, Baldwin Room, Laurent Quetton de St. George
    Papers, section II, Hector MacKay to Quetton St. George, Mar. 17 and 24, May 9,
    1810. Here the agreement took the form of a joint flour account between the two
    principal merchants at Dundas; on the other hand, prices moved upward
    despite the agreement, and the two often found it necessary to pay cash for flour
    in order to obtain it.
28 QUA, Tett Papers, vol. 1, p. 47, Tett to McKay, Jan. 21, 1842.
29 AO, Yonge Mills Records, MU 3187, letterbooks, J-1, Charles Jones to Tremaine
    and Moir, Sept. 18, 1836; see also AO, Wade Letters, MU 3074 (typescript), pp.
    140-45, Robert Wade to Ralph Wade, Jan. 10, 183[7].
30 QUA, Tett Papers, vol. 67, "Account of Potashes," Oct. 1834.
31 T.F. McIlwraith, "The Adequacy of Rural Roads in the Era before Railways: An
    Illustration from Upper Canada," *Canadian Geographer*, 14 (No. 3, 1970), 344-58.
32 QUA, Walter Beatty Papers, 1838-92 (copies). In 1848, the first year in which this
    diary covers a year fully and consistently, Beatty made 92 trips off the farm, 35
    of them to church, 20 to Brockville (about 10 miles away), and 10 to Yonge Mills.
    In August, his only trips were 3 to church; in January to March, he recorded 38
    expeditions.
33 AO, Crawford Family Papers, MU 755-6, diaries, 1837-50. Crawford farmed
    with grown sons, and it was they who made the journeys that are recorded. On
    the significance of such travels, see Winnifred Rothenberg, "The Market and
    Massachusetts Farmers, 1750-1855," *JEH*, 41 (No. 2, 1981), 283-314.
34 I have discussed this issue more fully in an unpublished working paper,
    "Produce Prices in Upper Canada," Apr. 1987. For example, with 1831 prices set
    at 100, those for 1842-43 are, for the Toronto-Hamilton area:wheat 84, oats 79,
    potatoes 83, hay 115, butter 111, beef 78, pork 81. On the significance of such
    local price indexes, see Winnifred Rothenberg, "A Price Index for Rural
    Massachusetts, 1750-1855," *JEH*, 39 (No. 4, 1979), 975-1001.
35 See for example B. Mitchell and P. Deane, *Abstract of British Historical Statistics*
    (Cambridge: Cambridge University Press, 1962), pp. 470-71, indexes for indus-
    trial products and for "domestic" (i.e. British) products. The post-war low for
    each, 1822, was 116 for the former, 83.9 for the latter; by 1851, another low point,
    the former stood at 89 and the latter (in 1850, the final year for the series), at 77.4
    (1821-5 = 100). A selection of produce prices for the Toronto area may be com-
    pared here:

	1822	1851
wheat (s/bu)	2/6	3/7
oats (s/bu)	1/-	1/5
potatoes (s/bu)	1/3	2/4
peas (s/bu)	2/4*	2/7
hay (s/ton)	50/-	52/9
butter (d/lb)	7.5	7.7
beef (d/lb)	3	3
pork (d/lb)	3.1	2.7

(*mean of 1821 and 1823 prices.)
For ocean freight rates, see D.C. North, "Ocean Freight Rates and Economic Development 1750-1913," *JEH*, 18 (No. 4, 1958), 537-55.

36 D. McCalla, "Forest Products and Upper Canadian Development, 1815-1846," *CHR*, 68 (No. 2, 1987), 159-98.

37 H.A. Innis, *The Fur Trade in Canada* (rev. ed., Toronto: University of Toronto Press, 1956), pp. 383-86.

38 W.L. Marr, "Tenant vs. Owner Occupied Farms in York County, Ontario 1871," *Canadian Papers in Rural History [CPRH]*, 4 (1984), 50-71.

39 See for example R.M. McInnis, "The Size Structure of Farms in Canada West, 1861," paper presented to the Conference on Agrarian Structures and Economic Performance in the Century of Industrialization, May 1984.

40 See also Peter A. Russell, "Forest into Farmland: Upper Canadian Clearing Rates, 1822-1839," *Agricultural History*, 57 (No. 2, 1983), 326-39.

41 D.A. Norris, "Household and Transiency in a Loyalist Township: The People of Adolphustown, 1784-1822," *Histoire Sociale/Social History*, 13 (No. 2, 1980), 399-415; early arrivals had some advantage here, but a far from absolute one. See also Norris's "Migration, Pioneer Settlement, and the Life Course: The First Families of an Ontario Township," *CPRH*, 4 (1984), 130-52.

42 See for example Bruce Wilson, *The Enterprises of Robert Hamilton: A Study of Wealth and Influence in Early Upper Canada, 1776 -1812* (Ottawa: Carleton University Press, 1983).

43 AO, McQuesten Family Papers, MS 434, item 161, John Fisher to Calvin McQuesten, June 16, 1838. See also B.L. Anderson, "Money and the Structure of Credit in the Eighteenth Century," *Business History*, 12 (No. 1, 1970), 85-101.

44 Rosemary Ommer, "Accounting the Fishery," paper presented to the 13th Conference on Quantitative Methods in Canadian Economic History, Waterloo, 1984.

45 Price V. Fishback, "Did Coal Miners 'Owe Their Souls to the Company Store'? Theory and Evidence from the Early 1900s," *JEH*, 46 (No. 4, 1986), 1011-29.

46 Lower Canada, Legislative Assembly, *Journals*, 1831-32, App. Ss. For the five years 1828-32, such imports averaged £1.1 million (F. Ouellet, *Economic and Social History of Quebec 1760-1850* (Toronto: Gage, 1980), p. 406).

47 Thus, in addition to goods valued for purposes of the ad valorem duty, Quebec in 1831 received over a million gallons of rum, over half a million pounds of tea, almost 7 million pounds of sugar, and smaller quantities of a number of other wines and spirits.

48 For the Rideau, see George Raudzens, *The British Ordnance Department and Canada's Canals 1815-1855* (Waterloo: Wilfrid Laurier University Press, 1979), p. 56; for the bank, see Upper Canada, Legislative Assembly, *Journals*, 1831, p. 31.

49 John J. McCusker and Russell Menard, *The Economy of British America 1607-1789* (Chapel Hill: University of North Carolina Press, 1985), p. 84.

POPULATION CHANGE ON AN AGRICULTURAL FRONTIER: UPPER CANADA, 1796 TO 1841

J. David Wood

In the settling of Upper Canada, a drama was enacted that was similar to that of many agricultural frontiers in the New World. "Upper Canada" symbolizes the frontier in the story of Ontario. For one generation, around the turn of the nineteenth century, it offered land seekers moving west in America an attractive alternative: it contained some millions of acres of good land, and it was recognized as a place of peace and order at a time when Indian hostility discouraged settlement in the Ohio Country and the "Prairie Peninsula" west of Lake Erie.

Although Upper Canada had much in common with other early agricultural settlements across North America, it also played out its own version of the drama. A considerable body of data on population can be assembled for Upper Canada, primarily from the annual reports submitted by township clerks to the justices of the peace (for the Court of General Quarter Sessions) and later to the Lieutenant-Governor's office.[1] These sources allow one to comment on the frontier debate on the strength of a data base that has not previously been fully assessed, and from a constituency (the settlers of Upper Canada) that has not usually been incorporated in the debate.[2] To that end, this paper will search for aspects of population that Upper Canada had in common with other areas of pioneer settlement and, in addition, will examine the variety of experiences that are often submerged in the emotive term "frontier." An analysis of population change does not tell us everything about the frontier, but certainly it can inform us about many fundamental conditions of frontier society.[3]

Upper Canada became a frontier rather suddenly, when it was transformed from little-known Indian territory into a refuge for hard-pressed Loyalists fleeing from the former American colonies.[4] It appears that the first farming settlers in what became Upper Canada crossed the Niagara River in 1780. They were followed by increasing numbers, especially after the peace treaty between Great Britain and the United States in 1783.[5] A prior French-speaking cluster that was attached mainly to the fur trade and eventually became amalgamated with newcomers had existed on the Detroit River for a generation.

For present purposes, the population that laid claim to Upper Canada can be divided into two main groups, contrasted by source area and period of arrival. The first was American and was composed of people born or having had long residence in North America, and thus familiar with the environment and essential life skills. The American period extends from 1780 to the War of 1812. It can be legitimately separated into Loyalist, 1780 to 1787 (by which time approximately 10,000 settlers had entered Upper Canada) and the so-called "Late Loyalist," 1788 to 1812. The population of 1787 had doubled by 1794, the mid-point of Simcoe's sojourn, and by 1800 it amounted to nearly 32,000 (not counting Imperial troops or approximately 3,000 transient Indians along the Shield edge and Georgian Bay). In the decade leading up to the war the growth diminished.

The second group was British, that is, an immigrant population from a relatively well developed Old World. The immigrants were largely from Ireland — more from the north than the south[6] — with English second, and Scots a distant third. The period marked by immigration began right after the War of 1812, with the well-publicized assisted passage of Scots into eastern Upper Canada, and continued well beyond 1840. The post-war immigration created new optimism, and the province's population entered a phase of rapid growth, 5 to 7 per cent a year, for most years up to 1840.

The pattern of population distribution went through a striking metamorphosis between the arrival of the Loyalists and the Union of the Canadas (see Figure 1). At the beginning the convenient gateways attracted the refugee settlers, and as a result, the 1794 population was clustered around the three river crossings into British territory: the St. Lawrence, the Niagara, and the Detroit rivers. By 1794, population was beginning to creep away from these clusters; but Simcoe still administered three virtually unconnected mini-colonies. By 1824, however, a major re-arrangement was under way. An expansion in search of good agricultural land, which had begun by the 1790s, had progressed well inland and had tenuously linked together the three corners of Upper Canada. By 1840, the main phase of the re-arrangement was complete, to the extent that the present-day distribution is not greatly different in pattern though the number of people is vastly greater.

Despite the continuity suggested by Figure 1, this essay will demonstrate that the peopling of Upper Canada is best seen as two rather different frontier expansions separated by the War of 1812 and its aftermath. This is not to deny that the two periods had a number of features in common, which indeed they shared with other frontiers. Certain ideas about frontier population can be successfully tested using the Upper Canada data. One that is fundamental to the common image

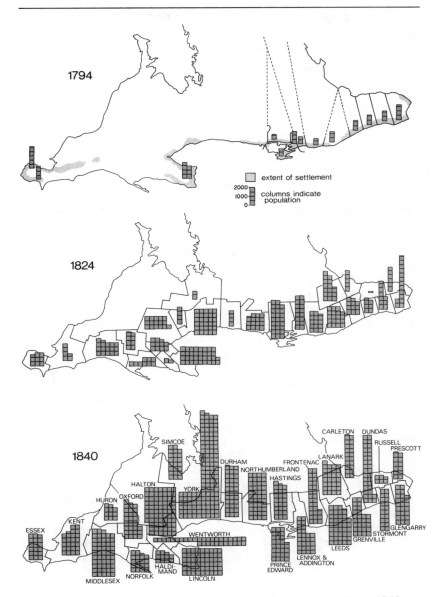

Figure 1: Distribution of Population, Upper Canada, 1794, 1824, 1840.
Sources: 1794 from J. D. Wood, "The Population of Ontario...", in
Robinson, A Social Geography of Canada, *forthcoming; 1824, from* Appendix of Journal of the House of Assembly, *1828; 1840 from* Census of
Canada, *1871, Vol. 4.*

of the frontier is that population, once established, grows unabated. Another, arising from the recognition of the frontier as a rough and trying environment, is that adult males hold a large numerical predominance over adult females and therefore are the major ingredient in population change. A third, which has to do with the stability of the pioneering population, is a two-sided coin: on one side is the picture of the pioneer as a footloose nomad, but on the other, the pioneer as a salt-of-the-earth founding father.

The Evidence from Upper Canada:
An Equivocal Frontier

A closer look at population changes before the War of 1812 reveals that growth was neither continuous nor ubiquitous. In fact, in eight out of ten townships for which a number of population returns exist, there appear to have been decreases as well as increases.[7] A map of the earliest province-wide distribution of population, for fifty-odd townships in the years 1805 to 1808, reveals a pattern primarily but not exclusively of increases (see Figure 2A). There is one notable pocket of stagnation in the southwestern extremity and hints of a slowing of growth in many parts of the province.

When population change in specific townships is examined, the initial appearance of great variety is reduced to two main types — one due to the expansion of the frontier and the search for farm land, the other due to the urgent need to provide refuge for the American Loyalists. Before the War of 1812 all the townships seem to fit one of the following descriptions:

1. the refuge type, characterized by a Loyalist foundation in the 1780s (which introduced a virtually mature demographic composite) and a steady growth nurtured by a modest expansion into new farmland. Examples of this type are Augusta and Edwardsburgh, on the upper part of the St. Lawrence River (see Figure 3);

2. the expansionary type, which might be thought of as more typical of the frontier, having two variants:

(a) the persistent-growth variant, characterized by young families, rapid increase, a large supply of good agricultural land with possibilities for expansion, and considerable immigration. Examples of this type are Haldimand and Hamilton, on the north shore of Lake Ontario (see Figure 3);

(b) the intermittent-change variant, characterized by an initial influx of young families, but an early tapering off of growth because of the rapid exhaustion of the supply of good agricultural land. The limitations on agricultural use might be the roughness of morainic ridges, the lack of sufficient soil over limestone, soil infertility, or poor drainage. These were areas of ongoing challenge for agriculture, as suggested by the graphs of South Gower, Percy, and King (see Figure 3).

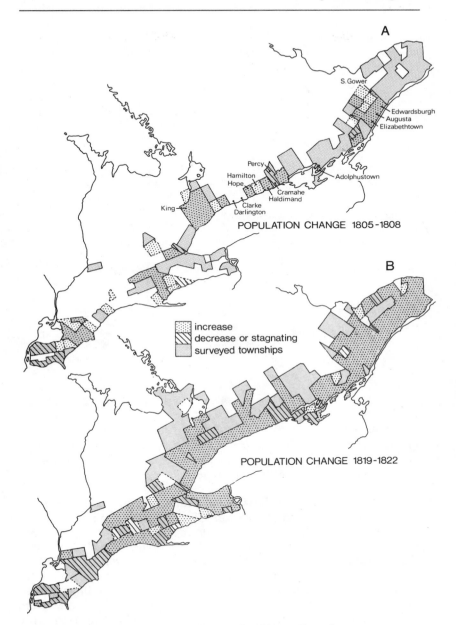

Figure 2: Population Change, by Township, Upper Canada:
A. c. 1805-08,
B. c. 1819-22. Sources: A. Only scattered data available, primarily from
RG 5 B 26, National Archives of Canada (hereafter NAC); surveyed
townships from Economic Atlas of Ontario, *plate 99. B. same sources as A.,*
and Archives of Ontario (hereafter AO), Municipal Records, RG 21.

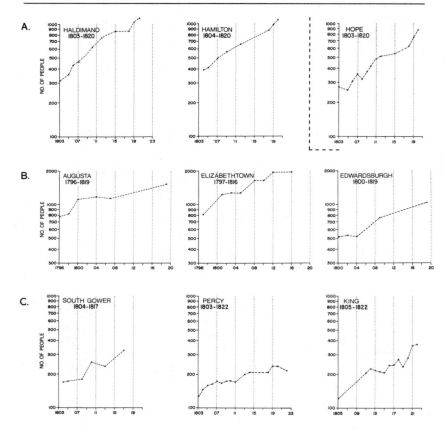

Figure 3: Population of Townships, by Type, c. 1796-1820: A. persistent-growth, B. refuge, C. intermittent-change. (The semi-log scale gives a more accurate view of the rate of change.) Sources: See sources to Figure 2.

There are some townships that appear aberrant. For example, one might expect Hope and Darlington/Clarke, which were in situations comparable to Haldimand and Hamilton, also to be of the "persistent-growth" type, but in fact they had significant losses as well as gains (see Figures 3 and 4). This suggests that in the first decade or so of the century (in fact, until about the time the government began to put renewed pressure on land held vacant) extensive speculative holdings limited the possibility of expanding existing farms or prevented new ones from being established, especially by the younger generation. A striking exception among the "refuge" townships is tiny Adolphustown on the Bay of Quinte.[8] After 1804 its population changed little, except to go into a decline ten years later (see Figure 4). It seems that Adolphustown was so small that all the promising agricultural land was fully occupied by the first generation of Loyalists and that new farmland had to be sought outside the township.

The half decade seriously affected by the War of 1812 appears on many of the graphs in Figures 3 and 4 as a retardation of growth or even a loss of population. Whereas Haldimand Township grew by 41 per cent between 1803 and 1806, it grew by only 14 per cent from 1812 to 1815. King Township had grown by 10 per cent a year from 1805 to 1811, but it lost population from 1812 to 1815. Cramahe added only fifteen persons between 1813 and 1815, and its neighbour to the north, Percy, lost population. In the absence of definitive evidence, the best explanation is that the war brought about a reduction in the birth rate,[9] since many of the men eligible for military service were away from home, even though they were enumerated in their own townships.[10] The population of Upper Canada at the outbreak of the war numbered about 65,000,[11] and by 1815 had probably not increased substantially.

The second common belief about the frontier, namely, the numerical predominance of men over women, comes close to being true for all parts of Upper Canada. At least in all kinds of townships in the pre-war period men were in a clear majority. There are some interesting distinctions that can be made, however, along the lines of the previous typology. For example, in persistent-growth townships in 1805, there were 130 or more men to every 100 women: Hamilton, 130:100, Pickering 150:100, West Flamborough, 132:100, Oxford, 133:100 (but there were townships that were notable exceptions). In the refuge townships (once again with exceptions), at about the same date, the ratio was markedly lower: Elizabethtown, 113:100, Adolphustown, 114:100. In most intermittent-change townships men had a surprisingly small predominance: South Gower, 100:100, King, 108:100, Beverley, 114:100 (with Percy something of an exception, at 117:100 in 1804, and 127:100 in 1805). The Western District is impossible to categorize, for it had a high surplus of men and yet underwent only spasmodic growth. The normal progression in this male-female ratio was from a sizeable predominance of men at the opening of settlement through a gradual levelling as the children entered the ranks of the adults.

Children were a major part of a rapidly growing frontier population; in fact it has been found that in most of the townships in Upper Canada for which pre-war evidence exists, children (under sixteen) made up 50 to 62 per cent of the population.[12] A preliminary analysis of the few runs of data that survive suggests that the lower proportion was characteristic of townships whose population was rising rapidly (such as those with persistent growth), whereas the higher proportion would have been found in townships where growth was modest or stalled (such as the refuge or intermittent-change types). This appears to agree with a suggestion made by Easterlin and by McInnis that the highest fertility rates were not on the cutting edge of the frontier, but in the

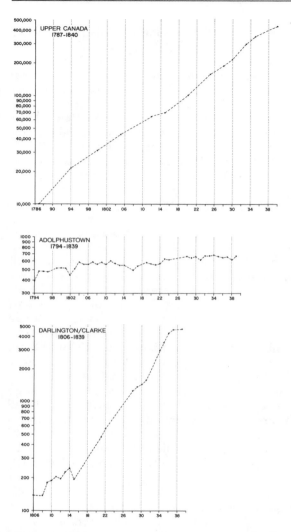

Figure 4: Population Change, Upper Canada, 1787-1840, and Two Aber-rant Townships. Darlington and Clarke were joined for reporting purposes from 1806 to the mid-1820s, and for this graph are kept together to 1839. Sources: The Upper Canada figures up to 1821 (except for the 1810 esti-mate from McCalla, in "The 'Loyalist' Economy...") are estimated by the author; the later data are taken from The Census of Canada, *1871, Vol. 4. The Adolphustown data up to 1823 are found in* The Appendix to the Report of the Ontario Bureau of Industries, *1897 (Ontario Department of Agriculture, 1899); the 1824-39 data are from NAC, RG 5 B 26, for both townships. The 1806-16 data for Darlington/Clarke are from AO, RG 21.*

partially settled areas just behind.[13] Much of the rapid growth in the more desirable townships was probably due to a predominantly adult male influx that would have counterbalanced the proportion of children (this is further analysed below through the longer post-war record). Thus there was variation even within what might be loosely described as "the frontier."

The scarcity of data for the early period and the capriciousness of much of those surviving, require one to be cautious in arriving at conclusions. The researcher wrestles with illegibility, inexplicable gaps, and apparent ignorance on the part of some clerks, and many findings must be considered tentative. But this said, extreme mobility of the population appears to be documented by some township returns that name the heads of households. It is not unusual for a household to disappear from a township and then to return after a few years. In Percy Township, for example, three families of Dingmans were resident in 1803 and 1804 but absent in 1805. The later records show that they were back in the township in 1806 and were still there in 1813. The Abel Conant household was in Darlington/Clarke from 1806 to 1810, after which it disappeared from the record to return in 1815, smaller in size. Rachel Lightheart, widow, was in the same municipality from 1806 to 1808. She then left, but was back from 1813 to 1815 with a smaller household. A record from the 1790s reveals Jacob Van Valkenburg in Augusta Township in 1796, gone in 1798, back in 1800, and gone again by 1804. David Covell also was in Augusta in 1796 but gone in 1798, then back in the township from 1800 to 1807.[14]

It is possible to trace a few people from township to township. Resolved Cleaveland was in Adolphustown Township in 1799 and 1800. He then showed up in Percy Township, forty miles west, from 1803 to 1805. Jeremiah Wood went from a long residence in Percy (1803 to about 1811) toward the Lake Ontario shore, into Cramahe Township (1812 to 1815), with a wife, two boys, two girls, and a servant. John Trull was resident in Hope Township in 1810, but then appeared in Darlington/Clarke in 1813-15, with a family that had grown to eight in 1815. The size of the family seems to have had little bearing on the decision to move.[15]

The fluidity of the population was a ubiquitous feature of Upper Canada. It occurred from the earliest days of settlement and was still a striking phenomenon in the mid-nineteenth century.[16] In both Adolphustown (1794-96) and Augusta (1796-98), one-quarter of the households disappeared in a two-year period. With this kind of "bloodletting," it might be predicted that the townships would have been empty after eight years. But in fact they increased in population. This points to the obverse of the transiency — the residential stability of a portion of the population (which was continually augmented by incoming transients).

An analysis of a few early-settled townships on the St. Lawrence and the north shore of Lake Ontario suggests some useful distinctions in the population.[17] There were the transients who stayed less than two years; there were the sojourners who tended to stay from five to seven years, probably farming rented land; and there were the long-term persisters who, in effect, were the founding families of the township. These founding families were not nomads, although contemporaneous with them were many souls just passing through. After ten years, roughly half the original households were still in the township. In Adolphustown, the proportion was lower (31 per cent), probably because, being a much older township the deaths of household heads removed their specific names from the available record. Another old township, Augusta, retained 51 per cent of its original households over an eleven-year span (1796-1807). In Percy (1803-13) 49 per cent persisted, in Haldimand (1805-15) 51 per cent, and in Darlington/Clarke (1806-15) 45 per cent.[18]

The persisters continued to account for a large proportion of the households in a township, usually a quarter to a third, and their households were larger than the average. At the end of an eleven-year period (1796-1807) in Augusta Township, the persisting households and the families of their male offspring (traced through surnames) accounted for 48 per cent of the 1,131 residents. They also accounted for 56 per cent of all households, many being new, small second-generation establishments. This pattern of persistence was characteristic of both fast- and slow-growing townships. The founding families quickly put down roots, expanding in size and influence, whereas the more noticeable streams of the footloose swirled around them and eventually moved on. In this way were the foundations of "Old Ontario" society laid.

After the War of 1812: Upper Canada's Second Generation

One might expect that with the war behind it and a renewed interest in the administration of Upper Canada ahead, the province would enter a period of accelerating growth. Certainly a new period emerged, but time was needed to replace old attitudes and old expectations, not least among the bureaucrats in Whitehall. The major new ingredient was immigration from the Old Country — "the redundant population of Britain", as Gourlay phrased it[19] — which began to flow towards Upper Canada by 1816. The effect of the fresh influx, however, was variable (as illustrated by Figure 2B). Eastern and central Upper Canada — generally the initial stopping places for immigrants — were already benefiting; but west of the Head of the Lake, population growth was very tentative and spotty, despite the rapid opening of new townships. The far southwestern sector continued to be generally beyond the reach of the immigrants and unstirred by the population growth. Other pockets of stagnation, toward the centre, seemed to occur in townships dominated by sandy moraines or thinly covered limestone plains.

In the next "period picture" of the population, displayed in Figure 5A, it is apparent that by the 1820s expansion was taking place in many parts of the province. There was a reinforcement and spreading of the booming sector of the Home District and the adjacent portion of Gore District. The Grand River Valley was being filled up, as was much of the rest of the north shore of Lake Erie. But there was continuing stagnation in the far southwest and in the middle Thames Valley, while newly opened townships just to the north were growing vigorously. Older-settled townships in Niagara and around the Head of the Lake actually lost population in 1829-30. Even some of the townships eastward on Lake Ontario, which had formerly been growing rapidly, lost population. The most striking change, however, was in the far eastern quarter, where settlers were abandoning the edges of the Shield and the very mixed-quality townships where drainage was poor and soils were stony and shallow.

The final cross-section of growth and stagnation, in the last year before the union of the Canadas, presents a marked patchwork (see Figure 5B). Although extension was still taking place at the edges, that is, toward the Lake Huron shore (especially in the Canada Company townships), north of Lake Simcoe, and north and west of Kingston, there were also losses in some townships, even near the edges of settlement.[20] Regional differentiation in the province was beginning to crystallize into the pattern we see today. Only the great peninsula from Niagara to Lake St. Clair would have its relative status significantly enhanced by the coming of the railways in the next generation. Regions of perennial slow growth or loss of population, such as the limestone flanks of the Shield, interior parts of the eastern end of the province, the Bay of Quinte, and the southern littoral of Lake St. Clair, had taken shape. The northwestern shore of Lake Ontario, with its tributary back country, was displaying the kind of persistent growth that eventually led to the heavy concentration of population dubbed the Golden Horseshoe. By 1840, all the townships in the Home District that fronted on Lake Ontario, as well as the tier behind them, had a population density of over thirty per square mile.[21] On the other hand, there was a lightly populated "pioneer fringe," with a density of less than six persons per square mile, stretching discontinuously up the Ottawa Valley, along the edge of the Shield north and northwest of Kingston, around the north end of Lake Simcoe and adjacent to Georgian Bay, through most of the Huron Tract, and along the St. Clair River and south to the mouth of the Thames River. The extremes in population density — the fringe and the heartland — are shown in Figure 6. The measures

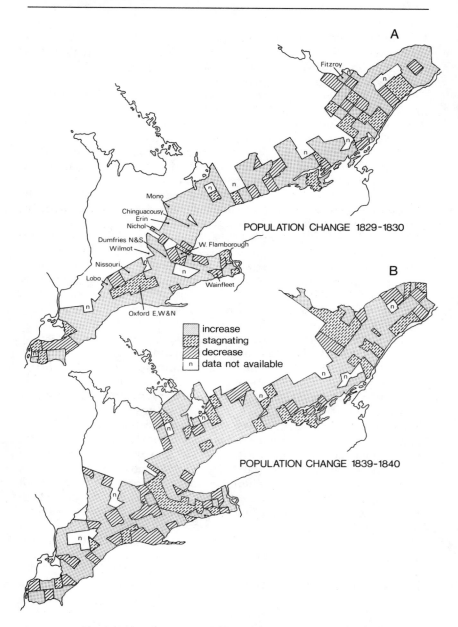

Figure 5: Population Change, by Township, Upper Canada: A. 1829-30 (increase was reckoned as 3 per cent or greater growth, stagnation as 0-3 per cent growth), B. 1839-40. Sources: NAC, RG 5 B 26. (To fill gaps in the 1840 returns, data were extrapolated from 1839 and 1841 for the townships north of Lake Simcoe and in Talbot District.)

are based on the average family size of six, the settlement fringe having less than one family per square mile, while the settlement heartland had more than six families per square mile.[22]

Variation in rates of growth in individual townships continued in the third and fourth decades of the century (see Figure 7). The persistent-growth townships of the first decade were showing signs of filling up. Haldimand Township, in fact, recorded a loss of population at the end of the 1830s, as did the majority of well-settled rural townships from one end of the province to the other. A comparison of Haldimand's near neighbour, Hope Township, reveals overall growth but also incidents of population loss. Only Hamilton Township enjoyed an unabated increase. The refuge townships, Elizabethtown, Augusta, and Edwardsburgh, continued a trend of modest growth, with the periodic setbacks that had characterized their demography almost from the beginning. The intermittent-change townships, except for King, generally remained hostage to an unfavourable environment. South Gower increased to 700 but then fell back. Percy, whose data could not be separated from the neighbouring township in the 1820s, might be represented by Wainfleet, a township settled near the opening

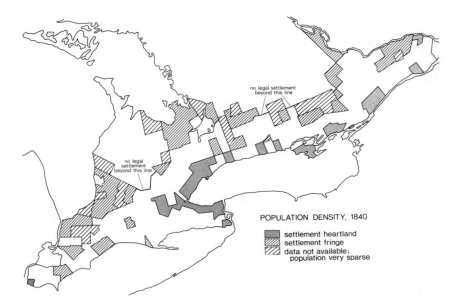

Figure 6: Rural population density in Upper Canada, 1840: the settlement fringe and the settlement heartland. The fringe is represented by a township density of less than six persons per square mile, the heartland by greater than thirty-six persons per square mile. Source: Journal of 1st Parliament of the United Canadas, *5 Vict., 1841, App. 22.*

of the century but dominated by poorly drained land on the dip slope of the Niagara Escarpment. King's environmental deficiencies were largely offset by development along Yonge Street, resulting in a steady growth of population after 1826.

The growth and distribution of the population varied considerably, both through time and from place to place in any given year (see Figures 2 and 5). Is the composition of the population similarly variable? We have enough data to compare the first and the second generations of Upper Canada and to assess whether newly opened townships always had similar demographic characteristics at similar points in their development.[23]

The ratio of men to women in the older-settled townships, whether they were persistent-growth, refuge, or intermittent-change types, continued to move toward a balance. By the end of the 1830s, when the

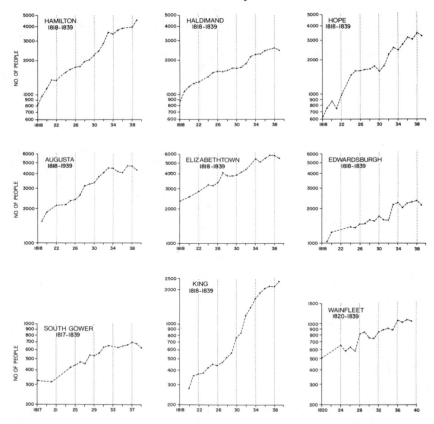

Figure 7: Population of townships opened for settlement before 1810, for the years c. 1819-39. (Compare with Figure 3.) Sources: See sources to Figure 2.

ratio for Upper Canada as a whole was 109:100, most townships were in that range, and some had even moved close to equality. There were exceptions, however, such as Elizabethtown, a Loyalist township, which had suddenly jumped to 131:100, and Hamilton Township, which had similarly jumped to 153:100. One could speculate on the reasons for such sudden rises, one of which, of course, could be inaccuracies in the data that have survived. In those two cases, the more likely reason was a rapidly growing town (Brockville and Cobourg, respectively) that might provide conditions for periodic fluctuations. A survey of the evidence does not lead to a clear picture of a process at work. In most townships the ratio could fluctuate greatly, even from year to year. In the relatively small populations characteristic of most townships — generally numbering only in the hundreds, and rarely over 2,500, through this period — a dozen or two movers could have a major effect. In a few fringe townships the coming and going of men engaged in the timber industry could drastically modify the number of adult males. In general, one can assume that the fluctuations were largely a result of migrant men; but, as is demonstrated toward the end of this article, men were not the only transients.

This raises the question of the amount of transience in the second generation of settlement, compared to the early years in a township. The evidence that is available allows us to carry out a detailed case study on one of the townships earlier identified as having intermittent growth — South Gower. It was a township that reached its maximum land occupancy shortly after the War of 1812, having been opened to settlers about the turn of the century. Of the forty-two households in South Gower in 1813, fifteen (36 per cent) were still there in 1825; some, in addition, appear to have been succeeded by offspring. This was a lower persistence rate than in Percy or Haldimand in the first dozen years of their settlement, but it was higher than in Adolphustown.

In the 1820s a great many new townships were being opened further west in Upper Canada, and one might expect this to be an enticement to residents of a township of variable quality, like South Gower. Our expectations, however, are not borne out by the comings and goings of the people of this township during the period 1825 to 1830. Not only did the population increase — albeit haltingly — during this period, but most of the households stayed put. In 1827, 78 per cent of the households of 1825 were still resident, and at the end of the five-year period 70 per cent remained. This does not mean that the demographic scene was stable. For example, of the households of 1825, the Joseph Barnes and Robert Kirkwood households were gone in 1827 but back in 1828. The seven-member Eder Wallon household was gone in 1828 but back in 1830. The William Adams household, of the same size, was away in 1827, back in 1828, and gone in 1830; and the Curtis Adams family does not appear in the 1828 record but is back in 1830, slightly reduced in size. The most notable loss was the Mahlon Beach household. He was a township assessor in 1825 and 1827, when his household totalled eleven, but he had left the township by 1828, following an earlier departure of one of the other half dozen Beach families. South Gower did not belie the characteristic fluidity of the population at the beginning of the nineteenth century, but at least for the five years at the end of the 1820s, it was not being depopulated by a rush to the West (or anywhere else).

"The West" for Upper Canada after the war was a gradually expanding belt of newly surveyed townships primarily in three locations: north of the Oak Ridges moraine, in the broad gore that had been Mississauga territory (later Peel County), and on the far side of the Grand and Thames valleys. This belt of recent settlement stands out on the maps of population change and the frontier fringe (see Figures 2B, 5, 6). It is to that area that we turn to re-examine a frontier population in the making.

Erin Township was initially in Gore District, part of the 648,000-acre cession by the Mississauga Indians in 1818. It was surveyed into lots in 1821. In natural endowments it was closest to the earlier townships that had suffered fluctuations in growth. It lay on top of the Niagara Escarpment and thereby was grudgingly blessed with shallow soils or with heavier morainic deposits of mediocre fertility, interspersed with wet patches. The population growth, however, seemed to be unimpeded by the natural deficiencies during the first fifteen years (see Figure 8). In 1822 there were 43 souls; by the end of the period, 1,200.

All the new townships had a similar exponential growth, shown most dramatically by Erin, Nichol, and Wilmot, such as had occurred in the first generation only in the persistent-growth townships. It is well-nigh impossible to classify the second-generation townships: they were all fast growers, even ones such as Fitzroy in the Ottawa Valley, which overcame an early destabilization by nomadic loggers. The fundamental distinction between the first generation and the second was that after the war the province was invaded by increasing numbers of overseas immigrants who pushed into most areas, but especially the newly opening townships, eager to try to make a livelihood in conditions with which they were unfamiliar. The rapid growth continued for a number of years until the farmers came to terms with the environmental limitations of a given township. In almost all the townships, after fifteen years of settlement the growth levelled off or receded.

Erin was similar to the pre-war townships in some important respects. The original households tended to stay: 52 per cent of the twenty-nine households of 1824 were still there in 1834. The loss of households was gradual: after two years (in 1826) 72 per cent were persisting, whereas after seven years 62 per cent were. Over the ten years, five of the households disappeared and then returned. Many

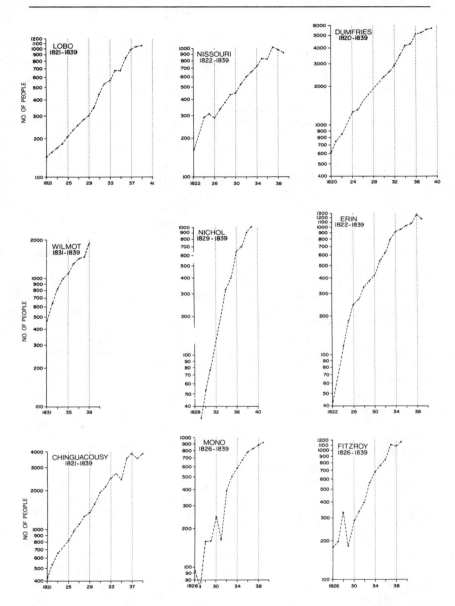

Figure 8: Population of townships newly opened after the War of 1812, for the years c. 1819-39. Sources: See sources to Figure 2.

households also appear to have had members coming and going from year to year.[24] Most households gradually added or, at a different stage, lost members. The Henry Barkley household, in the three years from 1824, went from seven to nine to six, and then settled at five through 1834. The Henry Trout household, from 1824 to 1830, went from eight to eleven, ten, eight, four, five, and then left the township.[25]

Erin Township was also different in some important respects. The founding families were inundated by the flood of newcomers, and certain demographic characteristics that had developed in the first generation settlements did not develop in Erin. Although over half the households of 1824 were still in the township in 1834, at the latter date they only accounted for 9 per cent of all households (unlike the 25 to 35 per cent in the townships in the first generation). The persisters, along with their relatives or offspring (based on surname), only made up 17 per cent of the 1834 population of 859. They did uphold the persisters' reputation of having larger households than the average — 7.1 compared with the township average of 5.3.

Erin differed from most other parts of the province in that the predominance of men gradually increased from 1825 to 1839. The only other township, of the twenty-five sampled, to have the same pattern as Erin was Hamilton, with its demographically volatile town. Erin fits the picture of a lightly populated township throughout the period. For example, it had a population of 185 in 1825 and an adult male-female ratio of 107:100. This looks like the pre-war examples of marginal areas (intermittent-change townships) that were first entered by small families. By 1828 (population 336) the ratio was up to 118:100, but in the following year it was down to 108:100. In 1834, with the population at 948, the ratio was 123:100. The ratios for Hamilton Township were even more irregular, beginning in 1819 at 107:100 and ending in 1839 at 153:100.

In one other respect Erin Township was unusual. It will be noticed that many of the population graphs show a setback between 1837 and 1838.[26] Just as the War of 1812 appears to have had more effect on the population in some parts of the province than in others, so the Rebellion of 1837 caused an eddy in the demographic processes in many townships. In most cases this was a loss of men. Erin lost men but at the same time reported a population increase. Further investigation of the demographic repercussions of the rebellion might provide a fuller understanding of this puzzling episode in Upper Canada's history.

The rise in the population of Erin in 1837-38 was brought about by a significant increase in the number of children and women. This brings our attention, for the last time, to the under-sixteen component of the population. Although it is difficult to get long, reliable runs of data, some rudimentary patterns may be identifiable. When some township populations are followed through thirty or forty years, a distinction between the pre- and post-war settlements appears. In the pre-war settlements, where there was very little immigration, the peak proportion of children — often 56 to 62 per cent — was reached within the first ten years. After that it descended into a long trough before rising somewhat with the next generation (usually from the mid-1830s). In the post-war settlements, the peak took twelve to fifteen years to be reached, and it was lower, in the range of 52 to 55 per cent. The distinction needs to be made that, although in gross terms the frontier was a men's domain, it rather quickly became a children's domain if it was conducive to agricultural (and therefore family) development. This was part of the "fertility explosion" before land began to get scarce and the younger generation began to consider leaving the farm.[27]

The importance of women and children in the changes in the population demonstrates that mobile men were not always the chief demographic influence. In fact, the generalization suggested earlier — that fluctuations were primarily due to the coming and going of unattached men — does not stand up without further qualification. An analysis of the long population series, some beginning before the War of 1812, reveals that although some fluctuations may have been caused by migrant men, as many were caused by changes in the number of children, or women and children, or by all components combined. Specific examples can be cited, in reference to graphs in Figures 3, 7, and 8. In Hope Township, the increase in 1818-19 was primarily of men, but the increase of 1810-11 was of children; and the decreases of 1820-21 and 1833-34 were losses of women and children. Men were involved in the decreases of 1829-30, 1836-37, and 1838-39, but certainly not alone. Among the post-war townships only a few appear to have been affected specifically by the movement of men. In Fitzroy, the increase of 1829-30 and the decrease of 1837-38 are among the examples. But the increases of 1827-28, 1832-33, and 1836-37 were related as much to the proportion of children as to that of adult males, as was the decrease of 1828-29. In Chinguacousy and Nissouri none of the changes can be attributed primarily to the men. Lobo Township, on the western frontier, appears to have been influenced by migrant men in the slowing of the growth in 1832-33 and 1838-39, but apart from that, any changes were broadly based.

Implications for Frontier Population Theory

The evidence from Upper Canada helps to clarify a few of the casual notions about what frontier population was like, at least in the mainly wooded lands of east-central North America. One important conclusion is that despite gross similarities, some of which arise from common conditions during the initial settlement, and some of which have emerged from the mists of frontier romanticizing, the "frontier experience" embraced considerable demographic variety. There were notable fluctuations in its population, including in the growth rate. All the townships in Upper Canada experienced setbacks, if not loss, in population in the first few years of their settlement; for the most successful, such as Hamilton or Dumfries townships, the growth continued for nearly twenty years before a break. Unabated growth was by no means the norm.

The ratio of men to women fluctuated dramatically both before and after the War of 1812. During the first generation, before the war, when township populations numbered only in the hundreds, the drifting of unattached men could have a major influence in population change. But, over the whole period, the best-established conclusion on this ratio is that men remained in a numerical majority in rural areas, except in half a dozen of the oldest-settled townships. The rough living conditions, the transiency, indeed all the trials of frontier existence were widely shared by men, women, and children. The records show that, after the War of 1812, women and children could be as responsible as men for striking variations in population.

The rate of immigration from outside the region had certain effects on the population. In Upper Canada's second generation the rapidly growing body of overseas immigrants "force-fed" the population increase (as can be seen in the graphs), and a township's population could rise much more quickly than had been true even for the persistent-growth townships in the first generation. In addition, it became common for people other than just men to be moving into new areas in large numbers.

Finally a township newly opened to settlement, no matter what the period and no matter what its ultimate agricultural potential, gave expression to some common characteristics. Among the initial body of settlers were the founding families: close to half the households involved in the first flush of land taking would remain in the township. They would soon develop households larger than the average for the township. Perhaps a legitimate extension also would be to visualize them as coming to dominate the township economically as well as genetically. Around the founding families milled large numbers of less fixed households that moved in and out (along with surplus members of the founding families). An Old Country visitor in the 1840s, struck by the apparent rootlessness of the population and the preponderance of immigrants, wrote

> There is a curious feature about Upper Canada ... that
> is, the exceedingly heterogeneous and exotic character
> of its population: ... the country has not been settled
> long enough for a generation born in it to have sprung
> up to any extent.[28]

A decade or two would pass before the native-born population would have "sprung up" enough to exert much influence in the townships newly settled in the 1820s and '30s.

NOTES

I am indebted to Gregory Finnegan for his effective research assistance and to Janet Allin for her excellent cartographic renderings; also to the reviewer (Prof. Brian S. Osborne) for a thorough and helpful reading. The research leading to this essay has been generously supported by grant #410-82-0925 from the Social Science and Humanities Research Council, by the York University SSHRC Travel and Small Grants Committee (1985), and by the Atkinson College Committee on Research, Grants, and Sabbaticals (1986).

1   Contained in Archives of Ontario, Municipal Records, RG 21, or in National Archives of Canada, Provincial and Civil secretaries' papers, RG 5, B 26. Familiarity with these clerks' reports does not breed unquestioning confidence; one feels obliged to make careful judgments about their accuracy and complete-ness, and as a result one discounts or avoids many of the returns. A point in favour of this kind of source is that, with the relatively small populations, the township clerk probably knew almost everyone in the township.

2   But see the recent account in Thomas F. McIlwraith, "British North America, 1763-1867," in Robert D. Mitchell and Paul A. Groves, eds., *North America: The Historical Geography of a Changing Continent* (Totowa, N.J.: Rowman and Littlefield, 1987), pp. 220-52, esp. pp. 235-50.

3   Many related questions are admirably addressed, on a broad basis, in Tamara K. Hareven and M.A. Vinovskis, eds., *Family and Population in Nineteenth Century America* (Princeton: Princeton University Press, 1978); and in "The American Population", in L.E. Davis, R.A. Easterlin, and W.N. Parker, eds., *American Economic Growth: An Economist's History of the United States* (New York: Harper and Row, 1972), pp. 121-83.

4   Howard Temperley points out that, because of the intrusion of money to reward loyalty, it was not a typical Turnerian frontier (if such existed): "Loyalists had a hard time of it.... Remarkably quickly, however, conditions improved." "Fronti-erism, Capital, and the American Loyalists in Canada," *Journal of American Studies*, 13 (1979), pp. 5-27, quotation on p. 5.

5   Bruce Wilson, *As She Began: An Illustrated Introduction to Loyalist Ontario* (Toronto: Dundurn, 1981), esp. Chaps. 3 and 4.

6   D.H. Akenson, *The Irish in Ontario* (Montreal and Kingston: McGill-Queen's University Press, 1984), esp. Chap. 1.

7   J.D. Wood, "The Population of Ontario: A Study of the Foundation of a Social Geography," in G.M. Robinson, ed., *A Social Geography of Canada*, forthcoming.

8   See Darrell Norris's exhaustive study: "Household and Transiency in a Loyalist Township: The People of Adolphustown, 1784-1822," *Histoire sociale/Social History*, 13, No. 26 (1980), 399-415.

9   Certainly in a few townships analysed the proportion of the population under sixteen years old (the only division between adults and children in the township clerks' annual reports) was lower than it had been for the previous decade. But extending the graphs to 1840 indicates that the war came near the beginning of a long-term decline in the proportion of under-sixteens, which started to rise again at the end of the 1830s.

10   Evidence is found in the 1813 clerk's report for Leeds and Lansdowne Rear, in the RG 21 microfilms, the Archives of Ontario, which gives military ranks for men who were almost certainly away on active duty.

11   Cf. Douglas McCalla, "The 'Loyalist' Economy of Upper Canada, 1784-1806," *Histoire sociale/Social History*, 16, No. 32 (1983), 279-304, esp. 283-86.

12   J.D. Wood, "The Population of Ontario...". The proportion accounted for by under-sixteens in the 1980s is less than 25 per cent.

13   As reported by H. L. Lefferts Jr., in "Frontier Demography: an Introduction," in D.H. Miller and J.O. Steffen, eds., *The Frontier: Comparative Studies* (Norman: University of Oklahoma Press, 1977), pp. 49-50.

14   This is the kind of personal detail behind the "complex local currents" that Michael Conzen treats at a different level and a different time in "Local Migration Systems in Nineteenth-Century Iowa," *The Geographical Review*, 64 (1974), 339-61.

15   Early evidence of this was offered by Merle Curti in *The Making of An American Community: A Case Study of Democracy in a Frontier County* (Stanford: Stanford University Press, 1959), p. 68. Hal S. Barron found that in a much older settlement, between 1860 and 1880, households with four or more children were the most likely to leave: *Those Who Stayed Behind: Rural society in nineteenth-century New England* (Cambridge: Cambridge University Press, 1984), p. 89. David Gagan, in *Hopeful Travellers: Families, Land, and Social Change in Mid-Victorian Peel County, Canada West* (Toronto: University of Toronto Press, 1980), pp. 117-19, found age — and, one would expect, also family size — not significant in transiency.

16   D. Norris, "Household and transiency..."; David Gagan and H. Mays, "Historical Demography and Canadian Social History: Families and Land in Peel County, Ontario," *Canadian Historical Review*, 54 (1973), 27-47.

17   I am indebted to Mrs. Rosemary Dubyk for the Haldimand, Percy, and Adolphustown calculations.

18   Cf. Gagan's analysis of "the persistent minority" in later Peel County, in *Hopeful Travellers...*, p. 116, passim. Also, H. J. Mays's thorough study of one township in "'A Place to Stand': Families, Land and Permanence in Toronto Gore Township, 1820-1890," *Historical Papers 1980*, presented at the annual meeting, Canadian Historical Association, pp. 185-211. Allan Bogue reports a remarkably similar finding, what he calls "the persistence of a substantial nucleus of settlers from the first census," in all the townships he studied in the midwest United States, and points to the inaccuracy of Turner's idea that "primitive" settlers were replaced by incursions of more advanced ones. *From Prairie to Corn Belt: Farming on the Illinois and Iowa Prairies in the Nineteenth Century* (Chicago: University of Chicago Press, 1963), pp. 26-27. And see a similar qualification of Turner, in Robert D. Mitchell, *Commercialism and Frontier: Perspectives on the Early Shenandoah Valley* (Charlottesville: University Press of Virginia, 1977), p. 133.

19   Robert Gourlay, *Statistical Account of Upper Canada* [1822], Carleton Library No. 75, ed. S.R. Mealing, p. 22.

20   For an illustrative analysis by lot of the expansion and retreat of settlement around the Shield edge, see Brian S. Osborne, "Frontier Settlement in Eastern Ontario in the Nineteenth Century: A Study in Changing Perceptions of Land and Opportunity," in D. H. Miller and J. O. Steffen, eds., *The Frontier: Comparative Studies* (Norman: University of Oklahoma Press, 1977), pp. 201-25.

21   Cf. Jacob Spelt, *Urban Development in Southcentral Ontario*, Carleton Library No. 57, Chap. 3 and Figs. 6 and 7. Thirty per square mile is a density similar to today's rates in southern Bruce County and in eastern Ontario away from the cities and major highways.

22   These measures in part hark back to F. J. Turner, or at least to the Superintendent of the Census from whom Turner took his cue. The 1890 Census of the
United States pointed out that a population density of only six per square mile
was the minimum for what can be considered agricultural territory. Cf. J. Fraser
Hart, "The Spread of the Frontier and the Growth of Population," in H.J. Walker
and W.G. Haag, eds., *Man and Culture...*, Vol. 5 of *Geoscience and Man*, 1974, pp.
73-81.

23   Bogue observed such similarities on the opening of successive townships
westward in Iowa: *From Prairie to Corn Belt*, Chap. 1.

24   See Norris's illustration of this for two families in Adolphustown, in "Household and Transiency...," pp. 412-14.

25   I presume this is the same Henry Trout who was a justice of the peace in some
part of the Gore District in 1840, when he swore in the assessor for Erin Township.

26   The population enumeration being an annual spring responsibility of the clerk,
the 1838 count would have been taken three or four months after the uprising.

27   Cf. R.M. McInnis, "Childbearing and Land Availability: Some Evidence from
Individual Household Data," in Ronald D. Lee, ed., *Population Patterns in the
Past* (New York: Academic Press, 1977), pp. 201-27; David Gagan, *Hopeful
Travellers...*, esp. Chap. 3.

28   From J. R. Godley, *Letters from America*, quoted in Gerald M. Craig, ed., *Early
Travellers in the Canadas, 1791-1867* (Toronto: Macmillan, 1955), p. 143. Great
transience seems to have been a characteristic of agricultural frontiers only with
the rise of overseas migration, since it was not significant in the earliest agricultural settlements in New England: see P. J. Greven, Jr., *Four Generations:
Population, Land, and Family in Colonial Andover, Massachusetts* (Ithaca and
London: Cornell Univerity Press, 1970), esp. Chaps. 6 and 7. The complex
migration paths leading to a new settlement in Grey County are discussed in
Darrell Norris, "Migration, Pioneer Settlement and the Life Course: The First
Families of an Ontario Township, *Canadian Papers in Rural History*, Vol. 4 (1984),
pp. 130-52.

RE-INVENTING UPPER CANADA: AMERICAN IMMIGRANTS, UPPER CANADIAN HISTORY, ENGLISH LAW, AND THE ALIEN QUESTION

Paul Romney

"A more interesting question was never agitated than that which has lately been started, whether all the inhabitants of the province who were either resident in the United States at the treaty of peace of 1783, or born there afterwards of British-born parents, are notwithstanding their residence here for seven years, to be now deemed aliens, ineligible as members of Assembly, unqualified to vote at elections, and incapable of inheriting lands, or even holding them by purchase, except as tenants at the will of the Crown." In these measured phrases, a writer signing himself "Simcoe" alerted the readers of the *Upper Canada Herald* in March 1822 to the implications of an impassioned debate that had occupied the provincial House of Assembly for several days during the recent session.[1] At issue was the title of Barnabas Bidwell, recently victorious in a by-election in the incorporated counties of Lennox and Addington, to sit as a member of the provincial parliament. The debate had turned partly on questions of moral fitness peculiar to the candidate, but another point of contention had been his nationality. Was Bidwell, though British-born, still a natural-born subject at the time of his election in November 1821? An attentive house had heard the law officers of the Crown, Attorney General John Beverley Robinson and Solicitor General Henry John Boulton, argue that he was not. If their argument was correct, were not the thousands of Upper Canadians mentioned by Simcoe — perhaps more than half of the inhabitants, certainly more than half of the landowners and electors — also aliens, and therefore legally incapable of owning lands and exercising political rights which had been their unchallenged possession for decades? The legal conundrum was perplexing, the social implications frightening.

In due course, the "alien question" produced a sensation commensurate with its importance. It brought Upper Canadian reformers into contact with imperial ministers and British radical politicians; it taught aggrieved colonists that they could hope to thwart the provincial government by appealing to London. It imbued an important section of the electorate with a lasting distrust of the government's integrity.[2] It engendered important innovations in political organization as the two sides competed to influence public opinion and bring it to bear on imperial politicians and administrators.[3] In retrospect it appears as one of the chief events in a sequence that leads to both the campaign for responsible government and the Rebellion of 1837. Yet while this event figures prominently in almost every work bearing on the politics of Upper Canada in the 1820s, it has never been given the thorough scrutiny it merits. It has been discussed capably, but always within a broader context which has imposed restrictions of scope. Anyone interested in the alien question must resort to a variety of accounts, each of which is focused on one or two aspects at the expense of the whole and each biased towards the same side, owing to that side's success in impressing its position on the common memory.[4]

The object of this paper is to redress the balance by examining two aspects of the question that have never previously been considered. One is the nature of the legal issues involved in the controversy. Historians have tended to agree with Aileen Dunham that the alien question "was a legal one of a strictly technical sort, but like all other questions of the period it was dragged into politics."[5] This statement bears two erroneous implications: first, that the legal and the political aspect of the question were mutually distinct; secondly, that the legal problem was resolvable by the strict and impartial application of legal rules and that the messiness of the affair resulted from its political complications.[6] These misconceptions entail the belief that the provincial government's view of the law was "correct" and opposing arguments merely meretricious. This belief is quite unfounded: we shall see that the law could be made to yield several distinct conclusions and that nearly everyone favoured the conclusion that was agreeable to his political prepossessions. The government position was neither uniquely "correct" nor even based on a full and impartial assessment of the relevant facts; it was in fact strongly biased by ulterior political motives. The second major topic of this paper is the significance of the alien controversy as a phenomenon of political culture. Upper Canadians' sense of their community, and their place in it as individuals, was rooted in their understanding of the colony's history. The claim of the late Loyalists[7] to be members of the community relied heavily on one view of its history; their opponents challenged this view and hinted at an alternative. The controversy forced both sides to articulate their understanding of the character of the Upper Canadian community, and its relationship to the imperial power, in a way that had important political consequences.

I

We must begin with a little parliamentary history. It has been said that the provincial House of Assembly refused from the start to declare Barnabas Bidwell an alien, and that he was ousted from the Assembly at the beginning of 1822 on the ground of moral turpitude.[8] This error flows from the misapprehension that the Assembly finally disposed of the question of Bidwell's nationality in November 1821, when it rejected a motion to declare him an alien. The error is excusable, being one that Lieutenant-Governor Sir Peregrine Maitland made in a dispatch to Whitehall less than four months after the event.[9] In fact, though, the course of the debate was far more complicated than this interpretation implies and its outcome far more ambiguous.

The challenge to the return of Barnabas Bidwell, couched in the form of a petition to the House of Assembly, was introduced by Attorney General Robinson in his capacity as a member of the provincial parliament. The petition admitted that Bidwell met the residential and property qualifications required of a candidate by the law governing provincial elections; it relied, therefore, on "circumstances connected with his character which render him utterly unworthy of the high honor of sitting in your august House." As treasurer of the county of Berkshire, in Massachusetts, he had reportedly been guilty of a misapplication of public funds, as a consequence of which he had fled to Upper Canada in 1810 in order to avoid arrest and trial. Though he claimed to be a natural-born British subject, he had lived in Massachusetts throughout the war for independence and subsequently, as a citizen of the United States, had become first a member of the House of Representatives and later attorney general of Massachusetts. In these official capacities, he had been obliged to swear an oath — which the petition recited in full — renouncing and abjuring "all allegiance, subjection and obedience" to the British Crown. When required as a resident of Upper Canada to swear allegiance to the Crown upon the outbreak of war with the United States in 1812, he had remarked that since this second oath was compulsory he did not consider it binding. The petition contended that these circumstances "morally incapacitated" Bidwell as a member of the House of Assembly, and it prayed that his election be declared null and void.[10]

The petition spoke only of moral, not legal incapacity, but the reference to Bidwell's residence in the United States during and after the revolution was bound to invoke any doubts that existed as to his nationality. Indeed, the anti-Bidwellites emphasized this aspect of the question from the start. "The question to be considered was whether the sitting member was a natural born subject, or an alien," said Attorney General Robinson in the first debate on the petition. Christopher Hagerman echoed him: "The question to be considered was, whether

Mr. Bidwell was a natural born subject, and had he retained his allegiance or not?" Robinson's other main auxiliaries, the brothers Jonas and Charles Jones, also made Bidwell's nationality the main issue. At the conclusion of the first debate, Jonas Jones moved that Bidwell's own admissions were sufficient to prove him an alien and therefore ineligible to the Assembly.[11]

Jones's motion was defeated by twenty votes to twelve, but the nationality question was far from dead. When the Assembly next considered the petition, a month later, Solicitor General Boulton, acting for the petitioners, at once announced his intention to prove that Bidwell was an alien. William Warren Baldwin moved that this was out of order, since the house had already expressed its view on the question, but he was overruled by the Speaker and Boulton presented his case. In the ensuing debate, the Bidwellites gained an initial advantage when Thomas Nichol, the government's chief critic in the Assembly, successfully moved that the allegations as to Bidwell's misconduct in the United States, even if true, were not legal disqualifications for a seat in the Assembly and therefore could not be taken into consideration.[12] This decision apparently committed the house to the position that the only relevant matters in the petition were those of Bidwell's nationality and his conduct upon taking the oath of allegiance in Upper Canada in 1812; of these, the latter was rather neglected in the subsequent debate, probably because so much conflicting evidence had been given on it.[13]

Bidwell's supporters seemed to have achieved a position in which Bidwell's expulsion depended on the Assembly's readiness to accept a proposition it had decisively rejected a month previously — that Bidwell was an alien; but the anti-Bidwellites managed the revive the morality issue by moving, in very general terms, that the allegations in the petition had been proved and Bidwell's election was therefore void. To the objection that the only question now before the house was Bidwell's nationality, they replied that, even if the alleged misconduct in Massachusetts was no *legal* disqualification, the privilege of expelling a member as morally unfit was inherent in the Assembly. This argument was somewhat disingenuous, since expelling a member on moral grounds was not the same thing as declaring his election void on those grounds, and it was the second course that was envisaged by the motion under debate; still it achieved its object.[14]

The trouble with the new motion was that it was not vague enough. It implied that *all* the matters alleged in the petition, whether relating to moral fitness or to nationality, were grounds for voiding the election. This troubled members who were willing to oust Bidwell as an alien but felt that the house had committed itself on the morality question by adopting Nichol's resolution. James Gordon of Kent deferred to their scruples by moving an amendment, which Robinson seconded, to the effect that "sufficient of the allegations" had been proved to render the election void. This language could be supported by those who thought that Bidwell was an alien but not morally disqualified, and by those who thought him morally disqualified but not an alien. It sufficed to achieve Bidwell's expulsion by a single vote, after an identical division of the house had defeated Dr. Baldwin's motion that the charges "had not been proved in such manner" as to render the election void.[15]

It was partly in order to resolve the ambiguity of this outcome that Marshall Spring Bidwell was nominated in February 1822 for the seat from which his father had just been ousted. The voters who had been deprived of Barnabas Bidwell were not just making a bid for the next best thing, they were forcing the Assembly to declare itself unequivocally on the nationality question; for in the younger Bidwell's past there was no moral blemish to cloud the issue. As "Simcoe" observed in the *Upper Canada Herald*, if the larger part of the province's landowners and electors were going to be branded as aliens, the sooner it was ascertained the better.[16] Marshall Bidwell's candidature was rejected by the returning officer as being that of an alien, but Bidwell's supporters challenged the return. On February 14, 1823, after more than a year of equivocation, the House of Assembly at last committed itself on the nationality question by resolving that Marshall Bidwell was eligible.[17]

II

As a problem in law, the alien question flowed from Britain's recognition of American independence by the Treaty of Paris, 1783. Looking back nearly forty years, members of the Upper Canadian House of Assembly found themselves debating whether the treaty had affected the status of Americans as natural-born subjects of the British Crown. If so, how were individuals who had lost that status to be distinguished from those who had retained it? The Bidwells' opponents affirmed that the treaty had affected individual allegiance and that the Bidwells, and perhaps other Americans who had moved to Upper Canada after the treaty, were therefore aliens. The Bidwellites denied that the treaty had affected individual allegiance; and when, in 1824, the English Court of King's Bench handed down a decision that contradicted them, they were thrown into disarray. Yet *Thomas* v. *Acklam*[18] had no direct bearing on the status of Americans who had settled in Upper Canada during the past four decades, and even before its decision some of their advocates were edging towards the position that, even if the treaty had affected individual allegiance, neither the Bidwells nor any other Upper Canadian settler had lost their British nationality.

Both sides accepted the dictum of Sir William Blackstone, the authoritative mid-eighteenth-century English jurist, that a subject could not legally abjure his allegiance to the Crown, nor be absolved of it by the Crown alone; allegiance could be removed, just as it could be conferred, only by act of Parliament.[19] How, then, could there be any doubt as to whether American subjects of the Crown had lost their status as natural-born subjects? The trouble was that there was no statute on the books which expressly deprived them of that status; neither did the treaty itself say anything on the subject. The question, therefore, was whether the treaty had implicitly affected individual allegiance, and if so, whether the statute of 1782 that had authorized the king to negotiate a peace with the rebellious colonies — a statute couched in the most general terms, which did not even address the prospect of independence — could be construed as implicitly sanctioning that implicit effect.[20]

In the absence of explicit language in either the treaty or the statute, Bidwell's supporters denied that the peace of 1783 had affected individual allegiance. Dwelling on George III's reluctance to conclude a peace that would mean abandoning his loyal subjects to the rebels, Robert Nichol ascribed the treaty's silence to a design not to cut stranded Loyalists off from their sovereign.[21] William Baldwin maintained that both parties to the treaty had concurred in that silence, since United States residents who remained loyal to the Crown could be distinguished from those who had not only by requiring the former to abandon their possessions and livelihoods and move to British territory. This would have imposed great hardship on individuals, contrary to the spirit of reconciliation that was supposed to animate the treaty.[22]

In the absence of legislative contradiction, Baldwin affirmed, Calvin's Case governed the situation.[23] In that judgment of 1608, the Jacobean judge and jurist Sir Edward Coke had distinguished between *natural* allegiance, which was perpetual, and *local* allegiance, which was temporary. Natural allegiance was owed to the sovereign into whose allegiance one was born, and to his heirs. It persisted even if one moved out of the empire of one's birth, or if one's province of residence was transferred to another sovereign by conquest or accident of inheritance; when King John lost Normandy and several other provinces to France, therefore, the inhabitants of those provinces born before the cession remained natural-born subjects of the English Crown. Similarly, Americans born before independence retained willy-nilly their allegiance to the Crown and owed to the United States (in the eyes of English law) only the local allegiance due to any foreign sovereign while sojourning in his territory — an allegiance that ceased with the sojourn. This was true even of the president of the United States; even he, on moving to British territory with his family and effects, must be admitted to the rights, privileges, and immunities that were his by birth.

The anti-Bidwellites denied the relevance of Calvin's Case. Distinguishing between the surrender of territory to a foreign conqueror and to a rebel citizenry, they argued that the former was a transaction between sovereign potentates and the inhabitants of the transferred territory were merely passive subjects of the transaction. The recognition of American independence, uniquely in British history, belonged in the latter category. Every consenting resident of the United States at the time of the treaty must be considered as a party to it, not merely as a passive subject of its provisions; thus it was not analogous to the loss of Normandy by King John.[24] The English law of allegiance must be adapted to comprehend this unique event.

In addition to reasoning directly from the treaty and the events surrounding it, each side invoked legislation and administrative practice, imperial and provincial, that tended to support its view. The Bidwellites cited an imperial act of 1790, passed in order to entice settlers from the United States by letting them bring in goods to a certain value duty free.[25] The first lieutenant-governor, John Simcoe, a Member of Parliament when the act was passed, had vigorously executed the policy of encouraging immigration from across the line. From 1792 to 1812, American immigrants had readily been granted lands by the Crown and had been unchallenged in their exercise of the political rights that went with proprietorship.[26]

This policy, and this practice, presupposed that the beneficiaries were British subjects. The presupposition was confirmed by no less than four provincial statutes, passed at different times as a precaution against the entry of disaffected persons, which withheld political rights from immigrants from the United States until they had resided in Upper Canada for a certain period.[27] Unless such immigrants were inherently entitled to the political rights of British subjects, such legislation was redundant. Even more to the point was the Forfeited Estates Act of 1814. The statute provided that American immigrants who had voluntarily returned to the United States since the commencement of the war, or who did so in future without licence from the government, were to "be taken and considered to be Aliens born and incapable of holding Lands within this Province."[28] Why was such legislation necessary, unless other late Loyalists were to be taken and considered to be natural-born subjects, capable of holding lands and exercising the political rights that went with landholding?

For counter-examples, the anti-Bidwellites went abroad. Had Barnabas Bidwell fled to England instead of Upper Canada, observed Hagerman, he would have been treated as an alien by British customs officials. Robinson invoked a British statute of 1788, passed to regulate trade between British and foreign territories in North America and the West Indies, which treated Americans as aliens. Other speakers cited article IX of the Anglo-American Treaty of 1795 (Jay's Treaty), which protected the current claims of each country's nationals to property situated in the other country. Unless the settlement of 1783 had relieved Americans of their British allegiance, they contended, this guarantee of claims to estates in England was redundant. Articles of the Treaty of Paris that guaranteed to Americans the continuance of rights they had enjoyed prior to independence were construed in the same way.[29]

Of course, neither side was content with staking out its own position; each also attacked its opponent's. Bidwell's supporters dwelt on the speculative character of the anti-Bidwellite position, which entailed a departure from doctrine that had long prevailed. In Baldwin's words, it was "mere inference from general reasoning and expediency ... urged against absolute and indisputable right."[30] The anti-Bidwellites in turn denounced the Bidwellite view as ridiculous. As early as 1818, Robinson had written that unless Americans were aliens, English law entailed the "monstrous absurdity" that "they may become in 1815 under the sanction and protection of our laws the legal proprietors of our soil, which in 1814 they invaded in open war, without incurring the guilt of treason."[31] The Bidwell debates evoked several similar comments, with Robinson leading the way. Often this argument was emphasized by naming eminent Americans who were thus privileged — Presidents Madison and Monroe, Generals Hull and Jackson, and so on; hence Baldwin's insistence that even these had retained the status of a natural-born subject.[32]

While it might seem absurd to contend that every American born before the treaty had retained British nationality, the anti-Bidwellites found it difficult to say exactly who had retained that status and who had not. Their leading opponents — Baldwin, Nichol, and John Willson — attacked this point strongly. If the treaty had affected individual allegiance at all, they maintained, its failure to say definitely who was affected meant that it must have alienated every American domiciled in the United States at the time it went into effect. The Assembly could not vote that Barnabas Bidwell was an alien without committing itself to the view that every resident of Upper Canada then so domiciled was equally an alien. The anti-Bidwellite doctrine was one, intoned Nichol, "that disfranchised and ruined thousands." If carried into effect, it would "depopulate the greatest part of this country by exiling a great proportion of the population."[33]

At first the anti-Bidwellites laboured to apply their doctrine narrowly, in order to distinguish the Bidwells from the thousands whom their view of the treaty allegedly placed also at risk. Barnabas Bidwell had held high office in the United States. As a condition of office, he had taken not merely an oath of allegiance to the United States but one expressly abjuring allegiance to the Crown. These acts probably made him unique in the province. This "narrow" anti-Bidwellite argument contended that Barnabas Bidwell, perhaps alone of the inhabitants of Upper Canada, had performed acts that entailed a choice of American over British allegiance.[34]

Once the Assembly had rejected Jonas Jones's motion to expel Bidwell as an alien, however, the anti-Bidwellites began talking more and more as though residence in the United States at the time the treaty went into effect were in itself legal proof of alienage.[35] Even so, they did not concede that this applied across the board. Nichol was right in remarking that the treaty had stranded many genuine Loyalists in the United States, and no doubt supporters of the provincial government were to be found even among immigrants who were not Loyalists in the strict sense of the word. Despite the treaty's silence, therefore, the anti-Bidwellites clung to the notion that there was some test of action by which persons who had retained British nationality might be distinguished from those who had forfeited it. "There was no particular time specified when a person was to become a citizen of the United States or a British subject," said Charles Jones. "It was very properly left to his own option, and depended on his subsequent conduct how he was to be considered."[36] Yet what was the standard? "It cannot be that the Independence of America, absolved from their allegiance and divested of all its consequent rights, persons who never contended for it, and who were in principle and conduct attached to the Royal cause.... Where then shall we draw the line; what shall be the test?" So Attorney General Robinson had asked in 1818.[37] He seems never to have found a legally satisfactory answer.

If the treaty's silence was the anti-Bidwellites' bane, they tried to turn the silences in other instruments to their advantage. Robinson led the way. Reading a provincial order-in-council of November 1794, passed to facilitate American immigration, he emphasized that it contained no specific reference to Americans.[38] Charles Jones dealt similarly with the imperial statute of 1790 on which the Bidwellites relied so heavily. Given the scanty population of the colonies at the time, Parliament must have envisaged the immigration of farmers and their establishment as freeholders on lands granted by the Crown — a scheme that was impractical if the immigrants concerned were aliens, legally incapable of owning land until they had resided for seven years in British territory. Jones maintained, however, that Parliament might have meant to encourage the entry of tenant farmers or artisans.[39] Perhaps the crudest argument of this sort was the effort to explain away the provincial Forfeited Estates Act of 1814. The act clearly implied that any late Loyalist unaffected by the act was a natural-born subject; yet Hagerman and Jonas Jones tried to deny this implication even in the face of Nichol's authoritative assertion, as the member who had introduced the bill into the Assembly in 1814, that Robinson, then acting attorney general, had drafted it on that assumption.[40]

As well as directly rebutting the Bidwellite appeal to history, the anti-Bidwellites tried in different ways to evade it. One ploy was to cite imperial administrative policy towards Americans domiciled in the United States as though it were evidence of the late Loyalists' status; Hagerman's customs-house argument and Robinson's citation of the

North American trade statute of 1788 are examples of this. The Bidwellite invocation of administrative practice and the provincial election statutes to show that the imperilled settlers had historically *been taken as* natural-born subjects was met with a different ploy, that of misapprehending it as a claim that these things had *made them into* subjects. By scoffing that the legislature was not empowered to legislate on naturalization, and that the executive could not legislate at all, the anti-Bidwellites could evade the actual argument and pervert it into an absurdity.[41] A third sort of evasion consisted in rhetorical identification of the imperilled settlers with the invaders of the years 1812 to 1814. During the Bidwell debates, this rhetoric tended to be aimed at Barnabas Bidwell in particular, but the earliest example precedes Bidwell's election.[42] Applied to the nationality question, such rhetoric at once denied that the late Loyalists were distinguishable from Americans and identified them with the invaders of their own invaded land, much as Japanese Canadians were identified with the enemy during the Second World War.

On the Bidwellite side, the chief rhetorical excess consisted in plangent evocation of the late Loyalists' sufferings and ardent loyalty during the war, but at least this rhetoric had merit as an equitable presumption. In contrast to the writhings of anti-Bidwellite historical interpretation, the Bidwellite response to efforts to show that the imperial government considered Americans as aliens was generally quite reasonable. Baldwin pointed out that the treaty articles cited as evidence that Americans were no longer British could be read as prohibiting discriminatory legislation by one country against residents of the other in respect of the rights in question in those articles. He granted that the North American trade statute of 1788 treated Americans as aliens, but he denied it meant that individual Americans, on moving to British territory, would not be entitled to consideration as British subjects.[43]

Perhaps the most important contribution in this area of debate was John Willson's. In rebuttal of the argument that Bidwell, had he fled to England, would have been treated as an alien by customs officials, Willson remarked that "he could not be induced to think that Americans after residing seven years in Canada, and taking the oath of allegiance, would be considered as aliens in the customs house in England." He rejected Robinson's contention that imperial trade legislation was more authoritative evidence of the late Loyalists' legal status than the relevant provincial statutes.[44] Alone of the Bidwells' supporters in the Assembly, Willson took a position that distinguished between Americans who had remained in the United States and those who had emigrated to Upper Canada. Should it ever be authoritatively decided that the Treaty of Paris *had* affected individual allegiance, this was the necessary basis for a defence of the late Loyalists' claim to the rights, privileges, and immunities of British subjects.

III

It should now be clear that, according to English law, the claim of Americans of British ancestry to British allegiance were far from negligible, and moreover that a negative decision as to Americans resident in the United States need not apply to those who had opted for British allegiance by settling in Upper Canada. Yet historians have unanimously assumed that the provincial government was correct in its view that the mass of late Loyalists were aliens. John Garner unquestioningly assumes that the the the Treaty of Paris made the late Loyalists into aliens; Gerald Craig and Patrick Brode, a lawyer, agree that the government position was correct, Brode remarking in addition that "The York government had known since 1817 that the American settlers were aliens."[45]

One source of this error is an excessive reliance on government documents. Robinson and Lieutenant-Governor Maitland assiduously propagated the notion that their view of the law was not just their view — it was "the law." Since 1818 at the latest, as we shall see, Robinson had been labouring to impose his view on the imperial government; by the end of 1821, if not earlier, he and Maitland were intent on exploiting the situation for political ends. In January 1822 we find Robinson instructing the House of Assembly that Barnabas Bidwell's alienage was a matter of legal fact — that "it was utterly impossible that Mr. Bidwell could be a natural born subject" — and conjuring his fellow legislators, "as they were on their oaths, not to set their faces against law, & decide that a person was a natural born subject, who was to all intents & purposes, an alien."[46] When judgment was rendered in *Thomas v. Acklam*, the provincial government seized on it as proof that its view had all along been "correct," while the Bidwellite position was at best ignorant and at worst seditious. "Even before the late solemn decisions in England with respect to the rights of American Citizens," declared Lieutenant-Governor Maitland in typical fashion, "a correct view was taken of their situation by the Government."[47] True, he had the support of an opinion of the imperial law officers, but they knew of the matter only what Robinson had been pressing on them for several years past.[48] Deep political designs fed on ignorance, and the late Loyalists became, in the highly tendentious language of a document that bore the colonial secretary's signature but in fact had been written by Robinson,[49] "such Citizens of the United States as being heretofore settled in Canada are declared by the judgment of the Courts of Law in England and by the opinions of the Law Officers to be Aliens." Maitland reinforced this with a message to the legislature (which may very well also have been written by Robinson, as attorney general), declaring: "Whatever difference of opinion may have formerly prevailed with respect to the civil rights of persons so situated ... the solemn decision of the question in the

Courts of the Mother Country, whose laws we have adopted, leaves no room for doubt."[50]

At first this sort of rhetoric had an effect even on the leading Bidwellites. They had not begun to divine how deeply Robinson's view of the law was dyed in ulterior political motives, and the government propaganda was designed to play on a notion deeply imbricated in eighteenth-century Whig constitutionalism: the notion that law and politics, far from being mutually entangled, formed distinct departments of public discourse. Whig constitutionalism was predominant in the political culture of Upper Canada, as in that of the mother country, and members of the House of Assembly cannot have expected the attorney general, in his constitutional role as legal adviser to the legislature, to be influenced by a secret political agenda in his explanation of such a crucial point of law. It need not surprise us, then, to find even Nichol — stalwart though he was to be in the crisis — wincing under the barrage of lawyerly certainty, granting that the problem is "delicate," wishing out loud that they had more time to make up their minds, and falling back on the position that, after all, the judges of England had not yet made up theirs.[51] Early in 1823 Nichol introduced a set of resolutions calling on the imperial government to secure the position of "foreign protestants" who had inadvertently failed to comply with the imperial naturalization statute of 1740.[52] The resolutions were drawn so as to avoid the implication that the late Loyalists were among those affected, and the disguise gained colour from the fact that a number of German settlers were undoubtedly in need of such relief, but anti-Bidwellites hastened to include the Americans among the aliens in need of succour. John Willson would have nothing to do with resolutions that could be so construed and led a largely late Loyalist minority in voting against them.[53]

A week or two later, Dr. Baldwin fell by the wayside as the house considered the eligibility of Bidwell's son. Calvin's Case seemed to him to make Marshall Bidwell an alien as surely as it made Barnabas Bidwell a subject. Born in the United States after independence, the younger Bidwell claimed British nationality under two eighteenth-century statutes, which protected the allegiance of the foreign-born children and grandchildren of certain British subjects.[54] Baldwin held that these statutes could operate only if the father of the foreign-born child was "in obedience to the Crown" at the time of the birth; he did not think Barnabas Bidwell had been in obedience.

Baldwin drew an analogy between the Bidwells' case and that of Aeneas MacDonald and his sons. The father, born in Scotland but resident in France from childhood, had been convicted of treason for his part in the rebellion of 1745, but his sons, born in France, were held to be aliens despite their father's British nationality. More generally, Calvin's Case had decided that a Scot born after the union of the English and Scottish crowns in 1603 could inherit as an Englishman, but a Scot born earlier could not. From this Baldwin reasoned that, while all the *antenati* (Americans born before the Treaty of Paris went into effect) had retained their allegiance as natural-born subjects, all the *postnati* (persons born in the United States afterwards) were aliens, unable as such to inherit their *antenati* fathers' lands in the province, though children born in British territory might do so.[55]

Baldwin's reasoning focused on an aspect of the subject that every other speaker neglected. The circumstances which had brought the nationality question to public notice tended to focus attention on the status of the *antenati*, and every other participant in the Bidwell debates assumed that the status of the *postnati* would be the same as that of their parents. This was not a matter of course, however, and Simcoe, while taking the status of the *antenati* for granted, had wondered whether their *postnati* children could claim British nationality.[56] Still, the States-born children of late Loyalists had inherited from their parents on the tacit — but not unreasonable — assumption that they had acquired British allegiance as the dependent kin of *antenati* who had opted for that allegiance by moving to Upper Canada. If Baldwin was right, though, their claims to their inherited estates were void in law.[57]

In February 1823, then, the leading supporters of Barnabas Bidwell in the previous session were split over their reading of the law and their choice of political tactics, and in Baldwin the Bidwellites had lost their only professional spokesman in the house. Such confusion did not make it easy to formulate an unambiguous conception of the law in response to that pressed by the anti-Bidwellites. In the new house elected in 1824, from which Nichol and Baldwin were absent by reason of death and defeat respectively, Willson's view of the law was to command a clear majority and find unambiguous expression in the form of legislation; but legislation is usually perceived as "politics," though it may subsequently become reified as "law," and in this case the government used the same techniques as before to foster that view.[58] Since by then the decision in *Thomas* v. *Acklam* had contributed to the controversy what could be presented as an authoritative decision as to the legal status of the late Loyalists, it is not surprising that modern historians, writing within a political culture that has inherited the disposition to see law and politics as distinct, have tended to perceive the Bidwellite conception of that status as a political rather than a legal artifact.

It cannot be too strongly stressed, therefore, that especially where the law is unclear, judicial reasoning often boils down to making and justifying a political choice, and that even where the law is fairly plain, it is not unusual to find judges inventing new law, sometimes pretending for the sake of propriety that the innovation is merely a logical derivative of prior decisions.[59] It will now appear that *Thomas* v. *Acklam* was largely a product of political considerations, that its construction as proof of the late Loyalists' alienage was strongly influenced by political designs, and that the Bidwellite position, both before and after *Thomas v. Acklam*, was at least as valid an exercise in legal construction as that of Robinson and his allies.

IV

Thomas v. *Acklam* concerned the claim of a *postnata* to inherit an estate in England. Her claim to British nationality had been supported with precisely the same arguments as Marshall Bidwell's: first, that the Treaty of Paris had not affected individual allegiance; second, that though born on foreign soil, she had a statutory claim to British nationality as the child of a British father. In addition to Calvin's Case, her counsel cited three pre-war Scottish decisions, the earliest dating from 1791, which had upheld the claim of American residents (one an *antenata*, the others *postnati*) to lands in Scotland. Against her claim it was argued that the Treaty of Paris had implicitly affected individual allegiance and that Parliament had implicitly sanctioned the discharge of allegiance by the statute authorizing the peace negotiations. The defence too cited Calvin's Case, as Baldwin had against Marshall Bidwell, in order to argue that even if the plaintiff's father had not been discharged from his allegiance, he had been out of allegiance at her birth; but no case bearing directly on the allegiance of United States residents was cited, and the Scottish decisions were simply ignored. Instead, counsel for the defendant dwelt on the great inconvenience entailed in double allegiance.[60]

The court adopted the defendant's view of both the treaty and the statute as self-evident, and it commended the remarks on inconvenience, saying "If the language of the treaty *could* admit a doubt of its effect, the consideration of this inconvenience would have great weight toward the removal of the doubt."[61] Since it is manifest that the language of the treaty *could* admit a doubt of its effect, this expression of certainty has the hallmarks of a rhetorical posture. Judges may on occasion proclaim their willingness to be bold, but as I noted above, when acting boldly they like to claim that their decision is mandated either by judicial precedent or (as in *Thomas* v. *Acklam*) by the manifest tendency of the facts.[62] In choosing to interpret the treaty as it did, ignoring the Scottish precedents that authorized the opposite view, the court was doing exactly what it pretended not to be doing. It was reaching a decision according to the standard of convenience.

In doing so, the court was influenced by four decades of international political history, during which the reality of American independence was increasingly borne in upon the British government and people, most forcibly by the War of 1812. In the early years, it had been possible for British statesmen to think in terms of reconciliation, in the sense of a future return of the colonists to the imperial fold. Such notions lay behind the statute of 1790 that encouraged American emigration to Upper Canada, and behind Simcoe's attitude towards American immigrants to the province.[63] By 1824 it no longer made sense to Englishmen to maintain that United States citizens of British ancestry had retained, as individuals, their allegiance to the Crown; but if they had forfeited that allegiance, when could they have done so but in 1783? And how, but by participating in the treaty by which the political subjection of their country to the British Crown had been formally ended? These new attitudes coloured the thinking of the court in *Thomas* v. *Acklam*, leading it to disregard precedent in favour of an innovation suited to the new political conditions.[64]

Had the nationality question come before the English courts twenty-five years earlier, in *Marryat* v. *Wilson*,[65] it might have been decided otherwise. Marryat had refused to honour insurance policies on cargoes carried in a certain vessel trading between the United States and the East Indies. The trade was barred to British vessels. The vessel in question purported to be American, but Marryat argued that it was British because its co-owner and master, though he claimed United States citizenship, was a British subject; the illegality of the transport rendered the policies void. In rejecting Marryat's plea, the Court of Exchequer argued that John Collet's acquisition of United States citizenship, while it did not void his British nationality, was recognized by English law to the extent of affording him the privileges the law allowed to United States citizens.

Marryat v. *Wilson* did not decide the question because Marryat's case was based on the nationality of Collet, who had not become a resident of the United States until after 1783 and was therefore not covered by the argument that the Treaty of Paris had affected individual allegiance. But Collet's partner, Adam Butler, had been resident there in 1783. In omitting Butler from the case, Marryat's counsel may have been influenced by the possible effect of the Treaty of Paris on his relationship to the British Crown, but it is equally likely that the case was concentrated on Collet as being not only the vessel's co-owner but its master. At any rate, what is significant is an aside of Sir James Eyre, chief justice of the Court of Common Pleas, in giving judgment. "By the way I do not understand upon what ground the case of *Butler* was distinguished from *Collett's case*, unless Butler has been expressly discharged from his allegiance by act of parliament, in consequence of our acknowledgment of the independence of the United States. They were both natural-born subjects, they were both adopted subjects of the United States, and it is to be said of both Nemo patriam in quâ natus est exuere, nec legeantiae debitum ejurare possit [No one can cast off his native land, nor abjure the duty of allegiance]."[66]

The doubt expressed by Eyre in 1799 reflected much authoritative legal thinking and government practice during the early years of American independence. A decade later John Reeves, superintendent of aliens and law clerk to the Board of Trade, would rely heavily on Calvin's Case in arguing that the perpetuity of natural allegiance made it impossible for Americans to have become aliens by the Treaty of Paris. Like Baldwin during the Bidwell debates, Reeves construed the contentious clauses of the treaties of 1783 and 1795 as a ban on future discriminatory legislation and claimed to be "relying upon the established and known positions of law for maintaining juridical truth, against hypothesis and the speculations of *political* reasoning." This was the legal basis on which the British government justified the impressment of American seamen into the Royal Navy in the years preceding the War of 1812.[67] In fact, in so far as naval impressment was a cause of the hostilities, one motive of the United States in declaring war was precisely to make the British realize that Americans now were foreigners.

As evidence for the uniformity of English legal opinion in his favour, Reeves cited the lack of litigation on the subject. Whence, then, came the "hypothesis and speculations" he was so anxious to refute? His essay, which was in fact a series of memoranda, seems to have been evoked by a dispute within the Board of Trade. In its efforts to prove that Americans were foreigners, the United States government had an ally in George Chalmers, chief clerk to the board. A legal practitioner in Maryland from 1763 to 1775, the Scottish-born Chalmers had been arguing this position at least since 1784 — strong evidence in itself that British statesmen of the era of the Treaty of Paris did *not* suppose the treaty to have affected individual allegiance.[68] Not until the War of 1812, however, did Chalmers's doctrine begin to command broad assent.

A prolific author, Chalmers restated his views in an influential reference work published in 1814,[69] only to evoke a rebuttal from Reeves. Chalmers published Reeves's memoranda along with his own views, but before the year was out Reeves had republished them as a pamphlet, with the stated object of "vindicating the known and long established law of England, against the assumptions and speculations of general reasoners." Reeves's pamphlet is important for its brief postscript on the status of the *postnati*, whom the passage of time had brought into a debate that had originally been focused on the *antenati*. Untroubled by the doctrinal considerations that were later to vex Baldwin, he accorded them the full benefit of the statutes that protected the British allegiance of the foreign born.[70] Even after the War of 1812, then, the doctrine Marshall Bidwell was to invoke in 1823 continued to command authoritative support within the British government. In May 1823, Robert Nichol had a firm basis in precedent and in history for dismissing Chalmers's doctrine (which Hagerman had quoted earlier in the debate) as a post-war novelty.[71]

Robinson and Maitland seized on *Thomas* v. *Acklam* as a vindication of the provincial government's position, and in doing so they had the support of the imperial law officers. It must be emphasized, then, that the decision by no means destroyed the Bidwellite case — not as a matter of law, at any rate. Though the Treaty of Paris was now held to have released from his allegiance every British subject resident in the United States at independence, it remained possible to argue that the late Loyalists constituted a distinct case — that because the treaty contained no explicit statement as to individual allegiance, it must be construed as allowing a measure of individual choice, which exempted from the loss of allegiance Americans who had actively opted for British allegiance by moving to British territory. We have already encountered the premise for that argument. It was that the Upper Canadian community had a distinctive history, which was not noticed in *Thomas* v. *Acklam* because it was irrelevant to the case of an American resident claiming to inherit real estate in England.

This was, in fact, the fundamental issue in the Bidwell debates, although they occurred prior to *Thomas* v. *Acklam*. The Bidwellite case was founded on an appeal to the record of legislation and policy, which showed that both the imperial and the provincial government had considered the late Loyalists as possessing British nationality. This record was cited in the first instance as evidence that the treaty could not have affected individual allegiance; but if this argument was dismissed, the appeal to history still sustained the position that the late Loyalists were a special case. It could be argued that, having entered Upper Canada on the imperial pledge that they were entitled to the political and civil rights of natural-born subjects, they had an equitable claim to be sustained in the enjoyment of those rights.

This claim had nothing to do with the individual immigrant's self-conception at the time of entry; the crucial thing was that he had been led to act in the expectation of certain benefits. Such an argument might embrace even Barnabas Bidwell, an individual — as the anti-Bidwellites stressed — who had clearly conceived of himself as an American citizen rather than a British subject. It derived its force, however, from its applicability to the thousands of other immigrants who had entered Upper Canada, not as fugitives from justice, but as *bona fide* settlers. It would be contrary to the principles of the British government, said Baldwin, to seduce persons into her colonies to improve and enjoy lands, and take those lands from them afterwards. The persons principally interested had come in under the pledged faith of the British government, said Nichol, and he trusted they would not now be denied their rights or be swindled out of their property.[72]

The imperial law officers might well have found such a case appealing. As we have seen, the judgment in *Thomas* v. *Acklam* relied in part on "the inconvenience that must ensue from considering the great mass of the inhabitants of a country to be at once citizens and subjects of two distinct and independent States" (inconvenience, indeed, which had led to war).[73] But the late Loyalists were inhabitants not of the United States but of a British colony, and the consequences of declaring them aliens included the potential invalidation of any land title that had passed through their hands, even if it now belonged to an undoubted subject of the Crown. This was inconvenience indeed, as the provincial government was to emphasize in urging its policy on the House of Assembly in 1825.[74] An appeal to the doctrine of convenience must tend in the imperilled settlers' favour, and a historically based argument in support of that appeal might have been well received.[75]

But the law officers heard no such case. There was no whisper of it in any communication of the provincial government, and they knew of the nationality question only what originated with Robinson and Maitland,[76] who were secretly committed to exploiting it for political ends. We have seen the flights of fancy achieved by the anti-Bidwellites, led by Robinson, in their zeal to discredit the Bidwellite appeal to history. It will now appear that, in order to serve his and Maitland's political ends, Robinson may have invented not only history but law — the alien question itself.

V

In November 1817, acting on an opinion of the imperial law officers, Lord Bathurst instructed the provincial government that American immigrants were aliens and were to be denied the rights of natural-born subjects until naturalized according to the imperial statute of 1740. It is likely that Robinson had become aware of George Chalmers's doctrine while resident in England from 1815 to 1817. Chalmers's book had just been published, and as solicitor general for Upper Canada, Robinson must have had ample opportunity for discussions with any imperial official with an interest in the question. Ordered in the spring of 1818 to draft a proclamation of the new policy, Robinson volunteered the opinion that, if American citizens who had immigrated since the war were aliens, those who had arrived before it must be aliens too. The new policy must therefore cause alarm among the late Loyalists at large and should not be proclaimed until Whitehall had been consulted as to its implications.[77]

This story has always been told as if Robinson was merely pointing out the implications of a settled point of law; but now we know how ambiguous the law was, his initiative appears in a different light. Bathurst's instructions, aimed as they were only at curtailing current and future immigration, were compatible with the notion that the pre-war settlers constituted a separate case in law. While casually noting that the government might intend some equitable distinction that would safeguard the pre-war settlers' land titles, Robinson ignored the possibility of such a distinction in law. It was he, and no one else, who first proposed that the pre-war settlers were aliens.

Robinson's purpose remains obscure, but he must have understood the political significance of his opinion. It is well known that by the time of Barnabas Bidwell's expulsion, he and Maitland were intent on exploiting the situation to achieve at least a partial disfranchisement of the late Loyalists.[78] In propounding the doctrine that they were aliens and hinting at the desirability of protecting the land titles jeopardized thereby, and in remaining silent as to the need to protect their political rights, Robinson's statement of 1818 prefigured that policy.

A few weeks after Bidwell's expulsion in 1822, Robinson left for England to advocate the disfranchisement policy at Whitehall. The imperilled property rights could be preserved only by legislation to nullify the consequences of alienage; in view of the legislature's attitude to the nationality question, as revealed in the recent debates,[79] it was desirable that such legislation be passed at Westminster and presented to the province as a *fait accompli*. Robinson pressed the imperial law officers for an opinion on his statement of 1818; but they were reluctant to commit themselves and Bathurst was equally reluctant to compel an opinion from them. Finding the imperial authorities intent on reuniting Upper and Lower Canada, Robinson tried to exploit the scheme by having clauses on the nationality issue inserted in the reunion bill; but Bathurst demurred for fear of further perplexing an already controversial measure.[80]

In the spring of 1825 Robinson again visited England in order to press his and Maitland's policy. Judgment had been rendered in *Thomas* v. *Acklam*, and the law officers had given their long-awaited opinion, but Bathurst again balked at presenting legislation to Parliament. After talks with Robinson, though, the colonial secretary authorized the provincial legislature to pass an act conferring "the Civil rights and privileges of British Subjects upon such Citizens of the United States as being heretofore settled in Canada are declared by the judgment of the Courts of Law in England and by the opinions of the Law Officers to be Aliens." Maitland reinforced Bathurst's dispatch with a message to the legislature that *Thomas* v. *Acklam* left no doubt that the late Loyalists were aliens, and any legal test in Upper Canada must so decide "without regard to inconveniences which might be much regretted"[81] — so much for the doctrine of convenience. Robinson drafted a bill, which was passed by the Legislative Council in November 1825 and sent down to the Assembly.

At this point the disfranchisement policy collapsed under suspicions that the bill was a fraud, designed to persuade the Assembly that it protected political rights while in fact it only protected land titles. The likelihood of those suspicions has been canvassed elsewhere;[82] it is irrelevant to the present argument. What is relevant is the likelihood, which emerges from the sequence of events just recounted, that the law officers of the Crown declared the late Loyalists to be aliens, not on an "objective" analysis of "the law" but on the basis of a legal construct invented by Robinson — a construct favourable to the government's secret policy.

This secret policy may explain Robinson's leading role in the Bidwell affair. The petition against Bidwell's return was bound to expose the question that Robinson had been anxious three years earlier to repress. It has been suggested that, carried away by his loathing of Bidwell, he simply overlooked this consequence of his action. Robinson seems to have been capable of such stupidity when his pride was galled,[83] but in this case the interpretation is unsupported by the evidence. It relies on the circumstances surrounding Jonas Jones's motion in the Assembly, on November 29, 1821, that Bidwell's election was void on the ground of alienage. After persuading the house to resolve that the petition contained "grounds and reasons of complaint sufficient, if true, to make void the Election of Barnabas Bidwell," Robinson moved to defer consideration of the petition for a month, obviously to give the petitioners time to prove their charges. Jones offered his motion as an amendment to Robinson's. It is said that the "over-enthusiastic" Jones thereby exposed a matter that Robinson desired to suppress.[84]

As we have seen, though, Robinson proclaimed from the very start that Bidwell's nationality was one of the points at issue. This makes it more likely that he deliberately exploited Bidwell's election in order to expose the question; at any rate, by presenting the petition himself, he lent the prestige of the provincial government and the authority of its chief legal adviser to the arguments in favour of Bidwell's alienage that the petition must evoke.[85] His motion and Jones's amendment probably represented concerted tactics. Jones would try to procure Bidwell's immediate expulsion on the ground of alienage; should the house object, Robinson would pursue the regular procedure of hearing evidence on the matters alleged in the petition. This would keep alive both the issue of alienage and the alternative thrust of moral incapacity.

Robinson was committed to both lines of attack. He was undoubtedly affronted at the prospect of sitting in the Assembly with a man of Bidwell's Jeffersonian political views and clouded personal history. Accordingly, a week before presenting the petition, he wrote to his friend John Macaulay of Kingston, a leader of the anti-Bidwell forces, proposing to share the cost of digging up dirt on Bidwell in the United States. Four weeks later he was asking Macaulay to procure evidence that Aaron Burr, the former vice-president of the United States, had been expelled from England some years previously as an alien.[86] By then the defeat of Jones's amendment had revealed the reluctance of the Assembly to accept that Bidwell was an alien, and Robinson wanted to place the matter beyond doubt.

Why was Robinson willing to air the alien question in 1821, when three years earlier he had been anxious to keep it a secret? In 1818, the Scottish agitator Robert Gourlay was in full career; by 1821 he had been expelled from the colony two years since. Perhaps the provincial government now felt that the question could safely be exposed; on the other hand, perhaps it needed airing because political tranquillity was *not* sufficiently restored. The general election of 1820 had resulted in the return for the fourth riding of Lincoln of Robert Randal, an ill-educated, insolvent Yankee, whose very disreputability (from Robinson's point of view) was part of his appeal to an alienated local electorate. Randal had defeated Isaac Swayze, who had played a key role in the muzzling of Gourlay. The veteran parliamentary malcontent, David McGregor Rogers, was back to vex the government after four years out of office. The Quaker radical Thomas Hornor was returned for Oxford; Robert Nichol, the government's leading critic, for Norfolk; William Warren Baldwin — impeccably conservative in his social views but waywardly liberal in his politics — for York and Simcoe.[87]

Bidwell's election in place of the deceased Loyalist Daniel Hagerman may have persuaded the government that it was time to restrain the refractory element of the electorate; but owing to the need for legislation to protect land titles, this could be done only with Whitehall's concurrence. By November 1821, the provincial government had been waiting more than three years for the colonial secretary to reply to Robinson's initiative of 1818. The challenge to Bidwell's return offered a means of forcing Bathurst's hand.

VI

In addition to its obvious political importance, the alien question altered the way Upper Canadians conceived of their community and its relationship to the empire. The legal controversy evoked two incompatible visions of Upper Canadian history. The Bidwellite case rested on the premise that the late Loyalists formed an integral part of the community: to use a concept deeply engrained in the political culture of Whig constitutionalism, the invocation of the imperial statute of 1790 and the name of Simcoe was an appeal to the founding compact of Upper Canadian society. The anti-Bidwellites' refusal to acknowledge a distinction in law between Americans resident in the United States and those who had settled in Upper Canada reflected an urge to read the latter out of Upper Canadian history — to achieve a unilateral revision of the compact, so to speak. Similarly, the anti-Bidwellite efforts to discredit the Bidwellite appeal to history were the corollary of an attempt to install an alternative vision of the origin of Upper Canadian society: that of a providential boon to Americans who had proved themselves loyal to God and King in the hour of trial.

The urge to historical revision shines forth from the rhetoric in which the anti-Bidwellite interpretation was embedded. "This province could no longer be considered a safe retreat for the loyal people who left that country, and came here for asylum, if they allowed them to be followed by the very men who had committed treason, and destroyed the constitution," warned Hagerman in arguing that Americans must be aliens. "Shall the guest, who is admitted to the feast prescribe the dishes, to which he has not contributed?" declaimed a writer in the *Kingston Chronicle.* "Shall we, who have sought for ourselves through wildernesses, with the greatest difficulties and exertion, a new home, after having lost all which we once considered our patrimony, yield up to interlopers an equal claim with ourselves to the highest offices in our Government?"[88] The impulse to deny any fact that contradicted the providentialist vision gave this anti-Bidwellite history a peculiar idealist cast. It was one thing to assert that, if Americans had retained British nationality after the Treaty of Paris, the course of history had produced a monstrous absurdity. It was quite another to reason — as Robinson did — that, because the course of history seemed to have produced such an absurdity, it could not have been as it seemed.

Anti-Bidwellite history was, then, an early stage in the formation of the "Loyalist" interpretation of Upper Canadian history. This does not mean that every Loyalist subscribed to it. David McGregor Rogers and Samuel Casey were two Loyalist MPPs who refused to consider the late Loyalists as aliens; Casey, the other member for Lennox and Addington, voted in 1822 to unseat Barnabas Bidwell but publicly recanted a year later.[89] Loyalist providentialism was among other things an ideological instrument, which justified the status of the provincial administrative elite by investing them with a superior claim to civic virtue.[90] In the early 1820s, the interests of the provincial elite seemed to require the reinvention of Upper Canadian society through a unilateral revision of its founding compact. Anti-Bidwellite history, and very possibly the alien question itself, were invented to serve that need.

This helps to explain why the attempt at historical revision continued even after the disfranchisement policy had been abandoned. Forced to admit the late Loyalists' equitable claim to political as well as property rights, Robinson conceded it only as a political matter, a proper subject for legislation, not as a matter of justiciable right. He continued to pronounce them aliens, who might be admitted into the Upper Canadian community as an act of grace but had no claim of right to membership.

Robinson first advanced this view in 1825, while defending his naturalization bill in the Assembly, but the classic text is the contemporary report of a Legislative Council select committee, a report said to have been drafted by Robinson's former mentor, John Strachan, and "corrected" by Robinson himself. According to this report, the goal of

Robinson's bill was that of "putting an end to all distinctions, and ... uniting the whole population" by conferring the rights, privileges, and immunities of British subjects upon the imperilled settlers, "a small, but industrious and respectable portion of the community." In meticulous reiteration of the Robinsonian view of law and history, the report quoted Simcoe's proclamation of February 1792 encouraging American immigration, the order-in-council of November 1794, and other documents in order to show that "no public encouragement [had,] at any time, been held forth to American citizens, other than loyalists, much less any invitation given them[,] to come into the province." Either explicitly or by innuendo, every line denied the imperilled settlers' claim to distinction from Americans who had retained their domicile in the United States. The report even discussed the alien laws of the United States, as though these were somehow relevant to the settlers' case.

This document, written by a clergyman at the dictation of a lawyer, was perhaps the first classic text of the Loyalist interpretation of Upper Canadian history. Its publication as a pamphlet, and the publication of Robinson's speech, testify to the government's eagerness to propagate that interpretation — an eagerness that may also explain why the Executive Council's report on the alien question ended with a statement of the need to establish a provincial university.[91] On the anti-Bidwellite side, at any rate, the Loyalist interpretation of history was the chief cultural legacy of the alien question. In view of the subsequent historiography, few will deny its durability.

The chief legacy on the other side, an enhanced sense of the Upper Canadian community as a distinct entity within the empire, was a natural response to anti-Bidwellite history. Intent as they were on reading the late Loyalists out of Upper Canadian history, Robinson and his supporters were forced to assert the superiority of British over Upper Canadian experience in the determination of an Upper Canadian legal question. Imperial legislation and administrative practice were cited against Upper Canadian; a legal doctrine that reflected British experience was invoked against one that reflected provincial history; ultimately, an English judicial decision was erected as an authoritative negation of that history. Every rebuttal of the anti-Bidwellite position entailed an assertion of the integrity of the Upper Canadian community — an Upper Canadian community of which the late Loyalists formed an integral part.

The fate of Robinson's bill can be understood in these terms. It was amended into a declaratory enactment that the persons affected "are, and shall be considered to be, and to have been to all intents, purposes, and constructions whatsoever, natural born British Subjects."[92] The amendment was ridiculed in typical anti-Bidwellite fashion as declaring "that to be law which is not law — that to be fact which is not fact."[93] To objective assessment, however, it seems a logical response to the attempt to set up *Thomas* v. *Acklam* as the last word on the late Loyalists' legal status. The Assembly justified its action in an exceedingly able address, which recited Calvin's Case and the act of 1790 in support of the old doctrine and stressed the inconvenience that must result from its sudden reversal.[94]

The alien question may well have contributed to the complex of cognate political perceptions that attracted agrarian radicals to the Baldwinite ideology of responsible government. Elsewhere I have noticed a symmetry between the Baldwinite emphasis on the disfranchisement of the colonial community, which flowed from the imperial denial of colonial internal sovereignty, and the radicals' sense of disfranchisement, which flowed from the impotence of the House of Assembly under the colony's authoritarian political institutions.[95] A similar symmetry is evident between the Baldwinite perception of the colony's founding Constitutional Act as a treaty between the imperial government and the colonists, not to be fundamentally revised without the colonists' consent,[96] and the Bidwellite perception of the late Loyalists as party to a compact which the imperial government could not equitably repudiate. One can imagine these cognate perceptions suddenly snapping together as the imperial government, after amending the Constitutional Act to empower the legislature to confirm the late Loyalists' political rights, tried to dictate the terms of the provincial enactment that was to accomplish this purpose. The attempt chafed a sore by requiring the settlers to admit as the price of relief that they were indeed aliens, while the dictation outraged colonists who believed in colonial internal sovereignty. Responsible government was first debated in the Assembly in the session following this ill-advised attempt.[97]

The ideology of responsible government fostered the identification of the administrative elite as outsiders: not members of the community but agents of the power that wrongfully denied local sovereignty. One can imagine the anti-Bidwellite campaign, with its persistent invocation of British authorities (the trade statute of 1788, customs policy towards Americans, *Thomas* v. *Acklam*) against a claim rooted in Upper Canadian history, having a similar effect. We are left contemplating the ironic possibility that the anti-Bidwellite attempt to appropriate provincial history, undertaken in order to expel the late Loyalists from the Upper Canadian community, induced in its intended victims a conception of that community in which their traducers had no place.

NOTES

1   Quoted in *Quebec Gazette*, Apr. 4, 1822; reprinted in Public Archives of Canada, *Documents Relating to the Constitutional History of Canada*, 3 vols. (Ottawa, 1914-35), Vol. 3, p. 87 [hereafter *Docs. Const. Hist. Can.*]. Comments in *Kingston Chronicle*, Mar. 15, 29, 1822, show that the letter was signed "Simcoe."

2   Aileen Dunham, *Political Unrest in Upper Canada, 1815-1836* (1927; reprinted Toronto: McClelland and Stewart, 1963), p. 81; Gerald M. Craig, *Upper Canada: The Formative Years, 1784-1841* (Toronto: McClelland and Stewart, 1963), p. 122.

3   On this see Hartwell Bowsfield, "Upper Canada in the 1820's: The Development of a Political Consciousness" (Ph. D. thesis, University of Toronto, 1976), pp. 251-91.

4   John Garner, *The Franchise and Politics in British North America, 1755-1867* (Toronto: University of Toronto Press, 1969), pp. 164-72, is generally accurate but takes it for granted that the imperilled settlers were aliens. Also generally correct, though biased by an excessive reliance on government correspondence, are Craig, *Upper Canada*, pp. 87-91, 114-22, and Dunham, *Political Unrest in Upper Canada*, pp. 73-82. Patrick Brode, *Sir John Beverley Robinson: Bone and Sinew of the Compact* (Toronto: University of Toronto Press, 1984), pp. 41-43, 70-73, 96-97, 122-41, is too much influenced by Robinson's perspective. Paul Romney, *Mr Attorney: The Attorney General for Ontario in Court, Cabinet, and Legislature, 1791-1899* (Toronto: University of Toronto Press, 1986), pp. 182-204, is reliable to the extent that it is based on original research but repeats some of the errors of earlier accounts. William Renwick Riddell, "The Bidwell Elections: A Political Episode in Upper Canada a Century Ago," Ontario Historical Society *Papers and Records*, 21 (1924) shows that Riddell was a judge who knew how to misread a statute: see his construction of Upper Canada stat. 40 George III (1800), cap. 3, sec. 2 at 239.

5   Dunham, *Political Unrest in Upper Canada*, p. 73.

6   Similarly, Gerald Craig has stated that Lieutenant-Governor Maitland and his advisers, in contending that the post-Loyalist American settlers were aliens, "were on sound legal ground ... although everyone knew that their motives were essentially political in reaching this position." This remark has been criticized as presuming "that John [Beverley] Robinson, a cool methodical lawyer, reached an important constitutional decision using something other than legal reasoning." Both writers can be faulted for assuming that "the law" in this case had an existence independent of politics. Craig, *Upper Canada*, p. 117; Brode, *John Beverley Robinson*, p. 130.

7   The crux of the alien question, as a matter of law, was whether all, some, or any of the Upper Canadians resident in United States when the Treaty of Paris went into effect had lost their British nationality. In view of the uncertain nature of the group in question, I have used the term "late Loyalists" to describe it. It will appear that one definition of the group included devotees of the United Empire and another excluded them.

8   Craig, *Upper Canada*, p. 116, Garner, *Franchise and Politics*, p. 168, and Romney, *Mr. Attorney*, p. 88, are wrong; Brode, *John Beverley Robinson*, pp. 71-72, is confused. Dunham, *Politics and Unrest in Upper Canada*, p. 75, discreetly refrains from interpretation.

9   Great Britain, Public Record Office, CO 42 [hereafter CO 42], Vol. 368, pp. 88-91 (Sir Peregrine Maitland to Lord Bathurst, Apr. 15, 1822, disp. 60); reprinted in *Docs. Const. Hist. Can.*, Vol. 3, pp. 93-94.

10   Journal of the House of Assembly, Nov. 24, 1821, printed in Ontario Bureau of Archives, *Eleventh Report (1914)* (Toronto, 1915), pp. 7-9; reprinted in *Docs. Const. Hist. Can.*, Vol. 3, pp. 82-83. The Journal is cited hereafter as: JHA [date] (OBA [page number]).

11 *Kingston Chronicle*, Dec. 14, 1821; JHA, Nov. 29, 1821 (OBA, p. 37).
12 Nichol relied on the terms of the Constitutional Act of 1791, which specified disqualifications: U.K. stat. 31 George III, cap. 31, secs. 21-23.
13 *Kingston Chronicle*, Feb. 1, Feb. 8, 1822; JHA, Dec. 31, 1821, Jan. 1, Jan. 2, 1822 (OBA, pp. 125-48 passim).
14 *Kingston Chronicle*, Feb. 8, Feb. 15, 1822; JHA, Jan. 3, 1822 (OBA, p. 149).
15 *Kingston Chronicle*, Feb, 15, Feb. 22, Feb. 29, 1822; JHA, Jan. 4, 1822 (OBA, pp. 152-53). OBA mistakenly records Alexander Macdonell as voting for Baldwin's motion, instead of against it. The division is recorded correctly in *Kingston Chronicle*, Feb. 29, 1822.
16 Cited above, n. 1.
17 OBA, pp. 314-15.
18 *Doe d. Thomas* v. *Acklam* (sometimes cited as *Doe* v. *Acklam*), 107 English Reports 572.
19 Sir William Blackstone, *Commentaries on the Laws of England*, 4 vols. (Oxford, 1765-69), Vol. 1, pp. 369-70.
20 22 George III, cap. 46.
21 *Kingston Chronicle*, May 9, 1823.
22 *Kingston Chronicle*, Feb. 8, Feb. 15, 1822; ibid., Apr. 18, Apr. 25, 1823. Baldwin's second speech should be read with the aid of his notes: Metropolitan Toronto Library, William Warren Baldwin Papers, L11, box "Unbound Miscellaneous," file "Marshall Bidwell."
23 77 English Reports 377.
24 *Kingston Chronicle*, Apr. 18, 1823 (J. Jones); ibid., Apr. 25, 1823 (C. Jones).
25 30 George III, cap. 27: "An Act for encouraging new settlers in his Majesty's colonies and plantations in America."
26 *Kingston Chronicle*, Dec. 14, 1821 (John Willson); ibid., Feb. 8, 1822 (Nichol); ibid., Feb. 22, 1822 (Nichol, James Wilson); ibid., Feb. 21, 1823 (Willson).
27 35 George III (1795), cap. 2; 40 George III (1800), cap. 3; 54 George III (1814), cap. 4; 58 George III (1818), cap. 9.
28 54 George III (1814), cap. 9.
29 *Kingston Chronicle*, Feb. 28, 1823; ibid., Apr. 18, 1823 (J. Jones); ibid., Apr. 25, 1823 (Baldwin); ibid., May 2, 1823 (Hagerman). Robinson cited sections 2 and 13 of 28 George III (1788), cap. 6, a statute regulating trade between British and foreign territories in North America and the West Indies. See CO 42, Vol. 374, pp. 370-77 (Robinson to Bathurst, Oct. 30, 1822, and enclosures), reprinted in Public Archives of Canada, *Report for the Year 1898* (Ottawa, 1899), Note C [hereafter PAC Report], pp. 35-38, and *Kingston Chronicle*, Feb. 22, 1822, where the date of the statute is misstated as 1798.
30 *Kingston Chronicle*, Feb. 8, 1822.
31 CO 42, Vol. 368, pp. 92-97 (Robinson to S. Smith, Apr. 1818; reprinted in *Docs. Const. Hist. Can.*, Vol. 3, pp. 6-9).
32 For examples see *Kingston Chronicle*, Dec. 14, 1821 (Robinson, Hagerman), Feb. 15, 1822 (Vankoughnet, J. Jones), Feb. 22, 1822 (Robinson, Hagerman); ibid., Apr. 25, 1823 (C. Jones), and CO 42, Vol. 374, pp. 370-77 (Robinson to Bathurst, Oct. 30, 1822, and enclosures; reprinted in PAC Report, pp. 35-38).
33 *Kingston Chronicle*, Feb. 8, 1822.
34 *Kingston Chronicle*, Dec. 14, 1821.
35 Compare the debate reported in *Kingston Chronicle*, Dec. 14, 1821, with those reported in ibid., Feb. 1-29, 1822, and Apr. 18-May 9, 1823.
36 *Kingston Chronicle*, Apr. 25, 1823.
37 Cited above, n. 31.
38 *Kingston Chronicle*, Feb. 22, 1822; Lillian F. Gates, *Land Policies of Upper Canada* (Toronto: University of Toronto Press, 1968), p. 29.
39 *Kingston Chronicle*, Feb. 21, 1823.

40   *Kingston Chronicle,* Apr. 25, May 9, 1823. Robinson himself was in England at the time and could not speak to the question.

41   *Kingston Chronicle,* Feb. 22, 1822 (Hagerman), Apr. 25, 1823 (C. Jones, Hagerman), May 2, 1823 (Hagerman).

42   See the quotation from Robinson, above, p. 85.

43   *Kingston Chronicle,* Feb. 22, 1822; ibid., Apr. 18, Apr. 25, 1823. Baldwin's notes, cited above, n. 22, are an essential adjunct to the newspaper report of the second speech.

44   *Kingston Chronicle,* May 9, 1823.

45   Garner, *The Franchise and Politics,* p. 164; Craig, *Upper Canada,* p. 117; Brode, *Sir John Beverley Robinson,* pp. 122, 130.

46   *Kingston Chronicle,* Jan. 22, 1822.

47   CO 42, Vol. 381, pp. 44-55 (Maitland to Bathurst, Mar. 3, 1827, disp. 5; reprinted in PAC Report, pp. 50-54 — quotation at p. 53).

48   CO 42, Vol. 374, pp. 58-59 (Copley and Wetherell to Bathurst, Nov. 13, 1824), printed in *Docs. Const. Hist. Can.,* Vol. 3, pp. 234-35. The opinion was based solely on the authority of *Thomas* v. *Acklam.*

49   Archives of Ontario, Robinson Papers, draft, Robinson to R. Wilmot Horton, Mar. 6, 1827.

50   Both documents are reprinted in *Docs. Const. Hist. Can.,* Vol. 3, pp. 272-74.

51   *Kingston Chronicle,* Feb. 8, Feb. 22, 1822; ibid., May 9, 1823.

52   13 George II, cap. 7, provided for the naturalization of foreign-born Protestants and Jews who had lived in the North American colonies for seven years.

53   JHA, Jan. 28, Jan. 29, Feb. 3, 1823 (OBA, pp. 278, 280, 290-1); *Kingston Chronicle,* Feb. 14, Feb. 21, 1823.

54   7 Anne (1709), cap. 5, and 13 Geo. III (1773), cap. 21, conferred British nationality on persons whose fathers or paternal grandfathers were natural-born subjects.

55   *Kingston Chronicle,* Apr. 18, Apr. 25, 1823; and see Baldwin's notes, cited above, n. 22.

56   E.A. Cruikshank, ed., *The Correspondence of Lieut.-Governor John Graves Simcoe,* 5 vols. (Toronto, 1923-31), Vol. 1, p. 113 (Simcoe to Dundas, Feb. 16, 1792, disp. 4). Gates, *Land Policies of Upper Canada,* p. 331, n. 142, mistakenly cites correspondence between Lieutenant-Governor Alured Clarke of Lower Canada and the Colonial Office as pertinent to this issue.

57   There is an inconsistency to Baldwin's position that I find impossible to resolve. It would have been easy enough to distinguish the Bidwells, who were residents of Upper Canada, from the Macdonells, who were residents of France at the time of the '45. The analogy with Scots born before the union of the Crowns was also questionable, since they were not the sons of natural-born subjects. Baldwin's apparent confusion was reflected in his voting. He himself moved that Marshall Bidwell was "not qualified within the meaning of the 22nd Section of the [Constitutional Act] to be elected," but he voted against Jonas Jones's motion that Bidwell, "having been born in the United States of America since the independence of those States, is by Common Law an Alien." The obvious explanation for this position is that Baldwin distinguished between Bidwell, born to an official of the state of Massachusetts, and the average *postnatus;* but in fact Baldwin seems to have thought that all *postnati* had been born to fathers who were not in obedience to the King: JHA, Feb. 14, 1823 (OBA, pp. 314-15).

58   See, e.g., *Report of the Honourable Legislative Council on the Civil Rights of Certain Inhabitants* [York, U.C., 1825], p. 75.

59   For example, see Richard Danzig, "Hadley v. Baxendale: A Study in the Industrialization of the Law," *Journal of Legal Studies,* 4 (1975), 249-84, A.W.B. Simpson, "Legal Liability for Bursting Reservoirs: the Historical Context of Rylands v. Fletcher," ibid., 13 (1984), 209-64; Douglas Hay, "The Political History of Scandalizing the Court," *Osgoode Hall Law Journal* (forthcoming).

Danzig speaks specifically of the "invention" of a rule of law; Hay describes the manufacture from whole cloth in eighteenth-century England of the doctrine under which the lawyer Harry Kopyto was recently persecuted in Ontario. I am grateful to Hay for the first two references above, and for that in n. 75 below.

60   107 English Reports 572. The leading Scottish case was *Stewart* v. *Hoome* (1792; 10 Decisions of the Court of Session 440). In *Sheddan* v. *Patrick* (13 Decis. Court Sess. 259), the plaintiff's claim failed because of bastardy, not nationality. The third case cited was unreported.

61   107 English Reports 579.

62   Simpson, "Bursting Reservoirs," p. 213n. says of the decision in *Rylands* v. *Fletcher* that the judge "emphatically denied innovation; his opinion was cast in a historical form, claiming therefore that he was merely stating what had always been the law. But this is a convention of legal dogmatics, and the argument did not proceed on this basis." See also below, n. 75.

63   S.R. Mealing, "The Enthusiasms of John Graves Simcoe" in *Historical Essays on Upper Canada*, ed. J.K. Johnson (Toronto: McClelland and Stewart, 1975), p. 304; George Chalmers, *Opinions on Interesting Subjects of Public Law and Commercial Policy arising from American Independence* (London, 1784), p. 20.

64   Although in general *Thomas* v. *Acklam* adopted the anti-Bidwellite line, it negated the contention that Loyalists resident in the United States at the time of independence had preserved their British allegiance. A decision of 1826 modified the earlier judgment by finding that an American who had fought for the Crown, evacuated New York with the British forces, and subsequently settled in the United States after returning there as an official of the British government had not forfeited his allegiance, and moreover that he had remained in obedience to the Crown even after his government appointment was terminated: *Doe d. Auchmuty* v. *Mulcaster*, 108 English Reports 287. In *Doe d. Stansbury* v. *Arkwright* (1833), however, a Loyalist who went to Britain in 1783 to claim compensation for his losses but took up permanent residence in the United States in 1785 was deemed not to have retained British allegiance: 172 English Reports 1105.

65   126 English Reports 993.

66   126 English Reports at 999-1000. The discussion of this case in James H. Kettner, "Subjects or Citizens? A Note on British Views respecting the Legal Effects of American Independence," *Virginia Law Review*, 62 (1976), 959-60, is vitiated by the author's misapprehension that it was Collet, not Butler, who had been resident in America at independence. I am grateful to David H. Flaherty for the reference to Kettner.

67   Kettner, "Subjects or Citizens?" pp. 960-63. Reeves's discussion of this question, written in 1808 and 1809, appears in George Chalmers, *Opinions of Eminent Lawyers on Various Points of English Jurisprudence, chiefly concerning the Colonies, Fisheries and Commerce of Great Britain*, 2 vols., (London, 1814), Vol. 2, pp. 422-85, and in William Forsyth, *Cases and Opinions on Constitutional Law, and Various Points of English Jurisprudence* (London, 1869), pp. 286-324. Reeves also published it himself in *Two Tracts shewing that Americans, born before the Independence, are by the Law of England, not Aliens* (London, 1814). The quotation is from the last sentence of his essay (italics added). On Reeves, see *Dictionary of National Biography*.

68   Chalmers, *Opinions on Interesting Subjects*, pp. 3-20; Kettner, "Subjects or Citizens?" pp. 963-65. On Chalmers, see Lawrence Henry Gipson, "George Chalmers and the *Political Annals*" in *The Colonial Legacy*, Vol. 1, *Loyalist Historians*, ed. Lawrence H. Leder (New York: Harper and Row, 1971); John A. Schutz, "George Chalmers and *An Introduction to the History of the Revolt*" in ibid.; and *Dictionary of National Biography*.

69 Cited above, n. 67. Chalmers's opinion, as given in this work, is reprinted in Forsyth, *Cases and Opinions*, pp. 257-86.

70 Reeves, *Two Tracts*, pp. iii, 64-65.

71 *Kingston Chronicle*, Feb. 28, May 2, May 9, 1823.

72 *Kingston Chronicle*, Feb. 8, 1822; ibid., May 9, 1823. See also Willson's speech in the latter number.

73 107 English Reports 572 at 579, and see above, p. 91.

74 See below, p. 96.

75 In *Smith ex dem. Dormer* v. *Packhurst* (1742), the court, in upholding an essential element of the strict settlement as it had evolved in practice for two hundred years without being tested in the courts, said: "Surely it is a much less evil to make a construction, even contrary to the common rules of law (though I think this is not so), than to overthrow, I may say 100,000 settlements; for it is a maxim in law, as well as reason, *communis error facit jus* [a common error makes law]": 26 English Reports 881 at 884. Note that here, as in *Thomas* v. *Acklam*, the court did not admit that it was deciding on the basis of convenience. It is probably impossible to calculate how many thousands of titles were jeopardized in the alien question, but it cannot have been fewer than those imperilled in 1828 by Judge Willis's opinion that the provincial Court of King's Bench more often than not had sat without a quorum. On that occasion the provincial government eagerly cited the doctrine of convenience against him: see Romney, *Mr Attorney*, pp. 148-49.

76 See, for instance, CO 42, Vol. 374, pp. 370-77 (Robinson to Bathurst, Oct. 30, 1822, and enclosures), reprinted in PAC Report, pp. 35-38.

77 CO 42, Vol. 381, pp. 62-65 (Bathurst to Samuel Smith, Nov. 30, 1817); ibid., Vol. 368, pp. 92-97 (Robinson to Smith, April 1818), both documents printed in *Docs. Const. Hist. Can.*, Vol. 3, pp. 5-9; Brode, *John Beverley Robinson*, pp. 26-37, 41-43. The imperial law officers gave no reason for their opinion: CO 42, Vol. 360, pp. 22-23 (Shepherd and Gifford to Bathurst, Nov. 15, 1817).

78 Craig, *Upper Canada*, p. 122; Romney, *Mr Attorney*, p. 89. In 1822 Maitland expressly recommended depriving the late Loyalists of the right of eligibility, not the right to vote; neither in 1822 nor 1825, when urging legislation to protect their land titles, did he talk of protecting their voting rights, which also required express legislation. In the absence of such a recommendation, it is reasonable to assume that the goal was total disfranchisement. Of course, even the loss of eligibility, depriving the post-Loyalist settlers of the opportunity to be represented by the leaders of their community, would have dealt them a heavy blow. It is quite remarkable how little paper on this subject survives in CO 42. Both times the government pushed for disfranchisement, Robinson went in person to do so.

79 See above, pp. 80-87.

80 CO 42, Vol. 368, pp. 88-91 (Maitland to Bathurst, Apr. 15, 1822, disp. 60, reprinted in *Docs. Const. Hist. Can.*, Vol. 3, pp. 93-94); National Archives of Canada, Upper Canada Sundries, RG 5 A 1, Vol. 57, pp. 29619-26, 30270-79 (Robinson to Hillier, Aug. 23, 1822, same to same, Nov. 11, 1822).

81 Cited above, n. 50.

82 Romney, *Mr Attorney*, pp. 96-104. A reviewer of *Mr Attorney* has accused me "inventing" these suspicions: see *Ontario History*, 79 (1987), 279. I was not alive in 1825, let alone active in provincial politics.

83 Brode, *John Beverley Robinson*, pp. 57, 129.

84 Brode, *John Beverley Robinson*, pp. 70-71; JHA, Nov. 29, 1821 (OBA, 37); *Kingston Chronicle*, Dec. 14, 1821.

85 Craig, *Upper Canada*, p. 116, supposes that the initiative came from Kingston, but that the government "was happy to see the question before the Assembly."

86   Archives of Ontario, Macaulay Papers, Robinson to John Macaulay, Nov. 18, 1821, and same to same, Dec. 13, 1821.
87   On Hornor, Nichol, Randal and Rogers, see *Dictionary of Canadian Biography*, Vol. 6; on Baldwin, see ibid., Vol. 7 (forthcoming); on Gourlay, ibid., Vol. 9.
88   *Kingston Chronicle*, Feb. 22, Mar. 29, 1822.
89   *Kingston Chronicle*, Feb. 21, May 9, 1823.
90   On the "party" character of Loyalist providentialism see also Paul Romney, "From the Types Riot to the Rebellion: Elite Ideology, Anti-legal Sentiment, Political Violence, and the Rule of Law in Upper Canada," in *Ontario History*, 79 (1987), 132-38, and Romney, "Very Late Loyalist Fantasies: Nostalgic Tory 'History' and the Rule of Law in Upper Canada," in W. Wesley Pue and Barry Wright, eds., *Canadian Perspectives on Law and Society: Issues in Legal History* (Ottawa: Carleton University Press, forthcoming 1989).
91   *Report on the Civil Rights of Certain Inhabitants;* John Beverley Robinson, *Speech in Committee on the Bill for conferring Civil Rights on certain Inhabitants of this Province* [York, U.C., 1825]. The imputation as to the report's authorship is in Francis Collins, *An Abridged View of the Alien Question Unmasked* (York, U.C., 1826), p. 13. The Executive Council report of Feb. 3, 1826, is reprinted in *Docs. Const. Hist. Can.*, Vol. 3, pp. 303-5, and PAC report, pp. 42-44.
92   The bill is printed in Collins, *Abridged View*, p. 8. Despite historical errors, Collins's pamphlet is a major source for the Bidwellite argument.
93   *Kingston Chronicle*, Dec. 21, 1825. See also *Report on the Civil Rights of Certain Inhabitants*, p. 75.
94   The address, dated Jan. 13, 1826, is reprinted in PAC Report, pp. 39-41, and *Docs. Const. Hist. Can.*, Vol. 3, pp. 294-96.
95   Romney, *Mr Attorney*, p. 323.
96   Paul Romney, "A Man Out of Place: The Life of Charles Fothergill, Naturalist, Businessman, Journalist, Politician, 1782-1840" (Ph.D. thesis, University of Toronto, 1981), pp. 460-66.
97   Craig, *Upper Canada*, pp. 120-22; Paul Romney, "A Conservative Reformer in Upper Canada: Charles Fothergill, Responsible Government and the 'British Party,' 1824-1840" in Canadian Historical Association, *Historical Papers, 1984* (Ottawa, 1985), p. 49; Romney, "Man Out of Place," pp. 422-25.

THE MEANING OF MISADVENTURE: THE BAPTISTE CREEK RAILWAY DISASTER OF 1854 AND ITS AFTERMATH

Paul Craven

When George Barnhart finished his summer's labour as gang boss on the Susquehanna Railroad, he set out with his wife and four children from Williamsport, Pennsylvania, to establish a homestead in Illinois. The Barnharts reached Elmira, New York, on October 25, 1854, intending to continue their journey by the Erie Railroad. Persuaded by a runner for a competing line that he would save time and money by travelling through Canada from Niagara to Windsor and connecting with the Michigan Central at Detroit, George handed over $76.50 for five first-class through tickets, "two of [his] children being considered as one person." The family left Elmira at four in the afternoon: at two o'clock in the morning of October 26 they arrived at Suspension Bridge, where the New York Central connected with the Great Western of Canada. The Barnharts would have had twelve hours to view the natural and man-made wonders of Niagara Falls, including Roebling's magnificent double-decked road and railway bridge, then nearing completion. They crossed to the Canadian side and by two in the afternoon had settled into their seats on the Great Western's Mail Express. Hardly had their train left the Falls than the conductor, Grafton Nutter, ordered the Barnharts out of first class and into an unheated, crowded and uncomfortable second-class car, inadequately lit by a single lamp that extinguished itself two hours later. Then their troubles began.[1]

According to the Great Western's new timetable, the westbound Mail Express should have reached Hamilton at 3:45 in the afternoon, London at 6:55, and Windsor at 11:20 that night, for an average running time of about twenty-five miles an hour over the 230-mile journey. It was not to be. A poisonous broth of mechanical failure, mistake, stupidity, greed, and mischance was set brewing as the locomotive huffed out of Clifton station. Fifteen hours later it would boil over in Canada's first major railway disaster. After two inquests, a grand jury investigation, three criminal prosecutions, a dozen civil suits and a commission of inquiry, it was to congeal into a statutory mould of hardened attitudes.

The Barnharts' train left Hamilton on time, but some twenty-two miles further on it was delayed more than an hour by a derailed gravel train obstructing the single track. For financial reasons, and to satisfy the impatience of investors, legislators, and the public generally, the GWR had opened for traffic in November 1853, well before construction was complete. The gravel train was one of several operated by the railway's ballast contractors, who were hastening to make up their time before winter set in and froze the roadbed solid. Running trains on an unballasted roadbed vastly increased the risks of delay, derailment, and collision with unscheduled construction trains. Moreover, the right of way was still unfenced and road crossings were mostly unprotected. There was no technological barrier to substantial improvement in any of these respects, yet these failings contributed to very high accident rates. So far, the public seemed willing to accept that price for the convenience and excitement of railway travel.

The derailment cleared, the Mail Express continued on its way with a new impediment: it was preceded now by a slow freight that would normally have followed. Leaving London at 9:30, the Barnharts' train ran less than four miles before a bolt snapped in one of the piston heads, disabling the locomotive. The conductor had no choice but to send a man back to London on foot for another engine. Almost four hours were consumed in fetching the new locomotive, reversing the train to London, and setting off again, so that the Barnharts' unlit car finally passed through Chatham seven hours behind its time.

To the west of Chatham lay a broad expanse of marshy flatland, drained by Baptiste Creek. This inhospitable and largely uninhabited region had been the scene of a calamity only three months before, when a train of two second-class cars and three freight cars loaded with Norwegian immigrants was detained by a derailed gravel train. In the resulting muddle, the freight cars were left for hours on a swamp-bound siding, without food or fresh water, in sweltering heat, and at the height of a cholera epidemic. Several immigrants, already weakened by privation, died on the spot, and more succumbed in the next few days.

George Harris, the Hamilton businessman who had undertaken to ballast this section of the Great Western, operated a number of gravel pits along the line. His contract required the railway company to supply locomotives for the ballasting work and appoint the conductors, engine drivers, firemen, and switchmen who ran the gravel trains. Harris was responsible for maintaining the equipment and paying the crews' wages. Among Harris's pits was one on the shore of Lake St. Clair, close by the mouth of Baptiste Creek. Its foreman, D.W. Pollard, superintended a train crew consisting of a conductor, D.W. Twitchell, an engine driver, John Kettlewell, and a fireman. There had been a switchman, but he had left early in October and was not replaced. The gravel train crew was filled out with men hired by the conductor on Harris's account: the brakesmen, Henry Taylor, Irving Leslie, and Henry Mason, and the engine cleaner, Patrick Pine.

On the morning of October 27, Pollard was away at Windsor, so authority to start the gravel train rested with its conductor, Twitchell. At about four o'clock he sent Pine to rouse Kettlewell and get the locomotive in steam. At 4:30, just as the Mail Express passed through Chatham, thirteen miles away, they set off along the gravel pit siding with a train of eighteen loaded ballast cars. When they reached the main line switch, which was always kept locked, Twitchell handed Taylor the key. Kettlewell's locomotive pulled the train westwards until it cleared the siding, then reversed, so that the engine was pushing the train eastwards along the Great Western main line at about eleven miles an hour. Twitchell was standing in the rear car with Leslie. Taylor was manning the brakes at the middle of the train. It was a dense black night, with a heavy fog.

On the Mail Express, Conductor Nutter had been at work for more than fourteen hours. The passengers were fretting over the delays and urging him to make up time, but the night was so dark and the visibility so poor that he ordered his driver, Thomas Smith, to proceed cau-

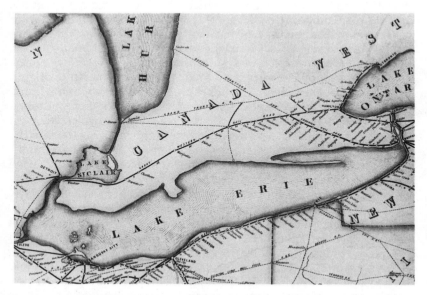

The western Ontario railway system and its American connections: detail from D.B. Cooke and company, Great Western Railway Guide *(Chicago, 1856). (Courtesy Archives of Ontario.)*

tiously; after all, they were too late to make their connection with the Michigan Central. In the second-class car just behind Smith's locomotive, George Barnhart had given up entreating the train crew to light the lamp. Windsor was only two hours away, and then he and his family would cross the border and leave this irksome journey behind them.

Twitchell was the first to see the danger, as the great white headlamp of the Mail Express loomed through the fog. He turned his revolving signal light to warn Kettlewell to reverse the engine, but it was too late. Twitchell leapt from the car and saved himself, but Leslie and Mason were killed as the loaded ballast cars collapsed from the impact. In the middle of the train, Taylor's leg was crushed and had later to be amputated.

In the cab of his locomotive, Smith was unaware of the peril until he saw "a kind of dim light like a shadow" no more than ten or twelve yards ahead. He had barely time to shut off the steam and blow one short blast on the whistle before the locomotive tumbled over, throwing live coals and cordwood in all directions. Scalded and dazed, Smith crawled from the wreck and met Kettlewell, who "came forward and enquired if anybody was hurt, and observed it was a bad job."

Nutter had just finished collecting tickets from passengers who had embarked at Chatham: he sat down to sort them when there was a crash, the seat gave way, the cars came to an abrupt halt, and he heard "dreadful cries." Rushing from the car, he came upon his brakesman, John Martin, both his upper arms and thighs broken; assisted by a passenger (the celebrated Irish "patriot" exile, Thomas F. Meagher, who, one newspaper reported, worked "like a Briton" to assist the injured[2]), Nutter managed to lift Martin into the car, where he was to die two and a half hours later.

Barnhart felt a shock; then all of a sudden his car was forced back, crashing through the first, second, and third cars behind. He found himself "jammed between some boards on top of several people," unable to free himself, with a broken jaw and several other injuries. His wife, a daughter, and a son were all injured. Barnhart's eldest daughter, a girl of sixteen, hung by one foot from the roof of the car: she "continued in this position for about two hours without my being able to render her any assistance as I continued jammed between the boards ... if she could have been extricated she would have lived, as I believe; she sustained no fatal injury from the collision, and died from being suspended with her head downwards."

All was confusion and terror. Until the survivors had built a string of fires from the smashed fittings of the cars, it remained too dark to assess the damage. Then, in the flickering light of the flames and the pale onset of dawn, the scale of the disaster was revealed. More than forty men, women, and children lay dead in the wreckage. Sixty more were injured, of whom ten would soon die. Nutter took charge. Fearing the arrival of the eastbound Express, he sent men with lanterns down the track. Messengers set off on foot for Chatham; others went in search of water, lamps, and tools. For five hours before help finally arrived, those of the passengers and train crews who were able tore boards from the cars to feed the fires and supply makeshift beds and stretchers, freed the wounded who remained trapped in the cars, comforted the dying, and laid out the dead. Surveying the scene, the mail conductor was heard to exclaim that his railroading days were over.

The catastrophe shocked the province. The railway, that long-awaited engine of progress and integration, now stood revealed as an agent of destruction:[3]

> Better, infinitely better, that the whistle of the locomotive had never awoke the echo of our forests, than that it should have sounded the death knell of so many human beings, who have dyed with their blood this road, within the past few months. What advantages, commercial or otherwise, arising from increased facilities of intercourse can compensate, if those facilities have to be purchased by severing the dearest ties of life, and leaving countless widows and orphans to mourn their bereaved condition? Death could appoint no surer engines of his power and will, than those fearful ones, that are now plentifully scattered over this Continent, and whose shrill whistle falls sadly and mournfully on the ear of thousands, whose existence has become one cloudless blank through their instrumentality. If the feelings of humanity are thus to be outraged day after day, by such an unparalled [sic] scene as we have lately witnessed, it is high time the Legislature, instead of increasing the cause, should put a stop to Rail roads altogether, and let us return to the slow coach and mirey roads, where we are free from the tortures of continued anxiety for present death.

The disaster cried out for an explanation, and no fewer than four official inquiries undertook to supply one.

As soon as news of the collision reached Chatham on Friday morning, October 27, the coroner, E.B. Donnelly, empanelled a twelve-man jury and conveyed it to the scene. Having viewed the bodies and ordered them removed to the Great Western freight house in town, he adjourned until the next day. The inquest sat almost daily until Thursday night, November 2, with intermittent breaks in the flow of testimony as the jury was taken to view the body of the latest victim.[4] In circumstances to be described below, a new jury of twenty-two persons was empanelled on November 3 and rendered its verdict the following night. In the meantime one of the injured passengers charged the directors of the railway with manslaughter, saying they were responsible for his parents' deaths. The local magistrates issued warrants and sent a constable to Hamilton to arrest the general manager, C.J. Brydges, who, it turned out, was already on his way to Chatham. When Brydges arrived he was brought before the magistrates, who remanded him into the custody of a bailiff pending the resumption of their investigation.

At the same time, the Kent winter assizes were in session, and on Monday, October 30, Chief Justice Macaulay delivered a lengthy if hastily drafted charge to the grand jury as it embarked on its own investigation of the catastrophe. On November 3, Brydges appeared at the assizes to ask the Chief Justice to discharge him from custody under the magistrates' warrant. Macaulay declined to take the matter out of the magistrates' hands but said in open court that he thought they should either proceed with an investigation at once or release Brydges on bail for his future appearance, "Notwithstanding that the whole Subject of the Collision was before a Coroners Jury, and the grand jury — Mr Bridges [*sic*] not being Criminally charged before either."[5]

Also on November 3, the provincial government appointed William Foster Coffin, a Montreal law officer and railway investor, and Matthew Crooks Cameron, a prominent Toronto lawyer, to "examine into and report upon the causes and circumstances," not only of the Chatham collision, but of all the Great Western's many personal-injury accidents to date. The Chatham magistrates saw in the commission a chance to let themselves off Macaulay's neatly impaled hook, for on November 9:[6]

> Mr. Brydges arrived in this town in company with Mr. Galt, of Toronto, his Counsel, to appear before the Magistrates, and to answer certain charges preferred, owing to the late Rail-road collision. The Magistrates postponed their investigation of the charges till that day, on account of the other judicial enquiries going on, Mr. Brydges in the mean time held *a prisoner on parole*, a somewhat novel position for an accused to occupy. It seems however that the prisoner was dismissed under the plea, that as the Government Commission was appointed to investigate the whole of this melancholy affair, the Magistrates did not consider it their duty to take any further proceedings.

Early in December Coffin and Cameron submitted a preliminary report about a collision between a locomotive and a cow that had resulted in the deaths of five passengers the previous July. Their final report, including a discussion of the Chatham disaster as well as the commissioners' personal depositions about a railway accident that befell them during the course of their investigations,[7] was transmitted to the government in early February, 1855.

Why so many enquiries? Part of the answer is undoubtedly the eagerness of officials to be seen to be doing something, the same spirit that led the local reeve to call a great public indignation meeting, "for the purpose of taking steps towards the care of the unfortunate sufferers by the Railway collision, and likewise to take steps for the prevention of a similar calamity in future, so far as a public demonstration of feeling can do so."[8] Part of the answer has to do with overlapping jurisdictions and their accompanying jealousies. Part of it is the simple wish common to all the inquiries: to get to the bottom of things, punish the guilty, avenge the victims, and safeguard the future. But another part of the answer, overlapping no doubt with all of these, is the magnitude of the issues and interests at stake. From the very day of the disaster the crucial question was whether the railway corporation or its managers could be held criminally responsible for the deaths.

Certain facts were clear. Twitchell, the man responsible for the ballast cars, was aware of the Great Western's rule that gravel trains must stay off the main line when passenger trains were due, and he had been reprimanded in the past for ignoring it. Kettlewell was also aware of the rule; indeed, he had reported Twitchell's disobedience on another occasion. Twitchell's first line of defence, sworn before the coroner's jury on October 28, was to claim that Patrick Pine, the engine cleaner, was supposed to watch for trains and had reported that the Mail Express had passed in the night. This was a convenient claim inasmuch as Pine had disappeared, but on October 31 he suddenly turned up and swore that immediately after the accident Pollard, the foreman, had given him two dollars, urging him to escape to Detroit lest he be arrested. He returned when he heard about Twitchell's testimony and proved that it was not his job to watch the line. The biter bit, Twitchell vanished in turn.

But it was also clear that the Great Western's arrangements left much to be desired. The railway's former chief engineer had protested in the strongest terms against opening the line when ballasting remained to be done. The practice of placing ballast train crews under the pay and control of the contractor while holding them to company rules was a recipe for divided responsibility; for example, one GWR worker testified that the day before the accident he had remarked to Pollard that his ballast cars were running on express time: "He answered that it was as well for him to be discharged by the [railway] Company for doing good work on express time as to be discharged by his employer [Harris]

for doing bad work." Nor was there any provision made in the ballasting contract for either the railway or the contractor to supply a
watchman. Harris testified that this was the conductor's responsibility,
but it is worth noting that there was nothing to this effect in the GWR rules
for conductors (which the company's division engineer testified were
perfect and complete in every particular) and that Harris was testifying
after Twitchell had fled. The contract relieved Harris of any responsibility for the negligence of train crew members appointed by the GWR,
unless they were acting on his express orders. The only other candidate
for responsibility to pay attention to the passage of trains was the switch
tender, who, the contract specified, was to be appointed by the railway
company and whose job was vacant at the time of the collision. Although neither Harris nor the Great Western officers who testified
considered it the switchman's job to watch for trains, the GWR rule book
stated it to be his duty, "before allowing a Train to pass, to satisfy
himself that the Line [was] clear."

All these facts were before the inquest's first jury, which heard
testimony from twenty-two witnesses, many of them cross-examined
extensively by the Great Western's counsel. On Thursday evening,
November 2, the jurors retired to deliberate. All the next day passed,
and at the assizes, where the trial business was complete, Macaulay
adjourned proceedings so as not to receive the grand jury's presentment until the coroner's verdict was known.[9] At four o'clock on Friday
afternoon, the jury asked to be released from its charge, stating that it
could not agree. The only evidence for what happened behind the
locked doors of the jury room comes from the *Western Planet*, not an
unbiased source, but it appears to have gone uncontradicted:

> The public may judge of the view which the Jury took
> of the matter before them, when we state, that 10 had
> agreed to bring in a verdict of *manslaughter in the first
> degree, against Twitchell, the Conductor of the Gravel
> Train, and culpable negligence on the part of the Directors
> of the G.W.R. Company*, in the management of the Road,
> which would have rendered them also criminally
> amenable to the law. As there were two dissentients to
> this verdict, who insisted on exculpating the Directors
> from all criminality ... the whole inquiry was quashed,
> the Jury dismissed, and a new one consisting of 22
> persons, immediately empanelled.

This new jury heard little additional evidence, and much of what it did
hear bore less on the causes of the accident than on a controversy that
had arisen concerning the subsequent medical treatment of the injured.
Otherwise, the new evidence seemed intended to underline Twitchell's

accountability and ensure Pine's exculpation. On November 4, the new jury delivered its verdict:

> *We, the Coroner's Jury,* after due deliberation, find that said collision was caused by *D.W. Twitchell,* Conductor of said gravel-pit Train of Cars, violating in a gross manner the rules and regulations of the G.W.R.W. Company, by causing said gravel-pit Train of Cars to go out on Main Track during Mail Express Train time; and *We, the Jurors,* do find that *J. Kettlewell,* the Engineer or Driver of the said gravel-pit Train engine St Lawrence, has violated the rules laid down and given him for his guidance by the G.W.R.W. Company, by driving his engine out on the Main Track during Express Train time; and we find said *J. Kettlewell* guilty of Manslaughter, but in a less degree, from his having gone out by direction of the Conductor of said gravel-pit Train, D.W. Twitchell. The Jury is also of opinion that the G.W.R.W. Company is censurable in not causing proper Guards and Watchmen to be placed at all points where there are crossings and sidings, but especially at ballast-beds or gravel-pits, where locomotives are placed, and where there is danger of collisions taking place; and are furthermore of opinion that G.W.R.W. Company are at fault in not having had a rule preventing gravel-pit Trains from running upon their road during foggy weather and severe snow-storms, which prevent persons discerning objects unless in immediate proximity to the same. The Jury are furthermore of opinion that all Officers of the Company, Watchmen especially, should be directly under the appointment of the G.W.R.W. Company's chief Officers. The Jury furthermore remark, that a double track would materially enhance the safety of Travellers, and almost preclude the possibility of collision.

This finding relieved the railway company of criminal blame. According again to the *Western Planet,* six jurors signed it under protest and only after the coroner had interrupted their deliberations to tell them that the grand jury had just returned true bills against Twitchell and Kettlewell.

Several aspects of the coroner's conduct of the inquest are open to criticism.[10] Although he organized the first jury and set it to work with commendable despatch upon learning of the collision, it seems unfortunate that it should have had only twelve members. The law placed no upper limit on the size of a coroner's jury, but it did require a minimum of twelve. Given the scale of the disaster and the public interest that he might have anticipated, Donnelly would perhaps have done better had he summoned a larger jury, even at the cost of a little time.[11] A more serious matter was his decision to empanel a new jury when the original one failed to reach a unanimous verdict.[12] The authorities were divided as to how the coroner should proceed when twelve could not agree. The better view was that he could take no verdict but should adjourn the jury to the next assizes, where it could be directed by the presiding judge. This was consistent with the theory that the coroner's inquisition (if it contained an accusation) was equivalent to the grand jury's indictment.[13] The alternative view held that in the absence of a unanimous verdict the coroner should conduct a vote of the jurymen and declare the majority, "into which the minority sinks, and the finding ... is from necessity, taken and considered as the verdict of all."[14] The assizes were already in session, and the presiding judge had charged a grand jury to inquire into the accident. Indeed, Macaulay had adjourned in anticipation of the coroner's inquisition. Donnelly could have reported the majority verdict, or he could have placed the divided jury under Macaulay's direction. Instead he took the apparently unprecedented step of replacing or enlarging the divided jury.[15]

More extraordinary even than this was the *Planet*'s charge that Donnelly interrupted the new jurors' deliberations to acquaint them with the grand jury's presentment. At the close of evidence in an inquest, the jury was to withdraw to a private room to consider its verdict, accompanied by a constable sworn to this oath:

> You shall well and truly keep the Jury upon this Inquiry without meat, drink or fire; You shall not suffer any person to speak to them, nor speak to them yourself, unless it would be to ask them whether they have agreed upon their verdict, until they shall be agreed - So help you God.

The strictures about the jury's creature comforts may have been relaxed somewhat, but the privacy of its deliberations remained sacrosanct.[16] In this respect, for Donnelly to drop in and supply the substance of the grand jury presentment would have been as improper as the judge in a modern criminal trial interrupting the jury with news that the defendant had just been held liable in collateral civil proceedings.

The grand jury had assembled on October 30 to hear the Chief Justice's charge.[17] It turned on the question whether and under what circumstances a railway corporation or its officers could be held criminally responsible for deaths on the line. Macaulay began by stating that the legal issues, new as they were for Canada, had yet to be fully settled even in England. He proposed, therefore, to deal with the question as one of first impression, expressing his view of what would be reasonable and just. The principle of criminal responsibility to be considered was negligence. Gross and wilful neglect involving wanton disregard of consequences and resulting in the loss of life was a felony: manslaughter. Manslaughter differed from murder in that intent or malice was absent. Corporations, lacking a mind to form the necessary intent, could not be indicted for murder. So the narrower question, in Macaulay's analysis, was whether a corporation could be indicted for manslaughter. Manslaughter was always sudden and unpremeditated; accordingly there could be no accessories before the fact. The principal in a crime must be present at the scene, aiding and abetting its commission or, if absent, must act through innocent agents. Macaulay doubted that the corporation itself could be prosecuted for manslaughter but allowed that its directors or managers might be, so long as the agent on the scene was entirely innocent:

> Death by accidents may occur in either of two ways. First, the absent principal may have furnished his innocent agent with dangerous and insufficient means to accomplish the end proposed, whereby the loss of life may be incurred, or Secondly, the means being ample, the agent may be guilty of gross neglect in their use. In the latter case the agent alone would be criminally liable, in the former he would be exculpable, and the blame would attach to his employer, and if his conduct could be regarded in so obnoxious a light, as to display a wilful purpose to kill, it would be malicious. If there existed no such intention, express or implied, and yet the defects were palpable, known, and the negligence so great as seriously to endanger and show a wanton disregard of life, he might be treated as the principal in manslaughter. I am not prepared to say he could not, notwithstanding the force of the technical difficulty, that if there was no design to incur, or expectation of, any accident, he was not actually present and could not be accessory to that offence; for if the thing was criminal — if the whole blame was imputable to him, and his conduct reprehensible to the degree supposed, — it seems to me he ought to be made responsible in some form of criminal prosecution.

"If there be criminality," Macaulay told the grand jury, *"and it rests no where else,* I cannot perceive any good reason why the only guilty party should not be regarded as the principal."[18]

This left the difficult case, however: the case of inadequate means and a careless agent. While there ought to be some avenue for prosecuting a company that knowingly and wilfully adopted a dangerous system of working, the mere fact that railway travel was hazardous could attract no liability. The legislature had approved of railways, and it was not for the courts to say that the trains must not run. To find that the man on the scene was at fault was to find that but for his carelessness this particular accident would not have happened, so that there could be no charge to bring home to the company or its management. In any event, if the man on the scene was guilty of manslaughter, then the company could be charged neither as an accessory, because the crime did not admit of accessories before the fact, nor as a principal, for it was not on the scene and its agent was not innocent.

It followed from this analysis that if the man on the scene was at fault personally in any degree — if he had disobeyed the company's rules, for example — then the chain of criminal liability could be traced back no further. One of the crucial consequences of Macaulay's analysis was the dual significance it attached to the company's own rules. They were both the standard against which the agent's culpability could be tested and the measure of the principal's innocence:

> I am disposed to think that if judicious and well-considered arrangements and regulations were made — such as if faithfully and correctly carried out were well calculated to prevent accidents — and yet if in carrying them out, those employed to do so, or any of them, did not strictly adhere to them, but disregarded or deviated from them, under circumstances displaying gross negligence, wilful inattention and disregard for human life, the Directors or governing members would not be criminally responsible for the event — but those only whose misconduct constituted the culpable character of the offence. To hold the former criminally liable, under such circumstances, would be equivalent to holding the running of railroad trains illegal — which it is not.

On these tests, the grand jury's verdict was a foregone conclusion. Twitchell had proved his guilt by running away. His criminality absolved the railway corporation's directors. On November 4, after waiting in vain for Donnelly's first jury to render a verdict, the grand jury made its presentment. It found that common prudence should have prevented Twitchell from entering the main track before daylight in so dense a fog and that he and Kettlewell should have obtained correct information about the whereabouts of the mail express.[19]

The Jury further present that great blame is attached to the Conductor and Engineer, for venturing out in distinct violation of the rules laid down by the Great Western Railway for the guidance of their officers and employees. Had those rules and regulations been obeyed, the accident would not have happened.

The Jury also present that D.W. Twitchell, the Conductor, and Kettlewell, the Engineer ... are guilty of manslaughter, they having, by reason of wilful negligence, caused the death of J.P. Bodfish, Nathaniel Oakes, and about 50 others.

They also present an opinion that no Gravel Train should be allowed to use the main track at night, and that proper watchmen should be appointed, as far as possible, to keep the line clear, and to give timely warning to Conductors of Gravel trains, if there is an impediment or hindrance on the Road.

The Chief Justice thanked the grand jury for its labours, issued bench warrants for Twitchell and Kettlewell, and hurried off to Sarnia, the next stop on the western circuit. Kettlewell was arrested and lodged in the county jail to await his trial at the spring assizes. There he was visited by the ever-solicitous editor of the *Western Planet*, whose blood, he reported, ran cold at the thought of the injustice done to the young engineer, a mere "passive agent," locked in a damp cell while Twitchell was beyond the reach of justice and those "in whose hands he was but a mere machine, and who [were] — morally and criminally — responsible for the carnage and slaughter" went free.[20] If justice was not to be found in the legal system, it must be looked for elsewhere:

> We are glad however to perceive that the government have appointed a commission to investigate the whole of this melancholy affair, and we hope that it will be done promptly, impartially and effectually and that the blame, wherever it lies, will be placed on the right shoulders — until then the public mind will not be satisfied.

Coffin and Cameron reached Chatham on November 28 and took evidence there, as well as at numerous other points along the line of the Great Western and in Detroit and upper New York State. They heard a good deal of testimony about the sorry state of Great Western management, particularly from disgruntled former employees and from Americans who deplored what it pleased them to consider the railway's overly British character. They learned very little that was in any way new about the circumstances of the Chatham collision.

On November 29 they interviewed Kettlewell, who was still in jail. He continued to say that he had taken the train out on Twitchell's orders, after Pine had told him the express had passed. He insisted that when he reported Twitchell for running on express time, Gregory, the division engineer, told him that if anything went wrong again, Twitchell would be solely responsible. Gregory more or less confirmed this evidence in his interview, and he submitted the letter he had written Twitchell on October 14 in response to Kettlewell's report: "I have to request that you do not run on Express time, but be off the *Main Track twenty minutes before it is due, and remain so till it has passed....* The whole weight and responsibility of any accident that may happen from a transgression of this will fall upon your shoulders." This evidence had been before the earlier inquiries, but never so clearly stated and carefully emphasized as now. Kettlewell now claimed that he had remonstrated with Pollard, the foreman, on October 23, objecting to the practice of running gravel trains before dawn:

> He then said the winter was coming on, and the time was short to get the work done; and he said all the rest were willing, and there were plenty of chances to make short runs in the morning. I then said I did not care, and would go out if a good watch was kept, and he replied that Pine would watch as usual.

Shortly after his appearance before the commission, Kettlewell was released on bail. At the Kent assizes the following May, the grand jury refused to indict him for manslaughter and he was discharged without trial.[21]

The commissioners' final report, completed in February, consisted of twenty-two pages of analysis and recommendations and some 200 pages of transcribed testimony and exhibits. The keynote of their account was the recklessness and perversity of train crews. In their preliminary report on the collision with a cow, the commissioners reported a coroner's verdict exculpating the engine driver and urging the Great Western to fulfil its statutory duty to fence the line.[22] "We give the verdict at length," Coffin and Cameron explained, "to show that the most important feature... does not appear to have attracted the attention of the Jury." This feature was the habitual carelessness of railway employees:

> The fact is, and it has been exemplified in the worst results on all Rail Roads that there is no more common nor more dangerous practice that that in use by engine drivers of *"running stray cattle off the track."*... The driver is, in fact, while his train is in motion, the sole, and almost the irresponsible Arbiter of the fate of all

those entrusted to his care. It is most important for the
future safety of human life, on every possible occasion
and in every legitimate way, to teach this class of men,
that they cannot always elude responsibility and punishment, and that the Government is determined on all
future occasions, as on this, to supply defects in the
Administration of Justice, arising from the inadver-
tence or inexperience of Coroners Juries.

While the commissioners considered the "fact" of this reckless practice
sufficiently urgent to warrant a preliminary report and a call upon the
government to institute criminal charges, they were content to leave
other issues, such as the want of fencing that permitted cattle to stray
onto the line in the first place, for later.

The commissioners' tendency to assume the negligence of railway
employees in the absence of evidence to the contrary and to thrust other
causes into the background is plain in their discussion of the Chatham
collision. They were aware, as their account shows, of the complexity of
the situation: the decision to run passenger trains before the line was
complete; the competing interests of contractor and railway manager;
the divided responsibility inherent in the contractual arrangements for
ballasting; the failure to appoint a proper watchman or switchman; the
ineffectiveness of Gregory's meagre effort to discipline Twitchell. Yet
all of these faults paled before the fact of Twitchell's "perverse and
desparate [sic]" act. The railway's decision to contract out its ballasting
was to be "deplored"; the inadequacy of the rules was to be "regretted";
the failure to appoint a proper switchman was "unfortunate." But even
though the commissioners found that "proper attention to any one of
these particulars would have prevented the appalling catastrophe," the
fault was entirely Twitchell's: "With him rests the blame."

Coffin and Cameron took a remarkably dim view of railway
employees. Train workers were "invested with an ill understood and ill
defined degree of responsibility, and not always taken from the most
intelligent classes of society." Engine drivers were prone to act rashly
and endanger themselves as well as others: "He may be of a perverse
and desparate [sic] nature, and habit may have deadened a sense of
danger in him." Indeed, "If occasionally a reckless driver falls a victim
to his own perversity and perhaps an attendant fireman, the deaths of
these men are no reparation for the lives of hundreds, sacrificed at the
same time." The commissioners seem to have come by these "facts" less
by weighing the evidence than by some extra-judicial instinct. For, "in
the event of his surviving, the engine-driver is almost always the only
witness to his own case. The fireman is too much occupied, to observe
what is going on, and in most cases it would be found difficult to prove
the facts." Hence, one supposes, the need for just such a presumption
as they furnished.

While they called for a variety of prophylactic measures, including regular safety inspections and improved equipment, the commissioners' principal recommendations were for publicly supervised discipline of the railway work force:

> The punishments and penalties employed should ... be clearly defined and invariable.... [F]or the proper control of men employed on railroads, as well as for the future safety of the public ... the Legislature should prescribe rules and regulations for the government of railroads, and of the men employed thereon, any violation of which, should be made a misdemeanour punishable with fine or imprisonment, independent of instant dismissal from the service of the Company.

There should be a uniform code of operating rules for all railways. Intemperance or disobedience should be punished by summary discharge from the company and summary conviction before a magistrate with a penalty of up to one month's imprisonment. Companies that reinstated rule breakers should be fined. Engine drivers running on another train's time should be fined if no injury resulted and convicted of manslaughter if death ensued.[23] The venue of railway workers' trials should be changed, to overcome the propensity of their neighbours to acquit.[24]

Meanwhile, the Great Western's management had not been idle. Like Twitchell, Pollard, and the rest, its first instinct had been to try to shift the blame. Its solicitor inserted an advertisement in the Quebec *Chronicle* on October 30, stating that the accident "was caused by Gravel Train being improperly on the track; and the fault lay with the Contractor or his men in charge of the Gravel Train, not with the Company."[25] But the attribution of blame was not the railway's only worry. Whether or not the accident was the GWR's fault, it would be liable in damages to the paying passengers. As Macaulay had told the grand jury, railways had an implied contractual duty "to provide in all respects for the safe carriage of the passengers. Carrying for hire, this is well understood in a civil point of view." As soon as he learned of the accident, Brydges journeyed to Chatham with a doctor to take care of the injured passengers and a lawyer to take care of the company's interests during the inquest.[26] He met with his board of directors on October 30 to report developments and to have them suspend a rule that limited his discretion to compensate accident victims to £20 each. Perhaps the news that the Chatham magistrates had issued warrants for their arrest helped persuade the directors to authorize Brydges and the company solicitor, along with the lawyer and doctor they had left at Chatham, to "effect compromises for indemnifying those persons who were injured at the accident near Chatham on 27th last, on such reasonable terms as they [might] judge proper, reporting to the Board as progress [was] made."[27] On November 6 the company deposited £1,000 at the Chatham branch of the Bank of Upper Canada for Brydges' use in meeting "immediate requirements." By the end of December the amount had quadrupled.[28] Some of the settlements with injured passengers amounted to between $2,000 and $3,000 each, and in March 1855 Brydges estimated the ultimate cost of the accident to be about £11,500 currency, enough to pay the Great Western's engine drivers' and firemen's wages and keep its locomotives in fuel for almost six months.[29] It would likely have been even more had the company not won its bid to have the venue for civil trials changed from Chatham to Sarnia, much to the disgust of the watchful *Planet*.[30]

The company also took what steps it could to persuade the Chatham justices to rescind their warrants. There was some discussion about a lawsuit against the magistrates, and on November 7, once the inquest and grand jury investigation were closed, the Great Western board decided to offer a $1,000 reward for Twitchell's apprehension, "so soon as the charge against the Directors before the Chatham magistrates shall have been disposed of."[31]

When it came to the Coffin-Cameron commission, the railway company was pleased with neither the procedure nor the outcome. The board criticized the commissioners for failing to give the company notice of their proceedings, for declining to permit GWR counsel to cross-examine witnesses, for taking evidence in private, and for exceeding their terms of reference in the questions they asked. The directors published a detailed refutation of the commission's findings and had it distributed to the shareholders.[32] Almost the only aspect of the report with which the company could agree was its account of where responsibility for the Chatham accident lay.

The commission's recommendations came in for as much criticism as its procedure and interpretation. The railway company denounced the proposal for legislation establishing a uniform system of rules:

> This must necessarily fix responsibility with the Government to a great extent, and transfer to the country liability for damage in accidents, since it must be manifestly unjust to thus place responsibility on parties who do not control the working. But such a system goes further: it takes from trustees, appointed by owners of property as its guardians, the right of management.

The idea that dismissal should be the invariable punishment for an employee's misconduct was "unjust and impracticable, neither [was] it likely that men would be found long to take employment under a law so degrading." In general, the Great Western's response to the commission's recommendations rested on an argument that the industry was to make repeatedly over the course of the next half-century, not only with respect to safety but in other regulatory spheres as well:

> To load the Statute Book with restrictive regulations on Railways, is only taking a direct method of preventing the natural extension of those great but difficult and often unremunerative works, on which the progress of Canada in wealth and prosperity now so mainly depends.

Recalling the events of 1854-55 in the wake of another railway catastrophe two years later, a journalist complained that the Baptiste Creek tragedy "was quietly consigned, after six month's investigation, to the pages of a Parliamentary document of some two hundred pages."[33] This judgment was unfair. The Chatham collision and the ensuing debate over the criminal liability of railway companies had important consequences, although their significance lay less in any diminution of accident rates than in enhancing the autonomy and discretionary power of the railway companies.

The lasting legacy of the Chatham collision was a legislative compromise between the commission's call for regulation to curb the outrages of a reckless work force and the company's demand for the right to manage its own affairs. "An Act for the punishment of the Officers and Servants of Railway Companies contravening the By-laws of such Companies, to the danger of person and property," proclaimed in 1856, made breach of company rules a misdemeanour punishable by a fine of up to £100 and imprisonment for up to five years.[34] The criminalization of workers' misconduct remained the Canadian state's principal legislative response to railway accidents for the next quarter century. It was reaffirmed following the next great railway catastrophe, the Desjardins Bridge disaster of 1857, when the legislature extended the provisions of the 1856 statute to non-observance of the Board of Railway Commissioners' orders.[35] Of course, disobedient workers in any industry could be punished by fine or imprisonment under the Master and Servant Act of 1847, albeit the penalties were less severe.[36] But when, in 1877, Parliament declared breaches of the employment contract to be "in general civil wrongs only, and not criminal in their nature," it specifically excepted certain breaches by railway employees.[37] Moreover, the general railway legislation made wilful or negligent contravention of company rules or official orders a misdemeanour punishable by substantial fines and jail terms, and these provisions were not repealed by the Breaches of Contract Act.[38] At the same time, the 1856 act and its successors imposed few substantive obligations on the railway companies or their employees.[39] The rule-making power was essentially delegated to the companies, which could then use the public courts to enforce their privately legislated codes.[40] In other words, the criminalization of railway workers' misconduct also implied that the courts would defer to the employer's version of the substantive law. This was also to be a persistent and decisive aspect of state regulation of railway employment.

Railway workers were in fact prosecuted under these provisions. In Ontario between 1856 and 1880 there were perhaps twenty-five occasions on which railway workers were prosecuted for manslaughter in accidents, one per year on average.[41] Kettlewell's experience was prophetic: in the ten prosecutions for which detailed records have survived, convictions were returned against only two of the prisoners, and in one of them the punishment was merely a token fine. In several of the acquittals the presiding judge either directed a conviction or noted his disagreement with the jury's verdict. The criminalization of workers' misconduct and the application of the theory of the culpable agent to the etiology of railway accidents had more far-reaching implications than the occasional trial of an engine driver or switchman. In particular, it shielded railway management from public investigation and criminal sanctions, if not always from civil liability. The proximate cause of the Chatham accident was Twitchell's blunder, but the remoter causes included a long series of questionable management decisions. The new legislation made certain what Macaulay had only surmised: that once a breach of company rules had been established, it was unnecessary for the law to inquire any further. Whether or not the accused employee was convicted, issues of corporate responsibility — the purposeful construction of the remoter causes of accidents — were beyond the reach of the law.

NOTES

Research for this chapter, and for the larger Canadian Railways Industrial Relations History Project, has had the generous support of the Social Sciences and Humanities Reseach Council of Canada. We gratefully acknowledge the research assistance of Lynne Brenegan, Rose Hutchens, Robert Nahuet, David Sobel, and Margaret Watson. Some of the research discussed in this paper was presented at the Canadian Law in History Conference, Carleton University, June 8-10, 1987. I am grateful to Harry Arthurs and Dick Risk for their comments on that presentation.

1   This account of the events of October 25-27 is compiled from reports of the accident in the Chatham *Western Planet*, the Hamilton *Spectator*, the Toronto *Globe* and *Leader* and the Montreal *Gazette*, and from testimony before the coroner's inquests and commission of inquiry as reported by the press and in the commission's report: Canada (Province), Legislative Assembly, *Journals*, 18 Vict. (1855), App. Y.Y., "Report of the Commission of Enquiry into Accidents and Detentions on the Great Western Railway."

2   For Meagher's own account, copied from the Detroit *Tribune*, see the Hamilton *Spectator*, Nov. 1, 1854. The Great Western officially thanked Meagher "for the energetic and valuable assistance rendered by him to the sufferers" (National Archives of Canada, RG 30, vol. 2, Great Western Railway Company minutes, no. 613, Mar. 16, 1855).

3   Chatham *Western Planet*, Nov. 1, 1854.

4   Coroner's inquisitions, which were courts of record, did not sit on Sundays.

5   Archives of Ontario, RG 22, series 390, box 14, Macaulay bench book, C.P. and Crim., Oct.-Nov., 1854, p. 296, entry for Nov. 3, 1854.

6   Chatham *Western Planet*, Nov. 15, 1854.

7   The Chatham accident and its aftermath inspired some gallows humour, like this attempt attributed by the Chatham *Western Planet* to the Hamilton *Spectator*: "EXCELLENT CHARACTER OF THE GREAT WESTERN RAILWAY. — It is said that the accidents on this line have become of such frequent occurrence, that even Mr. Cameron, the Government Commissioner, declines to travel upon it without his *Coffin*."

8   The meeting was postponed pending the outcome of the judicial investigations and then forgotten, much to the chagrin of the *Western Planet*'s editor, who pointed out that Woodstock had held a large meeting, "at which strong resolutions were passed, condemnatory of the management of this road, and expressive of the most lively sympathy with the wounded sufferers lying in our very midst," despite its distance from the scene. He hoped that Chatham would redeem itself and hold just such a meeting while the Coffin-Cameron commission was in town.

9   This adjournment was requested by the Crown attorney: Macaulay bench book, p. 296.

10   The account of the law of inquests relied on here is drawn primarily from the following sources: W.C. Keele, *The Provincial Justice, or Magistrate's Manual ...*, 3rd ed. (Toronto, 1851), pp. 202-18; "On the Duties of Coroners," 1 *Upper Canada Law Journal* (1855), 45-46, 64-65, 83-85, 103-6, 122-23, 143-45, 183-85, 203-5, 223-24; W.F.A. Boys, *A Practical Treatise on the Office and Duties of Coroners in Upper Canada*, 1st ed. (Toronto, 1864). There were two provincial statutes in force, "An Act for improving the administration of Criminal Justice in this Province," 4 & 5

Vict. (1841) cap. 24, and "An Act to amend the Law respecting the office of Coroner," 13 & 14 Vict. (1850) cap. 56, but neither touched directly on the issues raised in the present discussion.

11 Compare Keele, *Provincial Justice*, p. 213: "There must be twelve at the least to constitute a jury, but it is usual to swear thirteen or more."

12 Unfortunately the surviving records do not disclose whether any of the original jurors sat on the second jury.

13 Boys, *Practical Treatise*, p. 185: "When the inquisition contains the subject-matter of accusation of any person, it is equivalent to the finding of a grand jury, and such person may be tried and convicted upon it. And it seems as if an indictment be found for the same offence, and the prisoner is acquitted on the one, he ought to be arraigned on the other, to which he may, however, plead his former acquittal. In practice, an indictment is always preferred to the grand jury, and the party supposed to be tried upon both proceedings at the same time, so as to avoid a second trial."

14 For the former approach see Boys, *Practical Treatise*, p. 131. The alternative view is expressed by Keele, *Provincial Justice*, p. 216. The *Western Planet* (Nov. 8, 1854) cited English authority for the proposition that Donnelly ought to have accepted the majority opinion.

15 I have found no authority for this practice in the contemporary texts.

16 For the oath, 1 *UCLJ* 144; for the relaxed strictures, Boys, *Practical Treatise*, p. 131: "In modern practice this harsh law is mitigated.... If, after some delay, there is evidently no chance of a verdict ... the Coroner should adjourn the jury to the assizes."

17 Macaulay's charge was reprinted verbatim by many newspapers across the province, including the Toronto *Leader* (Nov. 6, 1854) and the Toronto *Globe* (Nov. 8, 1854).

18 Emphasis added.

19 Toronto *Globe*, Nov. 7, 1854.

20 Not to taint the *Planet* with the charge of consistency, it should be noted that later in the same leader the GWR directors were "morally, if not criminally, responsible." Barely a paragraph further, they were merely "virtually ... morally responsible," and Kettlewell was "not ... altogether free from blame" (Chatham *Western Planet*, Nov. 8, 1854).

21 Kent *Advertiser*, May 18, 1855.

22 For a consolidation of the statutory requirements see *The Acts of the Legislature of Canada: incorporating the Great Western Railway of Canada, and Acts Relating to the Same* (London, 1864). In civil litigation the Canadian courts had determined that only the owner occupier of trackside land could recover damages against the railway for failing to meet its statutory obligation to fence the line: Gillis v. Great Western Railway, 1 *Upper Canada Law Journal* (1855) 27; 12 *Upper Canada Reports* 427.

23 On this recommendation, Kettlewell should have been convicted. But it seems likely that Coffin and Cameron intervened to have him bailed. They were impressed with his testimony and credited him with "a degree of moral courage equally rare and commendable in a man of his class" for having informed on Twitchell. Certainly their emphatic condemnation of Twitchell as the solitary malefactor was intended (among other things) to exonerate Kettlewell.

24 In their discussion of the Princeton accident, the commissioners commented that as the employee on the scene "was tried for the offence and acquitted by a Jury of his countrymen, it is not for us to express any further opinion on the subject. We conceive it, however, to be very desirable for the security of the public as well as for the just protection of Railroad Companies, that all cases affecting such Companies or of individuals against such Companies, or in which the public safety and interests may be involved, should be removed to the jurisdiction of tribunals remote from the operation of local or personal influences."

25 For an exchange of correspondence about this advertisement, see Toronto *Leader*, Mar. 6 (really Mar. 7) 1855.

26 Donnelly's willingness to exercise his discretion and allow the railway company's counsel to cross-examine witnesses at length had been among the *Western Planet*'s complaints about his conduct of the inquest.

27 GWR minutes, no. 286, Aug. 1, 1854; nos. 435-36, Oct. 30, 1854.

28 National Archives of Canada, RG 30, vol. 5, Great Western Railway Finance Committee minutes, Nov. 6, 1854; Dec. 22, 1854.

29 GWR minutes, no. 565 (Eccard settlement), Jan. 9, 1855; no. 603 (Luscher settlement), Mar. 2, 1855; GWR finance committee minutes, Mar. 12, 1855. Employees injured or killed in the accident had no legal recourse against the railway. On T.F. Meagher's application, the Great Western donated £20 to the father of James Martin, one of the brakesmen killed in the accident: GWR minutes, no. 613, Mar. 16, 1855. The cost comparison is based on the company's revenue account statements for the half-year ending Jan. 31, 1855.

30 Chatham, *Western Planet*, May 16, 1855.

31 GWR minutes, no. 445, Nov. 7, 1854.

32 Great Western Railway of Canada, *Report of the Directors to the Shareholders upon the Report made by the Commission, Appointed to Enquire into Certain Accidents Upon the* GWR (Hamilton, 1855).

33 Toronto *Leader*, Mar. 17, 1857.

34 Province of Canada, 19 Vict. (1856), cap. 11. The statute also permitted railway companies to fine rule breakers, a disciplinary power which they would not have had at common law.

35 Province of Canada, 20 Vict. (1857), cap. 12, "An Act for the better Prevention of Accidents on Railways," s. 15. This statute also implemented a number of the commission's recommendations for government inspection and related topics.

36 Paul Craven, "The Law of Master and Servant in Mid-Nineteenth-Century Ontario," in D.H. Flaherty, ed., *Essays in the History of Canadian Law*, Vol. 1 (Toronto, 1981), pp. 175- 211.

37 Province of Canada, 40 Vict. (1877), cap. 35, "An Act to repeal certain laws making Breaches of Contracts of Service criminal, and to provide for the punishment of certain Breaches of Contract." This statute made any wilful and malicious breach of contract with the forseeable consequence of serious danger to person or property a misdemeanour punishable by a fine of up to $100 or imprisonment for up to three months. In addition, wilful and malicious breaches of contract by municipal employees with the foreseeable consequence of cutting off local gas or water supplies, or by railway employees with the foreseeable consequence of delaying the running of trains, were made subject to the same penalties.

38 Province of Canada, 22 Vict. (1859) C. 66, "An Act respecting Railways", s. 158, and its successor statutes.

39 There were a few of these in the general railway legislation, which required that certain classes of employees wear uniforms, that bells be rung at level crossings, and so forth. These requirements were largely redundant, given the much more encompassing codes in the company rulebooks.

40 The rules had to be formally adopted by the railway corporation and a copy deposited with the government before they could be enforced in the courts. At least one prosecution was dismissed because compliance with these procedural requirements was not strictly proved.

41 Gross negligence causing death would have amounted to manslaughter at common law; what was new in the statute was the notion that noncompliance with company rules amounted to criminal negligence.

BEYOND SUPERIOR: ONTARIO'S NEW-FOUND LAND

Elizabeth Arthur

In the mid-nineteenth century, the pioneer province of Upper Canada was being transformed "by technology, by the railway, by the telegraph and the stationary engine, by decimal currency and the Toronto Stock Exchange."[1] A vibrant and self-confident community, soon to be re-named Ontario, was reaching out to the north and west into regions about which it knew little and assumed much. Lack of knowledge is apt to produce over-generalizations and simplistic judgments,[2] and the portrayal of Ontario as imperialist and insensitive has become a common feature in studies of the development of the Canadian west. But a sense of alienation can be all the more poignant among those who believe themselves forgotten by the province in which they live. Caught within the political framework of Ontario, the region north and west of Lake Superior was to feel the full weight of southern numbers and southern assumptions.

Part of this region had been included in the original boundaries of Upper Canada; part of it had been claimed and later secured only after the transfer of Hudson's Bay Company territories to the Dominion of Canada. But lack of contact had made all the distant north a new-found land for Ontario in the 1870s and 1880s. For decades, only fragmentary information about the fur-trading companies that ruled in the north ever reached the centres of population. Indeed, what little was known became, amid the expansionist surge of the 1850s, the basis for a mythology. The Hudson's Bay Company became the villain of the piece. "The natural course of history was said to have been diverted by the schemes of a tyrannical monopoly. The North West Company, for its part, assumed almost mystical stature as a symbol of the past that had been wrenched unjustly from Canada."[3]

The North West Company belonged to a period more than thirty years in the past, and when it had existed its partners had had few contacts with Upper Canada. In the first decade of the nineteenth century, under a threat of war with the United States, the company had attempted to secure land on Lake Simcoe and at Penetanguishene,[4] and to develop a new route to the north less vulnerable to American attack.

Had these plans materialized, there might have been greater opportunities for future contact. But community of interest barely survived the restoration of international peace, for the North West Company had become embroiled in a bitter contest with its rival, a contest that culminated in its absorption into the new Hudson's Bay Company in 1821 and the virtual severance of ties with Upper Canada. It was known that there were spates of violence preceding the merger; indeed some of the resulting trials took place in York. One Scottish visitor described the town crowded with supporters of warring companies and expressed his fear that violence would erupt. He compared York to the Edinburgh of those distant days when rival barons and their retainers had descended upon it, "when the brawls of half-civilized mountaineers endangered the lives of citizens."[5]

There is little evidence that many Upper Canadians shared this concern[6] or were disposed to favour one company's claims over the other. But they did harbour an impression that northerners (including Nor'Westers) were by nature violent, and thus it was that a few

The boundaries of Ontario a century ago.

episodes remained in the folk memory through the quietude of the ensuing years. There was, it seems, in the settled parts of Upper Canada a consciousness, seldom expressed but nonetheless pervasive, of essential differences between a "civilized" agricultural society and what were believed to be disruptive and violent fur traders. Lieutenant-Governor John Graves Simcoe had enunciated this belief even before he reached Upper Canada: the fur trade, he declared, was "ultimately debasing the morals of the country by the ill habits of the coureurs de bois."[7] Others, often on the basis of even less knowledge, adopted the same view.

In justice, it ought to be stated that it was almost impossible for Upper Canadians to acquire any knowledge, for the Hudson's Bay Company, dominant and secretive, organized the only economic development then thought possible, the fur trade and the lake fisheries. It made international agreements with an American company to defend its monopoly. Above all, it determined the direction of trade (and, largely, of information) from Lake Superior northward to James Bay and thence to Britain and, to a lesser extent, eastward to Lake Temiskaming and down the Ottawa River to Lachine.

Moreover, its chosen personnel were the only European influence in a vast area, and not one of the men who commanded posts north of Superior before 1870 had been born or educated in Upper Canada's heartland. About half of them came directly from Scotland; the second largest group, the Métis, had been born in Rupert's Land and educated in Britain or Lower Canada. The wives of all but three or four of these post managers were Métis (or, in an earlier period, Indian). The rare exceptions were women who, like their husbands, had come from Britain or Lower Canada. Three of these men did have relatives who settled in Upper Canada. Francis Ermatinger had a brother in business in St. Thomas to whom he sent his younger daughter for her education.[8] Two others were members of prominent Loyalist families. Angus Bethune, brother of a future Anglican Bishop of Toronto, retired to the capital in the 1840s and served for two years as alderman.[9] John Dugald Cameron's brother was, for a number of years, secretary and registrar of Upper Canada, and it was to Toronto that some of the Cameron children were sent for their education.[10]

These men did maintain a correspondence with the south, but their letters usually dealt with family matters; there is little indication that any of them attempted to acquaint those north of Superior with the latest deeds of derring-do in Muddy York. The weight of other forces, which they saw no need to explain, meant that much Upper Canadian experience was irrelevant to them and that their experience was irrelevant to Upper Canada in their time. Residents of the Lake Superior District of the Hudson's Bay Company did not even think of themselves as living in Canada. One of them, for example, wrote of travellers headed east from Fort William, one to Canada and the other to the Pic post on the north shore of Lake Superior, as though neither Fort William nor Pic was situated in Canadian territory.[11] As well, copies of laws enacted by the Upper Canadian assembly seldom reached the north, and if they did, enforcement depended upon the Hudson's Bay Company.[12]

That some post managers sent their children to be educated in Upper Canada, and eventually chose to retire there themselves, did constitute a tenuous link between north and south, but not all the associations were happy or enduring ones. Some of the children pined for the homes they had left and chose in later life to distance themselves from an Upper Canadian society that perceived their fathers as having forsaken civilization. Ultimately, two regions became home to clusters of Hudson's Bay Company retirees, one around Cobourg and Port Hope, the other around Brockville, with easy access to Montreal and its links with a fur-trade past.[13] But it is questionable whether the flocking together of retirees, exchanging reminiscences of an active life in the north, would have much impact on the society as a whole.

In the early nineteenth century, printed accounts of life in the north were rare. To be sure, a few records of journeys across the wilderness had been published by 1820, and works like Ross Cox's *Adventures on the Columbia* (1831) and Washington Irving's *Astoria* (1836) did contain fragments of information about the region north of Superior. But all these books dealt with an era that had ended in 1821. Reliance on more nearly contemporary travellers' accounts was equally unsatisfactory, for such accounts inevitably chronicled individual experiences, which were not necessarily typical, and detailed the hearsay evidence of other itinerants along the way. By the 1840s, however, a number of travellers, whether or not their accounts were immediately published, were circulating their impressions of the north in Upper Canada.

J.H. Lefroy had travelled west in 1843; then, on his return, he had settled in Toronto, where he married a daughter of Sir John Beverley and Lady Robinson. He can hardly have failed to communicate to Toronto society the impressions he had already detailed in a letter to his sister in England:

> Rather than send a son of mine to become a clerk in the HB Company, I would see him a day labourer at home. He would there be within the influence of civilization, would have society, would suffer (probably) less from privation, and enjoy as high a standard of comfort. These boys lose all that, without a compensating prospect of acquiring wealth in the long run. They lose all religious influences and restraints, frequently marry squaws and return to civilized life as old men, if they do return, with habits that make it no longer enjoyment to them.[14]

Although Lefroy's comments were the most explicit, others seem to have reinforced this negative picture. Bishop Mountain, en route to Red River in 1845, saw the land west of Superior as empty and inimical.[15] There was no hint of the wilderness as any source of "inspiration, natural wisdom, or moral health."[16] Paul Kane's 1846 journey through the same territory produced paintings of Kakabeka Falls just west of Fort William and of the arduous Mountain Portage around the falls that would seem to support the contention that artists as well as writers saw the landscape as oppressive and frightening. With reference to other Canadian paintings, Gaile McGregor has observed that "waterfalls are typically seen from below and at short range. The human figures, usually diminutive and almost always placed at or near the base of the falls, often seem to be trapped in the bottom of a deep bowl."[17]

By the mid-1840s the minds of some enterprising southerners were being stirred by accounts of mineral wealth around Lake Superior. Soon a variety of highly specialized knowledge would become available, but it rested on a precarious foundation of assumptions and opinions about the north that no surveys of potential wealth would be likely to challenge. Mention has already been made of the belief that, in a harsh landscape remote from civilizing influences, violence and even barbarism were the norm. More insidious was the assumption by Upper Canadians that they did know the north because the words "northern" and "Indian" were so familiar. They used the more easily available information from the Ottawa Valley and the Lake Nipissing area as the basis for dubious generalizations about the world north of Superior. They assumed that the meagre knowledge they possessed about Indian life applied throughout the province. Yet, by 1847, Torontonians were fifty miles from the nearest reserve,[18] and all reports available to the government relied on the testimony of Indian agents and missionaries from Manitoulin Island southward.[19] It is perhaps not surprising that legislators should have concluded that the land north of Superior was a *tabula rasa* upon which Upper Canada might write what it would.

It was the reports of mineral discoveries on the American side of Lake Superior that first stimulated interest among Canadian businessmen looking for similar profitable investments. To the flood of applications for mining locations in 1845 the government responded by dispatching W.E. Logan, director of the Geological Survey, to examine what possibilities existed on the north shore. Logan, careful to specify the limits of his enterprise, showed a scientific scepticism of generalizations made without data that few chose to emulate. The only work he described as anything more than a reconnaissance was that undertaken by his assistant, Alexander Murray, in the valleys of the Michipicoten and Kaministikwia Rivers.[20] If it was assumed that river valleys might become centres of civilization, Murray's report cannot have been encouraging. It described the upper Kaministikwia valley, for example, as

Paul Kane's Mountain Portage. *(Courtesy Royal Ontario Museum, Toronto.)*

"a vast swamp, usually more or less covered with a stunted growth of evergreens and white birch."[21]

As to mineral lodes along the shoreline, Logan suggested that the government might give some limited encouragement to "such companies of respectable persons as might be found willing to risk their capital in mining adventures."[22] Twenty-seven mining locations on Lake Superior were accordingly granted by an order-in-council of November 2, 1846. The list of grantees provides some insight into the nature of the new interest in the north. It was not surprising that nearly half the grantees came from Lower Canada, where the tradition of linkage with the Lake Superior region was already strong. Among Upper Canadian investors from the Toronto area there were the Macdonnell brothers (who also had fur-trade connections) and W.B. Jarvis, S.B. Harrison, and John Ewart; from St. Catharines, W.H. Merritt; from the Windsor area, the old political rivals, Arthur Rankin and John Prince; from Chatham, Joseph Woods, notable only because his mining location, long after he had disposed of it, became the site of the Silver Islet mine. Such men, already established in successful businesses, were unlikely, for the most part, even to visit their newly acquired locations. John Prince, who was later to become a resident of Sault Ste. Marie, was at this time entirely caught up in the view from the south. His speech in the assembly in 1847 was devoted to a defence of speculators and an appeal to government and public to remember the risks they took in investing in the north.[23]

In fact, the risks were apparently too great for most of the original grantees, for within a year or two they had disposed of their locations to the new mining companies chartered in 1847. Companies, like individuals, found that large-scale exploitation would have to wait for the construction of a canal at Sault Ste. Marie. Two of the grantees, Allan and Angus Macdonnell, applied unsuccessfully for a charter to build such a canal, but others were unwilling to support the venture. The Macdonnell brothers were unique among the grantees in several other ways: they visited their locations at the eastern end of Lake Superior, near Michipicoten, interested themselves personally in the mining operations, and made contact with the Indians of the region.[24] Allan Macdonnell in particular insisted that the Indians ought to be fairly compensated for their lands, and when, in 1847, the initial request for a northern treaty came from Indians living from Michipicoten eastward to Thessalon Point on Lake Huron, government officials saw it as proof of Macdonnell machinations. Two years later, the brothers with about 100 Indians set out to halt, by a show of force, the mining operations at Mica Bay near Michipicoten. A military detachment was ordered to the scene, but bad weather prevented it from venturing onto Lake Superior. The Macdonnells were arrested when they returned to Sault Ste. Marie in December 1849, and, along with several Indian chiefs involved in the incident, taken to Toronto to be tried.[25]

Such a dramatic incident—and the details lost nothing in the telling — seized the attention of the Toronto press. But rival newspapers expressed diametrically opposite views on justice, law, and order in the north. The *Patriot* blamed the government's slowness and insensitivity for the confrontation at Mica Bay,[26] expressing outrage that the chiefs had been brought so far from their homes and, it claimed, left destitute in Toronto. It was gleeful when the legality of the warrants under which the arrests had been made was successfully challenged in a Toronto court.[27] The *Globe*, on the other hand, denounced its rival for condoning the actions of the Indians and, more particularly, "the whites who seduced them into so flagrant a violation of the laws."[28] The *Globe's* view, it would appear, was the more common one, for the assembly proceeded to enact a statute "to deter evil-disposed persons from inciting the Indians and half-breeds to commit an indictable offence."[29] It was generally assumed that the legislators had Allan Macdonnell in mind; in any case, the threat of a five-year prison sentence removed him from the centre of Indian controversies. It did not, of course, eliminate the controversies. Northern Indians meeting at the annual present giving on Manitoulin Island had the opportunity to learn for themselves about the direction of government policy, without instruction from men like Macdonnell. The whole history of the charges against whites for what was called "tampering" throws an interesting light on the mid-century Upper Canadian view of Indian intelligence.

Lamentably slow as it was, the process of gathering information for a northern treaty had already been set in motion before the Mica Bay incident. The Superintendent of Indian Affairs for Canada West, Thomas G. Anderson, had been appointed to investigate the Indian claims. He had met with a number of Lake Superior Indians at Sault Ste. Marie on their way back from Manitoulin Island and was then persuaded to undertake a journey to Fort William, where he held a council. A detailed description of that event by the Jesuit missionary Father Nicholas Frémiot provides some insight into a number of difficulties that Anderson may not have fully appreciated: the problem of determining the influence wielded by individual Indian leaders among their own people; the extent to which rumours of activity at the other end of the lake had reached Fort William; the possible significance of the decision to exclude Métis from the council.[30] That Anderson devoted so much of his own journals to descriptions of the scenery underlines the fact that this was his first visit north of Superior. Years of service in the Indian Department did not necessarily make him an expert on the north, and much of what he reported was second-hand. Details of the murderous character of the Nipigon Indians, for example, he heard from the manager of a rival post.[31] Inevitably, much of his evidence was of the hearsay variety, since his return trip along the shore of Lake Superior took place so late in the 1849 season that most Indians had already departed for their hunting lands in the interior.[32] Even what Anderson observed for himself revealed the difference between southern assumptions and northern practices. In praising the hospitality of the Fort William post manager and his wife, he commented that Mrs. McKenzie "being white commands that respect which would be due to a gentleman's wife in a more respectable sphere of life."[33]

Even the presence of Canadian government officials as far west as Fort William was a clear indication that the old days of isolation and Hudson's Bay Company dominance were drawing to a close. Canadian customs were at last being collected on imported goods.[34] Very soon, the company, fearful of any challenge in Canadian courts to its squatters' rights, would take steps to acquire title to the land around its trading posts.[35] But the investigations preceding the Robinson Treaty of 1850 also showed the dependence of the Canadian government on post managers north of Superior for information essential to the development of government policy. It was men on the scene who could supply census details and provide negotiators with some insight into native opinion. Even a decade later, the Indian Department was appealing to company representatives for information that only they were believed to possess.[36] The Province of Canada never appointed an Indian agent north of Superior (and the Dominion government delayed such action until 1876). For twenty-five years, therefore, it was the company managers at Michipicoten and Fort William who distributed annuities under the Robinson Treaty.[37] But there was increasing scepticism about the reliability of information derived from company sources. By 1855, the completion of the railway line from Toronto to Collingwood and of the American canal at Sault Ste. Marie permitted steamers to make regular summer runs to Fort William. The commercial revolution had reached Lake Superior, and the technology of the mid-nineteenth century had at last made the distant north comparatively accessible to southerners.

This new era was marked by criticism of both monopoly and secretiveness, especially by Upper Canadian expansionists, who saw the Hudson's Bay Company as a barrier to settlement. The dispute was fuelled as well by stories of tension between Methodist missionaries and post managers. William Mason and Peter Jacobs both encountered such difficulties north of Superior, and one fur trader wryly observed that, in his opinion, the moral character of both of them was "as bad as may be, but the comp'y have got tired of denouncing clergymen, as we always get the worst of it. They tell the greatest lies with perfect coolness and are always believed."[38]

Harsh judgments based on individual grievances against the company were also being spread by a few former fur traders now living in Upper Canada. Three of these men were John McLean, who had settled in Guelph in 1847 and who was the most vitriolic; and Robert

McVicar, then of Owen Sound, and George Gladman of Port Hope, who both had personal reasons for leaving company service well before the usual age for retirement. These three men were cited by the *Globe* as its sources of information,[39] and few of its readers were likely to question their testimony or to appreciate how slight was their acquaintance with the country north of Superior. Still less was the public in a position to judge the grievances each felt. There was no one to inquire, for example, whether the slowness in receiving promotions that had frustrated Gladman and his brother was due to their being Métis, or to consider whether the Upper Canadian society of the time was any less prone to racial discrimination than the Hudson's Bay Company was.

The *Globe* construed every example of alleged arbitrary action by company officials as proof of its general belief that the organization as a whole behaved with shocking cruelty toward the Indians.[40] On some subjects, like the climate and the suitability of the land for agriculture, editorial writers came perilously close to assuming that the converse of any report from the company must necessarily be true.[41] The Upper Canadian public was thus bombarded with statements highly critical of previous development in the north, and the *Globe*'s readers must have found it easy to mistake repetition of an argument for demonstration of its truth.

Ambiguity of language is most evident in the celebrated series of articles on the desirability of expansion to the northwest that the *Globe* began publishing in the summer of 1856. One editorial writer, having urged the extension of Toronto's hinterland "beyond the limits of Simcoe," then launched into a discussion of the western grain trade that would in future enrich the metropolis. Some detail on mineral exports and Lake Superior fisheries was followed by an expression of hope that "a rich interior country" would soon be opened up.[42] But where was this land of promise? Other sources make it clear that primary attention was focused on the prairies; Lake Superior lay well east of Eden.[43] Yet this distinction was far from clear in the repeated and careless use of the term *northwest*.

As for what became northwestern Ontario, the chief interest of the day seems to have been in crossing it, as cheaply as possible, to more hospitable lands. The *Globe* assumed that the road west would pose few difficulties now that there was easy transport as far as Fort William. "There would be some portages between Lake Superior and Lac de Pluie [*sic*]," it rather airily informed its readers, "and then there was navigation the whole way to the Assiniboine country."[44] Deeming that enough was already known about the land between Lake Superior and the Red River, the *Globe* was less than enthusiastic about the exploratory expedition sent west in 1857. The objective was at first described as desirable, "but the way it is being carried out has very much the aspect of a farce."[45] When a dispute among the principals led to the removal of

George Gladman from the command of the expedition early in 1858, the *Globe* defended him, its long-time source, as the most knowledgeable about the north and urged that the enterprise now be abandoned. It continued, however, under the joint leadership of Prof. Henry Youle Hind (whose academic credentials the *Globe* did not query but whose practical knowledge of the North it found reason to doubt) and Simon J. Dawson (whom the *Globe* did not bother to mention in this analysis).[46]

When Dawson's report became available to the public, it was found to challenge some of the assumptions of other explorers and several of the opinions of both Gladman and Hind, for it advocated the construction of a series of wagon roads to link navigable rivers and lakes west of Lake Superior, and the building of locks at Fort Frances. But the southern press and public could envisage only the high cost such a plan would entail.

Road building was thus delayed for nearly a decade, although contact with the north in other matters did increase and the body of information available in the south began to grow. By the 1860s even the Hudson's Bay Company was using the faster and less expensive Great Lakes route for transporting its goods, an obvious advantage that was weighed against "the publicity thereby given to our operations."[47] Publicity was inevitable in any case, now that Canadian government officials were at last paying visits north of Superior. John Prince, now of Sault Ste. Marie, was judge for the provisional District of Algoma, which included all of what is now Northern Ontario. In 1863 he made a trip to Fort William and there issued a warrant for the arrest of an Indian accused of murder.[48] The rarity of such occurrences and the problem in apprehending the suspect cannot have failed to make an impression upon him, but Prince was not always successful in conveying the significance of his northern experience to southerners. The exigencies of travel and the enormous area of the region to be served convinced him that the broader powers of magistrates at quarter sessions, which Upper Canada had ended in 1842, should be reinstated in the north. This suggestion seems to have marked him as "a hopeless anachronism,"[49] a judgment that offers an insight into a curious association of time and progress in Upper Canadian thought.

Progress was much in the mind of D.Y. Leslie when he was sent on an inspection tour of mining locations on the Canadian side of Lake Superior. He was immediately struck by the rapid pace of development on the American side. He compared the American population (19,696 according to the census) with his own unofficial Canadian tally in which he claimed that, outside the Hudson's Bay Company posts, the white population north of Superior in 1860 consisted of seven men and two women. If previous generalizations arouse scepticism, so too does this specificity! Leslie advised that surveys of townships on the American model be begun at once and that the price of land be lowered to attract settlers.[50] Surveyors began their work, and their reports provided some valuable information hitherto unavailable. The mineral development was followed by a few settlers, notably the McKellar family of Fort William, who moved there from Middlesex County by way of the copper mines of Upper Michigan and who thus combined knowledge of the north with connections in the south. A cousin, Archibald McKellar, who represented Kent County in the assembly from 1857 to 1876, may well have been the first member of the Ontario legislature with direct information about the distant north. In the summer of 1867 a group of members, led by the Hon. Stephen Richards, travelled to Fort William and were there greeted by advice on mining policy from the McKellars who were on the scene.[51]

The Confederation period was marked by the extension of representation to the region north of Superior. The vast constituency of Algoma sent its first members to Toronto and Ottawa in 1867. More immediately significant was the impetus given by Confederation to the old drive to acquire the Hudson's Bay Company lands. In 1867, the Canadian government revived its plans for a road to the west and called upon Simon Dawson to superintend the building of the eastern part of the route. The fact that much of the line still lay in Hudson's Bay Company territory not covered by any Indian treaty created some difficulties for him, and he urged his work parties to remain aloof and refrain from any disputes with the native people; in his report, he cautioned readers in the south that these northern Indians in no way resembled "the timid and cringing creatures who are the sole representatives of the Indian Race in the back settlements of Canada."[52]

But it was at the western end of the projected route that tensions mounted and that a Métis challenge to Canadian authority created what was seen as a national emergency. In the spring of 1870, Col. Garnet Wolseley and his troops landed on the shore of Lake Superior at the spot he named Prince Arthur's Landing (later Port Arthur) and proceeded westward over the uncompleted Dawson route. It is hardly surprising that Wolseley knew little of the country or the distances involved. But what he knew of events in the south also betrayed him, for he left part of his military force at the Landing to guard against Fenian raids,[53] although the nearest supporters of the brotherhood were in St. Paul, Minnesota, more than 400 miles away.

The Wolseley expedition had an enormous impact upon northern development. Its difficulties at Sault Ste. Marie, where the U.S. government denied the use of the canal to foreign troops, and then its slow and tortuous struggle through the wilderness west of Superior — taking almost three months to cover a route the *Globe* had assured its readers would be relatively easy — drew national attention to the necessity for faster and more secure communication with the real northwest.

Over the population of the north — Indians, Métis, and a smattering of white prospectors and fur traders — there washed in the 1870s the early waves of settlement. First, newcomers joined residents in work crews. The thousand men working on the Dawson route at the beginning of 1870 included "Iroquois from Caughnawaga, Algonquins from Lac des Deux Montagnes, Métis from Penetanguishene and Sault Ste. Marie, raftsmen from the Trent Valley, and 'pure Indians from Lake Superior' "[54] — hardly a typical Ontario work force of the time. The American company that developed the Silver Islet mine claimed to have brought in several hundred Canadians, but most of its correspondence relates to Americans, Cornishmen, and Norwegians.[55] The survey parties that fanned out to search for a suitable route for the transcontinental railway line, like the surveyors of townships, were usually Canadians, most of whom returned to their southern bases when the work was completed. But from construction crews, mines, and survey parties, some remained; all, wherever they might go afterwards, possessed first-hand knowledge of the north.

All this new activity attracted tavern owners, shopkeepers, professionals of various types, and, with the rumours of agricultural wealth, even farmers. The villages of Prince Arthur's Landing and Fort Frances expanded, although no census returns agreed with their own proud estimates of their population, probably because the censuses of 1871 and 1881 were both taken in early April and hence did not take into account the influx of seasonal workers that may well have doubled or tripled the population of these villages.[56] The surveyor of Oliver Township urged that it be settled immediately to solve the problem of the high cost of produce at nearby Prince Arthur's Landing.[57] Stories of this new land of promise seem to have been widely circulated, and a flood of applications for free grants poured in, largely from the counties of Simcoe and York. The accuracy of the picture conveyed may be judged in part by the large number of applicants who never settled on the land they were originally granted, sight unseen. Some moved north and later applied for, and settled on, land they had already inspected. Within two or three years, the largest number of applications were coming from Fort William and Prince Arthur's Landing, but often they bore the same names as earlier applicants from the southern townships of Adjala and Markham.

Among the townspeople, there was a small but significant group who moved from Bruce Mines, on Lake Huron, after the mine there was closed; whatever their place of origin, they already had a couple of decades of northern experience to sustain them in the Lake Superior country. But many of the new residents came from southern Ontario, bringing with them a conviction that their way of life there was good and exportable.

Within this group of newcomers, there was an influential core who might be described as missionaries. They attempted to spread their faith not only in the religious institutions that had taken root in the south, but also in the entire society that had evolved there. The first Methodist and Presbyterian congregations north of Superior were served by ministers who had been educated in Toronto, and southern influences prevailed in other denominations as well; the shore areas belonged to the Roman Catholic diocese of Peterborough and the Anglican diocese of Toronto. Only the remote regions as yet untouched by Ontario influences lay in the Anglican diocese of Rupert's Land with its headquarters at Red River.

Not unnaturally, the new communities needed the expertise of settlers with experience on church and school boards, as officers of lodges, and as members of municipal councils. When the new municipality of Shuniah (which included Prince Arthur's Landing, Fort William, Silver Islet, and the neighbouring townships) was formed in 1873, it selected as its first reeve an Ingersoll lawyer, Peter Brown, who was not even a permanent resident of the municipality. Among the most prominent of the newcomers were three former members of the Ontario legislature: Adam Oliver, who had represented South Oxford; Amos Wright from York County; and Dr. John F. Clarke, the former member for Norfolk.[58] Oliver established the first planing and saw mill near Fort William; Wright served as both Indian and crown lands agent; Clarke, having already made frequent visits to his sons who owned a pharmacy in Prince Arthur's Landing, moved north himself and in 1879 became the first sheriff of the District of Thunder Bay. All of them were important in promoting the outreach of institutions they already knew well. All of them served briefly as conduits for northern opinion, as they saw it, in their travels and in their contact with former colleagues.

Future spokesmen for the region were also moving north in the 1870s. Glowing predictions of the Lakehead's future led Dr. T.S.T. Smellie of Fergus to set up a practice in Prince Arthur's Landing. Love of adventure had already led the teen-age James Conmee from Grey County into service with General Custer, but well before the battle of Little Bighorn, he was installing machinery in Adam Oliver's new mill. He remained in the north to establish a variety of business enterprises of his own. Both he and Smellie would later represent northwestern Ontario at Queen's Park, but in their first years north of Superior, they were too much engrossed in their own careers and specific issues that affected them personally to develop any broad concept of the relationship of the north with the society they had left behind. On the other hand, men like Oliver, Wright, and Clarke were nearing the end of their lives, and decades of experience in the south outweighed their new connections with the north.

By the 1870s, however, there were at least two spokesmen who could already qualify as northerners. Neither E.B. Borron nor Simon Dawson had been born or educated in Upper Canada; its influence had reached them in transmuted form. Both men had been public servants and then elected representatives in the north. Both had established

E.B. Borron. (Courtesy National Archives of Canada, neg. no. 33352.)

Simon J. Dawson. (Courtesy Thunder Bay Historical Museum Society, No. 972.22.1.)

some rapport with the native peoples. But these two voices crying out of the wilderness offered conflicting advice. Janus-like, they looked forward and backward from the 1870s. Borron saw his task as facilitating the spread of Ontario's influence in the north and its assimilation of its new-found land; Dawson, on the other hand, denied that the north was part of Ontario.

Borron had been born in England and had emigrated in 1850. For some years he served as manager at Bruce Mines. In the early 1870s, he was a land agent and mining inspector; then, following a four-year term in the House of Commons, he served the Ontario government as stipendiary magistrate for the former Hudson's Bay lands north of Superior to which Ontario laid claim. He journeyed thousands of miles on his annual visits and provided Toronto legislators with meticulous and thoughtful analyses, the kind of information that till then they had so lamentably lacked. He noted the reluctance of several of the Hudson's Bay Company traders to provide information to a government they viewed as hostile; at the same time, he pointed out that the province, for the time being, had to rely on these men. In the distant north near James Bay, it was not yet possible for Ontario to assert its direct authority.[59] In all this, Borron was merely advising caution in the pace of development, not questioning the development itself.

Simon Dawson, on the other hand, saw himself as a proponent of a national interest that did not always coincide with that of of Ontario. He was Scottish by birth, but since his youth he had been associated with the lumbering industry of the Ottawa and St. Lawrence valleys. The Roman Catholic and conservative convictions he had brought from Scotland and the sympathy with French Canadian society that had grown out of his associations in this country together alienated him from the nonconformist Clear Grit tradition within which Oliver, Wright, and Clarke moved. Yet he saw no opportunity of winning an election in 1875 as a Conservative, so that it was as an independent pledged to support a Liberal government that he stood for office and was elected to the Ontario legislature. His decision may well mark the first example of the way in which northern experience could erode political loyalties.

In his first year at Queen's Park, Dawson sought to inform his colleagues and the public of the history of the north and its traditional links with Quebec rather than Ontario. No friend of the Hudson's Bay Company, he nevertheless tried to make the point that decisions by the Ontario government were too often based on a general hostility to that company, rather than on proven facts. His speech of February 5, 1876, does not seem to have evoked much response either in the assembly or in the press. His was a message Ontario did not wish to hear. When later, as a member of the House of Commons, he urged separate provincial status for the north, the *Globe* denounced him as a traitor.[60]

His efforts to prevent Ontario from securing the disputed territory were in vain, for the province's claims rested solidly on laws and treaties extending back more than a century. Who, on the grounds that the laws and treaties, in their time, had been based on ignorance of the country could now question their validity?

By the 1880s, the hopes of the north rested on the accuracy of the information its citizens could now send southward and upon their ability to persuade politicians whose power base lay elsewhere to listen to the voices from north of Superior. The *Globe* had delineated the problem in another context: "To legislate for communities at a distance must ever be one of the most delicate and difficult tasks falling in the path of conscientious and patriotic statesmen." There followed a list of factors that "make it hard to maintain a just attention to the modest force of views which have no friend at court and whose utterance, though that of the united force of a community, is yet greatly softened by distance."[61] But there was no editorial indication that the warning issued to imperial London might also apply to imperial Toronto.

NOTES

1   J. K. Johnson, ed., *Historical Essays on Upper Canada* (Toronto: McClelland and Stewart, 1975), p. viii.
2   Padraic O'Malley, *The Uncivil Wars: Ireland Today* (Boston: Houghton Mifflin, 1983), p. 96, discusses the effects of lack of information; p. 64 contains the apposite remark: "The South took its own indigenous attributes to be the attributes of the whole."
3   Doug Owram, *Promise of Eden* (Toronto: University of Toronto Press, 1980), p. 53.
4   Edith G. Firth, ed., *The Town of York, 1793-1815* (Toronto: University of Toronto Press, 1962), pp. 153-54. William McGillivray to Francis Gore, May 1810.
5   Edith G. Firth, ed., *The Town of York, 1815-1834* (Toronto: University of Toronto Press, 1966), pp. 303-4.
6   Ibid., p. 304n.
7   E.A. Cruikshank, ed., *The Correspondence of Lieutenant-Governor John Graves Simcoe* (Toronto: Ontario Historical Society, 1923), Vol. 1, p. 141, Simcoe to Henry Dundas, Quebec, Apr. 28, 1792.
8   Lois H. McDonald, *Fur Trade Letters of Francis Ermatinger* (Glendale: Arthur H. Clarke, 1980), pp. 290-93.
9   Hilary Russell, "Angus Bethune," in *Dictionary of Canadian Biography*, Vol. 8 (Toronto: University of Toronto Press, 1985), pp. 85-86.
10   Sylvia Van Kirk, "John Dugald Cameron," in *Dictionary of Canadian Biography*, Vol. 8 (Toronto: University of Toronto Press, 1985), pp. 121-22.
11   Provincial Archives of Manitoba, Hudson's Bay Company Archives (hereafter HBCA), B231/a/16, Fort William Journal, Aug. 15, 1836.
12   Ibid., B162a/9, Pic Journal, Feb. 8, 1836.
13   Jennifer S.H. Brown, "Ultimate Respectability: Fur Trade Children in the 'Civilized World, '" *The Beaver*, 68 (Spring 1978), 54.

14   George F.C. Stanley, ed., *In Search of the Magnetic North* (Toronto: Macmillan, 1955), p. 16. Lefroy to Mrs. Frances Rickards, Fort William, Lake Superior, May 30, 1843.

15   George J. Mountain, *The Journal of the Bishop of Montreal* (London, 1845), p. 15.

16   Gaile McGregor, *The Wacousta Syndrome* (Toronto: University of Toronto Press, 1985), p. 47.

17   Ibid., p. 19.

18   Donald B. Smith, "Aboriginal Rights a Century Ago," *The Beaver*, 67 (Feb.-Mar. 1987), 8.

19   Canada, Parliament, *Journals of the Legislative Assembly, 1847*, App. T, Report on the Affairs of the Indians of Canada.

20   Elizabeth Arthur, ed., *The Thunder Bay District, 1821-1892* (Toronto: University of Toronto Press, 1973), p. 46.

21   Ibid., p. 48.

22   Ibid., p. 44.

23   R. Alan Douglas, ed., *John Prince* (Toronto: University of Toronto Press, 1980), p. 89.

24   Donald Swainson, "Allan Macdonnell," in *Dictionary of Canadian Biography*, Vol. 11 (Toronto: University of Toronto Press, 1982), pp. 552-54.

25   Lise C. Hansen, "The Anishinabek Land Claim and the Participation of the Indian People Living on the North Shore of Lake Superior in the Robinson Superior Treaty, 1850" (Research report, Ontario Ministry of Natural Resources, Toronto, 1985), p. 38.

26   Toronto *Patriot*, Nov. 21, 1849.

27   Ibid., Dec. 29, 1849.

28   Toronto *Globe*, Nov. 11, 1849.

29   Province of Canada, *Statutes*, 1853, Vict. 16, cap. 176, pp. 720-24.

30   Lorenzo Cadieux, ed., *Lettres des Nouvelles Missions du Canada* (Montreal: Editions Bellarmin, 1973), pp. 592-98.

31   Arthur, *Thunder Bay District*, p. 72, Anderson Journal, Oct. 4-5, 1849. Account of conversation with Louis de la Ronde at Pic.

32   Hansen, "The Anishinabek Land Claim," p. 29.

33   Arthur, *Thunder Bay District*, Anderson Journal, p. 71, Sept. 25, 1849.

34   HBCA, D5/16 f. 134, John Swanston to Sir George Simpson, Michipicoten, Jan. 29, 1846.

35   Ibid., D4/48 p. 55, Simpson to John McKenzie, Lachine, Aug. 23, 1854.

36   Ibid., D5/52 f. 578, George Barnston to Simpson, Michipicoten, Sept. 4, 1860.

37   Hansen, "The Anishinabek Land Claim," p. 85.

38   Margaret A. Macleod, ed., *The Letters of Letitia Hargrave* (Toronto: Champlain Society, 1947), p. 212, cites the opinion of William Mactavish.

39   Toronto *Globe*, May 23, 1857.

40   Ibid., July 15, 1857, and Jan. 9, 1858, cite incidents at Sault Ste. Marie and Norway House; the generalized indictment appears in the Dec. 10, 1856 issue, as one example.

41   Ibid., Aug. 28, 1856.

42   Ibid.

43   This point is illustrated by Owram, *Promise of Eden*, in which map and text make clear that the "Idea of the West" begins at the Lake of the Woods.

44   Toronto *Globe*, Dec. 4, 1856.

45   Ibid., July 24, 1857.

46   Ibid., Apr. 20, 1858.

47   HBCA, B3 c/2, f. 444, Duncan Finlayson to John McKenzie, Lachine, Dec. 28, 1860.

48   Douglas, *John Prince*, pp. 184-85, Prince Diary, Fort William, June 22, 1863, and Sault Ste. Marie, Oct. 21, 1863.

49   Ibid., p. lvi.
50   Arthur, *Thunder Bay District*, p. 99, Leslie's report, Jan. 8, 1861.
51   Peter McKellar, "Early Mining," Thunder Bay Historical Society, *Papers* of 1918, pp. 15-16.
52   Simon J. Dawson, *Report on the line of route between Lake Superior and the Red River Settlement* (Ottawa, 1869), p. 28.
53   Arthur, *Thunder Bay District*, p. 118.
54   Simon J. Dawson, *Report on the Red River Expedition of 1870* (Ottawa, 1871), p. 13.
55   Arthur, *Thunder Bay District*, pp. 145, 147, 151-52, includes letters from A.H. Sibley, the president of the Silver Islet Mining Company, and W.B. Frue, the manager of the mine.
56   Thorold J. Tronrud, "Frontier Social Structure: The Canadian Lakehead, 1871 and 1881," *Ontario History*, 79 (June 1987), 147.
57   Archives of Ontario, Crown Lands Papers, Oliver Township, Department of Crown Lands, *Report* (Toronto, 1871), pp. 30-31.
58   George N. Emery, "Adam Oliver," *Dictionary of Canadian Biography*, Vol. 11 (Toronto: University of Toronto Press, 1982), pp. 651-53; Elizabeth Arthur, "Amos Wright," in the same volume, pp. 938-39; John F. Clarke, who also died in the 1880's was not included in the *DCB*.
59   Morris Zaslow, "Edward Barnes Borron, 1820-1915," in F.H. Armstrong et al., eds., *Aspects of Nineteenth Century Ontario* (Toronto: University of Toronto Press,1974), pp. 297-304.
60   Elizabeth Arthur, *Simon Dawson, C.E.* (Thunder Bay: Thunder Bay Historical Museum Society, 1987), pp. 19-22.
61   Toronto *Globe*, Mar. 22, 1856.

FINDING THE RIGHT SIZE: MARKETS AND COMPETITION IN MID- AND LATE NINETEENTH-CENTURY ONTARIO

Ben Forster

We assume that Ontario's late nineteenth-century Industrial Revolution[1] resulted in collusion, consolidation, and giant enterprises.[2] That, after all, is what seems to have happened in the United States. But at least until the 1890s, and quite probably beyond, there was an *expansion* of competition, not a decline. There was more competition not because there were necessarily more competitors, but because competition was made more possible by market integration and significant increases in industrial productive capacity.

An emphasis on collusion and consolidation is misleading on another score. The search for nineteenth-century antecedents of twentieth-century business life distorts the era's business and economic history and ignores the great persistence of small producers and manufacturers. The consolidation that did take place before the eighteen-nineties was slow.[3] The phenomenon of mid- to late-nineteenth-century business life in Ontario is the continuing strength of the small firm, rather than the emergence of the large corporation.[4] The era was marked by competition and persistence in business; for a few decades irreconcilable opposites were reconciled.

Among the Canadian provinces, Ontario (the term here covers both pre- and post-Confederation periods) had an especially diffuse pattern of small, vigorous manufacturers. Rural incomes were high in the province by the 1850s and rural demand consequently great. Artisanal and manufacturing shops, scattered throughout the province, produced a broad spectrum of goods.[5] Such shops, especially outside the main towns and cities and during the middle decades of the century, had sheltered *local* markets,[6] sustained by high transportation costs, limited organizational channels for the distribution of goods, and tariffs first British, and later Canadian. These fragmented markets were characterized by the restricted physical capital and economies of scale of small producers, an absence of national or even regional advertising, and local collusion of the sort so pithily described by Adam Smith in his *Wealth of Nations.*[7]

In the latter part of the century, the existence of these local producers for limited markets was increasingly challenged, as changing conditions obliged many manufacturers to cultivate large-scale, integrated markets and forced some of them to grow and consolidate. But at the same time smaller producers undertook an ever-changing battle with the aim of maintaining some control over their economic space. Collusion was therefore partly a mechanism for maintaining a crumbling structure of local or regional markets for smaller manufacturers struggling against outside competition, whether national or extra-national. Indeed, the motive for many early mergers in Canada was to continue the control of limited markets by equally limited producers.[8] Protective tariffs, traditionally viewed as the instrument of big business in Canada, were actually strongly supported by small producers eager to maintain an established way of doing business.[9] And social and political conditions restrained wholesale consolidation beyond the turn of the century.

Moreover, technological change did not lead only to industrial consolidation and giantism. What technological change did, constantly and rapidly, was to make existing equipment obsolete.[10] But in places where labour was especially cheap or transportation costs particularly high, outmoded machinery and tools could remain in use for a long time. Even more to the point, ingenious machinery for small-shop or individual production was being designed, constructed, and sold in considerable quantities. Thus resistance to consolidation and giantism did not appear necessarily futile, even at the beginning of the twentieth century.[11]

The pressures which led to greater market integration in the second half of the nineteenth century affected Ontario directly. To a considerable degree they were related to transportation, for high shipping costs were barriers to trade[12] and protected small markets from outside interference. The general improvement of canal transportation, culminating in the completion of the St. Lawrence canal system in 1849, helped to reduce somewhat the cost of manufactured goods brought from metropolitan centres outside Ontario. The construction of an extensive North American railway network and its later rationalization, caused steeply falling railway tariff rates. Ocean freight rates also declined sharply under the pressure of technological improvement.

Although numerous railways were in place by the 1860s, the first plans for railway building consisted of fervent efforts by the business elites of major entrepôts to develop market control over specific hinterlands. Such railway lines were built with the intent of *excluding* competitive carriers at almost any cost.[13] Consequently the railway "system" was chaotic and unintegrated, a mishmash of varying railway gauges and systems of ownership which did not permit reciprocal carrying rights or through-freight arrangements.

By the end of the American Civil War, considerable efforts were being made throughout North America to rationalize and restructure the railway systems. These attempts reflected the emergence of railways as business propositions independent of any particularistic business elite's desire for regional commercial hegemony. In the last two decades of the century, infill railway construction took place on a considerable scale, linking smaller towns into the rail system. The growing acceptance of standard gauge (at least seven different gauges had been in use) in North America after the end of the American Civil War lowered the cost of moving goods. So did the rapid adoption of steel rails to replace iron. Many carriers came to fast freight and car-exchange agreements, and joined the pooling arrangements expedited by the American Albert Fink. Canadian railways participated in these developments and copied them.[14]

At the same time, vigorous competition and ongoing deflation were reducing transportation rates. In 1858 it cost 38.61 cents a bushel to ship grain from Chicago to New York by rail; by 1890 it cost only 14.3 cents. A rate war broke out in 1876-77 between the major lines in the United States as well as in Canada. Passenger fares fell by one-half on long east-west runs; fares on first-class freight going west dropped by one-third; all eastbound goods obtained reductions of up to 85 per cent. Similar freight-rate wars took place in the early 1880s, despite Fink's attempts to limit the excesses of competition. In some instances, an instigator of the freight-rate wars was the Montreal-based Grand Trunk, which was seeking freight for its Ontario-and-eastward runs.[15] Rates for canal transport of staple products were likewise forced down, especially in the mid-1870s. Inbound canal rates on heavy items like iron fell, and even shippers of goods sent first class received substantial discounts.[16] Freight-rate declines of this order integrated not only national but continental markets.

Oceanic transport costs underwent ragged and continuous declines from the mid-1850s to 1900 (they fell in an especially sustained and dramatic fashion from the mid-1870s onwards), dropping by roughly one-half. Increasingly efficient steam-driven ocean-going vessels were developed, larger iron vessels were built, and technological improvements in wooden vessel construction reached a peak. The use of iron components in wooden vessels lengthened their lives; the rapid increase in the use of compound steam engines beginning in the mid-1860s and triple-expansion steam engines by 1890 forced freight rates down on all types of vessels.[17] "Freights to and from all parts low, and in most cases not sufficient to pay expenses," explained one laconic shipper in the midst of the depression in 1878. "Unless some improvement takes place, it will be very difficult to work ships, especially wood ships — the rate of insurance is so much more and less rate for freight, so that it cuts two ways on wood ships."[18]

Higher levels of market integration also followed from more advanced methods of distribution and selling. Stanley Chapman, writing about Britain's international commerce, has outlined the powerful reordering of international distribution networks that began in the 1860s. During much of the nineteenth century, the distribution of goods had depended on a system of specialization in which wholesalers, independent commercial agents, and banks acted as intermediaries between manufacturer and retailer.[19] It was the structure of commerce under which much of Canadian economic life had been established. In the 1860s, this system began to be assaulted by new methods that emphasized direct connections between manufacturer and retailer, Chapman concludes. It is clear that business in Ontario participated fully in these developments.[20]

The growing tribe of commercial travellers who represented manufacturers and manufacturer-wholesalers was evidence of this market restructuring. These salesmen penetrated markets formerly the preserve of local and regional manufacturers. In turn, businessmen struggled to exclude the travelling salesmen from their markets through municipal bylaws, taxation, and other expedients.[21] But these "restless emissaries of trade" became so pervasive in central Canada that in 1871 they organized into the Commercial Travellers' Association. Four years later, there were three such associations with a total membership of 1679.[22] Such salesmen "spread over the land like locusts," offering easy credit and high discounts to retailers.[23]

A further important step in the development of integrated markets was the emergence of brand-name recognition. The advertising of mechanized agricultural equipment and the test trials of such machinery that began to take place in the late 1850s helped establish the concept of "brands" in the public mind. In the 1870s and 1880s the Edwardsburgh Starch Company of Prince Edward County had a solid grasp of the usefulness of brand names. The firm protected its premium brand from price-cutting competition by producing an inexpensive product as well.[24] Hiram Walker's defence in their advertising of the phrase "Canadian Club" in the United States in the 1880s and 1890s was yet another example of the growing importance of brand names. Brand names also offered advantages to consumers, for they were a modest guarantee of quality for widely distributed products.[25] Other manufacturers shook the staid world of distribution and sales by pushing direct factory-to-consumer sales or holding mass auctions in distant markets.[26] Intense competition predictably resulted in collusion by some producers, or consolidation of ownership in order to maintain local markets or penetrate larger ones.[27] Most manufacturers hoped that higher tariffs would maintain some semblance of the older distribution and marketing systems while, at the same time, not prohibit the emergence of newer methods and larger markets within a sheltered provincial and national economic space.

If the tariff inhibited industrial consolidation, so did a variety of other social, economic, and political processes. Although brand names were beginning to have their attractions, customers often preferred to buy from local producers. Credit arrangements could be more flexible, and faulty goods might be more readily repaired. Despite the powerful impact of railway transportation on market integration, railways were not the flexible medium for moving goods that trucks have become in the twentieth century. Concentration was also inhibited by a lax system of insolvency and by high American tariffs that made the American market inaccessible to Canadian manufacturers. At best, technological enhancements altered production unevenly: human skill remained vital, and in many industries there was limited need for capital equipment. There was a profound difference between the use of occasional pieces of machinery to avoid production bottlenecks, and modern automated, flow-line production tended by low-skill labour.[28]

Yet, despite the relative absence of the twentieth-century phenomena of consolidation and concentration, the business environment was changing rapidly. Those changes were reflected in the evolution of two important industries, woollen textile and wooden furniture. They were not "artificial" industries created by protection, but were rooted in the period before 1850 in domestic, artisanal, and shop production. These industries were thus continuing elements in regional, national, and international competition.

The wool textile industry is an elegant example of the mid- to late-nineteenth-century development of an industry from the local to the regional and beyond. The early woollen manufactories were mostly carding mills serving local needs. At such mills, raw wool brought by farmers was carded so that it could be spun into yarn and woven at home. Such processing was usually for cash or kind. John Haggart of Perth, for example, carded wool in exchange for grain, which he then ground and sold; in this "generalist" milling environment, there was really no suggestion of factory production. John Rosamond in Carleton Place began to demand cash payments for processing by the late 1830s. Even in 1870, the small Schofield and Forbes mill in Hespeler did most of its trade by barter, often for raw wool — and, as it happens, that mill was far from unusual.[29]

The owners of these small wool manufactories tended, given the dispersed demand for their services, to establish themselves where water power was available. Inadequate transportation made it impossible for any single mill to meet the needs of a wide geographic area. The mills processed local wool, which was only suitable for coarse tweeds, rough worsteds, and blankets, all of which were so tough on the wearer that they "had inherent tendencies to impart what might be termed 'school-girl-complexions' to the skin."[30] In any case, woollen textile manufacture was heavily localized and bound into a system of domestic cloth production.

Several significant developments altered these characteristics of the industry. Ontario farmers became less self-sufficient in the 1840s and later. The "transportation revolution"[31] had a profound impact on the wool textile industry. It permitted expanded markets for textile producers; it forced relocation of plants; it encouraged the adoption of technological innovations that made higher production levels possible; it required, if expansion was the aim of the producer, higher levels of capitalization.

Yet the opportunities for expansion did not fully manifest themselves until the 1860s, after the recovery from commercial depression, the establishment of a railway network, and the increased demand and reduced foreign competition resulting from the American Civil War. Considerable growth followed, and in the Ottawa Valley, one of the chief centres of woollen textile production in Ontario, entrepreneurs who wanted to take advantage of larger markets moved their mills to ensure easy access to railways.[32]

They also had a magnificent opportunity to take advantage of recent improvements in the technology of woollen production. It is true that woollen textile machinery was adapted from the cotton industry and that all the main inventions had been made in cottons by 1800, but the transference of the technology to wool was not smooth. There were important differences in the raw material which stood in the way. A number of major adaptations took place beginning in the 1830s, but the power loom was not widely adopted in worsted production until between 1856 and 1867. (Worsted textiles are significantly different from woollens. Worsteds are made from long-staple wool which is combed rather than carded, is spun differently, and is not fulled.)[33] And the production of short-staple woollens was not fully mechanized as an industrial norm in Britain until the 1890s — developments in Ontario were surely slower than that.[34] Tweeds, which became a major item of production in Ontario, could be produced on the first wave of machines adapted to the woollen textile industry. In the Scottish tweed trade, the use of power looms increased very rapidly between 1856 and 1867. The carding process for coarse tweeds could mingle all lengths and diameters of wool, so that relatively unspecialized carding machinery could be used.[35]

But few mill owners at that time had the resources for rapid plant enlargement. The most notable expansions of the 1860s were financed through systems of interlocking partnerships, in which some of the major textile wholesalers, such as George Stephen (of later Canadian Pacific Railway fame) were heavily involved.[36] This gave an oligopolistic flavour to the industry: it was amenable to price leadership and other marketing dicta from central figures like Stephen.

The Rosamond Woollen Mill was a choice example of this progression in its relocation from Carleton Place to Almonte in the Ottawa Valley. The move was dictated by the greater water power available at Almonte, and by the transportation provided by the Brockville and Ottawa Railway, in which the Rosamonds invested. The original mill had been financed through a partnership which Rosamond took occasion to buy out; further expansion in the 1860s — which involved the importation of new machinery from Britain — was financed through retained earnings and through the inclusion of George Stephen as a partner. And while Bennett Rosamond, the dominant figure in the firm, remained largely independent of Stephen and his dictates, Stephen nevertheless had considerable influence with him.[37] In this case, relocation, expansion, and greater mechanization followed on the development of access to a larger market. Indeed, by the 1880s, there were large, heavily capitalized factories with hundreds of employees to be found in the industry: the Rosamond Almonte plant was one of them.

In sum, the changes of the 1860s brought some geographical concentration to the industry and some level of consolidation. The scope of markets widened, and inter-local, inter-regional competition became more intense. Even during the expansionary times of the 1860s and the early 1870s, the small local carding mills that had predominated in the earlier era faced serious competitive difficulties as the markets for the large producers expanded beyond the local to the regional and to a limited degree even the international market.[38]

Moreover, cheap woollens, frequently shoddy imported from Britain, began to appear in quantity in Canada in the 1870s, creating considerable pressure to reduce the high level of Canadian production.[39] This was but a forerunner to the developments of the depression-ridden 1870s. In this industry the depression also accentuated the oligopolistic tendencies created by the system of interlocking partnerships established in the 1860s.[40]

Yet small producers displayed enormous persistence. The boom of 1879-83, combined with higher protective tariffs and a tremendous upsurge in demand[41] encouraged small manufacturers to remain in the field. John Newton, for example, a small producer of blankets made from coarse domestic wool, vigorously supported protection as a means of permitting him to keep in the business with old machinery of limited capacity.[42] At the end of 1880, 37 of the 324 woollen textile producers that the Toronto *Monetary Times* could find in Ontario were still engaged in custom work, and as the business journal freely admitted, this number was undoubtedly an underestimate. Indeed, the paper noted some sixty-three carding or fulling mills in existence at that date in Ontario, many of which must have supported very small scale production of woollens.[43] After all, hand-loom weaving in the tweeds industry, under a regime of relatively low wages, could be competitive with power looms.[44] While producers already in a good position took the opportunity to expand, the number of employees per wool-manufacturing concern actually fell from 16.5 to 5.4 from 1871 to 1881.[45] Small producers maintained market presence as local markets became less isolated by accepting the dictates of manufacturers or selling agents — who, in turn, often had investment stakes in the larger woollen textile manufacturers. This fostered oligopolistic conditions in the industry further.[46] Moreover, the tariff permitted minor manufacturers with limited markets much better play than they would have had in open, competitive conditions.

The tariff may have also discouraged existing producers from changing their methods. The oligopolistic conditions of ownership in the larger mills permitted this, and it seems likely that consolidation in the industry slowed down. As a result of protected domestic markets, oligopolistic attitudes among larger producers, and the limited capital of small producers filling constricted market niches, the industry as a whole became unwilling to improve production methods. The prevalent interlocking partnerships among the larger producers in the industry undermined entrepreneurship at the managerial level.[47] Such partnerships certainly did not pave the way to any substantial consolidation and rationalization of the industry. So, at the turn of the century, some 300 firms participated in the Canadian industry in geographically dispersed locations, and usually in smaller towns.[48] This was not much different from the 324 firms of all sizes that the *Monetary Times* had listed as operating in Ontario in 1880.[49]

The harsher international competition after 1897 led to the 1900 Canadian Woollen Syndicate, which was an effort to develop a nominally consolidated industry for purposes of price and production control.[50] The organization drew together a variety of mills, not with any intent to eliminate the least productive or to undertake physical consolidation and rationalization, but simply to permit some of the existing mills to have longer runs of the goods they each produced most efficiently. Some advantages in marketing were also hoped for by the participants. This "merger" was barely distinguishable from collusion for purposes of market control. The syndicate was typical of a certain type of industrial consolidation in which effective rationalization was not pursued.[51] And it collapsed in short order.[52]

By the 1890s, if not before, the industry was in decline, only partly because of the tariff or systems of ownership. Canadian woollen textile production became increasingly driven by changing fashions. Cottons were becoming more popular and cut into the market for wool textiles; Canadian cotton production rose sharply.[53] Tastes in woollen textiles were also changing significantly. In Europe, beginning in the mid-1870s, coarse worsteds lost their popularity. French fine worsteds made from merino wool penetrated the British market heavily. The British worsted industry was unable to compete, largely because its retained earnings were too low to re-equip to produce the finer cloth. Meanwhile, light British woollens (short-staple cloth) were being exported in greater quantities to Canada, where they had an appeal far greater than the coarser domestic cloth.[54] Canadian raw wool, only useful for coarse tweeds, blankets, and the like, was thus first supplemented, and then replaced, by imported softer raw wool.[55] Both manufacturers and textile wholesalers were singularly unsuccessful in persuading Canadian sheep raisers to change to breeds that produced the softer wool.[56] The failure of that exercise in persuasion dictated higher costs for the manufacturers. Even more telling, only a handful of manufacturers chose to adopt new technology.[57] The reputation of Ontarian woollens, throughout the late nineteenth century, was not high. Few people of the middle class chose this product if they had alternatives.

Grafton and Company, for example, a manufacturer and retailer of clothing with branch stores by 1910 in Dundas, Hamilton, Owen Sound, London, Woodstock, Brantford, and Peterborough, did virtually all its buying in Europe, especially Britain. Twice a year, from the 1860s to the turn of the century and beyond, buyers from the chain went to Britain to buy textiles and clothing for the chain's middle-class clientele. While the store offered some Canadian tweeds, they were not vigorously advertised. No more telling comment can be made about the perceived quality of Canadian woollen textiles.[58]

When the Canadian tariff was lowered in 1897 to give British woollen cloth preferential access to the Canadian market, the largely uncompetitive industry suffered enormously. Only a few companies like the Rosamond firm of Almonte, which produced specialized goods, could readily endure the international rivalry.[59]

The major bout of geographical relocation and productive consolidation in the woollen textile industry that had occurred in the 1860s and early 1870s was not repeated. Heavily protected by tariffs and tainted with oligopolistic tendencies, the industry had limited flexibility. Larger manufacturers seemed to depend on the combined effects of tariff protection and oligopoly to avoid the rapid changes that might have made them internationally competitive once tariff barriers were removed. Small manufacturers continued to produce for local markets. It was, alas, an industry in decline.

In contrast, the furniture industry in Ontario did not appear to be in decline at the turn of the century; it seemed on the verge of substantial growth. The manufacture of wooden furniture ("case goods" such as dining room and bedroom suites, as well as chairs) was in a transitional phase in the second half of the nineteenth century in Ontario.[60] Although until recently the industry was relatively unconcentrated,[61] there were significant technological advances in woodworking machinery, and substantial transportation improvements, which permitted the development of a fair degree of geographical and firm concentration after 1870. At the same time, there was an undeniable continuation of small factories and shops.

The forces that led to the development of the wooden furniture manufacturing business were locational and technological. The building of utilitarian furniture for the settlers was an early, and necessary, industry in the province. Raw materials were universally available; high transportation costs made concentration in the industry difficult. The industry was highly diffuse as a craft. According to the census of 1851, in the settled counties there were at least six and as many as twenty-two cabinetmakers for each 10,000 people.[62]

Some sophisticated woodworking machinery had first been invented in the late eighteenth and early nineteenth centuries in the hothouse atmosphere of the Royal Navy dockyards in Britain. There, Sir Samuel Bentham (brother of the more famous Jeremy) developed a broad range of woodworking machinery.[63] But this machinery was not adopted more widely; in fact it practically had to be re-invented from the 1840s onwards, in Britain, the United States, and continental Europe.[64]

The Great Exhibition of 1851 in London England generated an international knowledge of improvements in woodworking equipment; the British in particular became aware of the American delight in high-speed machines and thought themselves backward because of it.[65] At the same time the construction of the Crystal Palace encouraged the development of woodworking machinery.[66] The exhibition and the publicity surrounding it speeded up technological diffusion.[67]

In North America the interest in high-speed machinery for replacing expensive labour was great. Even in Canada in the mid-1850s, as a boastful presentation of Canadian machinery at the Paris international exhibition indicated, machine manufacturers were producing some woodworking machinery, including a tongue-and-groove machine, a morticing machine, a planing machine, and a self-acting lathe.[68]

By the early 1870s, knowledge about a considerable range of machinery was widely dispersed. A major British technical manual published in 1872 on woodworking machines was widely distributed in Britain and North America.[69] In the United States, after the Civil War, the woodworking equipment that had been developed in the 1850s and somewhat earlier was perfected, methods of machine production were standardized, and new tools were invented. The spread of these innovations reduced production costs by speeding up the "basic procedures of cutting, planing, turning, boring, and sanding wood." Veneers cut paper-thin by machine-driven knives were readily available by the early 1880s. The "spindle shapers" with high-speed burrs that had first been used in the late 1860s were added to by machines that could create several copies of a three-dimensional carving at one time (in 1891 a device that produced eight duplicates at a time was introduced in Chicago); these were supplemented in the 1890s by embossing machines that pressed designs into wood.[70] The development of high-speed, specialized machinery in turn led to greater specialization in production in major American furniture-producing cities like Chicago and Grand Rapids, Michigan. The consequence in the United States was that "while small workshops would persist, the balance slowly tipped in favour of large factories, growing mechanization, and increased specialization."[71]

The impact of woodworking machinery was to be seen in a variety of industries, not just in furniture manufacture. Sash and door, as well as moulding, factories, with their array of saws, planes, and shaping machines, were widespread in Ontario. The well-outfitted moulding factory of Guggisburg at Preston was in 1866 subcontracting work from the major Toronto furniture manufacturer Jacques and Hay.[72] In carriage manufacturing, which involved much turning (lathe work), planing, shaping, and sawing, specialized machinery began to be widely adopted in the 1870s, at least in the United States.[73] The accelerated rate of technological change rapidly outpaced the ability of smaller manufacturers to adapt. But if their capital was sufficient and their adherence to traditional methods minimal, they could take advantage of the array of "combination" machinery. The industry consequently had a very broad spectrum of productive facilities, with a very great range of costs of production.[74]

Larger manufacturers of case goods had to balance several locational factors: access to concentrated markets, access to raw materials, and access to cheap, skilled, labour. Such a combination was to be found in the counties of Bruce, Huron, Gray, Waterloo, Oxford, and Perth.[75] Inexpensive transportation to a concentrated market was a decisive factor in the early history of the trade;[76] even after the development of railways, manufacturers of fine furniture did not like to consign their products to the uncaring hands of railway freight handlers, who, with the frequent repacking that commonly took place before the development of through-freight agreements, could do great damage.[77] The finished product had high bulk for its weight, and producers were constantly looking for cheaper transportation opportunities.[78]

Ready access to the bulky raw material became an important consideration with development of more sophisticated and integrated railway transport between the 1850s and the 1870s. This partly explains the efflorescence of the industry in Michigan and in southwestern Ontario, at the fringe of the deciduous forest.[79] The importance of railway links is evident in the explosive growth of the Knechtel furniture firm in Hanover after a railway link was established in 1881. Driven forward by vigorous family entrepreneurship, the firm became a national force in some twenty years. While Jacques and Hay's success was in large part based on the Toronto market, the firm's railway link to its lumber hinterland in Simcoe County was important in sustaining the firm when cost and accessibility of raw materials became vital.

When small-shop producers attempted to become large manufacturers with broad market penetration, they faced considerable difficulties. Not everyone had easy access to a large market, raw materials, and the capital necessary to adopt advanced technology. The George Moorhead Company of London, Ontario, gives some indication of the process and its problems. Moorhead, who ran a furniture shop in London beginning in 1857, developed it into a major manufacturing establishment by the mid-1870s.[80] He had been a single proprietor, but in order to expand he sold shares (overvalued as it turned out) in his business. By the mid-1870s he was able to advertise: "He has his workshops fully supplied with the latest and most approved machinery, all driven by steam power, and is prepared to produce every article of Furniture in the latest style as cheap as any house in the trade in the Dominion. Every new improvement immediately adopted, to keep up with the progress of the times."[81] Despite two fires that destroyed the premises, the Moorhead firm continued its headlong pursuit of progress, which included careful plant layout.[82] Before going bankrupt in 1878, Moorhead was the third- or fourth-largest manufacturer of furniture in the province.

Moorhead's market was initially London and the immediate vicinity, as is evidenced by the retail showroom at the factory premises in central London. The proprietor made large individual sales himself.[83] The fall agricultural and industrial exhibition in London also served to impress the product line on the mind of the local population.[84] By 1873 he had sales throughout southwestern Ontario, though evidently he did not open proprietary showrooms outside of London. In response to declining transportation costs (a major factor in pricing furniture in the nineteenth century), Moorhead made occasional forays far beyond this geographic area,[85] even undertaking auctions in Montreal. As was its stated aim, the company was on the verge of a very broad market penetration by the mid-1870s, though it did not have a clear strategy for expansion.

By that point, its aggressive growth was being driven by a desperate need to service a large debt. Production techniques became speed-oriented; some of the products were shoddy. The growth proved to be too headlong for the firm's capital base, and in 1878 Moorhead was looking for new investors to pay off his debt by an infusion of new equity. He was unsuccessful — and he became insolvent — as his financial ineptitude came to light.[86]

The management that took over the bankrupt firm was much less aggressive in its adoption of new technology and its search for new markets; rather, it concentrated on keeping the firm out of debt. This policy, combined with reduced accessibility to raw materials, condemned the former Moorhead firm to a protracted decline.[87] Still, the Moorhead episode showed that aggressive firms could pursue technological improvement and broader markets even in a depression and that there was room for a variety of larger, technologically advanced furniture manufacturers in the province. But it is striking that one of the province's largest furniture manufacturers in the 1870s served a market that was essentially regional and even sub-regional.

In the late nineteenth century, the Knechtel firm of Hanover, located in what became the Waterloo-Grey-Oxford-Bruce furniture-manufacturing nexus, followed a pattern similar to that of the Moorhead firm, in which local market dominance shifted to broader competitiveness. Daniel Knechtel moved to the village of Hanover in 1849; he had a background in carpentry and worked at it vigorously for a number of years with his brother, Peter. They established a sawmill, and by the late 1860s they were selling furniture. By 1874 they had built a furniture factory and had a steam engine to run it; their employees numbered roughly thirty.

Knechtel supplied much of the nearby demand for furniture at that point. Its future local competitors were at that time to be counted among the firm's employees. The market was served by their own retail outlet at their factory, and by wagon shipments of furniture to nearby towns. Longer-distance shipments were relatively rare.

These conditions changed in 1881, when the Stratford and Lake Huron Railway reached Hanover and a larger market opened up. The following twenty years were ones of very rapid expansion, with the erection of a new factory in 1884, the addition of more partners in 1887, the change to joint-stock organization for purposes of greater capitalization in 1891, and the purchase of part ownership in sawmills and factories at Southampton in 1895 and Walkerton in 1898. The opening of new factories was intended to maintain access to the declining regional supply of timber, a powerful locational consideration. By the turn of the century, the company had a strong regional, as opposed to local, presence. Under the leadership of the systematic and dynamic J.S. Knechtel, son of the founder, the groundwork was being laid for full national distribution of the Knechtel product line.[88] By 1901, four travelling salesmen had placed Knechtel goods in retail outlets in virtually every province; J.S. Knechtel hoped that all the main retail outlets in the country would be contacted by the next year.[89]

It is striking to note that, despite Knechtel's national presence by the first decade of the twentieth century the firm did not yet employ some important forms of machinery, such as the multiple-copy carving machine, which had been available for a decade. It is possible that tariff protection allowed the company to maintain outmoded technology despite its position in the market. Certainly its emphasis on good relations with highly skilled long-term employees militated against the quick adoption of machinery that would replace skilled labour. Yet the Knechtel example indicates the successful adaptation of a firm that at first dominated a local market to the emergence of integrated national markets. It was a challenge that other manufacturers, largely because of locational problems, failed to meet.

Some manufacturers found they could do well without immediate access to raw materials or cheap labour and could locate in large cities. One such was Jacques and Hay, a Toronto manufacturer. Jacques and Hay (in 1870 the firm became Robert Hay and Co., and later Charles Rogers and Sons Co.)[90] began as a small shop in Toronto in 1835, and by the 1850s had expanded into a factory with some ninety employees and a wide range of machinery. During the boom of the mid-1850s, the Toronto plant was producing 1,000 beds and 15,000 Windsor chairs as well as a variety of other wooden furniture each year.[91]

Jacques and Hay were well located. The Toronto facility was sitting on the largest and most sophisticated market in the province and because it was at a vital transportation node, it had some access to the rest of the province. Moreover, the Toronto base helped the company manufacture for the government, especially school desks and other high-demand items whose long production runs financially justified an investment in new technology.

The company's distribution facilities were enhanced by the opening of company showrooms in several Ontario towns in the late 1850s. The partners were not above using social emulation as a mode of marketing: they built the furniture for the Prince of Wales and his retinue during their stays in Montreal, Ottawa, Toronto and Niagara Falls in 1860. This they sold off at public auction in each city after the prince had left.[92]

The company did begin to face locational difficulties because of the diminishing availability of wood, high labour costs, and an orientation to large-volume production. It effectively dealt with these problems by buying land in Simcoe County (it owned about 1,100 acres by 1857) and establishing an outlying primary-processing plant there, at New Lowell. This location had the added advantage of being on a railway line to Toronto. At the new plant, only the simplest furniture and wooden objects were manufactured, while rough timber was cut and shipped to the Toronto factory and to other buyers for production. Such vertically integrated production enabled Jacques and Hay to cover the broad spectrum of the market.[93] By the 1860s, the firm was at the forefront of furniture production in Ontario both in terms of the technology used and volume produced. At that point, the well-organized factory had twenty circular saws, power planers, a belt sander, a jig saw, a moulding machine, and a multiple-drilling machine, all powered by steam.[94]

Jacques and Hay ultimately slid into oblivion. The absence of catalogues for the firm's products indicates some weaknesses in marketing, as such advertising mechanisms were in common use in the

United States by the 1870s. Their position was undercut by broad locational factors, despite their efforts at vertical integration and at reducing transport costs by cutting dimension stock at New Lowell. Moreover, despite the apparent technologically advanced state of the Hay firm, it was falling behind. By 1872, the range of machines available was stunningly larger than what Jacques and Hay had in 1864.[95] The firm was damaged further by rapidly falling transportation costs for finished goods that were produced close to sources of raw material and in places that happened to have a low-paid skilled work force.[96] The firm, under the Rogers name, declined until it was dissolved in 1922.

It needs to be stressed, however, that the emergence of large firms in the wood-furniture industry was not typical in the period from Confederation to the turn of the century in Ontario. Artisans and small-shop producers had great powers of persistence, in large part because the processes of market integration were not as effective or as complete as they might first appear.

Two useful examples of artisanal craftsmanship in furniture production date from the 1850s, and even later, when Jacques and Hay were already a power in the land. One of them, Friedrich Ploethner, probably did not even have a lathe during his career in the 1850s as a craftsman and cabinet-maker in Grey County: he worked with planes and chisels.[97]

Ploethner was perhaps unusual in his poverty of equipment. Francis Jones, who operated in the village of Ireland close to London, Ontario, from 1850 to the 1890s, left a collection of some 900 hand tools, which included those for rough carpentry and fine cabinet work. The tools themselves were not multi-purpose, which suggests that he probably made no real attempt to meet the competition that came from large producers like Jacques and Hay, among others. Jones, like virtually all artisanal cabinet-makers, did not specialize.[98] Ploethner and Jones were examples of the continuing dispersion of the woodworking industries even in the 1880s.[99]

The continuing localism and regionalism of the furniture industry was rooted partly in the craftsmanship which, until very recently, remained crucial to the making of furniture. Nonetheless, if small producers and owners of modest shops and factories wished to take advantage of the cachet[100] associated with improved fit and the increased speed of production that machines provided, they could make use of equipment specifically designed for the small shop. Some of this machinery — lathes, scroll saws, morticing machines, and others — was foot-powered, or made use of animal-driven windlasses. It was still being sold in quantity by American manufacturers after the turn of the century.[101] In addition, for small shops that had a source of power, "combination machines" could be obtained. The combination machines, readily available during the 1880s from the United States, were awkward for larger, more specialized producers of furniture, who found little use for machines that required constant readjustment for new tasks, but to a small shop they were a god-send.[102] Technology of this character made it possible to resist consolidation.

The uses of new sources of power, or the continued use of well established sources, made the persistence of small shops possible too. John Gemeinhardt, who was active as a furniture maker until just after 1900, used first a small steam engine and then a gas motor to run several pieces of machinery in his Bayfield shop, where he still received a significant municipal contract. Yet he employed only one other person, and that probably intermittently.[103] The Thomas McIntyre shop, which employed fifteen employees in the early 1860s, ran a variety of machines using water power.[104] In 1881, furniture shops with fewer than five workers still accounted for roughly one-half of all furniture production in the province, though the industry itself was shifting to areas that had ready access to markets or to raw materials.[105]

The imposition of a high protective tariff on furniture probably allowed the small producer to persist longer than otherwise.[106] In the later decades of the century, the larger Canadian manufacturers were protectionist, as were their smaller brethren. This attitude was due to the fear of American competition. The American furniture manufacturing industry in Michigan, Ohio, and Illinois emerged rapidly after the Civil War, and there manufacturing capacities were very large, and high-speed mass production was at a premium.[107] Michigan, in particular, was a rapidly expanding furniture producer, with a heavy concentration of production at Grand Rapids. By 1900 the city was one of the largest quantity producers of furniture in the United States, having overtaken Cincinnati. The great Chicago fire of 1871 enormously stimulated demand from the Grand Rapids producers; when that demand was slaked, they looked elsewhere, including north of the border. Imports of American furniture into Canada were very high during the mid- and late 1870s.[108] They dropped in a remarkable and sustained fashion when the National Policy protective tariff of 1879 was imposed, leaving a substantial market that Canadian producers of all sizes could fill.[109]

Even in the realm of marketing the persistence of the smaller firm in Ontario was apparent. Marketing mechanisms for the furniture industry reflected the limitations of the industry, and the degree of market integration that was taking place. In the United States, the chief method of distribution, already in use in the 1870s, was the furniture show, at which retailers examined and judged the products of the various manufacturers and ordered accordingly.[110] Such shows became major national events in the 1890s in the United States, revealing a very high level of market integration. The exhibitions were supplemented by company salesmen armed with catalogues and, later, photographs of products.

In Canada, where a less integrated market apparently existed, the furniture shows were much less crucial for gathering retailers and manufacturers together. Instead, manufacturers used travellers to place goods in retail outlets, and a number of manufacturers were directly involved in retailing, not only in factory showrooms (a procedure used by virtually all producers), but in captive showrooms in other towns and cities.[111] In fact, furniture shows in Ontario appeared to have been an extension of local or regional fall fairs. By the 1920s the most successful shows were those at Stratford and Kitchener. The earliest comprehensive manufacturers' organization dated from 1894, and the first general furniture exhibition from 1896, at an early dealers' convention. This was clearly following in the footsteps of the American industry, and it reflected the emergence of a relatively integrated market.[112] Yet the firms, rather than undergoing consolidation through competitive wastage or merger sought to maintain their independent existence. In 1900, for example, a "merger" aimed at market control was undertaken: some twenty-two furniture manufacturers in western Ontario were joined into one. But the new firm was based on nothing more than a share exchange; the board of directors was made up of the majority shareholders in the constituent companies; there was no consolidation of physical plant. At best, the new firm expected some savings in marketing.[113] The scheme did not last, for Knechtel left the organization. Knechtel's emphasis on representation by salesmen was repeated by other manufacturers, though in most instances, the salesmen were manufacturers' agents who represented more than one firm. Selling furniture from manufacturers to retail outlets through manufacturers agents remained the dominant method.

In conclusion, the developing geographical concentration of firms in southwestern Ontario did not necessarily mean that overwhelmingly large firms emerged, though some ongoing consolidation took place. Geographic concentration was due to the need for raw materials and skilled, cheap labour. A variety of economies could be achieved in transportation costs and availability of materials through geographic concentration, without alterations in plant size. The protective tariff sheltered all producers from intense American competition, and slowed down the trend towards consolidation.

Both woollen textile and furniture manufacturing were indigenous rather than "hot-house" industries. They were part of an efflorescence in rural industrialization that was the result of healthy, widespread demand in a well-to-do agrarian society. Because of the industries' deep roots, combined with protective tariffs, incomplete transportation integration, and certain technological developments, it was possible for them to resist consolidation and giantism successfully.

Recent scholars of the Industrial Revolution in Britain have begun to stress the persistence of established, smaller-scale means of production.[114] After a fashion, this paper has suggested that something similar happened in Ontario after 1850 and that such persistence stretched virtually to the end of the century. Yet it cannot be more than a suggestion in the absence full-scale studies for many industries. After all, the trend toward larger productive facilities and industrial consolidation in Ontario has only received episodic treatment by historians. Even the Canadian woollen textile industry, which has been relatively well studied, still offers much for the dedicated scholar. This paper is thus one effort towards redressing an imbalanced scholarly thesis which has not even been completely formulated. But the stubborn, continuing existence of small producers in the two industries examined, as larger producers reached widening bands of consumers, indicates the strength of ongoing competitive pressures. The industrial condition in late-nineteenth-century Ontario was characterized as much by the growth of competition as by the flight from it.

NOTES

1   The summary phrase is taken from Ian Drummond, *Progress without Planning: The Economic History of Ontario from Confederation to the Second World War* (Toronto: University of Toronto Press, 1986).
2   Michael Bliss, *A Living Profit: Studies in the Social History of Canadian Business, 1883-1911* (Toronto: McClelland and Stewart, 1974), pp. 33-54; B. Forster, *A Conjunction of Interests: Business, Politics and Tariffs 1825-1879* (Toronto: University of Toronto Press, 1986), Chap. 6; Gregory S. Kealey, *Toronto Workers Respond to Industrial Capitalism 1867-1892* (Toronto: University of Toronto Press, 1980), pp. 18-34; B.D. Palmer, *Working-Class Experience: the Rise and Reconstitution of Canadian Labour, 1800-1980* (Toronto: Buttersworth, 1983), pp. 96-99. T.L. Walkom, "The Daily Newspaper Industry in Ontario's Developing Capitalist Economy: Toronto and Ottawa, 1871-1911" (Ph.D. thesis, University of Toronto, 1983), shows how limited was concentration in some select industries.
3   Drummond, *Progress without Planning*, pp. 112-15.
4   R.C.B. Risk, "The Nineteenth-Century Foundations of the Business Corporation in Ontario," *University of Toronto Law Journal*, 23 (1973), 300-1 shows few significant corporate manufacturing businesses in Ontario before Confederation; most charters were for transportation or financial institutions. Nor did the use of the corporation did not rise sharply in the following two decades.
5   James M. Gilmour, *Spatial Evolution of Manufacturing: Southern Ontario 1851-1891* (Toronto: University of Toronto Press, 1972); John McCallum, *Unequal Beginnings: Agriculture and Economic Development in Quebec and Ontario until 1870* (Toronto: University of Toronto Press, 1980); Michael Bliss, *Northern Enterprise: Five Centuries of Canadian Business* (Toronto: Macmillan of Canada, 1987), pp. 232, 287. Despite his emphasis on the growth of larger manufacturers, Bliss suggests that this was the dominant characteristic of nineteenth-century production. *Monetary Times* (hereafter *MT*), Sept. 16, 1881, notes in connection

with the Toronto industrial exhibition, "One is struck with the great local diffusion which they [the manufacturers at the exhibition] present." The writer admits that geographical concentration of smaller firms was the wave of the future.

6   This has been argued effectively for the United States by Fred Bateman and Thomas Weiss in "Market Structure before the Age of Big Business: Concentration and Profit in Early Southern Manufacturing," *Business History Review*, 49 (1975), 312-36.

7   "People of the same trade seldom meet together, even for merriment and diversion, but the conversation ends in a conspiracy against the public, or in some contrivance to raise prices." A. Smith, *Wealth of Nations* (New York, 1937), p. 128.

8   Bliss, *Northern Enterprise*, p. 305, provides a Canadian example.

9   Archives of Ontario, Blake Papers, Vol. 22, D. Cornish to Edward Blake, Aug. 24, 1875, provides one example.

10   Canada, House of Commons, *Journals*, 1876, App. 3, p. 37, makes the case for technological depreciation in the sugar-refining industry. J. Schmookler, *Patents, Invention and Economic Change: Data and Selected Essays* (Cambridge, Mass.: Harvard University Press, 1972), p. 35, asserted that the 1874-88 period was one of "maximum technical change," according to the number of patents taken out in the United States.

11   Drummond, *Progress without Planning*, p. 113. Nathan Rosenberg and L.E. Birdzell Jr., *How the West Grew Rich* (New York: Basic Books, 1986), pp. 214-15.

12   Forster, *Conjunction of Interests.* Chap. 5, and review of same by Peter George in *Business History Review*, 61 (1987), pp. 346-48. See also Kris Inwood, "Effective Transportation and Tariff Protection: The Case of the Canadian Iron Industry" (unpublished paper, University of Guelph).

13   G.R. Taylor and Irene Neu, *The American Railroad Network 1861-1890* (Cambridge Mass.: Harvard University Press, 1956).

14   Bliss, *Living Profit*, p. 35.

15   MT, Aug. 12, 1881. Taylor and Neu, *The American Railroad Network*, esp. p. 2; E.C. Kirkland, *Industry Comes of Age: Business, Labor and Public Policy 1860-1897* (New York: Holt, Rinehart and Winston, 1961), pp. 79-80.

16   MT, Aug. 12, 1881. Canada, House of Commons, *Sessional Papers*, 1881, No. 6, cites a petition of 1880 from shipowners and others of St. Catharines which protested low canal freight rates.

17   D.C. North, "Ocean Freight Rates and Economic Development 1850-1913," *Journal of Economic History*, 18 (1958), 537-55. C. Knick Harley, "Aspects of the Economics of Shipping, 1815-1913," in L.R. Fischer and G.E. Panting, eds., *Change and Adaptation in Maritime History: The North Atlantic Fleets in the Nineteenth Century* (St. John's: Memorial University of Newfoundland, 1985), pp. 169-86; P.N. Davies, "The Development of the Liner Trades," in K. Matthews and G. Panting, eds., *Ships and Shipbuilding in the North Atlantic Region* (St. John's: Memorial University of Newfoundland, 1978), pp. 175-94. MT, Aug. 26, 1881. The crisis of wooden shipbuilding and the shift to composite ships is made clear in Canada, House of Commons, *Journals*, 1867-68, App. 11.

18   Quoted in A. Gregg Finley, "The Morans of St. Martins, N.B., 1850-1880: Toward an Understanding of Family Participation in Maritime Enterprise," in L.W. Fischer and E.W. Sager, eds., *The Enterprising Canadians: Entrepreneurs and Economic Development in Eastern Canada, 1820-1914* (St. John's: Memorial University of Newfoundland, 1979), p. 51; F.E. Hyde, *Cunard and the North Atlantic 1840-1973* (London: Macmillan, 1975), p. 96. E.W. Sager and L.R. Fischer assert the profitability of the shipping industry after 1874: "Atlantic Canada and the Age of Sail Revisited," *Canadian Historical Review* 63 (1982), 144. Others have been skeptical: see Fischer and Panting, eds., *Change and Adaptation in Maritime*

History, pp. 47-49; L.R. Fischer and E.W. Sager, eds., *Merchant Shipping and Economic Development in Atlantic Canada* (Saint John: Memorial University of Newfoundland, 1982), pp. 61-63.

19   Douglas McCalla, *The Upper Canada Trade 1834-1872: A Study of the Buchanans' Business* (Toronto: University of Toronto Press, 1979), provides a penetrating study of one firm in this system. It is worth stressing that wholesalers were nevertheless a healthy part of the business system long after 1900.

20   For an analysis of the alteration in marketing, see Stanley D. Chapman, "British Marketing Enterprise: The Changing Roles of Merchants, Manufacturers, and Financiers, 1700-1860," *Business History Review*, 53 (1979), 205-33. Drummond, *Progress without Planning*, pp. 277-78, provides a succinct outline of the conditions of distribution in Ontario.

21   Halifax *Citizen*, Nov. 24, 1874; Saint John *News*, Apr.25, 1877; *MT*, June 4, July 9, and Nov. 26, 1875.

22   *MT*, Jan. 2, 1874; Jan. 4, 11, 1878.

23   *MT*, Apr. 26, 1877.

24   E. Benson, *Historical Record of the Edwardsburgh Starch Company* (Montreal: Canada Starch Company, 1959), pp. 39, 46, 50-51.

25   *Industrial Canada*, May 1967, 205-6.

26   Saint John *News*, Nov. 20, 1874; Montreal *Witness*, Aug. 28, 1878; Canada, House of Commons, *Journals*, 1876, App. 3, pp. 37, 218; *MT*, Apr. 13, 27, 1876.

27   Forster, *Conjunction of Interests*, pp. 110-26. Bliss, *Living Profit*, pp. 33-54.

28   Polly Anne Earl, "Craftsmen and Machines: The Nineteenth-Century Furniture Industry," in I.M.G. Quimby and P.A. Earl, eds., *Technological Innovation and the Decorative Arts* (Charlottesville, Va.: University Press of Virginia, 1974), pp. 307-29. Forster, *Conjunction of Interests*, pp. 101-8.

29   Elizabeth Price, "The Changing Geography of the Woollen Industry in Lanark, Renfrew and Carleton Counties 1830-1911," (M.A. research paper, University of Toronto 1979), p. 36. R. Reid, "The Rosamond Woollen Company of Almonte: Industrial Development in a Rural Setting," *Ontario History*, 75 (1983), 267. The North Lanark Historical Society, *The Development of the Woollen Industry in Lanark, Renfrew and Carleton Counties* (Almonte: North Lanark Historical Society, 1978), pp. 4-7. David Seward, "The Wool Textile Industry 1750-1960," in J. Geraint Jenkins, ed., *The Wool Textile Industry in Great Britain* (London: Routledge and Kegan Paul, 1972), p. 43.

30   D.N. Panabaker, "Pioneer Woollen Mills in Preston, Hespeler and Vicinity," *Waterloo Historical Society Annual Report*, 21 (1933), 47, 51.

31   George R. Taylor, *The Transportation Revolution 1815-1860* (New York: Rinehart, 1951).

32   H.A. Innis and A.R.M. Lower, eds., *Select Documents in Canadian Economic History*, (Toronto 1933), pp. 607-8. Price, "Changing Geography," pp. 43-44.

33   For descriptions of the differences in modes of production of worsteds and woollens see *Industrial Canada*, Dec. 1902, pp. 242-49, and D.T. Jenkins and K.G. Ponting, *The British Wool Textile Industry 1770-1914* (London: Heinemann Educational Books, 1982), pp. 19, 103, 108, 110-13.

34   P. Ellis, "The Techniques of Weaving," and Hugo Lemon, "The Evolution of Combing," in Jenkins, ed., *The Wool Textile Industry in Great Brtiain*, pp. 31, 74, 76, 81.

35   Clifford Gulvin, *The Tweedmakers: A History of the Scottish Fancy Woollen Industry 1600-1914* (Newton Abbot: David and Charles, 1973), pp. 82, 91, 94, 103.

36   National Archives of Canada (hereafter NAC), Department of National Revenue Records, Series A-1, vol. 220, G. Stephen to A.T. Galt, May 28, 1866; Price, "Changing Geography," pp. 57, 78.

37   Reid, "The Rosamond Woollen Company," pp. 268-69; NAC, Sir John A. Macdonald Papers, vol. 267 pp. 121026-29, G. Stephen to Sir John A. Macdonald, Feb. 26, 1872.

38   Canada, House of Commons, *Journals*, 1872, App. 3, pp. 20-22. See also J.E. Middleton and Fred Landon, *The Province of Ontario: A History, 1615-1927*, Vol. 1 (Toronto, 1927), Part 2, Chap. 10, Manufactures and Trade.

39   Canadian production could meet between 60 and 85 per cent of domestic Canadian demand. These calculations are based on the Trade and Navigation Returns 1870-71 and 1871- 72, compared to Canada, *Census*, 1871, Vol. 3 and Canada, House of Commons, *Journals*, 1876, App. 3, pp. 268-69. Shoddy was made up of wool waste, either from the combing process undertaken in the manufacture of worsteds or from the recycling of woollen rags.

40   NAC, Sir John A. Macdonald Papers, Vol. 346, p. 158722, Jan. 1, 1875, Stephen circular.

41   *MT*, Jan. 7, 1881.

42   University of Western Ontario, Regional Collection, John Newton papers, end papers, Journal 20; J. Newton to Sir J.A. Macdonald, Sept. 1, 1876, draft follows entry of Oct. 8, 1876, Journal 20; Sir J.A. Macdonald to J. Newton, Sept. 17, 1876, copy follows entry of Oct. 8, 1876, Journal 20.

43   *MT*, Dec. 17, 24, 1880. The *Monetary Times* list is clearly of the larger establishments, as the census noted seventy-two carding and fulling mills and 993 wool-cloth-making establishments in the province in 1881 (*Census of Canada*, 1881, Vol. 3).

44   Gulvin, *The Tweedmakers*, p. 103.

45   Calculated from *Census of Canada*, 1871, Vol. 3; *Census of Canada* 1881, Vol. 3.

46   North Lanark Historical Society, *Development of the Woollen Industry*, pp. 22-25

47   Price, "Changing Geography", pp. 78-79.

48   *Industrial Canada*, Dec. 1902, pp. 242-49.

49   *MT*, Dec. 17, 24, 1880. That 1900 estimate was much smaller than the 993 wool-cloth making establishments the 1881 census counted. The 1871 census listed 233 establishments, and 158 carding mills. (*Census of Canada*, 1871, Vol. 3). North Lanark Historical Society, *The Development of the Woollen Industry*, pp. 8-10, notes great variations in plant size and modes of production in Lanark, Renfrew and Carleton counties.

50   *MT*, Jan. 5, 1900; Feb. 16, 1900.

51   George J. Stigler, "Monopoly and Oligopoly by Merger," *American Economic Review*, 40 (1950), pp. 23-34. M.A. Utton, "Some Features of the Early Merger Movements in British Manufacturing Industry," *Business History* 14 (1972), 51-60.

52   Reid, "The Rosamond Woollen Company," p. 281. Reid's reference is NAC, Minutes of the Fielding Tariff Inquiry Commission, Nov. 1905, pp. 802, 865, 876. The British were undertaking merger-combinations at the same time, which were aimed at maintaining prices without rationalizing the industry. (Jenkins and Ponting, *British Wool Textile Industry*, pp. 180- 81).

53   *MT*, Jul. 1, 1881; Jun. 17, 1881; Jun. 4, 1881; May 13, 1881; Apr. 29, 1881; Apr. 22, 1881; Apr. 1, 1881; Mar. 4, 1881; Jan. 21, 1881.

54   Jenkins and Ponting, *British Wool Textile Industry*, p. 38.

55   *MT*, Sept. 2, 1881; Jul. 1, 1881. Price, "Changing Geography," p. 81.

56   *MT*, Aug. 12, 1881.

57   Reid, "The Rosamond Woollen Company," p. 276. Though technological backwardness at the end of the century was common, it was not universal, as *Industrial Canada*, Dec. 1902, pp. 242-49 indicates.

58   Hamilton Public Library, H.F. Gardiner Scrapbooks Vol. 67, p. 22. Dundas *True Banner*, July 2, 1874, Apr. 19, 1883.

59   Reid, "The Rosamond Woollen Company," p. 281; Price, "Changing Geography," pp. 85-86.

60   J.L. Oliver, *The Development and Structure of the Furniture Industry* (Oxford: Pergammon Press, 1966), pp. 32, 54-56, 62-63, 81, 88. Sharon Darling, *Chicago Furniture: Art, Craft and Industry 1833-1983* (New York: W.W. Norton and Co.,

1984), pp. 38-39, 51-52. L.A. Koltun, *The Cabinetmaker's Art in Ontario, c.1850-1900* (Ottawa: 1979). And see also Barbara R. Robertson, *Sawpower: Making Lumber in the Sawmills of Nova Scotia* (Halifax: Nimbus Publishing, 1986), pp. 35-36.

61 International Labor Organization, Tripartite Technical Meeting for the Woodworking Industries, *Technological Changes in the Woodworking Industries and Their Social Consequences* (Geneva: s.n. 1967), p. 16. Steven S. Plice, *Manpower and Merger: the Impact of Merger Upon Personnel Policies in the Carpet & Furniture Industries* (Philadelphia: Industrial Research Unit, Wharton School, University of Pennsylvania, 1976), pp. 59-62. Wickham Skinner and David C. D. Rogers, *Manufacturing Policy in the Furniture Industry: A Casebook of Major Production Problems* (Homewood, Ill.: R.D. Irwin, 1968), pp. 1-3.

62 Robert C. Christie, "The Development of the Furniture Industry in the Southwestern Ontario Furniture Manufacturing Region" (M.A. thesis, University of Western Ontario, 1964), p. 3.

63 Edward T. Joy, *English Furniture, 1800-1851* (London: Ward Lock 1977), p. 225. J. Richards, *A Treatise on the Construction and operation of Wood-working Machines: including a history of the origins and progress of the manufacture of wood-working machinery* (London 1872), pp. 3-6.

64 Joy, *English Furniture*, pp. 226-30.

65 *Richards*, Treatise, pp. 17-20.

66 Robertson, *Sawpower*, p. 108. Joy, *English Furniture*, Chap. 9. Richards, *Treatise*, p. 17. Koltun, *Cabinetmaker's Art*, p. 127.

67 In the post-Second World War period the rate of technological diffusion was estimated at about ten years in the furniture industry, from inception to general use. International Labor Organization, *Technological Changes in the Woodworking Industries*, p. 15.

68 Toronto *Globe*, Aug. 25, 1855; Jeanne Minhinnick, *At Home In Upper Canada* (Toronto: Clarke Irwin, 1970), pp. 210-12.

69 Richards, *Treatise*.

70 Darling, *Chicago Furniture*, pp. 49-50

71 Darling, *Chicago Furniture*, p. 38. Christie, "Development of the Furniture Industry," p. 8.

72 A.E. Byerly, "Preston in 1866," Waterloo Historical Society *Annual Report*, 21 (1933), 55.

73 Edward P. Duggan, "Machines, Markets, and Labor: The Carriage and Wagon Industry in Late-Nineteenth-Century Cincinnati," *Business History Review*, 51 (1977), 308-25.

74 NAC, Department of National Revenue Records, Series A-1, vol 312, J. Rose to Commissioner of Customs, May 24, 1877; vol 393, Mr. Benson to J. Johnson, June 5, 1879.

75 Koltun, *Cabinetmaker's Art*, p. 127. Terence S. Green, "A Locational Study of the Furniture Industry in Southern Ontario," (B.A. research paper, University of Toronto, 1967). Christie, "Development of the Furniture Industry," pp. 20-47; Elliott R. Keizer, "Rural Industrialization: A Case Study of the Wooden Household Furniture Industry in the Georgian Bay Region" (M.Sc. thesis, University of Guelph, 1971).

76 Oliver, *Development and Structure*, pp. 32, 54-56. Green, "A Locational Study," p. 14.

77 Oliver, *Development and Structure*, p. 49.

78 Francis X. Blouin and Thomas E. Powers, *A Furniture Family: The Slighs of Michigan* (Ann Arbor: University of Michigan 1980), pp. 3, 7-8. Green, "A Locational Study," pp. 36-38; Darling, *Chicago Furniture*, p. 64.

79 Christie, "Development of the Furniture Industry."

80 Koltun, *Cabinetmaker's Art*, pp. 128-29.

81 London *Free Press*, June 30, 1870.

82 London *Free Press*, Nov. 5, 1874.

83 This in itself was common enough. Harry Ritz Yeandle, "Sales Promotion in the Canadian Furniture Industry," (B. Admin. thesis, University of Western Ontario, 1932), p. 6.

84 The fall fair saw Moorhead win a disproportionate share of the prizes for furniture; only London and area furniture producers competed: *MT*, Aug 5, 1881; London *Free Press*, Sept. 30, 1875.

85 London *Free Press*, Sept. 18, 1873.

86 London *Free Press*, July 18, 1878; *MT*, Feb. 8, 22 and Apr. 2, 1878; Toronto *Globe*, July 2, 1878.

87 Steve Coupland, "Joseph Seymour Fallows," seminar paper.

88 Hanover *Post*, Apr. 6, 1983; Feb. 11, 1954.

89 Hanover *Post*, Dec. 26, 1901.

90 Joan MacKinnon, *A Checklist of Toronto Cabinet and Chair Makers, 1800-1865*, (Ottawa: National Museums of Canada, 1975), p. 71-72.

91 MacKinnon, *A Checklist*, pp. 82-83; Ruth Cathcart, *Jacques and Hay: 19th Century Toronto Furniture Makers* (Erin, Ontario: Boston Mills Press, 1986), pp. 1-11. Some of the firm's work was clearly subcontracted.

92 MacKinnon, *A Checklist*, pp. 92-3.

93 Cathcart, *Jacques and Hay*, pp. 15-17.

94 Cathcart, *Jacques and Hay*, p. 15.

95 Richards, *A Treatise*. The book describes and illustrates gang and circular saws, band saws, jig saws, cross-cut saws, planing machines, scraping machines, moulding machines, mortising and tenoning machines, gang boring machines, fixed routing machines, carving duplicators, milling and shaping tables, chamfering and mortising machines, combination machines, lathes, veneer cutting machines, dovetailing machines, and pneumatic suction machines for clearing sawdust and shavings from a plant. Robertson, *Sawpower*, p. 128, describes a well-equipped Nova Scotian furniture factory of the early 1870s with rather less extensive machinery than Richards describes.

96 Green, "A Locational Study," pp. 14- 15.

97 Michael Bird, "Cabinetmaker and Weaver Friedrich K. Ploethner," *Canadian Collector* 15, No. 3 (May/June 1980), 28-32.

98 Koltun, *The Cabinetmaker's Art*, pp. 5-16. It is useful to cite Walter Peddle, *The Forgotten Craftsmen* (Saint John's: H. Cuff Publications, 1984), who shows that small shop furniture manufacturing in case goods went on in Newfoundland until the 1950s.

99 Philip Shackleton, *The Furniture of Old Ontario* (Toronto: Macmillan of Canada, 1973), p. 40. Indeed, the domestic production of furniture did not come to an end. See Brenda Lee-Whiting,"Furniture-Maker from Germany: Renfrew County's Albert Zadow," *Canadian Collector*, 16 (Sept./Oct. 1981), 37.

100 Koltun, *The Cabinetmaker's Art*, p. 128.

101 Earl, "Craftsmen and Machines," in Quimby and Earl, eds., *Technological Innovation*.

102 Richards, *Treatise*, pp. 57-58. Koltun, *Cabinetmaker's Art*, p. 129. Darling, *Chicago Furniture*, pp. 15- 22.

103 Michael Bird, "Perpetuation and Adaptation: The Furniture and Craftsmanship of John Gemeinhardt (1826-1912)," *Canadian Antiques and Art Review*, March 1981, 20-34.

104 John McIntyre, "Niagara Furniture Makers — II," *Canadian Collector*, 12 (Sept./ Oct. 1977), 52.

105 Christie, "Development of the Furniture Industry," p. 8.

106 David E. Bond and Ronald J. Wonnacott, *Trade Liberalization and the Canadian Furniture Industry* (Toronto: University of Toronto Press, 1968) argue that the tariff in the modern context does not insure more profit, but simply ensures the continuation of more inefficient plants. See especially pp. 15-17.

107 Blouin and Powers, *A Furniture Family*, p. 5. Oliver, *Development and Structure*, pp. 57, 89, gives some indication of the strength of the industry in Cincinnati.
108 Oliver, *Development and Structure*, p. 91; Plice, *Manpower and Merger*, p. 11.
109 Canada, House of Commons, *Journals*, 1867-1890, "Trade and Navigation Returns."
110 Oliver, *Development and Structure*, p. 92.
111 Henry B. Bowman, "Preston's Furniture Industry and Percy R. Hilborn," in Waterloo Historical Society *Annual Report* 60 (1972), 79. See also Miriam Hilborn, "The Poth Furniture Factory in New Dundee," Waterloo Historical Society *Annual Report* 50 (1962), 80, and MacKinnon, *A Checklist*, pp. 92-93.
112 Yeandle, "Sales Promotion," pp. 6-7. George Robert Munro, "A Sales Analysis of the Canadian Furniture Industry," (B. Admin. thesis, University of Western Ontario, 1932), pp. 18-19.
113 *MT*, Apr. 6, 1900.
114 See, for example, Maxine Berg, *The Age of Manufactures 1700-1820* (Tatawa NJ: Barnes and Noble, 1985).

STREETSCAPE AND SOCIETY: THE CHANGING BUILT ENVIRONMENT OF KING STREET, TORONTO

Gunter Gad and Deryck W. Holdsworth

King Street in Toronto has long been the city's premier business address and one of its most important thoroughfares, and through several phases of development it has maintained its position as the site of most of Toronto's highest buildings and most of its largest financial enterprises. The changing streetscape of King Street mirrors the evolution of Toronto's economy and society; in turn the streetscape is a setting for conducting business, communicating values, parading, and travelling. Through a comprehensive examination of one street, we shall probe the connections between the built environment and the social forces that have both produced and used it.[1]

This essay describes and analyses the built environment of King Street by paying special attention to morphological characteristics, that is, elements of the town plan (lot size, lot coverage, and the pattern of lots, blocks, and streets), buildings (height, bulk, materials, styles, and symbols), and land use (the activities carried out on the lots or in the buildings).[2] By adopting a morphological approach, we treat the streetscape as a whole, intentionally avoiding an emphasis on buildings in isolation.

Although King Street extends from the Don River in the east to the Parkdale district in the west, only the relatively short sections between Frederick Street and Simcoe Street have ever been part of Toronto's central business district.[3] Along this central part, the fulcrum of building cycles has shifted from east to west (see Figure 1). The shifts can be broken into four distinct periods: from the beginning to the middle of the nineteenth century, the section between Frederick and Yonge streets was the typical main street of a small government town; between the 1850s and 1880s, parts of the Georgian townscape between Church and York were transformed into a Victorian thoroughfare, lined by the high-order retail stores of Ontario's most important city; from the 1880s to the beginning of the First World War, the section between Toronto and Bay streets changed from retail axis to nascent office canyon, reflecting Toronto's rise to national importance; finally, ever larger office buildings and huge office complexes sprang up west of Yonge Street in the 1920s and after the Second World War as Toronto grew into the nation's most important business centre. Our emphasis here is on the time between 1850 and 1914 and on the section of King Street between Church and Bay.[4]

Prologue: Main Street in a Georgian City

By the 1840s, King Street was lined by continuous rows of buildings from the market at New Street (later Jarvis) almost all the way to Bay Street, and fragmented development had occurred between Bay Street and the group of government buildings beyond Simcoe Street (see Figure 2a). Although an important setting for public buildings, King was — at least between Church and Bay streets — a commercial axis.

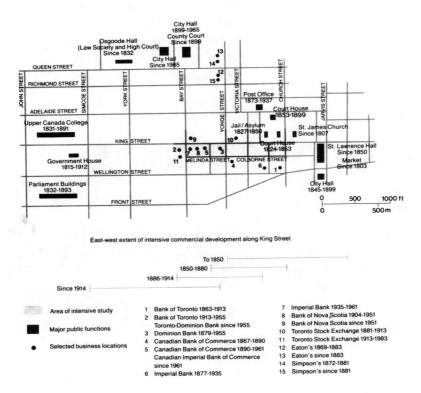

Figure 1: King Street in context.

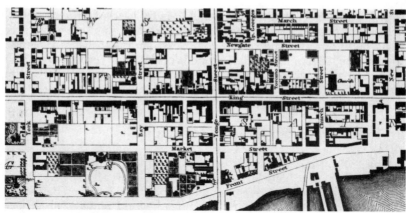

a. Detail of the 1842 Cane map.

*Figure 2: King Street in
the 1840s.*

*b. Courthouse Block as shown in the
1842 Cane map.*

*c. North side of King Street East between Yonge Street (left) and Church
Street, 1847. (From the* Illustrated London News, *Jan. 30, 1847, courtesy
Royal Ontario Museum, Toronto.)*

The commercial character of King Street is remarkable, since in the early decades of Toronto's growth, five large blocks had been reserved for prominent public buildings — courthouse, jail, market, hospital, school, and church — that would define the civic core of the city.[5] Although most of these public buildings were erected on the planned sites between the early 1800s and late 1830s,[6] business took over from government uses west of Church Street soon after.

In 1840, the insertion of a commercial row along the King Street sidewalk, directly in front of the public buildings of the Court House Square (see Figure 2b), marked the ascendancy of the merchants' world over that of government in the busiest section of the newly formed municipality of Toronto. This new row, the Wellington Buildings, was erected as a set of rental shops at the southeast corner of King East and Toronto streets[7] and was the inevitable consequence of earlier decisions to sell or lease real estate parcels in order to fund the public buildings of the Home District.[8] Even the new Assembly Hall of 1850 (St. Lawrence Hall) incorporated rentable commercial space on the King Street frontage, and the rest of the Market Block to the west of St. Lawrence Hall was developed by the young city and the buildings leased to commercial enterprises. Only part of the Church Block provided any long-term King Street frontage dominated by a public building; even there, commercial rows hemmed in the vista, and in 1851 the vestry of St. James' considered selling or leasing the King Street frontage for commercial uses.[9]

Although various schemes for an imposing landscape of public buildings never materialized on King Street,[10] there was nonetheless a strong sense of order in the way buildings accumulated on this Georgian main street. As early as the 1830s, there were some rather elegant structures, three or four storeys high with quoins, fire parapets, and gently pitched roofs, and with shops on the ground floors. The developments of the 1840s, with rows rather than isolated structures, contributed strongly to a unified Georgian streetscape. Victoria Row, designed by John Howard and built in 1842 on the south side of King Street opposite the Court House Square, provided five units, all in brick, along with two taller shops to the west.[11] Further west towards Yonge Street, the three-and-a-half-storey Albert Buildings, and the Adelaide Buildings (1847) also contributed to the emerging uniform brick wall along King Street, even if they were slightly taller and grander than the other three-storey structures on the street. These Georgian brick rows replaced earlier wooden buildings, which had been the first structures built by the colonists. Drawings of the 1840s (for example, Figure 2c) show the juxtaposition of one- and two-storey wooden buildings and the three- and four-storey Georgian rows.

In spite of the co-existence of two phases of development, King Street was seen as an elegant, orderly street, as one visitor wrote in 1845:

"The main street, King Street, is two miles and more in length, and would not do shame to any one, and has a more English look than most Canadian places have."[12] The Albert Buildings reminded the *British Colonist* of the quadrant on Regent Street, London.[13] By mid-century, King Street had evolved and solidified into distinctive clusters. There were groups of public buildings, wholesale and retail establishments, buildings where tradesmen or manufacturers produced goods, and even financial businesses, such as the Toronto branches of the Bank of Montreal at King and Bay and the Commercial Bank of the Midland District at Jordan Street. In many instances, residences could be found above shops, making King Street a truly multi-functional street.

The Victorian Thoroughfare: King Street in the Early 1880s

Between the early 1850s and the early 1880s, the appearance of King Street changed dramatically as many of the plain Georgian buildings were replaced by ornate Victorian structures. At the same time the function of King street changed considerably: it became a more special-ized street, its frontages lined by specialized shops and also by the first generation of purpose-built office structures. These changes were an expression of Toronto's growing economic importance as a wholesale and financial centre for a more far-flung region in the wake of the railway boom and also a result of the first major phase of industrial growth.[14] The growth of the city to more than 80,000 people by the early 1880s had resulted in a complex spatial pattern of economic activity; many of the functions such as retailing and manufacturing, once confined to King Street, could now be found in different parts of the city. Even the commerical district itself had begun to split into specialized nuclei of which King Street was only one component, wedged between the wholesale district to the south and the office cluster emerging near the courthouse to the north.[15]

From 1850 to the early 1880s the frontages of King Street were affected by a variety of architectural expressions (see Figures 3 and 4). The restrained Georgian brick facades were replaced; first by buildings with balustrades and shallow pediments and with ornamentation around the windows, and then, as the late Victorian styles gained popularity, by buildings with polychromatic brickwork, segmented window tops with keystones, and segmental pediments in the roofline. Especially eye-catching detail was displayed on many facades, such as Charles Robertson's store of 1850 with Gothic pinnacles, and Walker's Golden Lion with iron-framed display windows on the first two floors, elaborate ornamentation on the upper storeys, and a lion perched high above the street (see Figure 4, left of centre). In 1866, the drastic remodelling of the Victoria Row gave rise to the first example of the

Figure 3: Transition from Georgian main street to Victorian thoroughfare:
King Street West looking from Yonge Street towards Bay Street, c. 1870.
(Courtesy Metropolitan Toronto Library, T 12666.)

Figure 4: Victorian thoroughfare: King Street East looking west towards
Yonge Street from Toronto Street, 1880. (From the Canadian Illustrated
News, *July 31, 1880, courtesy Royal Ontario Museum, Toronto.)*

Second Empire style, followed in the 1870s by other commercial buildings, especially the Dominion Bank (1877-79), in a similar idiom. By the
early 1880s Victorian eclecticism was producing very ornate buildings:
steep roofs with iron crests and complex dormers, lots of little pediments, and complex bay windows.

The new buildings were larger than the Georgian rows, especially
in height. Almost all the buildings of the 1850-80 cycle had four storeys,
rather than three, and a few even reached five. More important was the
fact that the storeys were usually higher: about 15 feet rather than 11
feet. Thus the first two floors of a new building reached to the eaves line
of an old three-storey building, and the third and fourth floors of the
new buildings rose considerably above the roofs of the old rows. The
differences in height are clearly visible in the many photographs of King
Street that survive from the 1860s and 1870s. An exemplary photograph
of King Street West of c.1870 shows the prominence of the four-storey
furniture warerooms built in 1867 for the Robert Hay company (Figure
3, left middle ground). To the west, or right, is a four-storey Georgian
row building (housing the *Globe* newspaper until 1864) of lesser height
than its Victorian neighbour. The photo also shows the diagonal line of
a derrick being used in the construction of a building that would emerge
as another tall Victorian structure with a mansard roof extending above
the Georgian eaves.[16]

There were fewer changes in width and depth of the new buildings, however, since a great deal of redevelopment fitted into the lot
pattern of the pre-1850 period. Although lots varied in width from 8 to
56 feet, most were between 16 and 30 feet wide. In many cases several
adjacent lots were under the control of a single owner, and the Georgian
buildings had been erected in the form of two-to-five-unit rows with
total frontages of 32 to 50 feet or more. Thus, the fronts of Victorian
buildings could be 20 to 50 feet wide, without a dramatic change in the
width of the existing lot (see Figure 5a).

The depth of the Victorian buildings was similarly conservative.
Pre-1850 lots were between 50 and 100 feet deep and, at least in the case
of Georgian row buildings, there was a clear distinction between the
three- or four-storey front of a building, extending to a depth of 40 to 50
feet, and a one- or two-storey tail, filling most of the rest of the lot. This
pattern was not altered by Victorian redevelopment (or remodelling).
Even when lots were extended to a depth of as much as 210 feet, the new
four-storey front parts of the buildings only extended back about 50 feet
from the King Street facade. Only at street corners did the upper two
floors stretch back to a depth of 100 feet and more. It is quite clear that
the bulk of buildings was severely limited by the need to provide
adequate and safe lighting without electricity.

Although it is difficult to know how much of King Street was
affected by rebuilding or substantial alteration, a conservative estimate
is that about thirty buildings between Jarvis and Bay were involved.[17]

West of Bay, redevelopment occurred next to new buildings, largely owing to the scattered nature of development before 1850.[18] The combination of old and new and the different architectural features added between 1850 and 1881 resulted in an extremely lively streetscape. The *Globe* newspaper announced its presence by a globe on its roof (see Figure 4, right), the facade of Notman's photo studio incorporated the lens of a camera in the form of a circular window (Figure 4, left of centre), and various other businesses displayed signs and symbols that, together with less explicit architectural detail, expressed the exuberant spirit of commerce. King Street East was a Victorian streetscape par excellence (Figure 4), while King West was the frontier: one- and two-storey wooden buildings mingled with three- and four-storey brick buildings, and all were dominated by the five-storey Mail Building with its 120-foot tower.

The buildings constructed on King Street between Jarvis and York in the years 1850 to 1881 were of four kinds: retail stores, office buildings, hotels or hotel-restaurant combinations, and general commercial buildings. Noticeably absent from King Street were public buildings,[19] residential buildings, and even residences above the shops. Although we have no systematic study of the disappearing residences, many examples are reported, by John Ross Robertson for example, of merchants moving away from King Street in the 1850s.[20] By 1881 hardly any residents appear in the assessment rolls in the sections between Church and Bay. Even in the back streets (such as Colborne and Melinda) there were only about a dozen or so households.

In 1881, the south side of King Street between Church and Bay was lined by an almost uninterrupted facade of shops. The Dominion Bank premises at Yonge Street and two restaurants near Church Street were the only exceptions. The north side was quite different, however, since retail stores mingled with offices (including those of stockbrokers, coal merchants, real estate agents, newspapers, etc.) West of Yonge Street the mix of street level uses included, apart from retail stores and offices, a livery stable, a large vacant lot, and the last detached residence, that of the Cawthra family, at Bay Street (Figure 6a).

What happened above and behind the shops is of considerable interest for an understanding of the street. Again, the south side of King Street stands out, since in many cases retail establishments were the sole occupants of the buildings. But even here, amongst the grandest shops of Toronto, a more complex picture becomes apparent on close inspection. Many of the merchants, especially those who sold clothing, footwear, or jewellery, also made goods on their premises. An example is the dry goods business of W.A. Murray, an impressive enterprise according to one 1887 description. Praised as the "Swan and Edgars" or "Marshall and Snelgrove" of Toronto, this fashion store, which offered imported and home-made clothing, is said to have employed 100 salesmen (besides cashiers and bookkeepers).[21] Some of this clothing was made on the premises by between 100 and 200 workers.[22] Thus the establishment combined retailing and manufacturing. Other large enterprises of this kind were printing firms or stationery companies, where both printing and retailing occurred on the same premises. In the many general commercial buildings, similar combinations of activities were carried out, although in separate firms. The ground floor might have been occupied by a clothing retailer, and the upper floors, rear wings, or ancillary buildings at the rear by photographers, engravers, printers, cigar makers, or artists.

There were also many offices on the upper floors of these general commercial buildings, although they were different from later generations of offices. Most of those in the 1880s were extremely small and were occupied by real estate agents, manufacturers' agents, a few barristers, and a few financial businesses. Most of Toronto's offices were located elsewhere: banks, general insurance companies, and transportation-related companies were in the wholesale district south of King, and barristers, loan companies, insurance firms of various kinds, real estate agents, and architects were on Toronto, Adelaide, and Church streets near the court[23] and the post office. The concentration of offices on the north side of King just to the east and west of Toronto Street can be considered a spillover from this office cluster. Only stockbrokers were different: most of them were on the north side of King Street very close to the stock exchange at 24 King East (two properties west of Globe Lane).[24] Similarly, the important newspapers such as the *Globe*, the *Mail*, the *Telegram*, and the *World* had their premises on King Street, where they combined offices at the front with printing at the rear.

Undoubtedly, the most prominent use of the land and buildings on King Street in the early 1880s was retailing, whose visibility on the ground level, combined with the presence of Toronto's largest and most important retailers, shaped the street and its public image. Although retailing had spread to Yonge Street from the 1850s onward, observers like this writer in the *Canadian Illustrated News* of 1870 made a clear distinction between King and Yonge:

> Toronto possesses two principal streets — Yonge and King ... the only ones that are sufficiently broad, well lit, well paved, and lined with handsome shops. The buildings on King Street are grander and greater than their neighbours on Yonge, the shops are larger and dearer; and last, though far from being least, King Street is honoured by the daily presence of aristocracy, while Yonge is given over to the business-man, the middle class and the beggar.[25]

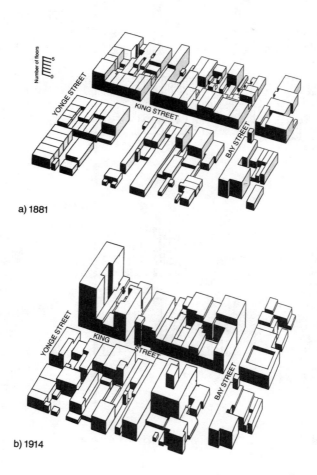

Figure 5: Building configuration, King Street West, 1881 and 1914. (Based on Goad's fire insurance plans, 1880, 1884, 1889, and 1914-18; city directories, 1880-83 and 1915; assessment rolls for 1882 and 1916. Computer-assisted design by D. Desousa, S. Schulte, and A.M. Baker.)

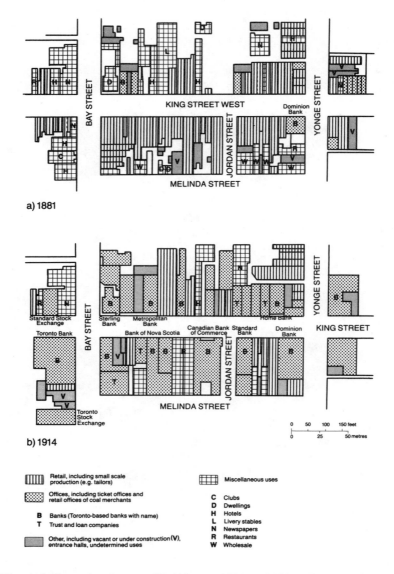

Figure 6: Street-level use on King Street, 1881 and 1914. (Based on city directories, 1882 and 1915; assessment rolls for 1882 and 1915. Goad's fire insurance plans, 1880 and 1914-18.)

As late as 1884, when the Yonge Street facades around Queen began to look just as impressive as the ones of King Street, commentators still heaped profuse praise on Toronto's principal business street:

> On the south side, the "dollar" or fashionable side, of King Street, continuously from York Street to the Market, are the spacious plate-glass windows, glittering with jewelry, with gold and silver plate, with elaborate china and brick-a-brac, with sheen of satin-shining tissues for Toronto's brides.... There are restaurants, where men and ladies can dine in comfort, and as luxuriously as in any in New York or London, photographers, art warerooms.[26]

Later in the decade, King Street is elevated above all other Toronto streets: "King Street, Toronto, has long been known to travellers as the centre of attraction, but the tourist of 1886, in describing the splendid plate glass fronts of immense establishments especially in the dry goods trade, would completely cast in shade all previous descriptions."[27]

The status of Toronto's showcase street was also reflected in front of the facades, that is, in the public spaces of the street. Not only written accounts but numerous drawings and photographs provide direct evidence of the use and importance of King Street.[28] The street of commerce was a place to shop and to promenade — one "did" King Street in the manner of an Italian "doing" a piazza. Pictures show men, alone and in groups, women in elegant outfits, and families with children. Many photos provide evidence of goods being loaded or unloaded, at times virtually blocking the street. Cutting right through the commercial district and separating the wholesale area from the office district, King Street was undoubtedly traversed by businessmen and messengers linking the wholesale houses and banks south of King Street with the post office, court and lawyers' offices to the north. Since most of the stockbrokers had their offices directly on King Street, one can also conjecture their presence in the street. Many blue-collar workers, such as printers and tailors, were employed in King Street businesses, and these workers undoubtedly contributed to the diversity of the crowd that used the street.

King Street was also an arterial road in the transportation system of the city beyond the confines of the commercial district. The first public transit line, the omnibus of 1849, linked the St. Lawrence Market and Yorkville via King East and Yonge. In 1861 the omnibus was replaced by a horse-car line and this was extended to the west and east of the Yonge-Jarvis section in 1874, 1877, and 1881. Thus, King Street became a link between the emerging mixed industrial-residential areas east and west of the commercial district.

Finally, King Street was a ceremonial street, a place to show off to visitors, a place to celebrate in and a place to mourn in. Royal and vice-regal processions like the one that marked the visit of the Prince of Wales in 1860, funeral processions like the one for Bishop Strachan in 1867, the Dominion Day parades of the 1880s, and many other events used King Street as the appropriate setting. Last but not least, there was the annual Orange Parade, which in most years in the 1860s, 1870s, and 1880s included King Street between Jarvis and York.

The picture that emerges is one of a specialized and special street. King Street had lost its residential function and had not gained any new public buildings in its main sections. It was wedged between the wholesale and banking district to the south and the Toronto-Adelaide Street office cluster to the north. The major economic function of King Street was retailing, with ancillary manufacturing (including publishing and printing) as a secondary activity. Offices were also of importance. Although retail activities could also be found on Yonge Street to a considerable extent and scattered along many arteries of the large nineteenth-century city, in size and quality of shops and its complexity and distinguished physical appearance, King Street in the 1880s was outstanding.

From Victorian Thoroughfare to Edwardian Office Canyon

Between 1881 and 1914 about three-quarters of the frontage on King Street between Church to just west of Bay was redeveloped. A substantial amount of this redevelopment occurred in the 1880s and 1890s, when three major retail stores (Lewis Rice, Michie, and John Kay) and about nine office buildings were constructed. Some of the results are seen in a photograph of King Street East taken before another wave of development took place (see Figure 7): in the foreground is an 1892 office building (Janes Building) on the northeast corner of King and Yonge, and in the distance is the domed corner of the Lewis Rice store of 1890. Prominent among the office buildings were the Manning Arcade of 1884 and the head office of the Canadian Bank of Commerce (1889-90). The Commerce, the largest of the Toronto banks and the second largest in Canada at the time, symbolized a renewed interest by banks in King Street locations. Between 1900 and 1914 a second wave of redevelopment inundated King Street: about twelve office buildings, three retail stores, and one large hotel (the King Edward) were built or substantially enlarged. Although retail facilities still had a foothold on King Street, they were clearly on the wane. The three stores that were part of this second wave of redevelopment were built or enlarged before 1910, and no major stores were built after that. Moreover, many retail establishments were displaced or disappeared. The King Edward

Figure 7: Transition from Victorian thoroughfare to Edwardian office canyon: King Street East, north side, looking east from Yonge Street, c. 1910. (Courtesy City of Toronto Archives, James 7227.)

Figure 8: Edwardian office canyon: King Street West, looking east towards Yonge Street, 1922. (Courtesy National Archives of Canada, PA-60412.)

Hotel and the CPR building (the latter on the southeast corner of King and Yonge) carved enormous gaps into the traditional frontage of retail stores on the south side of King East. Further west, the complex of early nineteenth-century public buildings disappeared.[29]

The transformation of King Street in this era involved more than just rebuilding and new architectural garb; rather there was a whole new scale of buildings. Some of the stores and offices still fitted into the older lots of 20- to 50-foot width, but in many cases new buildings were erected with frontages of 85 to 100 feet[30] and with great height: office buildings on King Street reached seven floors in 1890, fifteen floors in 1911, and twenty floors in 1914. For a brief period in 1911 a two-storey frame building of 1834 co-existed with a fifteen-storey office tower.[31]

Not all of King Street was equally affected by these redevelopment waves. Most of the changes took place between Toronto Street in the east and Bay Street in the west, and the Yonge to Bay stretch experienced an enormous upheaval through redevelopment (see Figure 5 to compare the building fabric of 1881 to that of 1914). Although the north side of the block between Toronto and Church was largely redeveloped or altered in the 1890s, the south side between Leader Lane and Church was only slightly affected. East of Church the pre-1850 building fabric was almost untouched.[32] West of Bay Street, the 1912-13 head office of the Bank of Toronto with its 120-foot-long King Street frontage represented a revolutionary change,[33] but otherwise the blocks between Bay and York remained unchanged until the 1920s and 1930s and even the 1960s.

By 1914 the increasing density of buildings on King Street was apparent: those of five or more floors cast long shadows, and a distinct canyon was beginning to take shape at King and Yonge (see Figure 8). The roofline was not consistently higher, however, for some three-and four-storey buildings survived from the pre-1880 period and even some newer buildings were relatively small. The banks had varying development policies: some, for example the Dominion Bank with its tall 1913-14 building on the site of its 1879 head office, were interested in substantial office towers with plenty of space for rent, whereas others, such as the Bank of Toronto or the Bank of Nova Scotia, built primarily to accommodate their head offices and Toronto main branches. Relatively low buildings with three- to five-storey facades were thus part of the streetscape, as were tall buildings whose ground-floor banking halls extended the equivalent of two or three normal storeys.[34]

The escalation in the scale of buildings was associated with an increase in the size of lots and in new patterns of ownership. In 1881 property ownership along King Street was highly fragmented. Three-quarters of the land fronting on King between Church and Bay streets was owned by absentee owners and estates; only a quarter was owned by family businesses, partnerships, and corporations (see Table 1).

Corporate ownership was restricted to five sets of parcels, which accounted for only 10.6 per cent of the land fronting on King Street. Significantly, four of these corporate holdings, namely those of the Dominion Bank, the North of Scotland Mortgage Company, the Canada Life Assurance, and the Mail Printing Company were on King West, while one King East parcel belonged to the Methodist Church (for use as a bookstore).

In 1914, 60 per cent of the land was controlled by corporations, most of them banks, mortgage, trust, and insurance companies, and to a lesser extent real estate developers, newspapers, hotels, and other companies (see Table 1). Absentee ownership had dropped dramatically from three-quarters to half of all land along the central King Street section, largely because most of the new corporate owners each at least partially occupied their buildings. Part of the revolution in land ownership was the creation of much larger lots than those of 1881. For instance, Toronto Hotel Ltd. managed to combine many parcels into one parcel of 166 by 197 feet; the Royal Bank owned a 46-by-110-foot parcel at 10-12 King East, and National Trust a 64-by-128-foot parcel at 18-22 King East. In other cases companies owned bundles of parcels, which were combined to form functional properties of 75 by 169 feet in the case of the Dominion Bank or 85 by 168 feet in the case of the Canadian Bank of Commerce.

Table 1
Property Ownership on King Street, 1881 and 1914,
by Percentage of Land Area

	1881			1914		
Type of Owner	1 Owner-Occupied	2 Absentee Owners	Columns 1 + 2	1 Owner-Occupied	2 Absentee Owners	Columns 1+2
Individuals, Partnerships and Estates	13.7	75.7	89.4	8.6	31.9	40.5
Corporations	10.6	0	10.6	41.2	18.3	59.5
Both Types of Owners	24.3	75.7	100	49.8	50.2	100

Note: For 1881, all properties fronting on King Street between Church and Bay streets, including nos. 50-52 and 55-57 west of Bay. For 1914, blocks south of King Street between Church and Bay and half-depth of blocks north of King Street between the same streets, including nos. 50-52 and 55-67 west of Bay.

The influence of banks and other financial businesses on the ownership of property and shape of buildings on King Street was substantial. Between 1850 and 1879 there had been no banks on King Street. The establishment of the Dominion Bank at the corner of King and Yonge in 1879 and the Quebec Bank at King and Toronto in 1886 started a movement of banks out of the wholesale district. By 1914 only the head office of the Imperial Bank, the Toronto main branches of the Bank of Montreal, and several less important banks were still missing from the King axis. Whereas banks and other financial businesses[35] began to dominate the street-level on King Street (see Fig. 6b), in many cases the floors above the banking halls provided space for a wide range of office establishments. Large buildings such as the CPR or Dominion Bank Building had 50 to 100 tenants each, and almost very sector of the economy was represented on the office floors above the banking halls.[36] Apart from being the street of banks, King Street was the core of the office district.

Other users of King Street were clearly in the shadow of the offices. There were six very large retail establishments in 1914 and about twenty or thirty small ones. By now, however, Yonge Street was the most important retail street in Toronto. Other important uses on King Street were the King Edward Hotel,[37] several large restaurants,[38] and newspaper offices-cum-printing-plants[39] (see Fig. 6b).

King Street had emerged as a street of increased national but decreased local importance. The most dramatic change was the decline of retailing activity on King and its increase on Yonge Street, where the two retail giants Eaton's and Simpson's became strong magnets. This shift had been gradual at first but had accelerated in the 1880s. Observers in the late 1880s considered King Street to be supreme but Yonge Street to be just as important.[40] In the 1890s, Robertson speculated that the volume of pedestrian traffic at Yonge and Queen was greater than at Yonge and King, "owing to the great retail shops there." [41]

The diminishing presence of high-order retail establishments also meant the disappearance of shoppers in the street and the end of "doing" King Street as a social occasion. Jobs in printing and garment manufacturing also disappeared, at least from the important Toronto-Bay section. Pictures from 1910-20 also show a King Street remarkably devoid of goods vehicles.[42] This change from earlier days was partially a result of the deeper lots and buildings that stretched to the streets and lanes running parallel to King (especially Colborne and Melinda). These increasingly became access routes to the back entrances of King Street buildings. The disappearance of goods vehicles from King Street was also due to the change in economic function: in the second decade of the twentieth century King Street accommodated the manipulation of abstract transactions rather than the handling of concrete goods.

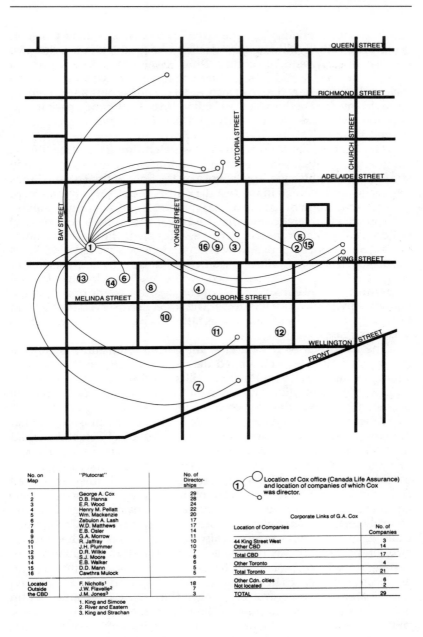

No. on Map	"Plutocrat"	No. of Director-ships
1	George A. Cox	29
2	D.B. Hanna	28
3	E.R. Wood	24
4	Henry M. Pellatt	22
5	Wm. Mackenzie	20
6	Zebulon A. Lash	17
7	W.D. Matthews	17
8	E.B. Osler	14
9	G.A. Morrow	11
10	R. Jaffray	10
11	J.H. Plummer	10
12	D.R. Wilkie	7
13	S.J. Moore	6
14	E.B. Walker	6
15	D.D. Mann	5
16	Cawthra Mulock	5
Located Outside the CBD	F. Nicholls[1]	18
	J.W. Flavelle[2]	7
	J.M. Jones[3]	3

1. King and Simcoe
2. River and Eastern
3. King and Strachan

Location of Cox office (Canada Life Assurance) and location of companies of which Cox was director.

Corporate Links of G.A. Cox

Location of Companies	No. of Companies
44 King Street West	3
Other CBD	14
Total CBD	17
Other Toronto	4
Total Toronto	21
Other Cdn. cities	6
Not located	2
TOTAL	29

Figure 9: Office locations of Toronto, "plutocrats," 1913. (Based on the Grain Growers' Guide, *June 25, 1913, and city directory, 1914.)*

It is not surprising that the street also entered a new phase as ceremonial setting, although the decline was gradual. In the first two decades of the twentieth century, King Street was still part of many processions, but it had strong rivals: Yonge Street was increasingly included, and the junction of Queen and Bay had become a strong focus since the opening of the new City Hall in 1898. The Orange parade was probably the first regular event that bid farewell to King Street for good in the 1890s.[43]

The impact of office work was now determining the street life on King. It was a much barer street in 1914; there were groups of men in straw boaters (which were even worn on the floor of the Toronto Stock Exchange) and women in modest dark attire, most likely members of the first generation of female office workers. It was not only a thinner but a much less diverse crowd that used the street. As the landscape and building patterns became simpler, street life paled. The real importance of King Street as a place of abstract transactions became hidden behind the Beaux-Arts stonefronts of the office buildings. The new function of King Street in 1914 was expressed on the one hand by the classical pillars and opulent banking halls, and on the other by the opacity of the many anonymous office windows. The street itself served the ebb and flow of commuters by streetcar lines rather than the public processions of earlier years.

The hundreds of large and small office establishments concentrated along King Street signified the rise of Toronto to the status of national control centre, a function still shared with Montreal at that time. The concentration and interconnection of powerful Canadian businessmen was at the very core of King Street. Of fifty "plutocrats" identified by the *Grain Growers' Guide* in 1913 as the most influential men in Canada, nineteen were residents of Toronto.[44] Ten of them had their offices on King Street, another six were not more than two blocks away, and only three had their bases in offices or manufacturing plants outside the commercial district (see Figure 9). All nineteen shared power in a tightly woven network of interlocking directorships. One crucial node in this network was occupied by Senator George Cox, who controlled seven financial companies from his base in the Canada Life Building at King and Bay; he was also on the boards of another twenty-two companies. Another node was occupied by the Mackenzie-Mann-Hanna trio, who controlled fourteen railway, utility, and other companies from their offices at the corner of King and Toronto Streets and participated in the control of another thirty-nine companies. From behind the grey stone facades of the Edwardian office canyon, these plutocrats controlled or helped to control banking networks from coast to coast (and beyond), steel making in Cape Breton, mining on the Shield, manufacturing and retailing in Toronto, railways on the Prairies, and sawmills in the Rockies; their insurance salesmen and railway engineers went to Europe, the Far East, and South America.

Epilogue: Corporate Redevelopment since 1914

The offices in these new tall King Street buildings were used to manage Ontario and national concerns. As the scale of business increased, the demand for space meant that enterprises even spilled over the large capacity created by 1914. During the next six decades, sites further west were redeveloped for larger and taller buildings in which to house larger corporations and the growing number of ancillary functions. This new phase of corporate development began in the 1920s and has continued in several dramatic phases of redevelopment until today.

The most impressive example of the 1920s wave of redevelopment was the Canadian Bank of Commerce Building of 1929-31 (see Figure 10). The new 34-storey building occupied the site of its 1889-90 head office and two adjacent King Street lots, and extended all the way back to Melinda. With a floor area of 450,000 square feet, this was by far the largest building in Toronto as well as the "tallest building in the British Empire."[45] The streamlined tower of the Bank of Commerce joined one built a few years earlier to the west of Bay, a new building for the *Star* newspaper (see Figure 10), that provided a slim 22-storey tower for rental offices and a large six-storey base for the newspaper plant. Although the 1920s saw important developments of office buildings along Bay Street, several other head-office expansion projects on King Street were scaled down or completely stalled by the Depression. The Imperial Bank downgraded an intended 20-storey redevelopment to a 7-storey modification of existing buildings at the southeast corner of King and Bay; the Bank of Montreal's 17-storey tower at the northwest corner of King and Bay was begun in 1938 but not completed until 1948; and the Bank of Nova Scotia's 26-storey tower of 513,000 square feet on the site of the former Canada Life complex[46] was not built until 1946-51. All the buildings erected between the late 1920s and 1951 were built to the lot line on King Street — at least as far as the lower floors were concerned. This mode of siting maintained the traditional street wall, established by the mid-nineteenth century. All of these structures were also built along the western part of King Street between Jordan and York streets; the corner of King and Bay and the north side of King between Bay and Yonge were the sections affected most strikingly by redevelopment.

A new wave of redevelopment in the 1960s did not significantly alter previous patterns[47] and also paled in comparison to the enormous change that swept King Street with the construction of the Toronto-Dominion Centre and other large complexes from the mid-1960s onward. Three corners of the King-Bay intersection underwent radical transformations that cut deeply into the nineteenth- and early twentieth-century fabric. The first, and perhaps most dramatic, amalgamation of property came with the development of the Toronto-Dominion Centre between 1964 and 1974. On most of an entire city block south of King and west of Bay, three giant office towers and a banking hall provided over 3 million square feet of space.[48] Even so, the buildings occupied only one-fifth of the site, which also contained a four-and-a-half-acre landscaped plaza. Designed by the famous U.S.-based architect Mies van der Rohe,[49] the project brought to Toronto a new sense of urban form: not only striking black towers, but also underground shopping and walkways, underground parking, and a set of open spaces. The Toronto-Dominion Centre also marked a new phase in the development process, for it was not the sole domain of a bank creating its head office building; rather, real estate interests, in consort with the bank and city council, were working to reshape urban spaces and create massive amounts of revenue-generating office space.[50] The contrast between the fabric in 1917, when there were several dozen distinct properties and buildings on the site, and the 5.6 acres and four structures of the Toronto-Dominion Centre in 1974 is startling (see Figure 12).

The Toronto-Dominion Centre and the similar Commerce Court (1971-72) created significant open spaces along the King Street sidewalk for the first time in more than a century. Whereas setbacks for the Georgian church, courthouse, and jail had quickly been superseded by commercial buildings, the new setbacks were provided by commercial interests, with the assistance of a city council keen to support open spaces in a "revitalized" downtown.

The development of the Toronto-Dominion Centre was encouraged by city politicians and planners, and the public did not seem to take notice initially. But by the time Commerce Court and First Canadian Place were under construction in the early 1970s, opposition had arisen. Critical voices were raised against the speed of redevelopment, the replacement of traditional buildings with those in the idiom of the International Style, the loss of street life, and the microclimate of wind and shadow. Office towers were also seen as symbols of corporate concentration and of American influence in the Canadian economy. A wide array of criticisms from reform groups and reform-dominated councils,[51] elected with a mandate to protect neighbourhoods and put a lid on development downtown, led to the formulation of new guidelines in the form of the Central Area Plan of 1979.[52]

In the case of subsequent developments, city planners grappled on the one hand with the pressures for expansion downtown in what was by then *the* national business centre and on the other with political desires for down-scaled and even decentralized growth. The large King Street projects of the late 1970s and 1980s (including the Sun Life Centre, Standard Life Building, and Scotia Place) adopted by and large the International Style but also tried to accommodate some of the past. The Sun Life project at King and University benefited from development

Figure 10: Transition from Edwardian office canyon to contemporary streetscape: King Street West looking east from York Street, c. 1936. (Courtesy City of Toronto Archives, Salmon 81.)

Figure 11: Modern large-scale complexes: King Street West looking east from York Street, 1980.

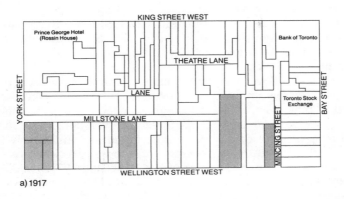

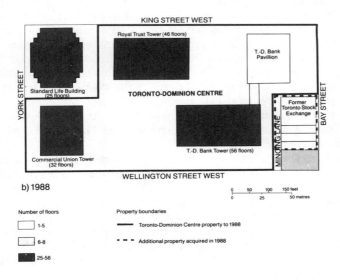

Figure 12: The impact of modernity: building fabric of Toronto-Dominion Centre block, 1917 and 1988. (Based on Goad's fire insurance plan, 1914-18; City of Toronto, Dept. of Public Words, property data map 506-123, Sept. 1985; City of Toronto Planning and Development Dept. staff reports.)

rights transferred across the street from St. Andrew's Presbyterian Church, and the latest of the mammoth corporate redevelopments, the Scotiabank complex, has amalgamated property but retained much of the extant street-side fabric—including the 1951 head office of the Bank of Nova Scotia. And the projects west of York Street, in an attempt to maintain some street-level activity, do not have large underground shopping concourses.

With the addition of each new office complex, the land-use pattern on King Street became simpler. First of all, office establishments displaced all other uses, at least above grade level, and even the newspapers, which had been part of King Street for a very long time. Shops at street level became a rarity; those catering almost exclusively to the office workers retreated to underground shopping concourses. Office occupancy in the mega-projects of the 1960s and 1970s has been as dynamic as that in earlier periods. The Toronto-Dominion Bank Tower, for example, had over 170 tenants in 1971, but the number of establishments had dropped to 55 by 1985; in the same period, the number of floors in this fifty-four-storey building that were occupied by a single tenant grew from 18 to 38. Moreover, the range of office activities seems to have narrowed. Architects, engineering firms, advertising agencies, and life insurance companies have either completely vanished or are strongly underrepresented. On the other hand, banks, trust companies, and stockbrokers have expanded significantly. As banks did not invade King Street until the 1890-1914 period and King Street accommodated all kinds of office establishments between 1914 and the 1950s, the period after 1960 was clearly the one in which King Street became the principal axis of a financial district.

And yet this picture of an emerging financial axis is only a partial one. King Street today is home to companies from many branches of the economy, from mining companies to law and accounting firms, and from real estate development companies to holding companies with wide-ranging investment portfolios. Even the public sector hides behind the inscrutable glass walls, where many offices of the provincial and federal governments occupy rented space. In many cases, and more and more so, the King Street offices are only part of an organization's head office or regional headquarters, since many of the routine functions and data centres are located at the fringe of the downtown office district or in the suburbs.[53] The principal offices of King Street are increasingly the site of high-level decision making on a national and global scale.

The importance of King Street as a public thoroughfare has continued to decline further. For all the cachet of the name for business, the street itself has become a shadow of its former self. Commuters scurry into and out of buildings in the morning and evening rush hours and spill out at lunch time, but in the evenings and on weekends street life is almost non-existent. The office towers cast long shadows and form unpleasant wind tunnels; pieces of sculpture that have been added in plazas or in front of buildings to humanize the scale merely confirm the street's lifelessness. Streetcars still trundle along the middle of the street and their overhead wires clutter up the architectural geometry (see Figure 11). The logistics of supplying the office towers with furniture, office machines, paper, and food is now taking place on Adelaide and Wellington, reducing these streets to mere back alleys. On King Street itself taxis and messenger vans park fleetingly and keep an eye out for the traffic police at rush hours. The peddlers of the "post-industrial" society sell scarves and attaché cases on street-corners, also with one eye out for the police.

Although the commercial axis has become a much more simplified place, public buildings have again become an element of King Street. On the western edge of the office frontier, Roy Thomson Hall was built on the railyard in 1982 as a new home for the Toronto Symphony and thus returned the site to a more "public" use once present in Government House. If they are built, the new CBC head office and a Metro Toronto City Hall (on the parking lots north of the CN Tower and the Metro Convention Centre and west of Roy Thomson Hall) they will probably reinforce the government presence in the years to come in a way that John Howard could never have imagined. Both new buildings, however, are likely to contain commercial space as well. The revitalization of the eastern end of King Street began with the $2 million renovation of St. Lawrence Hall in 1967 as the new home of National Ballet; then the spillover of popularity from the reinvigorated St. Lawrence Market in the "urbane seventies" brought public money for the development of a neo-Victorian park on the Church Block next to St. James Cathedral, and a small sculpture park on the Market Block. Ironically, all these attempts to inject public open spaces were preceded by an unrealized plan in the late 1940s to develop a public square (and underground carpark) on Toronto Street, thereby reviving the original plan for a major public space on King Street.[54]

Summary

Today, the panorama along the central section of King Street reveals almost two centuries of land division, building projects, and redevelopments, where public and private plans have ebbed and flowed. The survival of buildings from earlier eras is largely a result of the westward movement of development rather than of any conscious civic commitment to maintaining part of the past. Many properties have witnessed different eras of the city and have embodied the economic spiral of the city's growth: at the corner of King and Bay, for example, there have been five successive generations of buildings in 160 years.

In the balance of forces seeking public and private uses of land, private interests have largely won out, constrained periodically by municipal guidelines for development. Early on these public interests focused on defining a civic precinct. From the turn of the century, periodic attempts by councils to restrict height and density have been modified and countered by many instances of civic adoption of symbols of private success. The City's involvement in the building of the Toronto-Dominion Centre is but one instance of this.

There has been a staggering increase in the size of buildings, but it is still not clear what some of the implications are. Is it really a much denser environment? And is it a worse environment? Our research into earlier eras of the street has meant that we had to reconstruct the society and economy behind the facades of the buildings; as more archival material becomes available, the specifics of these worlds will become clearer. The complexity of those years bears comparison with the lives of the current occupants. Were the early occupants of King Street buildings not more crowded than their successors, who enjoy perhaps more and even better working space? And how high were the social barriers in 1880 between a merchant and his employees on the one hand and between the executives and professional workers in a modern corporation on the other? What are the implications of the increasing specialization of King Street? Are there people now who are excluded but who want to have a share of this street? How much time was spent getting to and from work in the different eras of King Street? How much influence does public opinion have in an environment so driven by market forces? To answer these questions we would need detailed information, not just about property ownership, building programs, occupancy and land use, but also about the relationship between boards of directors and employees, between owners and tenants, and between developers and the political bodies that have attempted to shape the history of one of Canada's most important streets.

NOTES

1 For a discussion of the commercial district as a whole and of selected large-scale office buildings, see Gunter H.K. Gad and Deryck W. Holdsworth, "Building for City, Region and Nation: Office Development in Toronto, 1834-1984," in V.L. Russell, ed., *Forging a Consensus: Historical Essays on Toronto* (Toronto: University of Toronto Press, 1984), pp. 272-322; "Corporate Capitalism and the Emergence of the High-Rise Office Building," *Urban Geography*, 8, No. 3 (1987), 212-31.

2 For an introduction to the morphological perspective, see Jeremy W.R. Whitehand ed., *The Urban Landscape: Historical Development and Management. Papers by M.R.G. Conzen* (London: Academic Press, 1981).

3 Further west, that is, west of Simcoe Street, an important cluster of public and semi-public buildings did emerge along and near King Street. After 1814, Gov-

ernment House was located at the southwest corner of King and Simcoe, and the Parliament Buildings first in the General Hospital at King and John streets in 1825 and then on the waterfront west of Simcoe Street in 1831. The nearby "Bishop's Palace" at Front and York and a preparatory school, Upper Canada College (built 1829-31) on the north side of King Street between Simcoe and John streets, contributed to give this western stretch of King Street the character of a government quarter insulated somewhat from the city. For most of the nineteenth century, this government quarter was undoubtedly a magnet that pulled a number of public and private institutions westward from the market node.

4   For primary sources, we draw on a wide range of fire-insurance atlases (especially those of 1880 and 1914-18), city directories (especially 1882 for 1881, and 1915 for 1914), and assessment rolls (especially "1881 made for 1882" and "1914 made for 1915"). As secondary sources for urban morphology, we rely on *Robertson's Landmarks of Toronto*, Vols. 1-6 (Toronto: John Ross Robertson, 1894-1914), Jacob Spelt, *Toronto* (Toronto: Collier-MacMillan, 1973); and R. Louis Gentilcore and C. Grant Head, *Ontario's History in Maps* (Toronto: University of Toronto Press, 1984); for the complexes of the 1960s, on Robert W. Collier, *Contemporary Cathedrals* (Montreal: Harvest House, 1974) and Patricia McHugh, *Toronto Architecture: A City Guide* (Toronto: Mercury Books, 1985); for the architecture of Toronto, on Eric Arthur, *Toronto: No Mean City* (3rd ed. rev. by Stephen A. Otto, Toronto: University of Toronto Press, 1986), William Dendy, *Lost Toronto* (Toronto: Oxford, 1978), and William Dendy and William Kilbourn, *Toronto Observed: Its Architects, Patrons and History* (Toronto: Oxford, 1986).

5   King Street was the main axis connecting the Old Town, laid out in 1793 east of what is now Jarvis Street, with the New Town, laid out in 1797 west of Yonge Street. Between Jarvis and Yonge, five blocks of six acres each were set aside for public buildings. See Spelt, *Toronto*, pp. 37-40. Various plans for these blocks are laid out in Gentilcore and Head, *Ontario's History in Maps*, pp. 249-51.

6   By the late 1830s the following public buildings were established: market with market buildings and town hall on a section of the "Market Square" (bounded by King, Jarvis, Front, and W. Market streets); St. James' church and later cathedral on the western half of "Church Square" (King, Church, Adelaide, and Francis streets); courthouse, jail, fire engine house, Wesleyan Methodist chapel, and St. Andrew's Presbyterian church on the "Square for Court House and Jail" (King, Toronto, Adelaide, and Church). The jail was first built on public land south of King Street between Yonge and Church streets; it was relocated in 1824. The "College Square" (Adelaide, Church, Richmond, and Jarvis) accommodated the Home District Grammer School and the Central (public) School; by 1827, however, most of the "College Square" was subdivided into small lots (see Plan of the Town of York, J.G. Chewett, 1827). No hospital seems to have been built on any of the five blocks set aside for public use.

7   Dendy, *Lost Toronto*, p. 78.

8   In 1819, four acres known as the Goal and Court House Block (also Court House Square, or Square for Court House and Goal) were granted to three Toronto citizens, in trust, for the purpose of a jail and courthouse for the Home District. An act of 1839 (2 Vict. cap. 44) validated these sales of King Street frontages to finance public buildings. See City of Toronto Archives, file "Engine House Lot."

9   Arthur, *Toronto: No Mean City*, pp. 131, 136.

10   Also never realized was an 1834 plan by John Howard to fill the space between the jail and courthouse with a prominent structure that would house guild hall, courthouse, post office, library, merchants' exchange, jail, police office, and holding cells (Arthur, *Toronto: No Mean City*, p. 70).

11   For the merchant Alexander MacDonell (one of the three men to whom the land was sold in 1819). Dendy, *Lost Toronto*, p. 72. This commercial row also arose on land set aside for public use in 1797.

12   Henry Scadding and John Charles Dent, *Toronto, Past and Present: Historical and Descriptive Memorial Volume, 1834-1884* (Toronto: Hunter, 1884), p. 193.

13   Arthur, *Toronto: No Mean* City, p. 146.

14   J.M.S. Careless, *Toronto to 1918: An Illustrated History* (Toronto: Lorimer, 1984), pp. 71-108.

15   Gad and Holdsworth, "Building for City, Region and Nation" in Russell, *Forging a Consensus,* pp. 277-88.

16   The building under construction, 31-33 King West, had "just [been] built" in 1872 for John Riddell, a merchant tailor (*Canadian Illustrated News*, Nov. 16, 1872). Photo T12666 of the Metropolitan Toronto Library is dated 1866. This means that it took some six years for 31-33 King to rise or that the photo is not dated correctly.

17   These buildings were very unevenly distributed: almost no change occurred east of Church Street and little on the north side of King Street between Church and Yonge. The south side of King East between Church and Yonge was affected dramatically, as was the south side of King West between Yonge and Bay, where only two out of nine properties were not redeveloped. The changes on the north side of King West between Yonge and Bay were also substantial, but even by the early 1880s wooden buildings and a large vacant lot remained.

18   The extent of this early development is problematic. The Cane map of 1842 and the Sandford Fleming map of 1851 show development west of Bay, but the Boulton map of 1858 shows many vacant lots, especially on the north side of King between Bay and York.

19   Some additions to, and rebuilding of, public buildings did occur, but only at the distant flanks of the commercial axis. St. Lawrence Hall was built at the eastern end in 1849-50 on the site of earlier market buildings, and St. James' Cathedral was rebuilt after the fire of 1849. Beyond the western extremity of the business section a new St. Andrew's Presbyterian Church was constructed on the south side of King at Simcoe in 1875 (its congregation sold the 1830s building at Church and Adelaide for commercial redevelopment), and Government House was rebuilt in 1866-70.

20   In discussing the south side of King Street in the vicinity of Leader Lane, Robertson mentions that in the early 1850s most storekeepers lived above their shops; but he also notes two business owners who moved away from this particular location on King Street in 1850 and 1851. See *Robertson's Landmarks of Toronto,* Vol. 3, 1898, pp. 21-22.

21   Conyngham Crawford Taylor, *The Queen's Jubilee and Toronto "Called Back," from 1888 to 1847: Revised Edition* (Toronto: Wm. Briggs, 1887), pp. 310-11.

22   Taylor, *The Queen's Jubilee,* p. 311. See also Anon., *History of Toronto and County of York, Ontario,* Vol. 1 (Toronto: C. Blackett Robinson, 1885) p. 454.

23   The courthouse was relocated from King to Adelaide between Church and Toronto in 1852. The jail, which served as Toronto's first asylum between 1840 and 1850, became part of York Chambers, a prestigious office building with a Toronto Street address.

24   In 1881, of nineteen stockbrokers, eight had offices on King Street East, five on Toronto Street, and the remaining six on King Street West, Adelaide Street East, and Yonge Street. *City Directory,* 1882, p. 528.

25   *Canadian Illustrated News*, Sept. 3, 1870, rep. in Charles P. de Volpi, *Toronto: A Pictorial Record, 1813-1882* (Montreal: Dev-Sco Publications, 1965), opposite Plate 66.

26   C. Pelham Mulvaney, *Toronto Past and Present* (Toronto: Caiger, 1884), p. 41.

27   Taylor, *The Queen's Jubliee,* p. 309.

28   Pictorial evidence is drawn from *Canadian Illustrated News*, 1863-1881 (many pictures reproduced in Volpi, *Toronto: A Pictorial Record* (also reprints of *Illustrated London News*). Photographs of King Street in the 1870s and 1880s were consulted in the City of Toronto Archives, the Metropolitan Toronto Reference

Library (Baldwin Room), and the National (formerly Public) Archives of Canada. For written accounts, see Mulvaney, *Toronto Past and Present*, pp. 41-42. "Doing King Street" is the title of an 1879 sketch by H. Glazebrook published in the *Canadian Illustrated News*, Jan. 25, 1879. (See also Volpi, *Toronto: A Pictorial Record*, plate 110.) On Orange parades, see the *Globe*, 1861-91. An illustration of the 1874 parade as depicted by the *Canadian Illustrated News* is included in Cecil J. Houston and William J. Smyth, *The Sash Canada Wore: A Historical Geography of the Orange Order in Canada* (Toronto: University of Toronto Press, 1980), p. 123.

29 The Parliament Buildings were abandoned when the legislature moved to Queen's Park in 1892-93; the buildings were demolished in 1900, and the Grand Trunk Railway built freight sheds on the site. Upper Canada College moved to a new site in 1891; the old buildings were demolished in 1900 and redeveloped for commercial use (including the Royal Alexandra Theatre). Government House was sold to the CPR in 1912 and replaced by freight yards. The entire area was redeveloped as a new goods transfer, wholesaling, and manufacturing district.

30 The largest of these frontages were 110 feet (Murray and Co. store), 120 feet (Bank of Toronto), and 166 feet (King Edward Hotel).

31 The last wooden structure on King Street between Church and Bay, at 35-37 King Street West, was demolished in 1911 to make way for a building of the Bank of Quebec. See *Construction*, Vol. 4 (1911), 65.

32 Only two stores (J. Thompson & Sons, 1887-88, and Oak Hall, 1893) and a bank branch (1907) were inserted.

33 This dramatic Beaux-Arts building, bedecked with Corinthian columns on both its King and Bay frontages stretched 120 feet along King Street and 134 feet on Bay Street. Dendy, *Lost Toronto*, pp. 98-99.

34 The Canadian Bank of Commerce Building of 1889 had a two-storey banking hall, the Dominion Bank Building of 1913-14 had a three-storey banking hall with a nine-storey shaft of office floors above, and the Bank of Nova Scotia's one-storey banking hall had the height of four floors. For a further discussion of the problems of assessing height and size of buildings in this era, see Gad and Holdsworth, "Looking Inside the Skyscraper: the Measurement of Size and Occupancy of Toronto Office Buildings 1890-1950," *Urban History Review/Revue d'histoire urbaine*, 16, No. 2 (1987), 176-89.

35 Insurance companies, trust companies, and stockbrokers were all there in the 1880s, and their scale of operation increased on King Street, but in 1914 King was still not the most important street for insurance companies (which were scattered throughout the business section) or trust companies (which were concentrated on Toronto Street). The Toronto Stock Exchange, and many stockbrokers, moved from King East to Bay Street in 1913.

36 In the Royal Bank Building, the "anchor" tenant had no visibility beyond the banking hall and rooms for the inspectors on the twelfth floor. A more significant presence was the Board of Trade, which occupied the top two floors for assembly room purposes. When it left the Board of Trade Building at Front and Yonge, its move was paralleled by over twenty grain dealers that had previously been housed in the old Board of Trade Building and now occupied several floors in the Royal Bank Building.

37 The King Edward Hotel was built by Gooderham and associated interests on the six lots west of Leader Lane (apparently as an attempt to stabilize declining real estate values on King east of Yonge).

38 Restaurants were not an entirely new phenomenon, but they were far more prominent than in 1881. Their presence can be seen as evidence of a large pool of labour along King Street. Company cafeterias like that of the Manufacturers Life (formerly Dorothy Jane Tea Room) underline this importance. See Manufacturers Life Insurance Company, *The First Sixty Years 1887-1947* (Toronto: Manufacturers Life Insurance Co., 1947), p. 129.

39   The *Star* joined the Mail on King Street, but the *Globe* went from King to Yonge and Melinda in 1890 and the *Telegram* from King to Bay and Melinda c. 1900. Newspapers shifted west along King Street or away from it. These locations continued from the 1920s to the 1970s, when newspapers finally left the core of the office district. Printing, especially the larger establishments, moved out almost completely, part of a more general pattern of movement of manufacturing to districts west of York and from there west to King and Spadina. This move was spearheaded by printing rather than garment manufacturing from c. 1905 to 1914.

40   Taylor, *The Queen's Jubilee*, p. 328. Taylor actually refers to an earlier description in the *Canadian Illustrated News* (see n. 25) and suggests that "in 1886" the writer "deserved(d) to be tarred and feathered."

41   *Robertson's Landmarks of Toronto*, Vol. 3, p. 62.

42   The following three paragraphs draw on photographs in the collections of the City of Toronto Archives, the Metropolitan Toronto Reference Library (Baldwin Room), and the National Archives of Canada.

43   It seems that the Orange Parade deserted a King Street segment on its route from 1899 onward. In 1898 the parade still included King Street (*Globe*, July 13, 1898); in 1899 it went along Queen but not King (*Globe*, July 13, 1899). Further checks of *Globe* articles for 1900, 1901, 1906 and 1911 do not reveal a return of the Orange Parade to King Street.

44   They were Cox, Flavelle, Hanna, Jaffray, Jones, Lash, Mackenzie, Mann, Matthews, Moore, Morrow, Mulock, Nichols, Osler, Pellatt, Plummer, Walker, Wilkie, and Wood; another twenty lived in Montreal and the remaining eleven in various other cities; see "Who Owns Canada," *Grain Growers' Guide* (later renamed *Country Guide*), June 25, 1913.

45   For details on the Canadian Bank of Commerce and its occupancy, see Gad and Holdsworth, "Looking Inside the Skyscraper," pp. 180, 185; and "Corporate Capitalism and the Emergence of the High-rise Office Building," pp. 220-23.

46   Canada Life had moved to a new site on University Avenue in 1931.

47   With up to twenty floors these new office buildings were of a modest scale. They were notable, though, for their plain International Style facades. Buildings that were part of this boom on King Street West were No. 4 (Prudential), No. 20 (Royal Bank), No. 15 (Montreal Trust); and on King Street East, No. 7-21 (National Trust), No. 10, No. 18 (Continental), all constructed between 1960 and 1970.

48   The Toronto-Dominion Centre's components are a low banking hall, which, in place of the classical Bank of Toronto, boasted 22,000 square feet under a single span; the Toronto-Dominion Bank Tower (1964-67, 56 storeys, 1,686, 875 sq. ft.), the Royal Trust Tower(1966-69, 46 storeys, 1,180,812 sq. ft.), and the Commercial Union Tower, (1972-74, 32 storeys, 603,800 sq. ft.). A fourth tower, the IBM Tower on a separate lot south of Wellington Street, was built in 1985. A fifth tower, on the site of the 1937 Stock Exchange, is in the planning stage in 1988.

49   With John B. Parkin Associates and Bregman and Hamann as the local Canadian architects.

50   The developer was Cemp Investment, a real estate development company controlled by the Bronfman-Seagram interests. The president of the Toronto-Dominion Bank, Allen Lambert, was a member of the Redevelopment Advisory Committe — a group of downtown businessmen who lobbied the Planning Board in favour of projects that might revitalize downtown. City planners also wanted something big. For a narrative of the process immediately after its completion, see Collier, *Contemporary Cathedrals*, pp. 122-31.

51   For the most poetic expression of this critique, see Dennis Lee, *Civil Elegies* (Toronto: Anansi, 1972), pp. 29-59; the issues are summarized in James T. Lemon, *Toronto Since 1918: An Illustrated History* (Toronto: Lorimer, 1985), pp. 151-62.

52 For the rationale of the plan, see Toronto, City Planning Board, *Proposals. Central Area Plan Review. Part 1: General Plan* (Toronto: City of Toronto, 1975). For the plan itself as approved in 1979 and amended to 1981, see Toronto, City Planning and Development Department, *City of Toronto Official Plan, Part 1, Office Consolidation* (Toronto: City of Toronto, 1981). The political background to the plan is discussed in Warren Magnussen, "Toronto," in W. Magnussen and A. Sancton, eds., *City Politics in Canada* (Toronto: University of Toronto Press, 1983), esp. pp. 111-21.

53 On the decentralization of routine work to suburban "back offices", see Gunter H.K. Gad, "Office Location Dynamics in Toronto: Suburbanization and Central District Specialization," *Urban Geography*, 6, No. 4 (1985), 331-51.

54 See Deryck W. Holdsworth, *The Parking Authority of Toronto, 1952-87* (Toronto: Parking Authority of Toronto, 1987), p. 18. LeMay also planned squares for the Civic Square and Market Block sites. Only the Civic (now Nathan Phillips) Square was built. The Toronto Street surface parking lot was managed by the Parking Authority for the Toronto Stock Exchange between 1957 and 1962 (carpark no. 46), and then by City Parking Ltd.

"A TERROR TO EVIL-DOERS": THE CENTRAL PRISON AND THE "CRIMINAL CLASS" IN LATE NINETEENTH-CENTURY ONTARIO

Peter Oliver

The Central Prison, Ontario's first intermediate correctional facility, which opened in Toronto in 1874 and closed in 1915, has much to tell us about attitudes in late nineteenth-century Ontario. The prison was designed to fill a gap in the new province's correctional system by holding offenders sentenced to less than the two-year term, which was served in a federal penitentiary, but to more than a brief period, which was served in a local jail. The few students whose work has touched upon the prison have viewed it in the context of the career of the progressive prison inspector, J.W. Langmuir, and have emphasized its reformist purpose and rehabilitative goals. For most late-nineteenth-century Ontarians, however, including convicts and those officials who controlled the criminal justice system, the prison acquired a well-earned reputation for punitive harshness, and one local jailer boasted that it was "a terror to evil-doers." A closer analysis confirms the accuracy of the contemporary judgment that first and foremost the prison was designed and administered as an instrument of terror and punishment.

J.W. Langmuir dominated Ontario correctional work from Confederation until his retirement in 1882. The general outlines of his career are well known. A young Scottish immigrant and businessman who served as mayor of Picton in the 1860s, he has emerged as the only genuine hero of social welfare administration in late nineteenth-century Ontario. Appointed inspector of prisons and public charities while still in his early thirties, he did much, by his energetic administration, to shape the Ontario system over the next decade and a half. Thus he appears in Richard Splane's history of social welfare as the official whose "capacity for strong administrative leadership may ... be identified as the key to the vigorous pace of social welfare development in the early post-Confederation era."[1] In a recent thesis on Langmuir as a correctional reformer, Stephen Connors argues that he was the architect of a system whose purpose was to "place inmate rehabilitation ahead of punitive impulses"; by the date of his retirement, Connors concludes, he had laid the "foundation of a modern system of corrections in Ontario."[2] A similar perspective informs the work of Donald Wetherell, who has studied a range of programs in Ontario prisons in this era, including labour, education, chaplaincy, and after-care services, and who concludes that their purpose was to maintain social control "by achieving rehabilitation." For Wetherell, Canadian practices, at least in intent, were more progressive than those of the United States. Long after the Americans had become "dissatisfied with their institutions as places of reform," he asserts, "many concerned Ontarians still placed substantial faith in penal institutions as the locale of rehabilitation."[3]

Correctional history offers one useful means of testing the idea that Ontarians in the late nineteenth-century were a compassionate people willing to enact fairly advanced legislation to address the problems of rapid industrialization and urbanization. The precise purpose and nature of social legislation in Oliver Mowat's Ontario are still a subject of some debate as students of labour legislation, education, mental illness, and public health reform offer varying interpretations. Since the Central Prison was established in this period as one of the provincial government's principal instruments of social policy, it is important to understand the objectives of its founders and the place it occupied in the Ontario welfare system.

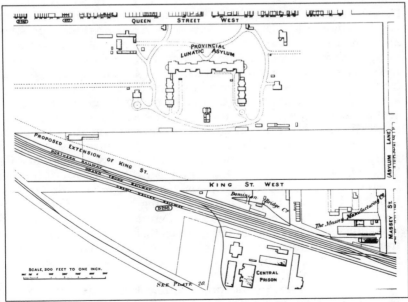

A map of Toronto in 1884, showing the Central Prison (south of King Street).

The Central Prison, Toronto.

Although what follows is only a preliminary statement and draws upon ongoing research, it is based on sufficient evidence to merit the conclusion that earlier students have failed to grasp either the real nature of the prison or the purposes it was intended to serve. Ontario's official prison reports in the late nineteenth century were similar to those of other jurisdictions in the sense that they were written so as to proclaim the virtues of the administrators and reveal as little as possible about internal problems and differences of opinion. John Langmuir's inspectoral reports were astute and remarkably selective documents intended to enhance his own reputation while flattering his political masters. Assertions like the one in his 1877 report that the reforms achieved through his office in the ten years since Confederation represented "an imperishable monument to the liberality and progressiveness of the Ontario people" need not be dismissed as mere hyperbole or hypocrisy, but this and all other official assertions must be subjected to analysis as a particular type of evidence and as only one part of a far larger historical experience. Doubtless the inspector regarded himself as a reformer and believed the Ontario record to be genuinely progressive, but Langmuir's reports were anything but disinterested documents. In any case the history of the Central Prison, when studied critically and in a wider context, reveals that Langmuir himself was frank about the purposes of the prison and that he used such terms as "progressive" and "rehabilitative" in a far different sense than recent historians and social critics.

In fact the Central Prison's origins cannot be traced to the reformist ideals of the 1860s and 1870s, whether to the Irish system of earned remission and indeterminate sentences associated with Sir Walter Crofton or to the American reform program associated with Zebulon Brockway's work at Detroit and Elmira and enunciated most fully in the famous Cincinnati Declaration of 1870.[4] Rather the prison was a product of local experiences dating back to the late 1830s and 1840s, when pauper migration and economic tensions caused the emerging middle class in Canada West's newly incorporated towns and cities to look with disfavour on the rapidly expanding population of the local jails. Although the growing jail population was seldom viewed as a serious threat to the social order, it elicited anger from the elite, especially from those who administered the criminal justice system, including judges, sheriffs, and, increasingly, a small number of bureaucrats whose responsibilities brought them in touch with the thorny problems of welfare administration. These groups came to regard the presence of repeat offenders in the local jails as an affront to community standards, even at times as a challenge to the prevailing concepts of moral order and social harmony. It was in this context, then, that the prison was established, and both those who promoted it and those who administered it firmly pronounced that its purpose was not to rehabilitate but to punish, not to "reform" criminals but to instil fear and to overawe that maladjusted and wastrel element of the community that was increasingly referred to by contemporaries as "the criminal class." Reform was an objective only in the limited sense that anyone who experienced hard labour in the Central Prison could be expected to go to almost any lengths to ensure that he did not return. In this sense the comment that the prison was intended to act as "a terror to evil-doers" was no casual remark but captured the very essence of contemporary attitudes to detention and rehabilitation.[5]

I

From the beginning Langmuir made it clear that his objective was to establish intermediate prisons along unrelentlingly punitive lines. In his first report, that of 1868, he urged that Ontario build several provincial prisons to receive persons sentenced to hard labour for periods of between sixty days and two years and drunkards committed for a third offence of disorderly conduct. Intermediate prisons, said Langmuir, would be industrial facilities designed to "teach this class of men ... that well-directed industry is better than sloth, vice and petty crime."[6] In its 1868 throne speech the Sandfield Macdonald government asserted its intention to establish centrally located prisons to house "hardened and habitual" offenders where they could be subjected to "rigorous discipline" analogous to that of the penitentiaries and in which inmate labour would defray costs. In 1868 these sentiments were embodied in a vague bill that did not specify the number of intermediate prisons that would be built or their cost. Nonetheless the opposition newspaper, the Toronto *Globe*, probably captured prevailing public attitudes when it applauded the intent to enforce hard labour unrelentingly. The *Globe* insisted that there was no reason why "criminals should not be made to clear the streets of our cities, if necessary with ball and chain, and why they should not be provided with at least so hard work as many an honest, deserving man has had to go through."[7]

Although the 1868 bill was withdrawn, there is no doubt that in its general outline it embodied a long-felt need in Ontario society. Indeed the Central Prison had its remote origins in the 1840s and 1850s, when many newly incorporated towns and cities passed by-laws designed to hold forms of behaviour in check that previously had excited relatively little concern. The migration to Canada West in the 1840s of thousands of poverty-stricken Irish immigrants posed a new kind of threat to those who lived in such cities as Toronto, Kingston, and Hamilton and led to strict by-laws aimed at drunks, vagrants, and other persons guilty of unruly behaviour. A Hamilton by-law of 1843 directed: "All vagrants, vagabonds, or other persons of ill-fame, or persons who are drunk or so conducting themselves to be a nuisance and found wandering in the Town at night shall be liable to be arrested and upon conviction thereof shall be liable to a fine of 30 shillings for each offence or in non-payment, 30 days in the District Gaol."[8] This particular measure, as John Weaver has demonstrated, led to as many as 50 per cent, or 516 of 1,105, of Hamilton's share of committals to the Gore District Jail between 1843 and 1851.

Municipal by-laws enforcing new standards of social behaviour were part of a larger movement to assert social control. This included the passage in 1845 of provincial Sabbatarian legislation, the proliferation of temperance societies and the tightening of local licensing laws, and, most of all, the movement to establish more efficient policing. Much of the impetus for police reform derived from widespread disturbances among construction workers on provincial canal-building projects. The Public Works Act of 1845 gave the government the authority to station mounted police on public works, and an 1851 amendment extended this provision to private projects so as to include the extensive railway construction then underway.[9] The police reform movement, a reflection of the mounting concern about social disorder, culminated in the mid-1850s, when a commission that had been established by the provincial government to investigate militia reform was also mandated to report on "an improved system of Police for the better preservation of the public peace."[10] The commission's recommendation that the government establish a centralized force along military lines was embodied in an 1856 bill, but, as Paul Romney notes, this measure "was swamped by the protests of municipal councils before it reached second reading."[11] Although the province rejected centralized policing in 1856, gradual reform continued, with the result that stronger local police forces charged with enforcing municipal by-laws arrested increasing numbers of persons whose behaviour in the earlier era had caused little concern and less official action.

Yet if the expanding social-control net swept ever larger numbers of petty offenders into the notoriously inadequate local jails, the crisis that led to the creation of the Central Prison was not primarily one of overcrowding in the jails. In some parts of the province, especially in the cities, jails did suffer from the press of numbers, but in such cases newer and larger jails were built, as in the case of Toronto in the 1850s. In the more rural parts of the province, existing facilities were readily able to accommodate the number of committals. By the mid-1850s, however, a strong sense developed in both city and countryside that the confinement of drunks and vagrants in county jails under conditions of idleness was serving more to encourage than to deter this persistent and annoying class of criminal. When Mr. Justice Robert Burns in 1854 submitted the reports of several county grand juries to the Provincial Secretary, he told the minister that there was an urgent need to make fundamental changes in the system of punishing criminals. "The County Gaols," he noted, "do not afford the means of employing convicts at any useful or profitable employment. There is a large class of convicts which it is not desirable should be consigned to the Penitentiary, and yet there are no means by which a proper reformatory punishment can be inflicted by incarceration in the County Gaols." Burns's remedy was to erect two or three "houses of correction" in different parts of the province; in other presumably more rural areas, counties should unite to construct larger more efficient jails.[12]

In the years ahead, judges, grand juries, sheriffs, and other judicial officers regularly expressed similar outrage about society's inability to enforce sentences of hard labour in the local jails; and always they suggested some variation or other on the theme of central prisons. In 1865, for example, W.H. Draper, the distinguished Chief Justice of Common Pleas and former head of the government, reported to the Provincial Secretary that he received "frequent representations from Sheriffs, that they found it extremely difficult to carry into effect in the County Gaols sentences of imprisonment coupled with hard labour. With few exceptions," Draper continued,

> such sentences are not carried into effect and the ordained imprisonment at hard labour degenerates into confinement with certain trifling occupations such as cutting and carrying firewood.... Systematic employment of convicts appears to exist only in the Provincial Penitentiary — and thus the convicts are a

useless burden on the community, contributing nothing to their own support and they are moreover but too
well aware, that unless they are sent to the Penitentiary
the sentence of hard labour is a merely idle form of
words.

Draper pointed out that it would probably be too expensive to equip
county jails with the means to enforce hard labour, and he added,
significantly, that in many counties the number of prisoners was so
small that the burden of establishing a labour system would be disproportionate to any benefits. Yet there was still no middle ground between a short jail sentence and imprisonment in the penitentiary for at
least two years, and for that reason, the Chief Justice lamented, "many
offenders will escape with inadequate punishment, a heavy and most
unprofitable burden will continue to be cast upon the community and
there will not be that wholesome dread of punishment which might
operate to check the repetition and increase of crime." A full eight
months passed before Attorney General John A. Macdonald responded
to his old chief's complaints. On August 27, 1866, Macdonald minuted
in reference to the grand jury reports and the comments of the Chief
Justice, "Worthy of all consideration, but in consequence of the speedy
alteration in the political system, no action is at present expedient."[13]

Certainly no action could be taken late in 1866, but John A.'s
disclaimer was not entirely frank, for no less a body than the Board of
Inspectors of Prisons, Asylums and Public Charities had been pressing
the government to act since 1859. The board, established by statute in
1857, had started to function late in 1858 and had devoted much of its
first year to an analysis of the state of the jails. Not surprisingly, the
inspectors, led by Dr. Wolfred Nelson and the capable E.A. Meredith,
reached conclusions that reinforced the recommendations the government had been receiving for more than a decade from informed sources
across the country. The new board, after studying all available documents in the government's files, sent its own comprehensive questionnaire to jail officials and, on the basis of the returns, concluded that the
jails were "schools of vice, to which novices in crime repair to receive,
in an atmosphere of idleness and debauchery, lessons in villainy from
hardened adepts older than themselves in crime." Because jail staffs
were inadequate and hard labour could not be enforced, most prisoners
"[were] not in the slightest degree punished by their repeated temporary sojourning in these places." Indeed for a certain class of offender,
the jails were "a harbour of refuge." For this debauched element,

a few weeks in the Government boarding house forms
a pleasant change in their street life; here they are
treated gratuitously for the ailments contracted by

> excesses in intemperance or vice. Here they freely meet
> old or new friends ... here they plot against society,
> organize their next campaigns, and enrol fresh recruits
> into their ranks.

Clearly the inspectors had worked themselves into a state of high dudgeon as they proceeded to denounce the sloth and cynicism of the criminal classes: "The majority [of jail inmates] enjoy their detention [and are] fully alive to the advantages of these asylums, where they can recruit their strength and invigorate themselves for fresh crimes." And of none was this more true than of the female offenders, who in 1859 constituted no fewer than 3,503 of a total of 11,131 persons confined that year in Upper and Lower Canadian jails. Almost all the female offenders, the inspectors wrote, were prostitutes, and for them the prisons were nothing but boarding houses, a resource in distress, a refuge during the inclement season.

What the jail statistics revealed, the inspectors emphasized, was "the actual state of petty crimes among us." The total number of persons imprisoned in the penitentiary in 1859 for more serious crimes came to a total of only 791 — when this was compared to the number of 11,131 in the jails, it was clear that minor offenders presented the community with a grotesque social and financial burden. The cost per prisoner of penitentiary confinement was $75.85 a year, and this for an institution fully equipped with a range of rehabilitative machinery; by comparison the annual cost of maintaining the petty offender in idleness in the county jail was $123.42.

For the inspectors the most disturbing statistic of all was the number of recidivists. For Upper Canada alone, out of a total jail population of 6,586, no fewer than 1,558 were repeat offenders. Repeated convictions, said the inspectors, "argue a settled habit — a fixed purpose of doing wrong. It constitutes of itself, an aggravation of the offence, calls for a more severe punishment, and proves the necessity of more energetic measures of repression." The detailed comments provided by sheriffs offered even greater cause for alarm on this score than did the statistical aggregates. These indicated that the same persons were returning to jail time after time, some as many as seventy-six times, one actually 163 times. Such figures, said the outraged inspectors, pointed to a fundamental defect in Canada's penal code, for such persons should be classed either as dangerous and incorrigible and "never be allowed to leave jail" or as monomaniacs who should be treated in an asylum.

For the inspectors, then, the jails were filled "by a class of persons who ... systematically [took] up crime and vice as a profession." Furthermore, under the existing situation of the jails, there was "no hope for any improvement among this unfortunate class." The board's solution was for the government to establish "in our principal cities District or Central Prisons, in which would be confined all misdemeanants and recidivists from the adjoining counties or districts." Furthermore, changes should be introduced in the criminal law to define the "inveterate offender" or recidivist and to ensure that he was sent to the new central jails.[14] Although the board made it clear that discipline in the new institutions would be rigorous, with the rule of silence firmly enforced, they believed as well that religious instruction and steady employment would rehabilitate prisoners in a way that the miserable county jails never could. The Board of Inspectors never deviated from this position. They pressed it on successive governments until the Confederation settlement of 1867 altered the situation fundamentally by giving responsibility for the jails to the new provincial governments. In the altered constitutional circumstances it fell to J.W. Langmuir to act on the concerns expressed so vigorously by E.A. Meredith and his colleagues in the pre-Confederation era. Regrettably, the Meredith board's sympathy towards rehabilitation was no longer in the foreground as the new Province of Ontario took steps to establish its own penal facilities.

II

The Central Prison was established during the period when Sir Walter Crofton's ideals of "reformatory prison discipline," which had transformed the Irish penal system, were at the height of their influence in North America. In the United States from the late 1850s, reformers disillusioned by the failure of the American penitentiary were casting about for new ideas. In 1867, under the sponsorship of the New York Prison Association, a 570-page study appeared that has been compared to Howard's *State of the Prisons* for its impact on penal reform. Written by E.C. Wines and T.W. Dwight, the *Report on the Prisons and Reformatories of the United States and Canada* "did not find a single prison that merited recognition as a reformatory."[15] In a sweeping condemnation of prevailing practices, Wines and Dwight reserved their praise for Crofton's Irish system, elements of which appeared in only a few reform schools, in a facility located in Charlestown, Mass., and most notably, in the recently established Detroit House of Correction. At Detroit the reforming warden Zebulon Brockway had established elaborate educational programs, a sophisticated chaplaincy service, separate facilities for women, and a grading system that allowed those who received the highest grades to be detained in a secondary facility with a more homelike atmosphere as the final stage in their incarceration. Brockway was the star performer at the 1870 gathering of American prison workers that issued the Cincinnati Declaration. One of the recommendations made at Cincinnati was for the establishment of intermediate prisons that would achieve rehabilitation through such Croftonian techniques of positive reinforcement as earned remission, indeterminate sentences and wages for prisoners.[16]

John Langmuir, when he was planning the Central Prison, made two pilgrimages to Detroit, one in 1869 and the other in 1871. Since he described Brockway's work as "a monument of perfect Prison administration," the influence on Ontario of the American reformatory movement seems clear and direct. Certainly there are marked similarities in design between Detroit and the Central Prison. After expressing his admiration for Detroit in his 1869 report, Langmuir referred to the report of the New York State commissioners on the prisons of the United States as the source of some of his own ideas on prison organization, and later references to the Cincinnati Declaration make it clear that he was also familiar with that document. For those who argue that during his inspectorate Langmuir was laying a firm foundation for prison reform, these American influences seem significant.

Sadly, however, Langmuir's interest in Brockway's experiment at Detroit was narrow and specific. There is little in Langmuir's references to Detroit to suggest that he understood or was interested in the program of "reformatory prison discipline." Indeed throughout his inspectorate until he retired in 1882, his reports offer few hints that he was conversant with international penological ideas. In the 1850s and 1860s the pre-Confederation Board of Inspectors had enriched their reports with discussions of foreign developments, while their vision of central prisons included the mobilization of a full penitentiary-style rehabilitative apparatus. On occasion Langmuir's reports employed some measure of rehabilitative rhetoric but always in the context of deterrence and punishment.

Most significantly, Langmuir's reports offer little sense of familiarity with the growing international literature on crime and punishment, nor do they suggest a reflective mind at work. The very range of his responsibilities as the province's only inspector of all correctional and welfare institutions must have precluded such a possibility. Regrettably Langmuir as sole inspector was unable to draw on the kind of collegial interchanges that had informed the work of the pre-Confederation Canadian board. Unlike several American states that possessed vigorous boards of charities and corrections, Ontario, out of a misplaced frugality, gave responsibility to a single powerful inspector; as a result the provincial system in the 1870s and early 1880s became increasingly inelastic and parochial. Langmuir did not attend the international correctional congresses of this period, and his occasional brief trips to inspect particular American facilities could not offset the intellectual isolation that increasingly beset the Ontario system.

Nowhere was this more evident than in the narrowness of Langmuir's reaction to Brockway's Detroit. After visiting that facility, the Ontario inspector in his 1869 report again strongly urged his government to establish an intermediate prison. But the case he made emphasized only two considerations. Firstly, he took up the old theme, made familiar by a generation of critics, that the jail system was "a delusion and a failure." Juveniles and those awaiting trial were contaminated by associating with old offenders who "lounge[d] their time out in idleness and sloth." Not only did the jails cost more than $100,000 a year to maintain and bring in only $700 in return, but over a third of the population were recidivists. Secondly, all Langmuir was able to see in Detroit was its balance sheet: it had turned a profit each year since opening in 1862 and had achieved a favourable balance of $56,000. If Ontario established an industrial prison, he promised, it would be self-sustaining if the average inmate could earn as little as 40 cents a day. Langmuir was also sanguine about the demand for prison labour and about his ability to dispose of the products it produced, although he believed that the plan under which the province itself controlled the convict workers and disposed of all goods produced was "far superior" to the contract system by which private businessmen purchased the labour of the prisoners.[17] The politicians were persuaded. When Premier Sandfield Macdonald presented his Central Prison bill in February of 1871, he concluded a brief debate by emphasizing that he expected that the new institution would save the province money.[18]

The guards at the Central Prison, c. 1879. Gilbert Hartley is the third man from the left in the front row; the warden is in the front at the far right. (Courtesy City of Toronto Archives, SC 214 #5.)

The statute itself was brief and unimaginative, little more than a framework to allow the government to develop the new prison as it saw fit. The government was authorized to buy land somewhere in the province and build a prison. Much was left to the inspector's discretion. The inspector was "to make rules and regulations for the management, discipline and police" of the prison and for "prescribing the duties of the warden and every other officer," subject to Cabinet approval. The rhetoric of rehabilitation that had characterized earlier Canadian prison statutes was notable for its absence and, in another striking departure, there was no provision for a chaplain. About the only evidence of progressive thinking was a clause that made it lawful for the inspector, "in order to encourage good behaviour and industry," to make rules so that a correct record of the conduct of each inmate should be kept "with a view to permit[ting] such criminal to earn a remission" of a portion of his term. The statute made ample provision for employing the convicts at hard labour, whether within or outside prison walls. And the Provincial Secretary was given the authority to transfer any prisoner sentenced to jail for a period of not less than fourteen days to the new prison.[19]

With that statutory framework in place, the decision was made to build the new institution in Toronto on Strachan Avenue south of King Street, a location served by two major railway lines. The prison was a three storey building consisting of a main section 100 feet wide with wings on each side and large workshops in the rear of each wing. There were cells for 336 prisoners. Its first warden, William Prince, a veteran of the British Army, had served as chief of the Toronto Police for fifteen years, earning a reputation for "arrogance and arbitrariness."[20] His principal assistants were a chief guard, James Beaumont, and a deputy chief guard, Richard Stedman. On Langmuir's recommendation all three men were sent on brief visits to industrial prisons in the United States to learn the fundamentals of their new duties. Most of the men hired as guards had previous police or military training, and the practice of arming guards with rifles or handguns strengthened the prison's military appearance.

Because the prison was designed as an industrial facility, Langmuir's most important task was to live up to his promise to Cabinet to establish industry in the new institution on a financially sound basis. When the Canada Car Company, which manufactured railway cars, offered to use all the labour not needed for prison domestic functions, Langmuir promptly abandoned his earlier opposition to contractors and jumped at the opportunity. In fact the prison workshops were completed and machinery installed to the specifications of Canada Car. For Langmuir the central if not exclusive place occupied by hard labour in the prison's regimen was readily justified. In numerous reports he argued that hard labour served several purposes equally well: it served as punishment; it provided industrial training; it inculcated an appreciation of the value of work; and it raised funds for the prison. For Langmuir and most of his contemporaries there was no suggestion of incompatibility among these several objectives. Ever sanguine where his own projects were concerned, Langmuir was euphoric in his 1874 report about the success of his industrial project and he liberally quoted officers of the Canada Car Company to the effect that prison workers were at least as good as free workers and in many ways better.

Within months the company was bankrupt, a victim of the trade recession of 1875. The years ahead saw Langmuir and his successors struggling constantly with a variety of approaches to prison labour, including the contract system, the state-use system, and the two in combination. With the Canada Car Company in debt to the Province for $45,000, a three-man commission composed of two Canadian business-men and Zebulon Brockway was appointed to investigate the thorny issue of prison labour. The words of its 1876 report must have been a bitter pill for Langmuir to swallow. They challenged the quality of prison labour in general and doubted in particular its financial value for the Central Prison because of "the class of prisoners confined, and the duration of their terms of sentence."[21] Such conclusions called into question the very rationale Langmuir had used to sell the prison to his political masters. In response he campaigned even more aggressively to persuade politicians and judges to take steps to stock the prison with healthy young men with longer sentences. This objective, as we will see, was never attained, and for the rest of its history the prison was beset with financial and labour problems. One reason cited prominently when it was closed in 1915 was the failure of the industrial system to achieve any of its objectives.[22]

Mired in the morass of problems arising out of the bankruptcy, Langmuir seized on these difficulties as an excuse for his failure to implement the earned remission system referred to in the statute. The subsequent history of earned remission in the prison, however, throws further doubt on the extent of his understanding of and commitment to reformatory principles. At this time remission was part of the rehabili-tative apparatus in Kingston Penitentiary, and in 1877 a federal statute marshalled through the House of Commons by Justice Minister Ed-ward Blake clarified the province's authority in this sphere. Blake's Act allowed a remission of up to a sixth of the sentence for Central Prison inmates and, as a concession to the view that sentences were already too short, judges received the authority to add another four months to the previous maximum of two years less a day. In presenting the measure, Blake stressed not its rehabilitative but its disciplinary purpose, com-menting that the prospect of a four-month remission was more likely than the fear of the dark cell to make prisoners orderly. To an interjection from John A. Macdonald he responded that the government "had another thing in view besides the reformation of the prisoner, viz., the good of the institution itself."[23] But remission even as a disciplinary instrument failed to take hold in the Central Prison. In 1884 James Massie, Prince's successor as warden, bragged that convicts preferred longer sentences in Kingston to a period in the Central Prison because "there is no remission earned here."[24] In contrast to many late nineteenth-century institutions, inmates in the Central Prison were there to stay for the duration of their sentences. Remission and pardons were seldom granted, even for special cases. In 1894, 1895, and 1896, there were two, one, and six remissions respectively and six, fifteen, and zero pardons.[25]

Other rehabilitation methods common in the nineteenth century were equally weak or absent in the Central Prison. Chaplains had played a significant role in Kingston Penitentiary from its establishment in 1835, and from 1851 full-time Catholic and Protestant chaplains not only offered religious sustenance but carried out many of the functions performed by trained treatment personnel in twentieth-century penal establishments. Probably ignorant of the chaplain's role in federal institutions, Langmuir believed the Central Prison could rely on volunteers. To this end he encouraged the establishment in 1874 of the Prisoners' Aid Association and solicited attendance by local clergymen. These volunteers were expected to provide religious services and to run a sabbath school. For several years divine services and the school could be provided only on alternate Sundays because not enough clergymen offered their services. Notwithstanding the notorious propensity of prisoners to participate in any activity to relieve the tedium, the school in 1877 was attracting an average attendance of only thirty-five. A measure of reform came in the 1880s, when the Toronto Ministerial Association was paid $700 annually and the Catholic church $350 for performing these services, but there was no attempt to institute a full-time chaplaincy.[26]

Educational training received equally short shrift. Not until 1879 was a night school for illiterates even considered. Whatever the deficiencies of educational programs in Kingston Penitentiary, such programs at least were available to all prisoners, and the nature of the education to be provided there was the subject of lively debate among penitentiary officials. When the Central Prison night school finally began operations in the 1880s, it was available only as a privilege. Attendance remained small, with the teacher reporting attendance in the winter months of between forty and fifty. Nor did officers place much importance on the prison library. When the few books available became too dilapidated to be read, the Warden could only suggest that money to replace them be raised by charging fees to visitors to the prison. Somewhat later occasional lecturers came to preach to the prisoners on uplifting topics, including the dangers of masturbation, much to the delight of the prison physician, who argued at length in several reports that this practice was the source of all evil.[27]

With the failure of earned remission to gain a place in the prison, the only hopeful innovation was the work of the Prisoners' Aid Association. Although Langmuir probably seized on volunteerism as a money-saving strategy, such prominent Torontonians as Samuel Hume Blake, Hamilton Cassels, and W.H. Howland did work that may have made a significant difference to the lives of many prisoners. As Sunday school teachers and through the efforts of a paid agent who worked in the prison, the association laboured diligently to instil middle-class values in its lower-class constituency. The association, which received both provincial and municipal grants, ran a temporary shelter for released inmates and was active in providing food and clothing and in finding employment for discharged prisoners. Yet however worthy their after-care activities, the association officials, perhaps fearful of being dismissed as do-gooders, appear never to have challenged the prison's punitive approach to rehabilitation. On occasion they even pressed for a still harsher regimen. For example they successfully urged that the use of tobacco, one of the few solaces of prison life, be ended because, like alcohol, it was deemed addictive and a leading cause of crime.[28]

The Central Prison's lack of interest in traditional rehabilitative processes, as they existed, for example, in Kingston Penitentiary, is striking.[29] When one considers as well the acclaim that Zebulon Brockway received in the late 1870s for his efforts at Elmira to reform a select group of first offenders aged sixteen to thirty, the reactionary character of the Ontario institution becomes even more glaring.

III

The Ontario facility, however, had not been established as a reformatory to rehabilitate younger or more hopeful offenders. Its purpose, as a statistical analysis of its population confirms, was to deter habitual minor offenders by punishing them with a maximum of rigour.

The most important single characteristic of the inmate population was its lower-class nature. As Table 1 demonstrates, out of a total of 17,512 inmates from the 1874-1900 period, fully 92.4 per cent fell into the three categories of unskilled, semi-skilled, or skilled workers. This compares to Michael Katz's calculation that in Hamilton in 1871 a total of 73 per cent of the entire male working population fell into these three categories.[30]

Unskilled workers were most grossly over-represented, making up 47.1 percent of the total Central Prison population, while Katz calculates that this group represented only 15 per cent of Hamilton's total male working population. Of the five most common occupations cited in the annual reports, labourer leads at 46.5 per cent, followed by tailor at 3.9 per cent (see Table 2). If the Central Prison population is compared with that of four sample jails and the Mercer Reformatory for women, it is significant nonetheless that skilled labourers made up fully 35.8 per cent of the prison's population but only 24.1 per cent of the jail population and 0.08 per cent of the Mercer (Table 3). Apart from what this suggests about the place of women in the late nineteenth century, it is apparent that prison officials were actively transferring workers with job skills to the prison to further institutional ends.

The type of crime committed provides another measure of the nature of the prison population. The most common offences by far were crimes against property, mostly minor, with larceny leading the list at 36.7 per cent (see Table 4); vagrancy followed far back at 15 per cent, assault at 10.1 per cent and drunkenness at 7.5 per cent. At first this would seem to suggest that the prison was used to protect society against property offenders to a far greater extent than against crimes against the person or moral offences. And in fact for the whole period, no fewer than 55.7 per cent of all committals were for property offences. This impression gains strength from Table 5, which groups offences by type and indicates changes at five-year intervals. This shows an increase in committals for property offences from 46 per cent in 1874-75 to 63.5 per cent in 1896-1900 and a correspondingly sharp decline in public order committals (primarily drunkenness) from 27.4 per cent in 1874-75 to 17.7 per cent in 1896-1900.

Percentage changes are far less distinct when considered for all five-year intervals, and in any case the common crime categories hide a good deal about the nature of the inmate population. It was natural, as V.A.C. Gatrell has demonstrated for the English situation, that property offenders should receive longer sentences than offenders against the person or morals offenders.[31] Assaults were often regarded as momentary aberrations or crimes of passion; property offences were more likely to be carried out by professional criminals. Gatrell appears to conclude that there was considerable justice to these sentencing considerations, and he argues that they give the lie to any "crude class interpretation" which suggests that the harshest punishments were unfairly meted out to the property offender. Because the jails were intended for the shortest-term offender, it seems inevitable that committals to the Central Prison should include so many property offenders.

Furthermore, officials seldom differentiated between petty thieves and drunks. It is true that the published statistics showed that only 19 per cent of Central Prison committals between 1874 and 1900 were for public order offences, a figure confirmed by our prison register analysis, which placed public order offences at 19.3 per cent for 1880-1900. (By contrast, 57.4 per cent of all jail committals, 1880-1900, were for

Table 1

Occupation of Central Prison Inmates, 1874-1900

	1874-1875		1876-1880		1881-1885		1886-1890		1891-1895		1896-1900		1874-1900	
	n	%	n	%	n	%	n	%	n	%	n	%	n	%
Professional	0	0.0	15	0.5	4	0.1	2	.06	2	0.1	15	0.5	38	0.2
Semi-Professional	61	7.7	277	9.1	258	7.0	232	6.4	215	6.5	248	8.0	1291	7.4
Skilled	274	34.4	1165	38.1	1263	34.5	1330	36.9	1105	33.5	926	29.9	6063	34.6
Semi-skilled	64	8.0	336	11.0	435	11.9	419	11.6	321	9.7	302	9.8	1877	10.7
Unskilled	397	49.9	1262	41.3	1705	46.5	1626	45.1	1651	50.1	1602	51.8	8243	47.1

Note: The tables have been compiled primarily from the published annual reports of the Prison Inspectors. Table 3 is derived from a computer analysis of four sample jails, the Central Prison register and the Mercer register. Sample sizes were as follows: Toronto Jail, approximately 1 in 10 (3,320 out of 33,391); Hamilton Jail, approximately 1 in 18 (1,042 out of 18,958); Guelph Jail approximately 3 in 4 (653 out of 872); Central Prison approximately 1 in 11 (1,095 out of 11,783); Mercer Reformatory 1 in 2 (834 out of 1,1668). All 1,012 jail register entries from Whitby Jail between 1881 and 1891 were included.

Table 2

Five Most Common Occupations of Central Prison Inmates, 1874-1900

	1874-1875		1876-1880		1881-1885		1886-1890		1891-1895		1896-1900		1874-1900	
	n	%	n	%	n	%	n	%	n	%	n	%	n	%
Labourer	449	56.4	1123	36.8	1687	46.0	1626	45.1	1651	50.1	1602	51.8	8138	46.5
Tailor	21	2.6	90	2.9	134	3.7	170	4.7	180	5.5	89	2.9	684	3.9
Carpenter	46	5.8	134	4.4	166	4.5	148	4.1	85	2.6	77	2.5	656	3.7
Painter	44	5.5	102	3.3	98	2.7	169	4.7	127	3.9	105	3.4	645	3.7
Sailor	39	4.9	116	3.8	135	3.7	97	2.7	60	1.8	66	2.1	513	2.9
All others	197	24.7	1490	48.8	1445	39.4	1399	38.8	1191	36.2	1154	37.3	6876	39.3

Table 3

Distribution of Sample Inmates by Class:Toronto, Hamilton, Whitby, and Guelph Jails, 1881-1891, Ontario Central Prison, 1874-1891, and Mercer Reformatory, 1880-1891

	Four Jail Sample		Central Prison		Mercer Reformatory	
	n	%	n	%	n	%
High-status business and professional	21	0.03	5	0.04	0	0
Small businessmen and clerical	517	8.5	83	7.5	32	4.4
Skilled labour	1,451	24.1	393	35.8	7	0.08
Semi-skilled	496	8.2	122	11.1	21	2.5
Unskilled labour	2,572	42.6	488	44.5	51	6.1
Not classified	970	16.1	2	0.01	723	86.7
Total	6,027	100.0.	1,095	100.0	834	100.0

Table 4

Five Most Common Offences Committed by Central Prison Inmates, 1874-1900

	1874-1875		1876-1880		1881-1885		1886-1890		1891-1895		1896-1900		1874-1900	
	n	%	n	%	n	%	n	%	n	%	n	%	n	%
Larceny	266	33.4	1376	45.0	1298	35.4	1439	39.9	1303	39.6	751	24.3	6433	36.7
Vagrancy	209	26.3	402	13.2	551	15.0	509	14.1	535	16.2	421	13.6	2627	15.0
Assault	80	10.1	365	11.9	387	10.6	364	10.1	301	9.1	270	8.7	1767	10.1
Drunkenness	76	9.5	220	7.2	562	15.3	323	8.9	117	3.6	9	0.3	1307	7.5
Theft	-	-	2	0.07	-	-	-		52	1.6	500	16.2	554	3.2
Other offences	165	20.7	690	22.6	867	23.7	974	27.0	986	29.9	1142	36.9	4824	27.5

Table 5

Offences Committed by Central Prison Inmates, 1874-1900

	1874-1875		1876-1880		1881-1885		1886-1890		1891-1895		1896-1900		1874-1900	
	n	%	n	%	n	%	n	%	n	%	n	%	n	%
Crimes against the person	116	14.6	459	15.0	436	11.9	464	12.9	378	11.5	361	11.7	2214	12.6
Crimes against property	366	46.0	1789	58.6	1742	47.5	1964	54.4	1926	58.5	1963	63.5	9750	55.7
Crimes against public morals	12	1.5	67	2.2	131	3.6	145	4.0	170	5.2	191	6.1	716	4.1
Crimes against public order	218	27.4	485	15.9	746	20.4	667	18.5	669	20.3	549	17.7	3334	19.0

Table 6

Sentence Length of Central Prison Inmates, 1874-1900

	n	%
1 month and under to 6 months	12,811	73.2
6 months, 1 day to 12 months	2,815	16.1
12 months, 1 day to 24 months	1,816	10.3
2 years, 1 day to 5 years	70	0.4

Table 7

Country of Origin of Central Prison Inmates, 1874-1900

	1874-1875		1876-1880		1881-1885		1886-1890		1891-1895		1896-1900		1874-1900	
	n	%	n	%	n	%	n	%	n	%	n	%	n	%
Canadian	313	39.3	1420	46.5	1777	48.5	1882	52.1	1962	59.6	2077	67.2	9431	53.9
English & Welsh	140	17.6	544	17.8	626	17.1	557	15.4	445	13.5	329	10.6	2641	15.1
Irish	178	22.4	517	16.9	587	16.0	477	13.2	305	9.3	200	6.5	2264	12.9
Scottish	56	7.0	143	4.7	184	5.0	163	4.5	120	3.6	86	2.8	752	4.3
American	86	10.8	347	11.4	385	10.5	405	11.2	345	10.5	327	10.6	1895	10.8
Other	23	2.9	84	2.7	106	2.9	125	3.5	117	3.6	74	2.4	529	3.0

Table 8

Canadian and Foreign-Born Inmates in Central Prison, 1874-1900

	1874-1875		1876-1880		1881-1885		1886-1890		1891-1895		1896-1900		1874-1900	
	n	%	n	%	n	%	n	%	n	%	n	%	n	%
Canadian-born	313	39.3	1420	46.5	1777	48.5	1882	52.1	1962	59.6	2077	67.2	9431	53.9
Foreign-born	483	60.7	1635	53.5	1888	51.5	1727	47.9	1332	40.4	1016	32.8	8081	46.1

Table 9

Country of Origin: Central Prison and Mercer Inmates Compared to all Residents of Ontario, 1881, 1891

| | 1881 | | | | 1891 | | | |
| | Ontario | | Central Prison & Mercer | | Ontario | | Central Prison & Mercer | |
	n	%	n	%	n	%	n	%
Canada	1,499,414	77.8	464	48.0	1,710,932	80.9	444	56.1
England	139,031	7.2	142	14.7	151,301	7.2	126	15.9
Ireland	130,094	6.8	189	19.6	103,986	4.9	94	11.9
Scotland	82,173	4.3	53	5.5	70,157	3.3	24	3.0
United States	45,454	2.4	98	10.1	42,702	2.0	67	8.5
Other	30,756	1.6	20	2.1	35,243	1.7	36	4.6

Note: The census did not consider the country of birth of men and women separately. Therefore the figures for the Central Prison and Mercer Reformatory in 1881 and 1891 have been added together. The census also did not consider the place of birth of adults and children separately. Therefore these tables are somewhat misleading since they compare the adult-only populations of the Central Prison and Mercer Reformatory to the entire population of Ontario.

Table 10

Index of Over-Under Representation in All Ontario Jails, the Ontario Central Prison and the Mercer Reformatory, 1880-1900

Country of Origin	All Jails	Central Prison	Mercer Reformatory
Canada	0.6	0.7	0.7
England & Wales	2.0	1.9	1.8
Ireland	3.3	2.0	2.9
Scotland	1.3	1.1	0.8
United States	3.1	4.9	4.0
Other	1.6	1.8	1.0

public order offences). Yet officials, noting that fully 77.9 per cent of Central Prison inmates were intemperate, believed that the vast majority of prisoners were drunks and vagrants who repeatedly committed minor offences. In their analysis, the distinction between minor larceny, vagrancy, and drunkenness did not loom large. All were attributable to the same lack of character and motivation in the offender population. The real significance of the higher proportion of larceny committals for the Central Prison would seem to be that occasional drunks went to jail and habitual drunks or drunks who committed another offence as well would wind up in the Central Prison. More research is necessary, however, before such a conclusion can be confirmed.

No issue was of more continuous concern to prison officials than length of sentence. Although these officers argued unconvincingly that longer periods of incarceration were needed to give the prison an opportunity to work its rehabilitative magic, their primary consideration was the needs of the prison industries. Despite numerous urgent pleas from inspectors and wardens, Ontario judges proved unwilling to bend their sentencing practices to accommodate the correctional philosophy of prison administrators. Stubbornly, the judges continued, as Table 6 indicates, to believe that petty crimes deserved brief sentences. Fully 73.2 per cent of the inmate population was sentenced to six months or less.

The analysis of the national origin of inmates is particularly revealing, providing little support for the popular stereotype that the hard-drinking Irish were disproportionately represented in the criminal class. Like other work, the Central Prison study confirms that immigrant status was far more important than national origin in contributing to crime.[32] The proportion of Canadian-born inmates increased gradually from less than 40 per cent in 1874-75 to over 67 per cent in 1896-1900 (see Tables 7 and 8). Using census data to calculate the relationship between committal rates by national origin and the place of birth of the entire provincial population, one confronts the problem that the census did not report the place of birth of men and women separately. Therefore the figures for the Central Prison and the Mercer have been added together. (Nor did the census consider the country of birth of women and children separately, and these figures are therefore somewhat misleading since they compare the adult-only prison population to the entire provincial population.) Nonetheless the results of these calculations as presented in Table 9 seem persuasive. In 1881, 77.8 per cent of the Ontario population was Canadian-born as compared to only 48 per cent of the population of the two intermediate prisons. Between 1881 and 1891 the Irish dropped from 6.8 per cent of the total population and 19.6 per cent of the prison population to 4.9 per cent of the total population and 11.9 per cent of the prison population. By comparison, the English, between 1881 and 1891, went from 7.2 per cent of the total population and 14.7 per cent of the prison population to 7.2 per cent of the total population and 15.9 per cent of the prison population. The analysis of aggregate statistics does not indicate very significant differences between Irish and English immigrants in criminal tendencies. The American immigrants stand out, moving from 2.4 per cent of the provincial population and 10.1 per cent of the prison population in 1881 to 2.0 per cent and 8.5 per cent in 1891, confirming the literary evidence, which included innumerable complaints by prison officials about the cost of confining American ruffians operating across the frontier.

The differentiation by place of birth stands out most clearly, however, in Table 10, an index of Over-Under Representation by country of birth for the 1880-1900 period in all Ontario jails, the Central Prison, and the Mercer. A score of less than one means that a national group was under-represented: a score of more than one means that it was over-represented. In this table, Canadians in the Central Prison score 0.7, the English 1.9, and the Irish 2.0; the Americans achieve the huge figure of 4.9. So much for the notorious criminal propensities of the wild Irish! Again the figures help to clarify the literary evidence, for not only are there frequent complaints in the prison annual reports about the Americans but there is a remarkable absence of comment on English and Irish immigrants. Indeed Ontarians in this period seldom made the connection between immigrants and crime. The Americans were regarded less as immigrants than as rootless drifters, tramps who came with the season, thus confirming the habit of Central Prison officials of thinking of their inmate population in terms of class, not ethnicity.

Other calculations serve to round out the picture. Understandably, those counties with large cities were most likely to send inmates to the Central Prison, and York and Wentworth with their cities of Toronto and Hamilton sent 41.3 per cent of all inmates between 1880 and 1900. In terms of religion, Roman Catholics were over-represented, contributing 34.3 per cent of the inmate population, although only about 16 per cent of the Ontario population was Catholic, providing further confirmation of the prison's lower-class constituency. The age breakdown shows 57.4 per cent of the population at thirty or under and three-quarters under forty, confirming the impression that this was a relatively young group. With respect to marital status, only 29.1 per cent of inmates of the 1874-1900 period were married. Most surprising, perhaps, was the literacy analysis. For the period 1880-1900, 79.5 per cent of the inmates were recorded as being able to read and write, and another 5.6 per cent could read only. While this was less than the provincial 1891 rate of 93.7 per cent, it was high enough to call into question the argument of those who equated ignorance and crime. For prison officials, perhaps the most strategically significant statistic of all was the recidivism rate. The prison register analysis between 1881 and 1891 demonstrates that fully 30.1 per cent of the inmates had been imprisoned in the Central Prison at least once before. Although fuller analysis of this category is needed, we can conclude tentatively that with so high a recidivism rate, the prison was failing in its most basic purpose.

All the above statistics demand extensive further analysis in conjunction with statistics for jails, the Mercer, and the penitentiary, and they must also be considered in comparison with other jurisdictions if their full meaning is to be grasped. Nonetheless, it is clear that this was a relatively young, disadvantaged working-class population, convicted of minor property and public-order offences and sentenced to brief periods of incarceration. Certainly there was enough here to sustain the belief of the criminal-justice officials, rooted in the pre-Confederation era and continuing into the later nineteenth century, that these people represented a hardened and degraded criminal class deserving of little sympathy and much hard punishment. Although the same figures provided ample room for a far more balanced and sympathetic judgment, few if any of those who came into contact with Central Prison inmates seemed willing to offer sympathy and support. In the circumstances, and considering the original financial rationale for the institution, the failure to commit scarce resources to traditional rehabilitation is eminently understandable in the light of contemporary attitudes and values.

IV

One of the most succinct statements of John Langmuir's correctional philosophy appeared in his 1876 report following a series of investigations into the prison's internal administration and discipline. To protect society, punish crime, and reform the criminal, Langmuir wrote, "the very first step" must always be "the entire subordination of the will of every prisoner to constituted authority." At first glance, this determination to begin the rehabilitative process by breaking the prisoner's will was nothing more than an echo from the 1820s and 1830s, when America's earlier generation of penitentiary ideologues had expressed precisely the same view. There was, however, a difference, which made Langmuir's assertion more brutal and repressive by far than that of the pioneers of the Auburn and Philadelphia systems. In the earlier day, penitentiary administrators, motivated by genuine idealism, were persuaded that such subordination was a necessary part of a far-reaching rehabilitative process. For those who shaped the Central Prison, however, repression and punishment were ends in themselves, all part of a program of deterrence aimed at the criminal class both within and beyond the walls of the Central Prison. Langmuir in 1876 expressed this frankly and forcefully:

The lives of habitual offenders having been one continued revolt against law and order, with little or no
subjugation of the will, or exercise of moral restraint,
the very first lesson that these men have to learn on
entering the Prison is implicit submission. Failing that,
the application of reformatory measures to those of
this class who are not beyond such influences, must
prove abortive — whilst deprivation of liberty only, to
those who are, is no punishment whatever, unless it be
accompanied by strict prison discipline and enforced
hard labour.

For Langmuir, then — to reverse a famous twentieth century penological dictum — men were sent to the Central Prison not as punishment but
for punishment. Yet not even this correctional philosophy, together
with an inmate population regarded as being composed of the dregs of
society, can fully explain the Central Prison's harsh regime.

John Langmuir and his colleagues never fully grasped the need to
come to terms with the power of the inmates as expressed through
prison subcultures. Elsewhere, harassed prison governors saw the
value of a range of techniques, including early release and payments for
over-stint industrial production, but Langmuir believed such methods
had little application to an inmate population such as existed in the
Central Prison. The result ensured that life in the Central Prison would
be characterized by a maximum of violence and a minimum of good-
will or co-operation.

This pattern emerged in the first few years of the prison's operation
and was accompanied by such serious administrative problems that
they almost resulted in chaos. Senior guards functioned at cross-
purposes and with slight evidence of control or direction from the
warden. The chief guard, James Beaumont, himself a former prisoner in
an Upper Canadian jail, over-indulged in alcohol, often in the prison
itself, and lost all semblance of control over his fellow guards.[33] Administrative staff, such as the bursar and the cook, refused to follow orders
from senior guards and fraternized with the prisoners to the detriment
of the discipline. The responsibility for some of this lay with Langmuir,
who had decided not to establish rules and regulations for the prison
until he had had an opportunity to observe the routine as it actually
functioned. In the absence of clear rules enforced by experienced administrators, the situation deteriorated to such an extent that several
internal investigations, conducted by Langmuir himself, had to be
carried out into the activities of the chief guard and related problems.

In one of these reports, Langmuir admitted that the failure of the administrative staff to follow orders had led to undue familiarity with
convicts, causing some of them to become unmanageable. The alcoholic

chief guard was dismissed along with some of his co-workers, and the former deputy chief guard, Richard Stedman, was promoted and evidently instructed to whip the institution into shape. Stedman, a powerful and determined man, proceeded to do so, leaning heavily on the prisoners and earning the dislike of many guards. Langmuir belatedly established a comprehensive code of rules, enforcing such essentials of the Auburn system as the rule of silence, the lock-step shuffle, and a restriction on letter writing by inmates to once a month and on visits to once every two months. In the area of punishment, however, the operative principle was "the discretion of the Warden" and no protection was offered prisoners against unfair or cruel treatment. Numerous escapes had occurred during the prison's first year, and this discretionary authority gave Stedman every opportunity to overawe the prisoners and punish them at will. There was a progression of punishments from solitary confinement through ironing to the wall and, finally, whipping. Stedman also used more direct methods, and many a prisoner received on-the-spot beatings from the burly chief guard.[34]

By early 1876 charges of maladministration and cruelty were a source of newspaper comment, and Langmuir urged that there be "a full and searching inquiry" by two members of the government.[35] Instead Langmuir himself and the minister to whom he reported, Provincial Secretary S.C. Wood, carried out an investigation. Unlike some American inquiries, this one did not allow prisoners to testify. Testimony from such persons as the bursar, the bailiff, the storekeeper, and even the acting chief guard made it obvious that many prisoners had experienced great brutality, much of it at the hands of Richard Stedman. The cook, for example, saw the chief guard kick one old man repeatedly; the bailiff who had conveyed another prisoner beaten by Stedman to the insane asylum related that the doctor there was shocked at how the prisoner had been mistreated; in another case the storekeeper had heard the screams from prisoners beaten after an escape attempt and reported, "I was unwell for two or three days after this from the effects, having never seen anything of the kind before." The formal report, however, exonerated the prison administration in every respect, while in a covering letter to his Cabinet colleagues the Provincial Secretary commented that the Central Prison was "second to none in America." Any laxity of discipline, he asserted, would "result in insubordination and mutiny." If the prison was "to be considered a place where crime was punished," it was "imperatively required that strict discipline be enforced." Although the report praised Stedman as being "in many respects a good officer," it did admit that on occasion he had been "unnecessarily severe," and his resignation was accepted.[36]

Almost as revealing as these confident assertions of official rectitude, however, were clear indications in the report of prisoners' resistance to authority. Many of the prisoners subjected to harsh punishments were being disciplined for attempted escapes, and in the prison's first year nine prisoners had actually escaped. Other prisoners had collected an assortment of weapons, including knives, and it was admitted that the prisoners had managed to defy the rule of silence and to communicate frequently among themselves. In subsequent reports there were many references to fires breaking out in the workshops and elsewhere about the prison. Most important, the day after Stedman's removal, Langmuir was forced to report that "the insubordination of a large number of the prisoners ... became so general yesterday, as to amount to a preconcerted mutiny." The disturbance had started in the dining hall as a protest over inadequate food. Langmuir had reasserted control by rushing to the prison and having three ringleaders whipped on the spot. Henceforth, to eliminate one obvious point of prisoner interchange, the convicts were served their meals in their cells. Following these events, the prison's officers seemed to have asserted a firmer control over the prison community.

The following year we are given an unusual glimpse into the inner workings of the prison in letters written by a young guard, Gilbert Hartley, to his fiancée in Hamilton. Hartley came to the prison in 1877 and before long was put in charge of one of the largest prison industries, the broom shop. From the correspondence he emerges as a sensitive, well-read young man, ultra-respectable, and a devoted Christian. His letters throw light on several aspects of the prison's operations, but what emerges most forcefully is the growing contempt he felt for the prisoners themselves. He was appalled, for example, that the Episcopal minister would conduct a communion service for such riffraff, but he could hardly keep a straight face himself when the first convict seized the communion wine and "drank almost the entire contents" before it could be seized from him. He complained:

> I see their daily conduct and I have no hesitation in saying that they are at best liars and thieves. I get so disgusted with them when I see much that is vile and evil among them. Heaven forbid that I should disparage Christian work among them or set myself up as a model of purity. I should be glad indeed if they could be converted to a man for it would save a great amount of vexation and work. I do wish that I was in a purer element. There is nothing that is elevating and refining all is base and vile. I cannot believe a word any of them says. I have often seen them doing things distinctly and when accused of it would deny it.[37]

A few months later Gilbert described to Mary the administration of a whipping. He began by informing her that several of his charges had just been punished by forty-eight hours in the dark cell:

> Do not think I am cruel but I find the only way to manage the thieves and roughs who number about three hundred and fifty is by stern measures, kindness to most of them is like throwing pearls to swine. At nine a.m. on Tuesday a prisoner named Kennedy was flogged getting fifty lashes. On Sunday last during Sunday-school he struck one of the guards. Flogging is not a very refining medium but it is one that cools down a man very quick.[38]

After edifying his fiancée with a vivid description of the mechanics of the operation, he related that for the first ten or twelve lashes, "it was fearful to hear him cry and beg and twist around," but after that he was silent. "His shoulders were all purple and blistered, a sore place for many a day to come. This marks the third time for him."

A little later he told Mary of another whipping, that of a man whose escape plans had been discovered. This prisoner took forty lashes, "without a murmur. His feet are now shackled and will remain so for near two years."[39] From this respectable young man who could urge his fiancée to read Milton and Macaulay and write movingly of the sunset on Toronto Bay, there was no expression of sympathy for any of his charges, only dislike and contempt.

Any prison that relied for its efficient administration on fear, punishment, and hard labour was bound to experience untoward incidents. In 1885 the Irish Catholic Benevolent Union charged prison officers with cruelty, ill-treatment, and excessive punishments, especially towards Irish prisoners, and following extensive publicity a three-man royal commission was appointed to investigate.[40] One of the commissioners, inevitably, was the retired inspector, John Langmuir, and he dominated its work. Unlike the previous investigations, this one allowed prisoners to testify, but their testimony was treated with unrestrained contempt. Again and again, the commissioners simply justified whatever punishment had been administered. In the case of William O'Neill, kept in his cell for three months on bread and water and then declared insane, they found the punishment "certainly not as severe as might have been meted out." Michael Wynne, a thirty-year old recidivist, kept forty days on bread and water for refusing to work, was pronounced to be thoroughly bad. He had brought his punishment on himself, and if he had been released with neither clothes nor money, that had been the result of his own behaviour. In the case of a convict from Albany, New York, who had threatened the warden, the lash had not been used because the physician had expressed doubts about the convict's sanity. The commissioners had no such doubts; they pronounced the man incorrigible and regretted he had not been flogged. In the case of a young man who had received fifteen punishments, the commissioners pronounced, "The recurrent jail-bird of this prisoner's type is worthy of no consideration," and "There need be no very great concern on the part of society if the very hardest usage under prison rules is meted out to him." In the case of a man who had been placed on bread and water for seven weeks for refusing to work, the commissioners commented, "We do not think that a man should be starved into submission." Instead they advised that he be beaten into submission.[41]

All in all, the report of the 1885 royal commission is a remarkably revealing document. The warden's administration was fully exonerated and the status quo staunchly defended. The state, the commissioners advised, was "not bound to treat vicious members so daintily in prison that they would be better off by reason of their vice, or to make unexceptional lodging for them, while many of its virtuous members outside [were] suffering from hunger." The commissioners were greatly concerned that "the vagabonds and criminal class" not be advised of the fact that comfortable lodging and first-class food were "to be furnished by simply breaking the law." Most of all, they reaffirmed the contrast between the penitentiary environment in which prisoners serving long sentences could be induced to obey the rules through the prospect of receiving good conduct remission, and the different circumstances of the Central Prison. In penitentiaries, they pointed out, prisoners might receive such luxuries as tobacco and newspapers, but "for the class of offenders who seek to make the Central Prison their occasional or permanent resting place, the Government should render this Prison as undesirable and as uninviting as the most rigid discipline, added to the hard labour contemplated by law, can make it." The Central Prison, they concluded, was entirely different from the penitentiary, for in the prison,

> a large majority of the inmates are drunkards, vagrants
> and petty criminals who are almost constant residents
> of one prison or another.... The lives of many of these
> prisoners have been almost one continued revolt against
> law and order, and the first lesson they have to learn on
> entering the Central Prison is to subjugate their wills to
> prison authority.

That this conception of the Central Prison's role in Ontario society should prevail through several investigations and be restated so forcefully time and again suggests emphatically that the prison was not the creation of any one man or the instrument of a few prison officers but that it reflected fundamental values and impulses rooted deep in Ontario society. Despite John Langmuir's early praise for Brockway's Detroit and his occasional references to the ideals of American prison reformers, the prison owed little if anything to foreign influences. Its origins are to be found in the changing definitions of crime and conceptions of criminality developed in the pre-Confederation era and expressed forcefully in the 1850s and 1860s by numerous sheriffs, grand jurors, judges, and, most eloquently, by the old Board of Inspectors. In establishing a prison designed to punish and deter, Langmuir was no more and no less than the voice of Ontario. This was a society with a strongly authoritarian strain, still largely agrarian in its values, still deeply committed to a traditional work ethic. Most Ontarians, whether urban middle-class or farmers, were deeply affronted by evidence of the existence of a class of men and women who refused to conform. As this element filled the jails and became an increasing burden to the pocketbook of respectable citizens, there were few who would have disagreed with the comment of an Ottawa newspaper in 1880 that "criminals must be recognized as a class, and brought under a system of control."[42]

A few years later, in 1891, evidence given by numerous individuals before the famous Commission to Enquire into the Prison and Reformatory System of Ontario, once again served to underline the broad foundation of support for the deterrent prison. Numerous sheriffs, jailers, police chiefs and others involved in the criminal justice system applauded the Central Prison with unrestrained enthusiasm. The jailer at L'Orignal expressed the view of all when he confidently asserted that a prison should be "a terror to evil-doers. I know that they dread the Central Prison and that many of them don't go into evil again."[43] In late Victorian Ontario, the Central Prison was an apt expression of middle-class beliefs, an institution applauded by most and all but impervious to criticism and scandal. It was only the prisoners who suffered and, as the 1885 commissioners saw it, few of them deserved the consideration or sympathy of their fellow Ontarians.

NOTES

The research for this paper was carried out as part of a larger, continuing study of Ontario correctional history in the nineteenth and twentieth centuries being done in association with the Ontario Ministry of Correctional Services. Financial support has been provided by the Ministry, the SSHRC, the Solicitor General (Canada) Fund for Independent Research, and York University. I thank all the above, and also my two research assistants, Michelle Corbett and John Choules, for their dedicated efforts.

1   Richard B. Splane, *Social Welfare in Ontario, 1791-1893* (Toronto: University of Toronto Press, 1965), p. 50.
2   Stephen B. Connors, "John Woodburn Langmuir and the Development of Prisons and Reformatories in Ontario, 1868-1882" (M.A. thesis, Queen's University, 1982), pp. ii, iii.
3   Donald G. Wetherell, "To Discipline and Train: Adult Rehabilitation Programmes in Ontario Prisons, 1874-1900," *Social History*, 12, No. 23 (May 1979), 145. And see D.G. Wetherell, "Rehabilitation Programmes in Canadian Penitentiaries, 1867-1914: A Study of Official Opinion" (Ph.D. thesis, Queen's University, 1980).
4   Sir Walter Crofton's Irish system is discussed in most of the literature on nineteenth century British corrections. See for example Leon Radzinowicz and Roger Hood, *A History of English Criminal Law*, Vol. 5, *The Emergence of Penal Policy* (London: Stevens, 1986). For an account by a zealous advocate of Croftonian principles see Mary Carpenter, *Reformatory Prison Discipline* (London, 1872). For an overview of correctional reform in the United States in the 1860s see Blake McKelvey, *American Prisons, A History of Good Intentions* (Montclair, N.J.: Patterson Smith, 1977).
5   Ontario, *Report of the Commissioners Appointed to Enquire into the Prison and Reformatory System of Ontario, 1891* (Toronto, 1891).
6   Ontario, *Annual Report of the Inspector of Asylums, Prisons, etc.* (hereafter *Annual Report of the Inspector*) (Toronto 1868).
7   Toronto *Globe*, Nov. 13, 1869, as cited in Connors, Langmuir, p. 80.
8   John Weaver, "Crime, Public Order, and Repression: The Gore District in Upheaval, 1832-1851," *Ontario History*, 78, No. 3 (Sept. 1986), 186-87.
9   Ruth Bleasdale, "Class Conflict on the Canals of Upper Canada in the 1840's," *Labour*, 7 (Spring 1981), 33.
10 Paul Romney, *Mr Attorney, the Attorney General for Ontario in Court, Cabinet, and Legislature, 1791-1899* (Toronto: University of Toronto for the Osgoode Society, 1986), pp. 231-39.
11 Romney, *Mr Attorney*, p.237.
12 National Archives of Canada (hereafter NAC), Provincial Secretaries' Papers, Justice Robert Burns to Provincial Secretary, June 3, 1854.
13 NAC., Prov. Sec. Papers, Justice W.H. Draper to Prov. Sec., Nov. 13, 1865.
14 Canada, *Board of Inspectors of Prisons, Asylums and Public Charities*, Preliminary Report (Ottawa, 1859).
15 Blake McKelvey, *American Prisons, A History of Good Intentions* (Montclair, N.J.: Patterson Smith, 1977), p. 68.
16 For a useful discussion of Crofton's influence in the United States see McKelvey, *American Prisons*, Chaps. 3 and 4.
17 Ontario, *Annual Report of the Inspector*, 1869.

18 Connors, *Langmuir*, pp. 81-82.
19 *Statutes of Ontario*, 1870-71, 34 Vict. cap. xvii, An Act to Provide for the establishment and government of a Central Prison for the Province of Ontario. (Assented to Feb. 15, 1871.)
20 Nicholas Rogers, "Serving Toronto The Good: The Development of the City Police Force 1834-84," in V. Russell., ed., *Forging a Consensus: Historical Essays on Toronto* (Toronto: University of Toronto Press, 1984).
21 Ontario, *Report of the Royal Commission appointed to enquire into the value of the Central Prison Labour* (Toronto: Hunter and Rose, 1877).
22 See especially Ontario, *Report of the Special Committee on Prison Labor* (Toronto, 1908).
23 Canada, House of Commons, *Debates*, Feb. 28, 1877.
24 Ontario, *Annual Report of the Inspector*, 1884.
25 Figures taken from *Annual Reports of the Inspector*.
26 Ontario, *Annual Report of the Inspector*, 1877; and see 1880 report.
27 Ibid., 1881, 1882, 1886.
28 Ibid., 1882.
29 For penitentiary studies see Wetherell, "To Discipline and Train" and William A. Calder, "The Federal Penitentiary System in Canada, 1867-1899: A Social and Institutional History" (Ph.D. thesis, University of Toronto, 1979).
30 See Michael Katz et al., *The Social Organization of Early Industrial Capitalism*, Chap. 6, "The Criminal Class: Image and Reality," esp. p. 213.
31 See V.A.C. Gatrell, "The Decline of Theft and Violence in Victorian and Edwardian England," in V.A.C. Gatrell et al., *Crime and The Law* (London: Europa, 1980), p. 299. Another important issue which I am now exploring relates to property crime and the economic cycle. Preliminary results show no very clear relationship between recession and the numbers of persons committed for property offences.
32 See Katz, *Social Organization*, pp. 210, 237, for a suggestive discussion.
33 Ontario, *Annual Reports of the Inspector*, 1875, 1876.
34 Ibid., 1876.
35 Ibid.
36 Ibid.
37 City of Toronto Archives, Gilbert Hartley Papers, Gilbert To Mary, Feb. 9, 1879.
38 Hartley Papers, Gilbert to Mary, Dec. 19, 1878.
39 Hartley Papers, Gilbert to Mary, May 17, 1879.
40 Ontario *Sessional Papers*, 1886, "Royal Commission Appointed to Enquire into Certain Charges Against the Warden of the Central Prison and into the Management of the Said Prison."
41 Ibid.
42 Ottawa *Journal*, Feb. 24, 1880, as cited in Connors, *Langmuir*, p. 77.
43 Ontario, *Report of the Commissioners Appointed to Enquire into the Prison and Reformatory System of Ontario, 1891* (Toronto, 1891). Inevitably this commission was chaired by J.W. Langmuir.

SCIENCE AND THE STATE IN ONTARIO: THE BRITISH CONNECTION OR NORTH AMERICAN PATTERNS?

Richard A. Jarrell

In the move towards an identifiable Canadian nationality before the turn of the century, Ontarians were leaders, simultaneously rejecting the bumptious American political and social styles and expressing a strong desire for a richer Imperial bond with the mother country.[1] This desire was expressed in diverse ways as avid participation in the Boer War, the formation of the IODE, and talk of "Imperial Federation." Were Canadian scientists immune to such sentiments? Sir William Dawson, renowned palaeobotanist and principal of McGill University, in his capacity as first president of the Royal Society of Canada, argued for an Imperial Union of Geological Surveys,[2] and his colleague, the physicist Howard Barnes, campaigned for active Canadian participation in the British Science Guild before World War I. The British Association for the Advancement of Science, in its first meeting outside the United Kingdom, met in Montreal in 1884, returning to Toronto in 1897 and to Winnipeg in 1909. The association's annual meetings — perhaps the most important scientific meetings held in the world — naturally sparked much patriotic fervour and a rush by Canadians to join the association when its meetings were held here. Canada was part of Britain's colonial empire; was Canadian science also part of a British scientific empire?

Recent work has emphasized the concept of "colonial science" first outlined by Basalla.[3] According to his description, Canadian science would have been in the position of providing data to the British while receiving from the mother country theoretical ideas, education, models of institutions, and in the early days, direct control of local science. Another important explanatory approach is that of "centre and periphery"[4] which, for example, would have present-day American science at the centre and third-world science at the periphery. In the Victorian era, one would identify British science as the centre, and Canadian, Australian, or American science at the periphery. Either approach leads to the notion that Canadian science in the nineteenth century was subordinate to British science, if not intrinsically inferior.

In his ground-breaking dissertation,[5] the late Vittorio De Vecchi argued that Canadian science in the late nineteenth century followed the lead of British science: Canadian scientists looked to the old country for support, institutional models, arguments for government financial assistance, research concepts, and organizations. He cited a number of examples of scientific initiatives by the federal government that were a result of British-inspired lobbying, direct financial aid from the British Association, or Canadian memberships in the British Association. He largely discounted — or ignored — any American influence upon Canadian science.

The hypothesis of the British connection might be re-stated in this way: Canadian science moved slowly towards independence before 1914 by following British examples and accepting British leadership. Canadian scientists — particularly academic scientists — wished to emulate their British peers and to form stronger ties with them. A major obstacle was the propensity of Canadian legislatures to finance practical science, science with a pay-off, rather than what we would today call "pure science." This argument would accord well with Berger's view that Canada's growing nationalism expressed itself as pro-Imperialist sentiment.

It is true that some Canadian scientific institutions were based upon British examples. Yet much of this seemingly pro-British scientific attitude of Canadians evaporates under closer scrutiny.[6] The British Association did attract large numbers of Canadians when it met in Canada, but almost all of them promptly dropped off the rolls in subsequent years. The American Association for the Advancement of Science — which also met in Canada — was almost equally attractive to Canadians. British financial support for Canadian science was infinitesimally small compared with funding from the federal government. Dawson's plea for an Imperial geological union came to nought, and Barnes persuaded very few to support the British Science Guild. After the turn of the century, university scientists, almost none of them trained in the United Kingdom, forged stronger ties with colleagues across the border, a practice long before established by the geologists and natural scientists of the Geological Survey of Canada and the Department of Agriculture.[7]

Given this equivocal evidence, the following questions arise: Did Canadian science, beginning in the second half of the nineteenth century, follow its own pattern of scientific development? Did this pattern have much in common with Britain's, and were its links with British science decisive factors in its own development?

The development of scientific activity in Ontario, the most populous and most developed province, offers an important case study.

Three lines of inquiry suggest themselves: the state of scientific education, the form of scientific organization, and the activities of the state. For the first two, Irish, rather than British, models were significant in nineteenth century Canada.[8] For the last, we must re-evaluate the place of science in government. Earlier analyses dealt primarily with the federal government. In some cases, one can demonstrate direct connections to British models or leadership; in others, American connections; in still others, what seem to be uniquely Canadian approaches. For example, the Geological Survey (established in 1842) was inspired by both the British Survey and individual American state surveys. The Experimental Farms (1885) and the Canadian Forest Products Laboratory (1913) were clearly American in inspiration.

It is evident that governments spent public funds on science for several reasons, the least important of which was the advancement of science *per se.* This was true for virtually all North American governments at any level.

For an analysis of the expenditure pattern in Ontario, a definition is required. In science policy literature, the acronym "GERD," meaning Gross Expenditure on Research and Development, is one measure of national financial support for science and science-based technology. But the concept "research and development" cannot be applied readily to the nineteenth century. An alternative is to adopt a looser formulation, "Science-Related Expenditures" (SRE), which would include direct aid to scientific and technical education at any level, assistance to scientific organizations (professional or amateur), and the use of science *as a tool of government,* a tool that was used primarily for economic development and, later in our period, for enhanced human safety, security, and comfort.

It is relatively easy to survey the expenditure statements of provincial governments but more difficult to decide what constitutes an SRE. For example, an entry for a "provincial bacteriological laboratory" is straightforward, but "assistance to the dairy industry" might include laboratory work, research, technological development, and direct subsidies for purchasing milk and cheese. What part is truly related to science? It is not always possible to determine. Therefore the simplest approach is to note the entire expenditure if that expenditure is demonstrably related to science, at least in part.

From the beginning in 1867, the Government of Ontario appropriated funds for scientific activities. These expenditures, like those of the federal and other provincial governments, fell into several broad categories:

1. direct or indirect aid to scientific education (universities, technical education, agricultural education, science teaching in primary and secondary education);

2. assistance to organizations and institutions fostering science and its application (grants to mechanics' institutes, libraries, horticultural and scientific societies, agricultural societies);

3. regulatory and statistical agencies (boards of health, safety inspections, food and drug supervision, labour acts, standards);

4. science-based agencies for development (fisheries, forestry, mining, surveying, agricultural ministries and agencies).

But the Ontario expenditure pattern alone would tell us little about the nature of Canadian science before 1914.[9] As a basis of comparison, a neighbouring American state is more useful than another province (where patterns were remarkably similar). If one could demonstrate that the pattern of SRE's in Ontario from 1867 to 1914 strongly resembled that of a comparable state, then we would have to question seriously the case for the British influence upon science in Ontario, especially if the British pattern were quite different. The obvious candidate for comparison is the state of Michigan for a number of reasons. This state is immediately adjacent to Ontario, had a similar land area during most of the last century,[10] and has a similar geology. There is rich, generally level or rolling farmland in the south, glaciated terrain with poor soils in the north, and a rich mining district in the far north. Both have extensive lakes and rivers, important economically for the fur trade, lumbering, and tourism, each in its turn. Both developed mixed agriculture with a grain basis, both have small regions with microclimates suitable for winegrowing and fruitgrowing despite climates that are about equally cold. Both were dominated by one big city — Detroit and Toronto — and both diversified industrially in much the same way. In both, the development of transportation, trade, and fisheries was influenced by the Great Lakes. Ontario's settlement dates from the early 1790s, Michigan's from the late 1790s (it was a *de facto* part of Canada to 1796), with immigrants from the American East significant in both populations.

The political patterns of Michigan[11] were, of course, purely American; yet the democratic outlook was similar. Local government differed little, the public education systems of both date from the 1840s, and both looked to New England and New York for models. The "internal improvement" rage — to build railways, roads, and canals to open up the hinterland and to stimulate the economy — which occurred in Michigan in the 1830s and 1840s, had its Ontario counterpart. Ontarians moved freely to Michigan in tough economic times, and the Canadian portion of the Michigan population was significant by the end of the century.[12] The fact that Ontario residents found little difficulty in establishing themselves in Michigan suggests there were few substantial social differences.

The demographic growth patterns of Ontario and Michigan were similar from an early date. The population growth of the two jurisdic-

Figure 1
Michigan and Ontario Science-Related Expenditures (1870-1914)

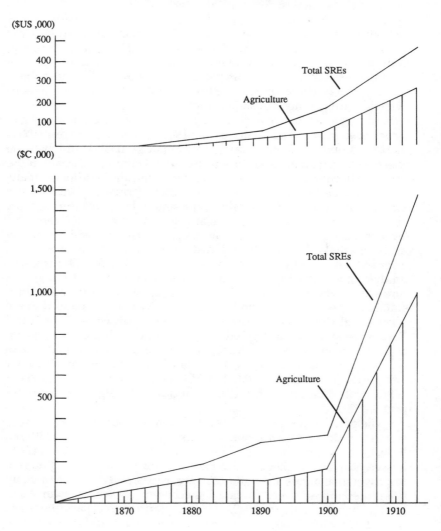

tions remained parallel from 1850 to 1911. The two are still almost identical in population. In both cases the earliest and heaviest settlement was in the southern regions, with sparser (and later) settlement in the poorer-soil areas of the north. Toronto and Detroit dominated their hinterlands by the latter part of the century, and both developed into diversified manufacturing centres after mid-century. The two cities remained similar in size: in 1890, Detroit counted 206,000 and Toronto (in 1891) 181,000, by 1900 and 1901, they were 286,000 and 260,000 respectively, and in 1910 and 1911, 466,000 and 375,000. Their current metropolitan populations are still close.[13]

The two economies were also very similar.[14] Michigan's lumber boom was earlier than Ontario's; Michigan sawmills produced some four billion board feet (mostly pine) annually by the early 1870s. Near the end of the century, Ontario was shipping much of its pine to feed the mills in Michigan, whose supplies were by then almost totally depleted. The Michigan copper and iron ore industries were well in advance of Ontario's, but the hard-rock mining boom of the north was just beginning. In agriculture, Ontario was ahead: in 1900, the value of Michigan farm products was approximately $110 million, whereas those of Ontario were worth more than $170 million. In the manufacturing sector, Michigan's total salaries and wages were $72 million compared to Ontario's (1901) figure of $44.7 million, and in 1909 the former reported $148 million to the latter's $117.7 million (1911). The furniture industry was a Michigan specialty, with $4.4 million in capitalization in 1900, about $1 million less than Ontario's furniture industry. And in the new century, each became the centre of automobile manufacturing in its own country.

Not surprisingly, the similarities in economy, population, and geography are repeated in government science. An analyis of the actual expenditures shows that in Michigan SRE's fell into four main categories: direct grants to organizations, development and conservation, agriculture, and public health. The same categories apply to Ontario, although some specific matters (such as food and drug administration, animal health, or fisheries) were federal responsibilities.[15] Table 1 tabulates total figures for Michigan at approximately five-year intervals. Despite some anomalies, partly political and partly economic in origin, the trend is clear: SRE's remained essentially stable at a relatively low level until the 1890s, followed by significant rises to much higher levels before World War I. The figures are only approximate because Michigan revenues and expenditures were not systematically published in state documents and must be reconstructed.[16] The nature of the specific expeditures will be outlined below.

Table 2 provides, for comparison, the Ontario SRE's at five-year intervals.[17] One important area of expenditure has been omitted, namely, scientific education in the public primary, secondary, and post-secon-

Table 1
Science-Related Expenditures, Michigan, 1862-1914
(rounded to nearest $US 100)

Year	Institutions	Development	Agriculture	Health	
Total					
1862	2,000	118,400	13,500	—	133,900
1871	—	5,100	3,000	—	8,100
1877	—	8,100	28,400	4,000	40,500
1880	400	14,500	12,000	4,000	30,900
1884	—	20,500	18,900	6,600	46,000
1890	—	60,200	27,200	2,000	89,400
1895	6,500	66,000	13,000	11,400	96,900
1900	300	89,800	75,100	23,700	188,900
1905	6,800	152,800	237,800	35,000	432,400
1910	1,300	115,200	177,400	41,400	335,300
1914	—	135,100	289,000	44,000	468,100

Source: See note 14.

Table 2
Science-Related Expenditures, Ontario, 1868-1914
(rounded to nearest Can. $100)

Year	Institutions	Development	Agriculture	Total
1868	8,000	10,600	64,400	83,000
1870	8,000	41,800	63,200	113,000
1876	25,200	39,700	96,200	161,100
1881	34,800	34,200	129,100	198,100
1885	42,400	49,900	113,300	205,600
1890	110,400	51,700	127,800	289,900
1895	42,400	42,300	202,600	287,300
1900	56,200	80,300	184,500	321,000
1905	184,000	192,500	395,900	772,400
1914	196,200	276,300	1,009,100	1,481,600

Source: Ontario *Sessional Papers*.

Table 3
Science-Related Expenditures, Michigan

Institutions

Occasional grants to state horticultural society, pomological association, farmers' institutes, dairymen's association; grants for national and international exhibitions

Agriculture

State agricultural society, 1849
Agricultural college, 1855
State board of agriculture, 1861
Division of agricultural statistics, 1881
County schools of agriculture, 1905

Development and Conservation

Geological survey, 1837
Board of geological survey, 1869
State salt inspectors, 1869
Board of commissioners of state fisheries, 1873
State oil inspector, 1875
Commissioner of mineral statistics, 1877
Michigan school of mines, 1885
State game and fish warden, 1887
Forestry commission, 1887
State weather service, 1887
Mackinac state park commission, 1897
Forestry reserve, 1904
Game, fish and forestry warden, 1907

Public Health

State board of health, 1876
State veterinarian, 1885
State livestock sanitary commissioner, 1885
Dairy and food commissioner, 1893
Bacteriological laboratory, 1907

Note: The dates are the years when the agency was created or the first appropriations were made.

Source: See note 14.

dary schools. Records of the education departments of Michigan and Ontario do not allow a differentiation of expenditures for purely scientific education. The figures under the agriculture head do include subsidies to the Ontario Agricultural College (now the University of Guelph) and the Michigan Agricultural College (now Michigan State University), and the figures listed under development include support for the Michigan College of Mines (now Michigan Technological University) at Houghton and the School of Mines at Queen's University. These are not entirely comparable, however;[18] no attempt has been made to isolate the science-education components in the budgets of the University of Michigan and the University of Toronto, the two chief state-supported universities. The School of Practical Science in Toronto *was* separately funded and is included under Institutions for Ontario in Table 4.

Figure 1 compares the growth patterns of the two jurisdictions. Subsidiary curves show the comparative rise of expenditures in the agricultural sector, the largest set of SRE's for both Ontario and Michigan.[19] Another indicator of the similarity of both government's approaches is the total SRE amount as a percentage of the general expenditures. For Michigan, although the figure went as low as 3 per cent or as high as 11 per cent, SRE's usually accounted for about 7 per cent of state expenditure. In Ontario, the figure was usually 7-8 per cent. A look at specific entries reveals a striking similarity in the approaches of both Ontario and Michigan, despite the total dollar differences. Table 3 shows the most important SRE's for Michigan, along with dates of creation of the agencies or dates of first appropriations. Table 4 provides a similar synopsis for Ontario. Agriculture and the development areas — mining, forestry, and fisheries — received the most attention. Few state governments took agriculture quite so seriously as Ontario. Michigan's primary expenditures were on the agricultural college, with sporadic grants for the state fair and to societies. Michigan believed in minimalist government even more than Canada, so we do not find any large-scale funding of local agricultural organizations. The State Board of Agriculture, created to reorganize the nearly moribund agricultural college, was expected to encourage organizations, import livestock, disseminate information to farmers, receive reports from agricultural associations, and promote domestic industry and household arts. This mandate was almost identical to that of the boards of agriculture created by the Province of Canada in 1857, and continued by Ontario. In the Ontario example, sufficient funds were available to attempt at least part of the program. Michigan's agricultural college was probably better financed than Ontario's, thanks to the state endowment fund and the Morrill and Hatch acts but towards the end of the century, Ontario's Department of Agriculture had widened its scope with a variety of regional specialized schools and experimental stations.

Table 4
Science-Related Expenditures, Ontario

Institutions

Grants to fruit growers, entomological society, mechanics' institutes, various scientific and engineering associations; grants for participation in national and international exhibitions
Education museum, 1858
School of practical science, 1871
Provincial museum, 1887

Agriculture

Grants to agricultural societies, 1846
Ontario agriculture and arts association, 1869
Ontario agricultural college and experimental farm, 1874
Bureau of industries, 1882
Dairy schools,1894
School of Agriculture (Kingston), 1895
Experimental fruit stations, 1896
Ontario Veterinary College, 1909

Development and Conservation

Surveyor-general, 1868
Inspector of mines,1890
Ontario Game and Fisheries Commission, 1890
Bureau of mines, 1891
Algonquin Provincial Park, 1893
School of mines (Kingston), 1894
Mining development grants, 1895
Summer mining schools, 1896
Mining exploration,1897
Commission of fisheries,1899

Public Health

Board of health, 1882
Vaccine farm, 1887

Source: Ontario *Sessional Papers*

For most of the nineteenth century the forestry sector was Michigan's economic mainstay. The general approach seems to have been to cut everything saleable and then move on.[20] A Forestry Commission received a single grant for a report, but systematic forestry work, with a reserve and designated warden, follow only after the turn of the century. The scientific approach to mineral resources dates from statehood; Douglas Houghton's geological survey pre-dates his friend William Logan's Canadian survey by five years. The mining boom in Michigan began just before mid-century, with copper and later iron ore in the Upper Peninsula. At first only geological surveying was necessary, and that was not financed every year or systematically. As the mining industry grew, the state required statistics and, finally, a specialized school for mining. The vast salt deposits near the St. Clair and Detroit rivers required the services of a salt inspector. As in Ontario, the Great Lakes and inland fisheries might soon be exhausted, leading to the establishment of a special commission to provide hatcheries and protection of existing stocks. Conservation was the last phase of the developmental area to appear, with a game warden and the first state park.

Central control of public health came late to Michigan, as it did to most jurisdictions in North America. The State Board of Health appeared only during the last quarter of the century, with expenditures for animal health — for agricultural purposes — pre-dating the inspection of food and dairy products for human consumption in the 1890s.

The evolution of Ontario's SRE's differ in degree rather than in kind from those of Michigan and, for several reasons, the chronologies vary. The government of Michigan approached development in two distinct phases: a short period of intensive development of its transportation and communications system — the "internal developments" program of the 1830s — which nearly led to bankruptcy, followed by a longer, slower phase of assisting natural resources development. Like most nineteenth-century legislators, those of Michigan were not anxious to spend money. So long as the timber and minerals were shipped outwards, there was no urgency to increase efficiency or to impose conservation measures. As Table 1 shows, the government's expenditures on development remained relatively static until after the turn of the century. The geological survey remained small and was not even funded every year. Ontario could rely upon the Geological Survey of Canada for most of its mineral exploration until nearly the turn of the century. In Michigan, the provision for mining education came much later than that for agriculture; Ontario's approach was similar.

As in Michigan, internal improvements in Ontario resulted in large debt loads, although much of the debt for railway development, for instance, passed to the federal government in 1867. Ontario's primary development concern, after agriculture, was mining. Apart from fire control, the government showed little interest in forestry until later in the century.[21] Catton remarks that "inexhaustible" was the fatal word of nineteenth-century Michigan.[22] The same might almost be said of Ontario.

In both jurisdictions government assistance to agriculture was centred on agricultural education and associated research, with Michigan a quarter-century in the lead thanks largely to assistance from the U.S. federal goverment. One significant difference was the weight Ontario put upon grants to agricultural societies. Upper Canada had financed local organizations very early and brought in systematic distribution and reporting with the Agricultural Act of 1857. Michigan had local agricultural societies, but these survived on local inititative. The legislators, perhaps still mindful of the near-bankruptcy brought on by too rapid internal development, were loath to support associations of any kind; during the last forty years of the century, only a few tens of thousands of dollars were expended in this way. In Ontario, from Confederation to the end of the century, the agricultural societies alone received nearly $2.7 million. Technical education, as one form of development, scarcely existed in Michigan, whereas in Ontario, unsuitable British models, such as the mechanics' institutes, absorbed considerable tax monies with few results. The University of Michigan and the School of Practical Science at Toronto provided engineering education, but not until nearly the end of the century did the two educational departments develop technical training at lower levels.

One might object that Michigan is not a good comparison because, as a northern state, it might not be representative. A brief comparison with the state of Indiana shows that the three jurisdictions differed little by the First World War.[23] Table 5 shows the range of SRE's in Ontario and Michigan by 1915. Indiana had all the same kinds of expenditures as Ontario or Michigan with only one exception.

If Michigan and Ontario exhibit similar evolutionary patterns, how do they compare with Britain? Table 6 lists the main types of SRE's at five-year intervals for the United Kingdom.[24] These figures, compared with Tables 1 and 2, show a very different pattern, with far more institutional support and little expenditure (for obvious reasons) upon development. The total SRE amounts, as a percentage of the gross annual expenditure, varied between 0.9 per cent and 1.3 per cent, considerably less than that of either Ontario or Michigan; Canadian federal SRE's averaged about 1.5 per cent of expenditures until the turn of the century, and then moved upwards towards 6 per cent before the First World War.

There is scant evidence that Ontario scientists emulated their British colleagues and yearned to join them in a larger Imperial system of science.[25] Neither can one substantiate any conception of Ontario as a conscious imitator of the British in its approach to science as a tool of

Table 5
Science-Related Expenditures of Ontario and Michigan by 1915

Type of Expenditure	Ontario	Michigan
Grants to societies	yes	yes
Geological survey	yes	yes
Mining bureau	yes	yes
Oil and gas inspection	no	yes
Forestry management	yes	yes
Game and fish protection	yes	yes
Fisheries research	yes	yes
Entomological research	yes	yes
Board of agriculture	yes	yes
Agricultural college	yes	yes
Veterinary services	yes	yes
Board of health	yes	yes
Bacteriological labs	yes	yes
Food and drug inspection	no	yes
Statistical bureau	yes	yes
Technical education grants	yes	yes

Table 6
Science-Related Expenditures, United Kingdom, 1870-1900
(rounded to nearest £100)

Year	Institutions	Development	Agriculture	Health	Total
1871	588,300	16,800	—	—	605,100
1875	716,100	16,300	—	—	732,400
1880	718,500	13,000	—	—	731,500
1885	902,800	19,100	—	—	921,900
1890	1,063,000	19,800	2,200	—	1,085,000
1895	1,133,400	28,700	49,000	85,000	1,296,100
1900	1,102,000	24,200	109,000	—	1,235,200

Note: Institutions include science and art institutions, technical instruction, museums, learned societies, exhibitions, official expeditions, public works surveys, and patents. Development expenditures pertain to the Scottish Fisheries Board. Source: Parliamentary Papers.

government.[26] Ontario resembled Michigan (and Indiana, and no doubt many other states) in its approach for several reasons. First was the nature of the development of the province. Like Michigan, Ontario had tremendous natural resources, first furs, then timber, agricultural land, fish, and minerals. The industrialization of both followed logical and similar paths: the first industries (mills, tanneries, breweries, and distilleries) were linked to early farm and forest production. They were followed by more sophisticated industries (founding, textiles, shoes, agricultural implements, furniture, carriages, railway equipment) after agriculture and urban life became more fully established. Finally, high-technology and consumer manufactures (food, confections, electrical equipment, and automobiles) appeared at the turn of the century.[27]

In the frontier American states, as in Canada, governments had to take a hand in promoting development. As each jurisdiction became more heavily settled, richer, and more diversified, government expenditures broadened. In those areas in which science could act as a tool, the demands increased enormously at the turn of the century. Up to that point, we see a quiet diversification in SRE's as development progressed; these amounts might well have been much greater except for the long periods of financial difficulty in the last quarter of the century. If somewhat greater reliance upon the state as the financier of development was typical of Ontario, that trait cannot be identified as British. The contemporary British government SRE's were different and not nearly so diversified as those of the jurisdictions around the Great Lakes; the United Kingdom was not a frontier society in the nineteenth century, and its expenditures were intended to improve existing systems as opposed to creating them *de novo*.

The marked similarity in the growth and nature of SRE's in Ontario and in Michigan allowed Ontario society to look to the states — and the reverse may have been true at times — for models for institutions and government agencies to deal with almost identical problems. The links are sometimes demonstrable, as in the case of the Ontario Agricultural College. Sir John Carling, when Commissioner of Agriculture and Arts in 1871, suggested such a college and requested a report from an agricultural journalist, the Rev. W.F. Clarke. Clarke, after a quick tour of neighbouring states, concluded that the Michigan Agricultural College was the best model for Ontario.[28] The operations of the provincial board of health, created in 1882, emulated those of the Michigan board.[29] Usually, the direct connection cannot be identified, but certain ideas were "in the air," as in the establishment of provincial and state parks, game and fish protection agencies, and bacteriological laboratories.[30]

Although we lack detailed studies of the role of science in government in pre-World War I North America, one can argue that Ontario (and most other provinces[31]), having a base population with a North American outlook and a similar set of developmental problems to solve as the neighbouring Americans, followed approximately the same path. Science, as a tool of government for development, was used in a North American fashion. Canada, like the United States, was a developing nation, its industrial revolution just underway after mid-century. The British approach to scientific advancement was a luxury Canada could not yet afford. Any belief in a greater Imperial science community was the preserve of a very small group of men and certainly was not an attitude shared by many in Queen's Park.

NOTES

1   See Carl Berger, *The Sense of Power: Studies in the Ideas of Canadian Imperialism 1867-1914* (Toronto: University of Toronto Press, 1970).
2   J.W. Dawson in *Proceedings of the Royal Society of Canada*, 6 (1887), vi-vii, xii-xiii.
3   George Basalla, "The Spread of Western Science," *Science*, 156 (May 5, 1967), 611-22.
4   A number of approaches are reviewed in R.A. Jarrell, "Differential National Development and Science in the Nineteenth Century: the Problems of Quebec and Ireland," in N. Reingold and M. Rothenburg, eds., *Scientific Colonialism: A Cross-Cultural Comparison, 1800-1930* (Washington, D.C.: Smithsonian Institution Press, 1987), pp. 323-50.
5   Vittorio De Vecchi, "Science and Government in Nineteenth Century Canada" (Ph.D. dissertation, University of Toronto, 1978).
6   R.A. Jarrell, "British Scientific Institutions and Canada: the Rhetoric and the Reality," *Transactions of the Royal Society of Canada*, Ser. 4, Vol. 20 (1982), 533-47.
7   See, for example, W.A. Waiser, "The Macoun-Merriam Connection," *HSTC Bulletin*, 6, No. 1 (1982), 3-9. The trans-border linkages were also evident in French Canada: see Raymond Duchesne, "Science et Société coloniale: les naturalistes du Canada français et leurs correspondants scientifiques (1860-1900)," *HSTC Bulletin*, 5, No. 2 (1981), 99-139.
8   R.A. Jarrell, "The Influence of Irish Institutions upon the Organization and Diffusion of Science in Victorian Canada," *Scientia Canadensis*, 9, No. 2 (1985), 150-64.
9   The year 1914 is chosen as an approximate cut-off date as World War I changed a number of peacetime expenditure priorities. In this analysis, only state and provincial government SRE's are counted; federal SRE's, in both countries tended to cover different areas depending upon constitutional jurisdiction. There is no space in this study to discuss federal expenditures, but they were similar in the U.S. and Canada. Municipal and private contributions are likewise ignored, as they were insignificant during this period.
10 The vast territory of northern Ontario was not completely part of the province at Confederation and did not undergo extensive development until after the turn of the century. In 1901, Ontario contained 222,000 square miles to Michigan's nearly 97,000, a third of which was Great Lakes waters.
11 The basic survey of Michigan's political history, with a good deal of material on development, is Willis F. Dunbar and George S. May, *Michigan: A History of the Wolverine State* (Grand Rapids: William B. Eerdmans, 1980). The work provides a useful annotated bibliography. Virtually nothing has been written about the history of science in Michigan, or the role of science in development. The most important serials, *Michigan Pioneer and Historical Collections, Michigan History,* and *Michigan Historical Review* offer very little.

12 For a recent statistical study of this phenomenon, see Gregory S. Rose, "The Origins of Canadian Settlers in Southern Michigan, 1820-1850," *Ontario History*, 79, No. 1 (Mar. 1987), 31-52.

13 Toronto figures (rounded to the nearest 1,000) are not from the official censuses but are revised figures reported in various editions of the *Canadian Annual Review of Public Affairs*. The Detroit figures, also rounded, are U.S. census figures.

14 No single source will provide a standardized set of statistics for either Michigan or Ontario. The following statistics are drawn from Michigan Department of State, *Michigan and its Resources* (Lansing, 1893); Walter L. Dunham, *Banking and Industry in Michigan* (Detroit, 1925); Leonard Bronder and John Koval, *Michigan's Economic Past — Basis for Prosperity* (Lansing: Department of Commerce Technical Report 10A, March 1967); *The Statistical Year-Book of Canada, 1901* (Ottawa, 1902); Third Census of Canada — 1901, Vol. 2 (Agriculture) (Ottawa, 1904) and Vol. 3 (Manufacturing) (Ottawa, 1905); *Fifth Census of Canada — 1911*, Vol. 3 (Manufactures) (Ottawa, 1913); "Report of the Bureau of Industries," Ontario, Legislative Assembly, *Sessional Papers*, 1901, No. 28.

15 Federal SRE's in this area appear mostly in the 1890s and later, with food and drug acts, animal health acts, and Customs Department and Inland Revenue Department laboratories. Ontario and the federal government shared certain responsibilities, such as fisheries, mining exploration, and forestry. This was also true in the U.S., but to a lesser extent during the period.

16 The sources of the earlier figures are the state Auditor-General's, Treasurer's or Board of Audit's reports in the *Joint Documents of the State of Michigan* (for 1862, 1871, 1877, 1880, and 1884), published by the legislature. For the later years, the source is the annual *Red Book* (later *Official Directory and Legislative Manual*), published for members of the state House of Representatives and Senate. The reporting system varied from time to time and was very different from the straightforward reporting procedure of the Ontario Legislature. Total state expenditures are not always evident (as with the Consolidated Fund in Ontario); therefore, the reconstructed figures should be regarded only as indicative of the level of expenditure.

17 The sources for Ontario figures are the annual "Public Accounts" records published in the *Sessional Papers* of the Legislative Assembly. Where the "Public Accounts" do not cover one of the five-year dates, the figures of the next year are substituted.

18 Michigan, like Ontario, opted to provide state support for a few public universities while discouraging the proliferation of many small private or religious colleges. The primary difference is that Ontario made direct annual grants, whereas Michigan created endowment funds. In the case of the Michigan Agricultural College, the state provided direct subsidies and created an endowment, as did the federal government, through the Morrill and Hatch acts, by setting aside public land for education. There was no analogous financial support in Canada until the federal Agricultural Education Act of 1913.

19 The curves are not exact. Ontario figures are reasonably accurate, but individual salaries are not always identifiable. Some Michigan figures are reconstructed. The relative value of the Canadian and American dollar would, of course, vary from year to year.

20 This is the predominant theme in Bruce Catton's popular work *Michigan: A History* (New York: Norton, 1984). His over-concentration on the forestry sector gives a truncated view of the rise of the mining and manufacturing sectors.

21 Large gaps remain in the historiography of development in Ontario but two recent works should be noted: Dianne Newell, *Technology on the Frontier: Mining in Old Ontario* (Vancouver: University of British Columbia Press, 1986) and R. Peter Gillis and Thomas Roach, *Lost Initiatives: Canada's Forest Industries, Forest Policy, and Forest Conservation* (New York: Greenwood, 1986).

22 Catton, *Michigan,* esp. Chap. 10

23 Indiana, although physically much smaller than either Michigan or Ontario, had a large agricultural sector, rising manufacturing, important natural resources (coal, oil, gas, and limestone), and a population slightly larger than either Michigan or Ontario. Sources for Indiana statistics: *Year Book of the State of Indiana for the Year 1917* (Indianapolis, 1918). Total SRE's for 1915-16 were approximately $416,300, about 3 per cent of the total state budget. This does not include grants to the state universities.

24 The source of data is the annual "Finance Accounts" of the Exchequer, printed in the parliamentary papers. The categories are those under "Supply." Figures are provided only up to 1900; after that time, Irish science, technology, and agriculture were funded separately and the Science and Art Department was absorbed by the Board of Education; the expenditures for the latter cannot be differentiated. However, the pattern did not change in any significant way.

25 See note 6.

26 See D.S.L. Cardwell, *The Organisation of Science in England* (London: Heinemann, 1972). Details on the main scientific expenditures, including education, the geological survey, museums, specialized science, engineering, and technical schools, can be found in the annual reports of the Department of Science and Art (later Department of Science and Industrial Research) in the parliamentary papers.

27 For Canada, see R.A. Jarrell, "Government, Technology and Industry: The Emergence of the Canadian Pattern," *Atkinson Review of Canadian Studies,* 2, No. 2 (Spring-Summer 1985), 26-32. The focus of the turn-of-the-century industrial expansion in Michigan was the automobile industry. How it was linked to earlier industrial development is discussed in George S. May, *A Most Unique Machine: The Michigan Origins of the American Automobile Industry* (Grand Rapids: William B. Eerdmanns, 1975).

28 "Report of Rev W.F. Clarke," Appendix E to "Report of the Commissioner of Agriculture and Arts," Ontario, Legislative Assembly, *Sessional Papers,* 1870-71, No. 5.

29 Several state boards were visited by members of the Ontario board. Dr J.J. Cassidy visited Lansing to study the Michigan board's methods, which were in large part adopted. See "First Report of the Board of Health," Ontario, Legislative Assembly, *Sessional Papers,* 1883, No. 13, p. vii.

30 For the role of the laboratory in public health in Michigan, see C.C. Young, *The Development, Organization and Operation of the Bureau of Laboratories of the Michigan Department of Health* (Lansing, 1925). Young gives a synopsis of public health laboratories in the U.S. states and Canadian provinces in the early 1920s. Almost all of them bore a strong resemblance to one another.

31 The author has surveyed the public accounts of all provinces (except Newfoundland) up to 1915 and finds a similar evolution of SRE's Some provinces naturally expended more per capita than others, and the needs of governments varied across the country. Direct borrowing of ideas was common, especially in the western provinces.

FROM MODERN BABYLON TO A CITY UPON A HILL: THE TORONTO SOCIAL SURVEY COMMISSION OF 1915 AND THE SEARCH FOR SEXUAL ORDER IN THE CITY

Carolyn Strange

At the beginning of the twentieth century, sexual vice and the city were virtually synonymous in the minds of most North Americans. The metropolis was more than a jumble of streets and stores and stone — to those who dubbed it "Modern Babylon," it was a mythical representation of cravings, temptations and desires.[1] Sexual gratification and materialism were linked in the city's image as a "painted whore," the female personification of urban allurement. Progressive reformers vowed to transform "Babylon" into a modern "City upon a Hill" — the appropriate environment for a moral, industrial capitalist society. They believed that it was possible to eliminate the deplorable side effects of material progress by intelligently managing economic and social change. The conventional image of Progressives — experts, dedicated volunteers, and professionals who tackled the trusts and lobbied for child welfare — has, however, marginalized the importance of sexual reform.[2] In fact, the search for sexual order was central in their attempts to bring about a moral urban society. When hemmed in by the conventions and intimacy of social relations in small towns, sex, like business, was a natural, vital force. In the amoral cities, however, small shops ballooned into monopolies and sex burst its marital and procreative boundaries. Like a "painted whore," big cities reportedly lured innocents from the stability of their villages into the chaos of urban vice and depravity. A mere street light could be seen as "a strange, glittering night-flower, odour-yielding, insect-drawing, insect-infested rose of pleasure" in the eyes of those who believed the city to be the breeding ground of sexual immorality.[3] Accordingly, within the Progressives' campaign to rationalize urbanization, it was as important to reshape the urban sexual environment as it was to clear slums and purify water supplies. Indeed, they saw no contradiction between sexual reform and

the bureaucratic management of urban society since industrial capitalist development depended in part upon a harmonious work force that
could be counted on to reproduce a stable supply of workers and
consumers. If big business was to be efficient, rational, and well-
ordered, then sex would have to be as well.

The search for sexual order in Toronto inspired its urban reformers
to launch a formal investigation of the state of immorality in their city.
The record of their inquiry, the report of the Toronto Social Survey
Commission of 1915, expressed a typically Progressive approach to
urban sexual reform. Although the religious, civic, medical, legal, and
philanthropic representatives who headed the commission presented
themselves simply as "fact finders," they understood and portrayed
vice as the tawdry underside of the "Queen City." Thus, they operated
within a conceptual framework where women stood for the city's cheap
allure. Sexual vice for these Progressives signified a serious breakdown
in social organization generally, though they traced one of the greatest
sources of immorality to Toronto's working women and their changing
leisure patterns. The survey report presented "the working girl," not as
a worker, but as an index of urban immorality; her leisure received more
attention than her work because the commissioners believed that it was
in leisure pursuits that moral choices were made. The findings of the
report added a powerful voice to the rising chorus of alarm at the nature
of women's pleasures. Along with others involved in the fight against
vice, notably penologists and recreation proponents, they elevated
working women's leisure to the status of an urban problem that could,
they hoped, be solved by social and governmental supervision. Both the
commissioners' recommendations and the programs instituted later by
prison and recreation reformers illustrate how the Progressives constructed vice as a gender- and class-related concept.[4]

In many ways, Toronto was hardly a typical city for a vice commission to investigate. Its population of over 200,000 at the turn of the
century was dwarfed by the millions who crowded into New York and
Chicago, the sites of the two most famous vice surveys. Although the
number of Torontonians increased by 75 per cent between 1901 and
1911 and by a further 37 per cent over the following decade, most of the
increase was attributable to an influx of British immigrants. Together
with the native-born population, they constituted better than 93 per
cent of the city's population throughout the first two decades of the
twentieth century, when most major North American cities were struggling with problems of "alien assimilation." Toronto's religious homogeneity almost matched its ethnic consistency. Despite the growth of
the Jewish community, from just over 1 per cent in 1901 to almost 9 per
cent in 1921, the proportion of Protestants remained extraordinarily
large at 77 per cent in 1921, while Catholics accounted for just under 14
per cent.[5] Known as the "City of Churches," Toronto was also labelled

"Toronto the Good" as an affirmation of the Anglo–Protestant mores that set the city's tone. Montreal outrivalled Toronto in both size and economic productivity, but the Queen City began to challenge that dominance as new markets opened up in the hinterlands of northern Ontario and the West by the turn of the century. The major areas of growth were in secondary manufacturing and in the wholesale, retail, and financial sectors, so that Toronto could boast not only the highest productivity of any Canadian city (next to Montreal) but also the most diverse economic base.[6] Manufacturers, merchants, and bankers prospered most from Toronto's growth in the early twentieth century, and the propertied middle classes benefited as well, particularly through the expansion of the tertiary sector. Toronto's poor, primarily non-Anglo-Protestants and recent immigrants, not only saw little of the city's prosperity in their own lives but experienced an erosion of their already limited economic security when real wages declined after the First World War.[7] Despite this class stratification, the city did not house its densely packed groups of poor and immigrant labourers in anything resembling the tenements of New York, Chicago, or even Montreal. Toronto could certainly claim metropolitan status by the early twentieth century, but it could scarcely compare to the greatest cities of North America as an embodiment of the "evils" of industrial urbanization. Toronto at the turn of the century was a fledgling metropolis that remained in large measure a decorous Tory town.

There were those, however, at the religious, civic, and philanthropic helm of the city who were convinced that a lively trade in commercialized vice and "white slavery" flourished beneath Toronto's veneer of urban decorum. In the autumn of 1913, when a deputation from the Toronto Local Council of Women (TLCW) requested the civic board of control to appoint a "commission on social vice," they represented not only their more than sixty member organizations, but also a widely held conviction that Toronto was riddled with vice. This was, however, hardly the first time that North American moral reformers had taken upon themselves the task of social housekeeping; rather, their plan to establish a vice survey in Toronto was one in a series of responses to the alleged rise in immorality. Suspicions of white slavery were not unique to Toronto. Indeed, the goal of the international social purity movement was to bring the "traffic in young women" to the attention of authorities at every level of government and to demand action to combat the "evil." In the United States, for instance, social purity advocates successfully lobbied Congress in 1910 to pass an act to prohibit the "interstate traffic in women for the purpose of prostitution." In Ottawa, the National Council of Women (NCW), the Women's Christian Temperance Union (WCTU), and newer figures on the moral landscape, such as the Rev. Dr. Shearer of the Moral and Social Reform Council, urged the Dominion government to strengthen the criminal law as Canada's contribution to the "war on the white slave trade." Their efforts were rewarded in the Criminal Code Amendment Act of 1913, an expanded and more punitive version of existing legislation relating to prostitution.[8] Throughout North America, particularly in the cities, smaller local groups devoted exclusively to the promotion of individual and national purity sprang up in this climate of fear.[9] One local organization — the Toronto Vigilance Committee — lobbied for the "prevention, by education and other means, of young girls entering upon immoral careers," while its broader aim was "TO USHER IN A 'BETTER TORONTO.' "[10]

Protestant clergy were instrumental in gathering local support to combat vice, and the protestant churches provided the structure for organizing that support on a national basis. In 1913, the Board of Temperance and Moral Reform of the Methodist Church and the Board of Social Service and Evangelism of the Presbyterian Church combined their efforts to conduct social surveys of Canadian cities and rural districts. In that year alone the boards studied Vancouver, Sydney, St. Catharines, Regina, Port Arthur, London, and Hamilton. Members of the TLCW undoubtedly knew of the Methodist and Presbyterian surveys, but when they lobbied the municipal government to " 'study the problem of the white slave traffic, existing vice and social disease in the City of Toronto' with a view toward 'lessening these evils,'" they were following in the footsteps of the famous Chicago Vice Commission of 1911.[11] The members appointed to the Chicago commission — social leaders who "command[ed] the respect and confidence of the public at large" — had sought the aid of every "civic, protective, philanthropic, social, commercial and religious body in the city" to stamp out the "social evil." Their disapproving eye focused on everything from false advertisements for cures for venereal disease to the sexual exploitation of immigrant women and girls. In conclusion, they directed their recommendations to every conceivable authority, from parents to the president.[12] Encouraged by the fervour of the larger "war on the white slave trade" and convinced of the need for a municipal commission such as Chicago's, the TLCW delegates trooped up the stairs of Toronto City Hall, prepared to launch the local battle against vice.

But the forces they met behind the imposing sandstone walls were anything but hostile. Like many North American local governments in the 1910s, Toronto City Council was imbued with "a new spirit in social welfare, housing, land use planning and local government reform."[13] Local politicians began to promote social and economic welfare in the burgeoning city by expanding the range of physical and protective services, creating public utilities, and providing social, cultural, and recreational services.[14] As Mayor Horatio Hocken declared, municipal government could no longer confine itself to laying sidewalks and patching pot-holes as it had done in the days when ward bosses dominated city politics. "We have got a long way past that," he proudly stated,

> and the problems we have to deal with now are problems affecting human welfare, problems of prevention, the problems of looking to the betterment of the people of cities. In Toronto we ... look to the serving of those human instincts which when properly provided for, make a healthy, moral, and intelligent community.[15]

In his statement of municipal Progressivism, Hocken made it clear that the civic government was willing and prepared to take on social responsibilities previously thought to be the exclusive domain of the city's philanthropic organizations. Progressive politicians in Toronto tried to link the existing voluntary social reform groups to the growing administrative arm of the city government; indeed they depended upon both the energy and the expertise of those who had previously seen to the physical and spiritual welfare of Torontonians. The membership of the Toronto Social Survey Commission reflected city council's conception of the suitable blend of elected officials and other social leaders who they assumed would "command the respect and confidence of the public at large." The City approved the survey proposal on October 27, 1913, and appointed as commissioners six clergymen, four representatives of social service agencies, four elected city officials, three doctors (including the Medical Officer of Health, Dr. Charles Hastings), two lawyers, two businessmen, and an academic who acted as secretary and wrote the final report.[16]

With characteristic Progressive assurance, the investigators proclaimed that they were engaged in a fact-finding mission.[17] Like most Progressives, they considered themselves scientists who methodically explored social phenomena, and they regarded the city as their laboratory, full of troubling specimens of urban life. With the apparent detachment of anthropologists they gave accounts of their contact with the city's under classes as if they belonged to an exotic tribe. And finally, as social geographers, they undertook what the mayor of Toronto called a "moral survey of the city." Armed with scientific methods and infused with a religious commitment to reform, the Social Survey Commissioners vowed that their report on vice would "present statements of fact that fairly represented existing conditions" in their city.[18] It was not their intention to "play the alarmist and paint the conditions existing in the City in lurid colours, or on the other hand to 'prophesy smooth things' "; instead, they intended to provide accurate snapshots of the vice scene.[19]

It is apparent, though, that their pictures of Toronto resembled paintings more than photographs. Their distrust of the moral pitfalls of big city living, coupled with their association of women with urban allurement, washed over the canvas of the survey report. Just as they linked the city with sexual vice and likened urban temptations to feminine wiles, so they painted women's work and play in bold relief. In the background lay their interpretation of the broader economic and social changes that had transformed working women's lives in late nineteenth-century Toronto.

The debate on women's leisure in the Progressive period was an epilogue to earlier controversies about changes in women's work in the initial phases of industrial capitalism.[20] Women's work in manufacturing was unconventional because, unlike domestic labour, it entailed toiling for wages at relatively fixed hours. From the 1870s, when members of Toronto's female labour force first entered non-domestic wage labour, fearful observers predicted a breakdown in the prevailing standards of behaviour for working-class women. As long as these women worked behind closed doors in the "proper sphere" of either their parents' or masters' homes, they rarely attracted public notice. Domestics and daughters, however, proved equally eager to move out of their proper sphere once the diversification of secondary manufacturing multiplied the number of semi-skilled and unskilled jobs available in Toronto. Young women from working-class families were attracted to the small employment niches that opened up in the industrial sector as industrialists sought cheap labour in the persons of women and children. While male workers claimed most of the positions in Toronto's earliest factories, small groups of women could be found in paper box factories, shoe-making shops and cigar-rolling firms.[21] Though fewer than 10 per cent of the city's 5,500 women workers toiled in the nascent manufacturing firms in the 1880s, they attracted public attention that far outweighed their numbers.[22] It was clear to shop owners that women preferred factory work for they would accept as little as 30 to 60 per cent of men's wages,[23] while mistresses who had lost their domestics to alternative employment recognized that the rise of women's wage labour threatened to diminish the always inadequate pool of "good help." In 1887 a correspondent to the Toronto Bureau of Industry summarized this transition in women's work and sketched the economic and social reasons women gave for seeking wage labour:

> Many work through necessity that they may live, others that they may help their parents, while no inconsiderable number are daughters of country farmers who prefer city life and fixed hours of work, even at low wages, rather than remain at home, on the farm.[24]

The correspondent's observation suggests that women were attracted to the cities not just by waged labour but also by the prospect of freedom from family responsibilities and scrutiny. The workers who filled the city's growing number of non-domestic "women's jobs" led to the fear that patriarchal controls over daughters as well as employers' supervision over servants would be eroded. For those with an interest in maintaining those restraints, the female wage worker represented disorder.

The "woman adrift" was the phrase that came to be used in the late nineteenth century to describe this novel type of worker.[25] YWCA spokeswomen were instrumental in drawing public attention to what they believed to be the moral danger when these young women "liv[ed] independently, unsupported and unsupervised by family, community and church."[26] Despite poverty wages and the health and safety hazards of manufacturing jobs (which might have caused public concern), it was women's time *off* more than their time *on* the job that members of the YWCA and other evangelical organizations found problematic. Mayor W.H. Howland portrayed the working girl of the 1880s as a lonely soldier in the battle for respectability, forced to dodge her way through the minefield of urban dangers: "Now that women are reaching out to take part with men in the labour of the world, some form of protection for them is necessary, particularly when young women gravitate toward the large cities."[27] He added that the "home influence" of the YWCA Boarding House would be the best protection for "women adrift" in Toronto. Under the scrutiny of her family, or the keen eye of a mistress, a young woman was assumed to be safely anchored, but under a foreman's control for a mere sixty or seventy hours per week, or even less in periods of unemployment, the female worker seemed to be adrift in a sea of urban dangers and temptations. Members of the YWCA feared that the lack of communal, religious, and family supervision of women's free time created a vacuum that drew working women directly to vice.

In the late nineteenth century, though, the waif-like figure of the "woman adrift" commanded less public attention than the male members of the "dangerous classes."[28] Whereas working women were pitied, working-class men were feared on account of their alleged taste for public gambling and carousing — activities that led all too often to crime and violence. Accordingly, such organizations as the WCTU emphasized *male* vice in their campaign against immorality. They stressed that it was but a short trip (literally only a few steps, in some drinking establishments) from the saloon to the brothel, and from there to family breakdown and crime. The election of W.H. Howland as a reform mayor in 1886 signalled the Toronto electorate's support for a crusade against dissolute pleasure. Shortly after taking office Howland created a morality branch, and its director, Staff Inspector David

Archibald, diligently set about raiding Toronto's brothels, gambling dens, and saloons, the "most obvious threats to civic virtue" in their view. Complaints about the sweeping powers of the Morality Department show that disorderly drunks, vagrants, brothel "inmates," and young boys were the primary targets of Archibald's program to cleanse Toronto's blighted landscape.[29]

The heated debate over Sunday streetcars in the early 1890s revealed the belief of respectable Torontonians that the growth and increasing concentration of the poor in "the Ward" had produced a corresponding rise in vice. Sabbatarians gloomily predicted that if Sunday was violated by the intrusions of streetcars, Toronto would be threatened further by the "temporal adversities, poverty and misery" that already plagued nations which did not observe the Sabbath. Those who backed Sunday cars protested that their support "by no means involve[d] the desire for the open saloon or improper amusements"; rather they optimistically predicted that this urban amenity would actually lead to an improvement in the moral tone of the poor and thereby of the city as a whole. Sunday cars were touted as vehicles that would allow the poor and working class of Toronto to escape their unhealthy, cramped, unattractive dwellings for greenery, fresh air, and relaxation, if only for a few hours a week. And since the backers of Sunday cars believed that the city's beaches and parklands were more attractive than the littered laneways of the Ward, they predicted that the poor would no longer drift into the saloons and gambling dens, the breeding grounds of vice and crime.[30] The five-year battle for Sunday streetcars ended in the defeat of the Sabbatarians and a partial victory for those who asserted that the poor and not simply the "leisure-class" had the right to enjoy healthful amusement. Yet this right was highly qualified by the concept of what constituted legitimate leisure activities. Sunday car backers had painted bucolic pictures of families picnicking on river banks and stalwart men testing their athletic skill on playing fields, but they were as critical of youth "intent only upon spreeing" as were the Sabbatarians. Neither of these two factions, however, reserved a place for working-class women's amusement anywhere but in the context of family outings. In the dialogues between the various governmental and philanthropic groups that aimed to elevate Toronto's moral tone in the late nineteenth century, the "woman adrift" was discussed less as a source than as a victim of urban vice.

By the second decade of the twentieth century, when efforts to re-establish order in the urban community included an attack on Toronto's growing commercial amusement industry, the subject of working women did come to dominate public discussions of immorality. Indeed, Progressive literature, including the social survey, discussed vice overwhelmingly in relation to working women's pleasures. Urban reformers attributed sexual meanings to the increasing visibility of women's work and play. By 1912 an estimated 40,000 women were working for as little as $5 a week. Yet the "problem of the working girl," as it came to be defined in mainstream newspaper columns, mass circulation magazines, and philanthropic organizations, was not a class issue but rather a moral dilemma. Women's entry en masse into an industrial work force dominated by unethical men seemed, to these self-appointed spokespersons for working women, to herald a "grave and generalized social crisis."[31] Jane Addams had expressed the Progressives' sense of crisis in a 1908 address on the amoral state of women workers in "the modern industrial city":

> Never before in civilization have such numbers of girls been suddenly released from the protection of home and permitted to walk unattended upon city streets and to work under alien roofs. For the first time in history they are being prized more for their labor power than for their innocence, their tender beauty, their ephemeral gaiety.[32]

The new forms of pleasure provided by the expanding commercial amusement industry only underlined the suspicion that the freedom of waged labour had led women astray as well as set them adrift. Fixed hours and wage labour made leisure possible for women in a way that other forms of women's work (notably the domestic labour of servants, young daughters, and married women) did not. Although working women remained constrained by their parents' expectations that they would contribute to the family economy, as well as not dishonour the family through promiscuous behaviour, the changing conditions of single, working-class women's labour did open up new possibilities for leisure pursuits. Unlike both bourgeois and working-class women who did not earn money, they were able to socialize with co-workers and participate in public amusements in ways that more closely resembled the leisure patterns of working-class men. And female wage earners who flaunted their working-class finery on downtown streets had a bold public style that asserted their intention to claim the same freedoms in their pursuit of pleasure that were traditionally granted only to men. Progressives challenged the legitimacy of these claims by expressing their fear that working women's taste for fun would divert them from their duties to their families, their employers, and later to their husbands and children. For members of the Social Survey Commission, an analysis of Toronto's vice problem necessarily entailed mapping out the contested terrain of women's leisure.

The survey report reflected the investigators' belief that the immorality of women's leisure pursuits outweighed the problems they were mandated to explore, namely, commercial vice and white slavery. With noteworthy lack of concern, they dismissed houses of ill-fame and resorts of assignation as reasonably discreet and few in number, and as for white slavery, they concluded that there was no evidence that an organized traffic in women operated in the city. The equanimity with which they regarded commercialized vice was based on their belief in the potency of the law as a remedy for social problems. The Toronto police were not as effective in stamping out the city's red light districts as the law permitted, but the commissioners suggested that with greater vigilance and stiffer sentencing, the force's fight against commercialized vice would succeed. More troubling for them was the seriousness of a phenomenon they felt neither the law nor the police could attack directly, that of "occasional prostitution." The survey admitted that "out-and-out prostitutes, as a class, [were] known to have existed always, and in a large city their presence in considerable numbers [was] more or less to be expected." But this new form of vice seemed not to be containable within an easily defined class of fallen women, or even within the physical borders of the red light district. Illicit sex had long been associated with disorder (as "disorderly house," the legal synonym for "brothel" makes clear); yet segregated prostitution offered respectable citizens the sense that immorality could at least be confined to the "lower orders" within the physical borders of their urban dens.[33] "Occasional prostitution," however, unleashed sexual disorder upon the entire community. Surveying this scene of generalized vice prompted the investigators to predict:

> [When] more or less thoroughly commercialized immorality invades offices, shops and factories, takes up its abode in apartment and rooming houses, or even in the home, and lurks in amusement resorts, in such a form that those engaged in it are not a segregated and despised class, but outwardly respectable, and with a definite standing in the world of business and industry, there is a very much more serious situation.[34]

What did these moral surveyors mean by "occasional prostitution?" According to their definition, "women who, while living an immoral life, did not depend wholly on the proceeds of prostitution" could be labelled occasional prostitutes.[35] What constituted an immoral life, however, was not as well defined. It appears that women who socialized with a variety of men out of a desire for fun and not necessarily marriage conformed to the investigators' notion of prostitutes, though the lack of a clear monetary payment for sexual favours made them hesitate to place them with the "out-and-outs."[36] The women they called "occasionals" or "semi-professionals" were sometimes married women or young daughters who still lived at home, but more often they were working women who either worked during the day to avoid suspicion about their night-time trade or who worked legitimately, and "in the phrase of their circle 'sported on the side.'" Occasionals admitted that they "sported" out of a desire "'for fun' or 'for a good time,'" phrases the investigators translated into young women's search for "sexual passion," plus the "suppers, shows and drinks their male associates provided" in exchange for sexual gratification.[37] Absent from this picture were the seduced innocent and the degraded fallen woman: in their place was the coquettish working woman — the "good times" girl.

One explanation the Social Survey Commissioners considered to account for the rise of this figure on Toronto's social landscape was the possibility that low wages rendered working women dependent on men for money and material goods. The report in fact went to some length to consider whether poverty could be the prime motive for prostitution. Most women, it declared, earned between $6 and $9 a week, though some were paid as little as $5. Those who boarded, of course, suffered the greatest hardships, and many reported that they were often forced to choose between food and a roof. "It is plain," the report stated, "that the pressure of poverty must be felt often very keenly by very many working women and girls." Despite these telling observations, the investigators were convinced that working women's meagre wages were neither the only nor the chief cause of professional and semi-professional prostitution. The temptation to supplement wages with gifts or money was great, they admitted, "but most girls in such positions successfully resist[ed] the pressure and retain[ed] their virtue."[38] The commissioners concluded that long periods of unemployment and the need to earn enough for food and lodging could hardly explain the extent of working women's immorality since such a high proportion of "occasional" and professional prostitutes were domestics — women assured of meals and a home. Their portrayal of women's work as a moral test rather than as a class issue meant that poverty and alienation were never more than minor considerations in their explanations for vice.

In the social surveyors' search for the leading cause of urban immorality, they briefly considered a number of alternative explanations. They had already dismissed white slavery and were relatively certain that, aside from a few Jewish and Italian pimps tucked away discreetly in the Ward, there were not many procurers in the city. As moral reformers who looked for environmental causes of social disorder, they turned their attention to the troubling features of city life that they believed had led to a breakdown in morality. The growth of Toronto's commercial leisure industry caused especial concern because it encouraged a degree of heterosexual familiarity that reformers did not connect to the established patterns of courtship.[39] Investigators claimed that urban amusements were modern dens of iniquity disguised as pleasure resorts. Restaurants and ice cream parlours, where young men and women liked to meet over meals and treats, were actually "cloaks for the traffic in vice." Toronto's commercial amusement parks were equally suspect, since young women reportedly mingled with men who "picked them up and paid their way to various booths." In the winter, ice rinks contributed to the growth of vice since unescorted women were observed to allow "unknown men to accost and skate with them." But the worst offenders were the movie theatres and dance halls. In the dimly lit corners of nickelodeons, undue familiarity might easily take place between patrons, and in dance halls, undue familiarity seemed to be the object of the price of admission, the investigators concluded after they had seen men "dancing with girls they did not know." Since there were no chaperons, the surveyors assumed that the patrons themselves appreciated the "prevalence of immorality" when they visited the city's dance halls.[40] The spectacular growth of the leisure industry, from nine places of amusement in 1900 to 112 by 1915,[41] gave Toronto's moral overseers reason to fear that working women's taste for good times would find an increasing number of outlets. Thus there appeared to be a vicious cycle in which commercial amusements whetted young people's appetite for dubious pleasures and thereby created a demand for entrepreneurs to expand their facilities. Because the social surveyors believed that working women's familiarity with casual male acquaintances was tantamount to occasional prostitution, the city's leisure scene became a prime target in their war against vice. Their mission in the years following the report was to restore order to the "unregulated sexual market place."[42]

Progressives had little faith that women themselves could be trusted to impose the limits necessary to channel heterosexual familiarity into courtship and to confine sex within marriage. It was women's apparent freedom and independence in their leisure hours, more than anything else, that led the investigators to assume that intervention was necessary to re-establish sexual order. They pronounced Toronto's moral atmosphere unsatisfactory because it had become fouled by "the free and promiscuous intercourse of the sexes in public dances, [and by] the readiness with which young girls enter[ed] into conversations with strangers at public rinks, and ma[d]e free with young men to whom they ha[d] not been introduced."[43] They believed that women's contact with the world through urban wage labour stripped them of the modesty that had supposedly preserved female chastity in the rural past. Since women's work had become essential to the growth of labour-intensive industries in the city, however, it was hardly feasible to send them back to the country; instead, the reformers tried to steer women away from "good times." One approach was to reinforce existing morals laws and to urge stricter policing of the streets and parks where women could easily make the acquaintance of strange men. Another was to channel women's search for fun away from commercialized amusement and into organized recreation. These divergent approaches to the vice problem both stemmed from the larger attempt to establish order in the urban sexual environment.

The Progressives' most direct attack on the vice problem came in their calls for a more coherent criminal justice system that would emphasize reform rather than punishment. The Social Survey Commissioners were advocating such an approach when they recommended more arrests, longer sentences, and fewer options to pay fines, even in the case of juveniles, first offenders, and petty criminals.[44] The theory was that a strict system of reform at the first sign of criminal tendencies would ultimately benefit the individual offenders and the society to which they would be returned. In practice, however, Progressive penal theory weighed heavily on young, working-class women.[45] Often, it was not so much a young woman's behaviour as her location and the time of day or night that left her vulnerable to apprehension by the police. This is evident in prison and police records. Arrest reports frequently mentioned that women were apprehended as morals offenders if they could not give a satisfactory justification for their presence at night on one of the city's streets without parental supervision or a respectable male escort. The assumption in virtually all cases of female juvenile delinquency or vagrancy was that the woman must have had an immoral purpose for appearing in public beyond normal work hours. The superintendent of the provincial women's reformatory, Emma O'Sullivan, painted the entire inmate population (most of whom were serving sentences of a year or more for vagrancy or related morals offences) as "sex offenders," or what the social survey investigators might have called "occasionals."[46] With juveniles, it was enough to assume that a young woman had *probably* engaged in sexual misconduct. In 1917, for instance, a seventeen-year-old named Mary was apprehended in the company of another young woman at midnight on a downtown street. Though her companion was allowed to go home to her parents, Mary was sent to Toronto's Catholic training school for an indeterminate period of up to four years. When her parents engaged a lawyer to petition for her release after two years' detention, the head of the Toronto Children's Aid Society replied that Mary could be detained for the full term of her sentence because "she admitted wrongdoing with a man the night prior to her arrest" and because a doctor had determined that she was "mentally weak."[47] The mother superior of this training school labelled another inmate "unusually depraved," stating, "she is somewhat proud of the fact that she had been 'going around' as she terms it, for more than a year." Eva, a sixteen-year-old arrested on a typically vague charge of "petty crime," was equally defiant in her defence of her leisure pursuits. In juvenile court, testimony was introduced to the effect that she liked to go out in "autos" with young men and with girls older than she was. Eva declared that after working as a waitress during the day, she enjoyed spending her evenings at the shows. A Children's Aid worker added that "she assumed a defiant attitude and used very bad language." Such damning evidence of inappropriate leisure activities and Eva's unfeminine defence of her right to her pleasures earned her an indefinite term of up to six years.[48]

The justification for such long sentences for young women was the assumption that the purpose of the training school or reformatory was to re-educate morals offenders so that they would adopt the attitudes and behaviour deemed suitable to their class and gender. Both vagrancy and delinquency were *de facto* status offences in the eyes of keepers; to change the *status* of the offender — to re-form her — necessarily required extraordinarily long sentences. Reformatory records also suggest that penologists were influenced by a conservative impulse to resist the economic and social changes that drew working-class women from domestic service into the world of wage labour and exposed them to the temptations of urban amusements. One of Toronto's training school superintendents, for example, attributed what she believed to be an increase in female delinquency to working-class girls' inadequate training in sewing, cooking, and housework. Teaching "these most important lessons," she predicted, would help to keep them "off the streets."[49] Since most inmates were charged with offences that penologists connected to a lack of moral supervision, incarceration provided an opportunity for remedial lessons in domestic skills in addition to character reformation through the inculcation of proper attitudes. "It takes much longer to drive out bad habits," stated the reformatory matron, Emma O'Sullivan, "than to establish good ones."[50]

The good habits that she, like her colleagues, tried to develop in her charges were obedience, self-control, and diligence — all qualities highly desirable in a maid or a wife. Preparing a young morals offender to take a situation as a domestic (often the only route to parole or early release) was doubly beneficial: not only did it replenish the dwindling ranks of women willing to work in service; in addition, it ensured that the released prisoner would have little free time. O'Sullivan recommended that one of her reformatory inmates be paroled into domestic service because "a mistress with sufficient time and patience and with the power of enforcing her commands could do quite as much or more perhaps than commitment."[51] If no situation was available, then requests for domestic help from a young woman's family were usually deemed sufficient to secure a release. The overriding goal of reformatory commitment, however, was to set the morals offender back on the path that would lead to marriage and a family. Instruction in domesticity was intended to make inmates "so devoted to and skilfull at domestic chores" that they might attract prospective husbands on the lookout for dedicated housekeepers. If the prisoner did not marry upon release, she could still support herself by working in a respectable household.[52] In either case, reformatory officials could assure themselves that released inmates would lead home-centred lives under the supervision of guardians who had a vested interest in retaining the woman's domestic labour.

Penologists did concede that a strict regimen and domestic training might prove insufficient to the daunting task of character reformation. Prison superintendents were haunted by the knowledge that they could oversee women in prisons and even provide careful supervision in parolees' own homes or in situations upon release, but, as O'Sullivan observed, "we surely cannot protect them in our own streets."[53] To counter this problem, several superintendents spearheaded a penal recreation movement that would pit "systematic and enlightened recreation" against the lure of commercial amusements. Disciplined exercise and organized play were presented as necessary antidotes to the dissolute tendencies of women who were "products of a poorly planned and badly organized social life."[54] Progressive educators and members of the playground movement voiced similar sentiments. "This stupid experiment of organizing work and failure to organize play," an exasperated Jane Addams complained, had turned the normal "love of pleasure ... into all sorts of malignant and vicious appetites."[55] Toronto's social survey was in tune with the Progressive program to rationalize the urban leisure scene and to instill a desire for respectable pleasure among the city's youth. The leisure problem would not be solved, the social survey commissioners warned, by simply suppressing the injurious commercial amusements, but also by providing a wider range of "beneficial and wholesome" diversions.[56] Recreation was a compromise between the fast-paced excitements and temptations of the city and the commissioners' idealized vision of home-based, family, and Church-oriented leisure pursuits.

Recreation became the elixir in the reformers' formula for a refurbished moral and social order: "without it," they predicted, "our young people—and adults too, for that matter—will degenerate both in body and in mind."[57] The recreational schemes suggested in the survey report harked back to a time of non-commercial pleasures, yet they also looked forward to a future where Canadian youth would assume their proper places in the modern industrial order. Ideally, recreation would not corrupt morals as commercial amusements reportedly had done; rather it would pave the road to responsible citizenship and economic growth. The commissioners declared, "[Recreation] increases efficiency, and makes its subject better able to earn a living and 'make good' in the struggle of life; and it thus cultivates self-respect and self-control."[58] When it came to working women, they recommended that employers provide a social secretary who would supervise their leisure for the promotion alike of "health, morals and efficiency."[59] Recreation permitted none of the freedoms that commercial amusements allowed young women in their promiscuous mingling with men. In vigorous, outdoor exercise and well-supervised indoor sports, women and girls were to learn rules and respect for the authority of their leader. Thus the well-ordered basketball or volleyball team could foster the ideal of a restored sexual order for recreation enthusiasts.

Members of the playground movement were at the forefront of the Progressives' efforts to alter the urban landscape.[60] The first national organization to promote the construction of supervised play spaces for inner-city children was the Playground Association of America.[61] Soon after it was founded in 1906, Canadian women's groups began to lobby municipal governments to build playgrounds for the children of the urban poor. The TLCW approached City Hall in 1908 in the hope of convincing local politicians that the investment of a few dollars in playgrounds would save thousands in the future by fostering a happier, healthier citizenry.[62] By 1914, there were nine supervised playgrounds in Toronto plus a rapidly growing number of parks, ice rinks, tennis courts, and baseball diamonds[63] — all evidence of the civic commitment to bring about a "healthy, moral and intelligent community" by "properly provid[ing] for human instincts."[64] Settlement house workers urged that the restorative and reformative benefits of recreation be offered to the poor of all ages. Though they continued to concentrate on youth, they became spokespersons for the principles of disciplined play throughout the community. The investigators on the Toronto Social Survey Commission supported their efforts, declaring "Few things are of more importance to the general health and moral tone of any community than provision for healthy, satisfactory recreation."[65] In supplying alternatives to dance halls, amusement resorts, and movie houses they hoped to attract the city's poor to leisure activities that would sublimate rather than stimulate their sexual longings.

Several voluntary social service and reform organizations concentrated on young working-class women in their campaign to reshape urban leisure patterns at the same time that juvenile authorities and the police were focusing on the same women in their crackdown against vice. Some groups failed because of their rigid, openly moralistic attempts at character reformation. Such was the case in 1912 when the WCTU advocated that Toronto's working women form clubs dedicated to the eradication of "undesirable dress, deportment and conversation."[66] Other groups were slightly more aware of their constituents' desire for fun, even if they were unwilling to provide fast-paced amusements. The women who helped found the Toronto branch of the Big Sisters' Movement in 1912 were committed to providing "friendly intervention and supervision" while they taught their charges "the art of having a good time in a wise and safe way."[67] One of the Big Sisters' brochures cautioned volunteers against adopting a superior attitude toward "her girl" while at the same time it underlined the social gulf that separated the respectable lady from the "good times" girl: "Don't patronize," it warned, "you may know more about virtue, but the girl is probably a better expert on temptation."[68] The Big Sisters fought an uphill battle in their attempt to compete in the city's leisure market. Six years after they were founded, for instance, they decided that a "Little Sisters' Club House" would "offset the influence of unsupervised dance halls where far too many girls went to find doubtful forms of amusement." The club opened in 1918, featuring "safe, pleasant surroundings" to amuse the more than 500 girls under their supervision. Despite a large expenditure of $3,000 for a tennis court and an ice rink, they could not attract enough girls to warrant the expense. "A few lost interest after a while," a Big Sister explained, "admitting frankly to a preference for the public dance halls, and the company of young men who possessed or were able to borrow automobiles."[69] By 1920, they attempted to draw "pre-delinquent" girls under their influence as well through their art classes, dramatic clubs, debating societies, and sewing groups in the hope that filling leisure time with "wholesome activities" would prevent delinquency. Their efforts to offer a compromise between strict control over women's free time and the looseness of commercial amusement often backfired, however. Working girls with a taste for good times continued to find the Big Sisters' diversions dull, while more serious-minded girls found their activities frivolous. In 1921, faced with large expenses and small victories, the Big Sisters abandoned their recreational schemes to concentrate on case work.

The YWCA proved to be more successful in its attempts to substitute recreation for commercial pleasures. The Y leaders were veterans in the crusade to improve working women's leisure activities, and by the early twentieth century they had begun to learn from previous failures. As early as 1883 the executive of the Toronto YWCA declared it would "provide some legitimate amusement for [members] in order to prevent them from attending questionable places of amusement." Their solution, the "Girls' Friendly Society" never caught on with Toronto's young women, perhaps because the "amusements" it offered consisted of classes in practical bookkeeping and domestic skills.[70] The next generation of YWCA leaders was more responsive to popular leisure tastes. By granting its members a degree of self-determination in their recreational pursuits, they attracted and sustained the interest of a large clientele of working women. In 1921, the Toronto YWCA board pointed proudly to its roster of 3,000 members, over 2,600 of whom were single and employed. Spokeswomen for the organization stressed that their earlier emphasis on evangelical care had become outmoded.[71] They demonstrated their fresh approach to their clientele through their growing support for women's recreation. After much lobbying from the residents of YWCA houses, for instance, the dance committee grudgingly approved of "no more than one dance per month" to be chaperoned by at least two senior members. When it came to single-sex sports and outdoor exercise, however, the YWCA provided unequivocal support for working women's right to leisure. A pamphlet on YWCA work in the "home field," asserted, "All Girls Need Fun, " especially after a full day of monotonous work. "Commercialized Amusements are quick to take advantage of this, but so often the amusement provided is of a character detrimental to the best interest of the girl." The aim of the YWCA in contrast, was to organize "wholesome, clean recreation to keep life normal."[72] In swimming classes, baseball games, and folk dancing, women learned the importance of following rules, co-operating with their peers, and developing team spirit. The YWCA thereby tried to provide its members with a brand of leisure shorn of its subversive potential. Their aim in recreation was to de-sexualize fun while developing "loyalty to Home, School and Church" — the three elements necessary to "keep life normal."[73]

By the 1920s, organizations like the YWCA had conferred a new legitimacy to working women's leisure. Ironically, the recreationists began to worry about the working girl who did *not* want to have fun, because she was a subject who was difficult to reach. Reformers feared that such women would fail to develop healthy bodies and healthy attitudes if they did not adopt a play discipline to supplement the work discipline demanded of them by their employers. Recreational leaders encouraged working-class women to be efficient employees and dutiful daughters while they were working; yet they never lost sight of their goal to prepare young women for their future roles as wives and mothers. Well-supervised recreation was designed to keep girls and women from sinking into dubious pleasures, while at the same time organized games and sports would permit them to satisfy their appetite for fun before settling down. And working-class marriage and motherhood had nothing to do with fun, as a training school superintendent reminded a recently married ex-inmate:

> When a woman has a husband and child it is time for
> her to be very gentle and modest in all her ways. She
> can be cheerful and happy, but her days for fooling
> ought to be over.... You can be friendly and pleasant,
> but never forget that you are a wife and mother now.[74]

As long as working women's leisure did not entail unsupervised heterosexual familiarity, it did not threaten to disrupt her path toward producing healthy children within the sanctity of marriage. And if having fun involved games that taught respect for authority and rules, it received enthusiastic support from those who considered the young working-class woman an important source of cheap labour and also a valuable tool for raising the moral standards of her class. Wholesome and clean recreation was therefore both an antidote to sexual disorder and a blueprint for the stabilization of gender and class relations.

In prisons and on playing fields, Toronto's Progressives sought solutions to the problems they had constructed out of the changing forms of women's work and leisure in the city. That the social survey commissioners' exploration of vice led them to Toronto's commercial amusements is evidence that they approached the leisure scene as contested moral terrain. The surveyors' emphasis on women's public leisure pursuits suggests, however, that they regarded working-class women's pastimes as an index of urban morality. If "working girls" flaunted their finery unreservedly on the city's downtown streets and made dates with strange men at dance halls, they expressed a brand of sexual autonomy that the investigators could understand only as "occasional prostitution." Women's spirited pursuit of commercial pleasures raised fears that the Queen City had turned into a "Modern Babylon" of materialism and sexual gratification. For Toronto to become a "City upon a Hill," working-class women would have to alter their taste for amusement. Some, like the young women sent to training schools for four or five years, learned the hard way that their right to find their own amusement was extremely limited, while those who participated in recreation programs received subtler lessons about the boundaries that circumscribed working women's fun. Whether guilty or innocent of moral transgressions, though, the "working girl" was a prime target in the Progressives' attempt to rationalize social organization by eliminating urban sexual disorder.

NOTES

An earlier version of this paper was presented during the Berkshire Conference of Women's Historians at Wellesley College in June 1987. I would like to thank Suzanne Lebsock, Mariana Valverde, and the other members of the Informal Economy Study Group for their helpful criticisms. Karen Whyte assisted in the production of the final draft.

1   References to modern cities as Babylon were common in this period, but the most famous reference comes from William Stead's series on vice in London, called "The Maiden Tribute of Modern Babylon." See R. Schults, *Crusader in Babylon: W. T. Stead and the Pall Mall Gazette* (Lincoln, Nebraska: University of Nebraska Press, 1972).

2   See Robert Wiebe, *The Search for Order, 1877-1920* (New York: Hill and Wang, 1967), for the classic assessment of Progressives as reformers who tried to establish order in "modern" life. For a somewhat darker view of the "search for order" in Canada, see Carol Bacchi, *Liberation Deferred: The Ideas of English Canadian Suffragists, 1877-1914* (Toronto: University of Toronto Press, 1983).
3   Theodore Dreiser, *Sister Carrie* (Harmondsworth: Penguin, 1981 [1900]), p. 47.
4   In this paper, I will use "Progressivism" to label early twentieth-century Canadian as well as American urban reform. The term seems particularly appropriate for Toronto, where reformers looked to American cities (especially Chicago) for guidance on the improvement of urban living.
5   Michael Piva, *The Condition of the Working Class in Toronto, 1900 to 1921* (Ottawa: University of Ottawa Press, 1979), pp. 8-13.
6   James Lemon, *Toronto Since 1918: An Illustrated History* (Toronto: James Lorimer, 1985), p. 13.
7   Piva, *The Condition,* p. 58.
8   John P. S. McLaren, "Chasing the Social Evil: Moral Fervour and the Evolution of Canada's Prostitution Laws, 1867-1917," *Canadian Journal of Law and Society* (No. 1, 1986), 125-65, p. 149.
9   Mariana Valverde, "Constructing National and Sexual Purity — the 'White Slave' Panic in Canada, 1910-1925," paper presented at the Centre of Criminology, University of Toronto, Oct. 13, 1987.
10   Archives of Ontario (hereafter AO) Ontario, Attorney General of Ontario, Files, Criminal and Civil, 1912.
11   Toronto, Social Survey Commission, *Report of the Social Survey Commission, Toronto, Presented to the City Council, October Fourth, 1915* (Toronto: Carswell, 1915), p. 7. Both the Chicago and New York Commissions devoted the bulk of their reports to an examination of sexual immorality, whereas the Methodist and Presbyterian surveys dealt with a wide variety of concerns, including housing, health, unemployment, and church attendance. In most of those reports, sex received little of the authors' attention. In focusing on "existing vice and social disease," then, the Toronto commission followed more closely the American than the Canadian genre of urban survey reports in the early twentieth century.
12   The Vice Commission of Chicago, *The Social Evil in Chicago: A Study of Existing Conditions* (Chicago: Gunthrop-Warren, 1911), pp. 1, 55-65, passim. Between 1911 and 1913, eleven U.S. cities published vice reports, eight of which were published in 1913 alone.
13   Lemon, *Toronto,* p. 17.
14   Roger Riendeau, "Servicing the Modern City, 1900-1930," in Victor Russell, ed., *Forging a Consensus: Historical Essays on Toronto* (Toronto: University of Toronto Press, 1984), 157-80, p. 159.
15   Horatio C. Hocken, "The New Spirit in Municipal Government," Canada Club, Ottawa *Addresses* (1914-1915), 85.
16   Toronto, *Report,* p. 3. The twenty-two member Commission included three women: TLCW President Mrs. Heustis; social worker Elizabeth Neufeld; and St. James (Anglican) Rectory representative Adelaide Plumptre.
17   The scientific language of the Progressives obscured their highly subjective interpretations of the social phenomena they explored. The Chicago commission, for instance, claimed that it would expose "conditions as they exist" and base its conclusions, not on preconceived notions, but on "incontrovertible facts" (Chicago, *The Social Evil,* pp. 1, 32). The Progressives' extensive use of statistics has led some historians to assume that they were at least on the road to rationality. John McLaren, for instance, argues that reformers turned what might have been "rational law reform" in regard to prostitution into a moral panic: "the predominance of rhetoric and [their] tendency to avoid the discus-

sion of social data meant that the exact character and extent of the problem which the social purity crusaders were fighting was typically obscured" (McLaren, "Chasing the Social Evil," pp. 153-4). Likewise, Lori Rotenberg uses the Toronto Social Survey Report's "social data" on vice uncritically in her description of prostitution at the turn of the century and never questions the report's use of ill-defined terms such as "occasional prostitution." See Lori Rotenberg, "The Wayward Worker: Toronto's Prostitute at the Turn of the Century," in Janice Acton, ed., *Women at Work. Ontario, 1850-1930* (Toronto: Canadian Women's Educational Press, 1974), pp. 33-69.

18 Toronto, *Report*, p. 7.

19 Ibid., p. 8.

20 Gareth Stedman Jones, "Class Expression versus Social Control? A Critique of Recent Trends in the Social History of 'Leisure,'" in Jones, *The Languages of Class: Studies in English Working-Class History, 1832-1982* (Cambridge: Cambridge University Press, 1983), 76-89, p. 87.

21 Gregory S. Kealey, *Toronto Workers Respond to Industrial Capitalism, 1867-1892* (Toronto: University of Toronto Press, 1980).

22 *Census of Canada*, 1881, Vol. 2, pp. 292-303.

23 Ontario, Bureau of Industry, *Annual Report*, 1887, p. 28.

24 Ibid.

25 Lynn Weiner, *From Working Girl to Working Mother: The Female Labor Force in the U.S.* (Chapel Hill: University of North Carolina Press, 1895), chapter one, "Woman Adrift: The Era of the Working Girl."

26 Diana Pedersen, "'A Building for Her:' The YWCA in the Canadian City", *Urban History Review*, 15 (No. 3, Feb. 1987), 225-41, p. 227.

27 AO, Toronto YWCA, Minutes, May 1881.

28 See Paul S. Boyer, *Urban Masses and Moral Order in America, 1820-1920* (Cambridge: Cambridge University Press, 1978) for an analysis of changing conceptions of urban moral order in the United States.

29 Christopher Armstrong and H.V. Nelles, *The Revenge of the Methodist Bicycle Company: Sunday Streetcars and Municipal Reform in Toronto, 1888-1897* (Toronto: Peter Martin, 1977), pp. 7-8, and C.S. Clark, *Of Toronto the Good* (Toronto: Coles 1970 [1898]), pp. 19-27 passim.

30 Armstrong and Nelles, *The Revenge*, pp. 108, 58.

31 Alice Klein and Wayne Roberts, "Besieged Innocence: The 'Problem' and the Problems of Working Women, Toronto, 1896-1914," in Acton, ed., *Women at Work*, 211-59, pp. 211-12.

32 Jane Addams, "Address by Miss Jane Addams," *The Playground*, 2 (No. 13, 1908), 25-8, p. 26.

33 Neil Shumsky, "Tacit Acceptance: Respectable Americans and Segregated Prostitution, 1870-1910," *Journal of Social History*, 19 (No. 4, 1986), 665-81.

34 Toronto, *Report*, p. 13.

35 Ibid., p. 12.

36 In New York such women were labelled "Charity Girls." See Kathy Peiss, *Cheap Amusements: Working Women and Leisure in Turn-of-the-Century New York* (Philadelphia: Temple University Press, 1986), Chap. 4.

37 Toronto, *Report*, pp. 12-13.

38 Ibid., p. 36.

39 For an illustration of fears that young women were trading sexual favours for fun instead of marriage, see Mrs. Alice Kinney Wright's sermon, "Keep thyself pure," quoted in Clark, *Of Toronto*, pp. 185-87. She heaped praise upon the "sweet, pure girl who says, 'I do not believe in allowing my gentlemen friends those privileges which rightfully belong to the man I intend to marry. I have not met him yet, but he is going to be a good man, and I will reserve all right to myself for him,'" p. 186.

40   Toronto, *Report*, pp. 11, 50-51.
41   Figures tabulated from the listings under "Places of Amusement" in the Toronto City Directory, *Might's Greater Toronto City Directory*, 1900-1915.
42   Steven Schlossman and Stephanie Wallach, "The Crime of Precocious Sexuality: Female Juvenile Delinquency and the Progressive Era," in D. Kelly Weisberg, ed., *Women and the Law: A Social Historical Perspective*. Vol. 1, *Women and the Criminal Law* (Cambridge, Mass.: Schenkman, 1982), 45-84, p. 57.
43   Toronto, *Report*, p. 56.
44   See McLaren, "Chasing the Social Evil," pp. 149-50 for a summary of ammend-ments to laws relating to prostitution in the Criminal Code Amendment Act (1913), 3 & 4 Geo. V, cap. 13.
45   Schlossman and Wallach, "The Crime," p. 47. Both the number of arrests and the periods of incarceration for crimes such as vagrancy jumped in the second decade of the century. Vagrancy was, and remains, an extremely ill defined offence. In practice, vagrancy was treated as a status offence, in that it reflected the arrestee's social and economic status rather than defined a specific crime. For an analysis of women charged with vagrancy in Ontario, see Carolyn Strange, "The Velvet Glove: Maternalistic Reform at the Andrew Mercer Ontario Reformatory for Females, 1874-1927" (M.A. thesis, University of Ottawa, 1983).
46   Ontario, Andrew Mercer Ontario Reformatory for Females, "Annual Report," *Sessional Papers*, 1919.
47   AO, Ontario, Ministry of Correctional Services, St. Mary's Training School, Case files (reel 1, Feb. 13, 1913).
48   Ibid., July 28, 1924, and May 13, 1919.
49   Lucy Brooking, quoted in Toronto, *Report*, p. 55.
50   AO, Ontario, Ministry of Correctional Services, Andrew Mercer Ontario Reformatory for Females, Case Files (no. 3682, April 12, 1907).
51   Ibid. (no. 3974, Apr. 15, 1913).
52   Schlossman and Wallach, "The Crime," p. 57.
53   "Committee on Reformatory Work and Parole," American Prison Association *Proceedings* 1910, p. 51.
54   Mrs. J. K. Codding, "Recreation for Women Prisoners," American Prison Association *Proceedings* 1912, 312-319, pp. 319 and 315.
55   Jane Addams, "Address by Miss Addams," p. 26.
56   Toronto, *Report*, p. 54.
57   Ibid.
58   Ibid., p. 56.
59   Ibid., p. 39.
60   The most comprehensive study of the importance of playgrounds to the recreation movement is Domenick Cavallo, *Muscles and Morals* (Philadelphia: University of Pennsylvania Press, 1981).
61   Paula D. Welch and Harold A. Lerch, *History of American Physical Education and Sport* (Springfield, Ill.: Charles C. Thomas, 1981), p. 67.
62   TLCW President, Mrs. Florence Heustis, was the local leader of the playground movement. See Paul Bator, "'Saving Lives on the Wholesale Plan:' Public Health Reform in the City of Toronto, 1900-1930" (Ph.D. thesis, University of Toronto, 1979), pp. 117-18.
63   Riendeau, "Servicing the Modern City," p. 167. Spending on parks, recreation, schools, libraries, and welfare services in Toronto grew from $5 per capita in 1900 to $35 per capita in 1930.
64   Hocken, "The New Spirit," p. 85.
65   Toronto, *Report*, p. 54.
66   Toronto *Star*, May 1, 1912, p. 16.

67 Helen Robinson, *Decades of Caring: The Big Sister Story* (Toronto: Dundurn, 1979),
    p. 20. Settlement house organizer Dr. Ware felt that ladies of the leisure class
    were naturally endowed with the ability to teach sewing, cooking, and the "art
    of having a good time." He used this argument to explain the disproportionate
    number of women engaged in settlement house work. Wayne Roberts, "'Rock-
    ing the Cradle for the World': The New Woman and Maternal Feminism,
    Toronto, 1877-1914," in Linda Kealey, ed., *A Not Unreasonable Claim: Women and
    Reform in Canada, 1880s to 1920s* (Toronto: Women's Press, 1979), 15-45, p. 33.
68 Undated brochure quoted in Robinson, *Decades of Caring*, p. 34.
69 Ibid., pp. 38, 42.
70 AO, Toronto YWCA, Minutes, 1883.
71 Wilena Crawford, "Recreation for Girls," *Social Welfare*, 5 (Aug. 1923), 232.
72 AO, Dominion YWCA, "The Home Field," n.d., p. 8.
73 Ibid., p. 5.
74 AO, Alexandra Case Files, (Mar. 14, 1913).

ONTARIO WORKERS AND THE DECLINE OF LABOURISM

James Naylor

As the year of the Winnipeg General Strike and the emergence of the One Big Union, 1919 was a landmark in Canadian working-class history. Yet dramatic class confrontations were not confined to western Canada. Ontario workers were similarly angry at their employers for using the war emergency to erode working conditions and for profiteering from the international catastrophe. They were frustrated by the relentless battle against soaring inflation, and feared an incipient "kaiserism" for, on the eve of the armistice, the government of Robert Borden had greatly expanded the powers of the federal state banning all meaningful forms of trade union activity through orders-in-council. In the spring and summer of 1919, such sentiments contributed to a level of industrial conflict unknown in the province's history. Over 35,000 workers left their jobs in strikes that hit entire industries, particularly the metal, building, and garment trades, and that culminated in the brief, but dramatic, Toronto General Strike in late May 1919.

Yet the end of the war also held great promise. Workers could hope that the wartime spirit of co-operation and sacrifice in the interests of democracy could be turned against class privilege on the home front. Such a campaign could be waged at the ballot box as well as on the picket line. Labour's arrival, that same year, as a significant, independent force in the Canadian electoral system has not received much attention from historians. Yet the achievements of labour on the "political" as well as the "industrial" front — to use the terminology of the day — were an integral part of the working-class upsurge in the era of the Great War and are crucial for understanding its character. Moreover, in spite of the attention given by historians to the west, it was Ontario workers who were in the vanguard of electoral action. In view of the scale of class conflict and the rapid emergence of a working-class political presence in Ontario, the *Globe's* assessment of the provincial election of October 20, 1919, as a "political revolution"[1] expressed a widespread feeling that great changes were in the offing. The contest had been fought between the old order and the new. For growing numbers of workers and farmers, the old parties — the Conservatives and the Liberals — seemed to belong to a world that had been destroyed by the Great War. The past five years had confirmed that they were political machines, tied to the "interests," and not truly interested in making the world safe for democracy, or entrenching it at home. The United Farmers of Ontario and the Independent Labor Party (ILP), which together overthrew Ontario's party system, were "natural allies" in the "Battle for Democracy" on the homefront.[2] As a local ILP secretary told an election rally on the eve of the victory, their candidate "represent[ed] the people and the Grit and Tory candidates merely represent[ed] the special interests which [had] permitted profiteering and exploitation of the people for their own benefit."[3] Through their elected members, Ontario's farmers and workers would at last hear their own voices at Queen's Park. The new order, it appeared, had been born.

In the provincial parliament, the new farmer and labour parties held power only narrowly: forty-five UFO and eleven ILP members sat on the government benches in a 111-seat legislature. Despite historians' preoccupation with these events as the precursor of the "agrarian revolt" of the 1920s, the urban component of this victory was no less significant. The Independent Labor Party of Ontario, scarcely more than two years old, had received 124,564 votes in the twenty-three constituencies it had contested. In Hamilton, Brantford, St. Thomas, Peterborough, Waterloo, St. Catharines, and Galt, as well as in smaller industrial towns across the province, Labor candidates placed first in the polls. In London, the ILP candidate defeated Adam Beck, Ontario's foremost champion of public ownership, itself a popular working-class cause. In the aftermath of the election, ILP activists celebrated the culmination of the long, slow advance toward independent working-class political action. Yet, for ILP partisans, the gains were ephemeral. Two years later, in the 1921 federal election, old party allegiances were re-established and only one ILP member made his way to Ottawa. In 1923 they were also unable to repeat their success in the provincial election.[4]

Why was the ILP unable to consolidate the gains it had made in 1919? In large part, the answer is to be found in the fortunes of the post-war trade union movement upon which the ILP was based. The party's base of support was shaken by union defeats during a severe economic depression beginning in mid-1920. But the vicissitudes of the labour movement can only partly explain the sudden collapse of independent working-class electoral power. Demoralization over trade-union defeats alone cannot explain why working-class voters abandoned the ILP in droves after 1919. Moreover, despite its long and deep roots in sections of the Ontario labour movement, "labourism" ceased to be a political tendency of any consequence in Ontario and soon disappeared. By the mid-1920s, those who espoused working-class political action could more properly be considered socialists, specifically social democrats or communists. This major political discontinuity can best be explained by examining the weaknesses in labourist ideology and the frustrations its proponents felt in the wake of its electoral breakthrough.

I

Essentially, labourism was little more than the impulse of skilled workers for direct access, as workers, to the halls of political power. The experiences of the war demonstrated forcefully to them the consequences of their exclusion. Labour shortages during the war created conditions for the growth of trade unions, but workplace struggles against individual firms proved less and less adequate in the face of more powerful employers and growing government intervention. Union struggles regularly brought workers face to face with the state, particularly the police and the courts, as well as with new government bodies such as the Imperial Munitions Board. Moreover, although organized workers had long intervened in municipal politics through local trades councils, the war drew them into a wider range of national issues. The mounting cost of living, the struggle for recognition of unions and shorter hours in war industries, and opposition to orders-in-council banning strikes combined to focus workers' attention on the state. A paucity of legislative gains in the wake of labour's annual "cap-in-hand" lobbying sessions with legislators convinced more and more workers of the need to send elected representatives, rather than delegations, to Ottawa and Toronto. Advocates of independent working-class political action found themselves receiving an unprecedented hearing in trades councils, local unions, and working-class neighbourhoods; the war revealed the class interests behind the old parties and convinced many workers that they could only rely on their own representatives in the nation's legislatures.

Although Independent Labor Parties were formed in city after city, the ideological break with the past was less dramatic. In fact, labourism's most notable feature was the absence of a systematic political program. When the Greater Toronto Labor Party was formed in 1917, for instance, the committee that was struck to draw up a "Declaration of Principles" had little enthusiasm for the task. "It is the belief of your committee," it reported, "that there is no necessity for the formation of an old-time party platform because their [sic] never was any virtue in any of them."[5] An organizer of the tailors' union expressed the same sentiment. A "hard and fast platform," he said, would cause "too much dissension." All that labour wanted, he added, was to have its representatives in power.[6] If the new labour party was truly democratic and acted in workers' interests, why would it be necessary to adopt a program? Along with corruption and patronage, election promises — usually empty — were part of the repertoire of the old parties and of the political system that sustained them. Programs only divided workers against themselves and maintained the "moneyed interests" in power. The ILP was out to defeat "partyism."

Despite such disclaimers, this political project reflected a substantial measure of political unanimity which was all the more remarkable given the decentralized nature of the Ontario labour movement. When fifty delegates representing sixteen local ILPs met to form a provincial party in Hamilton in July 1917, there was little disagreement on either the form or the substance of the new political movement.[7] Most notable was a faith that workers could gain power through electoral means. The reasoning of Joseph Marks, the editor of the region's main labour paper, the *Industrial Banner*, was implicitly accepted by all the delegates. "The under dogs are in the majority," he argued, "and the ballot paper marked by the horney handed twelve dollar per week paw is just as effective as the one marked by the five thousand dollar kid glove."[8] The inability of workers to use the ballot box effectively was due to a blind allegiance to the old parties and the manipulation of the political system by capitalists. Consequently the ILP's main demands were for the democratization of the political system. To this end, the core of the ILP's program demanded the abolition of property qualifications and election deposits, direct legislation — the initiative, referendum, and recall — and proportional representation. If unfair obstacles to working-class electoral expression could be removed and the grip of the old parties loosened by educating workers, labour's political power could no longer be restrained. This reinvigoration of the political system had its roots in a Radical Liberal tradition reminiscent of Gladstonian Liberalism in Britain and populism in the United States, whose mantle had clearly passed to the labour movement. Labourism did not go very much further, for the other elements in its program consisted of reforms embodying either immediate working-class goals, such as old age pensions and soldiers' pensions, or reforms proposed by social reformers from outside the labour movement, such as mothers' allowances and, occasionally, the single tax. Not only was such a program considered "moderate" by both friends and opponents of the party, the provincial ILP discounted its own demands by adding as a postscript:

> We believe that performance is better than promise, and we rest our claim for the support of the workers on the general declaration that we stand for the industrial freedom of those who toil, and the political liberation of those who have been denied justice.[9]

The election of representative workers to all levels of government was both the primary and ultimate goal of the movement.

Labourism had its strongest base in local trades and labour councils, which served to focus the otherwise disparate interests of skilled workers divided into separate craft unions. Whereas national and provincial labour organization was rudimentary, trades councils had a long history of intervention in local politics. As the *Industrial Banner* noted, trades councils had become centres of wartime militancy because they provided a forum for unionists who were increasingly concerned about the status and future of their class. Trades and labour councils, then, often took the initiative by nominating and supporting their own candidates for municipal office. In St. Catharines, a long-time alderman and secretary-treasurer of the trades council, James A. Wiley, was elected mayor in 1918. Harry Symons, secretary of the Brantford trades council, was elected alderman in 1917. In Kitchener, both the president and past president of the Twin City Trades and Labor Council, W.F. Gallagher and C.C. Hahn, were endorsed by the council and repeatedly elected as aldermen. The Peterborough trades council established a committee in 1915 to search for labour candidates to contest the municipal election, and the body's president, J.J. Hartley, made a strong bid for the mayoralty. President James Hughes of the Welland trades council was regularly re-elected alderman and was considered the "labor representative" on the town council. Although their electoral success varied, by the end of the war nearly every trades council in Ontario was participating directly in municipal politics by nominating "labour" candidates. For many, elected leadership in local labour bodies had become the stepping stone to public office. The weight of labour's endorsement could be seen in London, where two incumbent aldermen — Fred Daly and Henry Ashplant — sought the trades council's backing and regularly attended its meetings.[10]

In town after town, then, labourism was forged in municipal politics. Elaborate programs were unnecessary if labour's representatives on city council were answerable to a trades council that met, in most cases, fortnightly. Labour candidates' programs varied little from city to city: everywhere the main planks included municipal ownership of street railways, "fair wages" for civic workers, and improved educational opportunities for working-class children. The unanimity that existed among organized workers on such questions made debate superfluous. The selection and election of labour candidates were explicitly considered of greater importance.[11] A growing enthusiasm for labour representation and a concerted campaign carried on by Joseph Marks, through the *Industrial Banner*, led to the establishment of local Independent Labor Parties to carry out these tasks, but the individuals concerned and the political program remained the same. The 1919 provincial election campaign, although run by local labour parties (except in Port Arthur and Fort William where the trades council played this role) differed little from civic campaigns. The greatest emphasis was placed on selecting the candidates and getting out the vote. Once in Queen's Park, labour representatives would be guided by their debt to the labour movement, just as Liberal and Conservative MPPS were loyal to capital.

These developments were most apparent in Hamilton, where, with its strong tradition of craft unionism, labourism was most deeply entrenched as a political current. A local stove mounter, Allan Studholme, had been repeatedly elected as Labor MPP from Hamilton East since a street railway strike in 1906. At Queen's Park, Studholme had carefully maintained his political independence, despite overtures from the Liberals, while pushing organized labour's legislative program and supporting democratic rights, such as the enfranchisement of women.[12] At the same time, Studholme shared the ideological stance of his city's labour paper, the *Labour News:* opposition to socialism and violence, and support for the American Federation of Labor, the wage system, and "the justice of workers to collectively maintain a minimum scale for craftsmen."[13] Labourism did not directly challenge either the social order or the structure and ideology of the craft union movement. The two ILP members elected from Hamilton to the provincial legislature in 1919, Walter Rollo and George Halcrow, had solid credentials in the city's labour movement as leaders of both the trades council and the ILP. Unlike in smaller communities, labour political activity was directed by the local Independent Labor Party rather than the trades council. However, since both bodies were led by the same individuals, it is difficult to draw any real distinction between the two. Although Hamilton workers experienced their first electoral success at the provincial level, they too developed a community focus. In 1915 Halcrow became the Hamilton ILP's first alderman, and by 1919 the party elected two members of the board of control, five aldermen, a school trustee, and the Hydro commissioner. Their 1919 program stressed municipal "fair wages" and public ownership, but the main point was that labour must have "a fair hand" in reconstruction.[14]

In Toronto a pre-war Independent Labor Party had been little more than a Liberal appendage, and not a very successful one. Workers who found themselves drawn to independent political action were more likely to align themselves with the vigorous socialist movement in the city, which was dominated by the Social Democratic Party (SDP). On the eve of the war, the Toronto SDP had perhaps a thousand members and had succeeded in having one of its most prominent members, Jimmie

Simpson, elected to the board of control with the largest number of votes for the post in the city's history.[15] The growing sentiment for independent political action among non-socialist workers created a dilemma for the SDP and other socialist groups. Many were uneasy with the call made by Joseph Marks and Laura Hughes to "lay aside their Socialism in order to be united against the boss."[16] Nevertheless, the appeal had a certain logical consistency to socialists who, like their international counterparts before 1919, had engaged in revolutionary propaganda while their practical activity was confined to the tasks of organizing trade unions and fighting for reforms. Marks and Hughes were only suggesting that socialists and non-socialists unite electorally as they had done in the unions. Among the socialists who applauded the suggestion were those who, like Simpson, held leadership positions within the union movement.[17]

The 1917 federal slate of the Toronto ILP reflected this alliance. John Bruce and D.A. Carey — one a socialist, the other a conservative — had surprisingly little trouble in sharing the ILP platform. Local unions and the trades council contributed generously to the campaign.[18] By 1919 the Toronto ILP had 3,000 members and had undertaken a campaign to raise $25,000.[19] The first real sign of conflict did not arise until the abortive Toronto general strike of late May 1919 brought political differences to the fore.[20] Still, in the provincial election that followed, the majority of the city's unions rallied behind candidates who stood well to the left of those who ran outside Toronto. Although not elected, two socialists, John MacDonald, a central figure in the general strike, and Jimmie Simpson, each amassed a substantial number of votes in the industrial west end. Despite the relationship of forces in the Toronto labour movement favouring socialists, the campaign had a strongly labourist tone. "People to-day are disgusted with both political parties," MacDonald told an ILP rally shortly before the election. "They cannot get a corporal's guard at their meetings since patronage has gone out of business, and the labour movement will clarify politics."[21] The appeal for "straight" working-class representation, regardless of program, echoed that heard around the province. In view of the divisions in the labour movement in Toronto, only such a vague appeal could hold the electoral movement together. The decision of the Tories to run W.D. Robbins, a leader of the street railway union, and leading opponent of the general strike, against the ILP in Riverdale testifies to their recognition that working-class representation was widely recognized as the main issue in the campaign.

The unanimity evident in the ILP's provincial conventions and election campaigns was more remarkable given the deep divisions within the provincial labour movement. Although the labour movement was considered "more advanced" in Toronto, pockets of socialism existed elsewhere in southern Ontario as well. In Hamilton in particular, Fred Flatman had cultivated a base for more radical ideas in the suburban branches of the ILP and developed a wide following for his ideas through the pages of the *New Democracy*. In Brantford, divisions in the local party dated from the 1917 nomination of M.M. MacBride, whom the well-known co-operative leader, George Keen, described as "in" but not "of" the ILP. Keen thereupon resigned from the party to protest MacBride's dealings with the Unionist Party. In the fall of 1919, however, such differences seemed to disappear. More specifically, the different political currents found their own reasons to support a political movement that was clearly in the ascendancy. The socialists saw a development that parallelled the emergence of the British Labour Party and, like the socialist Independent Labour Party in that country, felt that they could appeal to a wider working-class base by participating in a broader party.[22] Many in the Social Democratic Party had long argued that the ballot was labour's "strongest weapon."[23] Revolutionary socialists, such as John MacDonald, were obviously less sanguine about electoral change but saw the movement as a legitimate expression of working-class unrest and therefore worthy of their participation.[24] Less radical participants often saw electoral activity as an alternative to militant industrial action. The *Labor News*, for instance, urged its readers: "Vote as you strike — it is more effective and it don't cost so much."[25] Even Tom Moore, the conservative leader of the Trades and Labor Congress, got on the bandwagon and briefly supported the ILP campaign at its height.[26] Few working-class leaders, it seemed, wanted to risk being isolated within the labour movement by attacking the popular movement for political action. The inchoate character of the ILP program made it easy for all to participate.

II

The new labour caucus in the provincial legislature mirrored the dominant features of labourism. Most members had a long history in the labour movement but were not representative of the emerging radicalism in many of the province's unions. The electoral failure of the Toronto ILP contributed to the conservatism of the caucus as did the tendency of some ILP branches to select members already experienced in municipal office such as the mayor of Brantford, Malcolm M. MacBride, and the former mayor of London, Hugh Stevenson. In a survey of the composition of the new labour caucus, *Maclean's Magazine* considered the Peterborough MPP Thomas Tooms to be "the most radical perhaps in the Labor party."[27] Yet Tooms, a supporter of Henry George's views on taxation, was no more able to provide a coherent conception of the ILP's role in the provincial parliament than were his colleagues.

Not surprisingly, given the lack of programmatic focus, divisions quickly emerged as personal animosities, often fuelled by individual ambitions. M.M. MacBride — "Me-Me" MacBride as the Hamilton *Labor News* christened him — created repeated dilemmas for the provincial ILP in this regard. MacBride's style of political discourse was highly personal and, despite his avowed allegiance to the labour movement, his highest praise went to the renegade Tory, Sir Adam Beck, while Jimmie Simpson served as personification of the socialist evil.[28] Matters quickly came to a head at the first meeting of the ILP caucus, where MacBride played a leading role in moving that the ILP co-operate with the United Farmers' caucus in the legislature and drafting a joint program which was adopted unanimously. Then, condemning the failure of the ILP to fight for a legislated eight-hour day, MacBride bolted from the meeting. As details of the episode became known, it was clear that MacBride's actions were motivated by his failure to receive a cabinet post in the new government. Although MacBride was lured back to the party, *Maclean's Magazine* commented in an aside to an appraisal of Labour Minister Rollo's performance that "[this] writer has talked with Mayor MacBride of Brantford, and knows what would have been done had he been minister," adding "[MacBride] is not cursed with that so prevalent quality of modesty."[29]

Though unfortunate, the MacBride affair was not necessarily debilitating for the caucus and the party. Yet the ILP's lack of direction could only exacerbate such divisions, particularly as it became evident that the ILP caucus was being drawn in the wake of the United Farmers without a clear conception of its own mandate. Points of demarcation from the UFO were clear and acknowledged. Committed to small government, the UFO had little interest in public ownership, such as Beck's expensive "Radial" scheme, which would see electrical railways run by the Hydro Commission criss-cross the province. Local trades councils, on the other hand, were actively promoting it. More seriously, farmers had little conception of trade unionism and, as employers of labour, opposed legislation to reduce the length of the working day. Yet ILP candidates had not generally campaigned on specifically trade-union, or even working-class, issues. As the letterhead of the Guelph ILP read, the party had been organized to "Fight for the Rights of the People."[30] Outside the largest cities many local ILPs had united with the UFO to run candidates in mixed rural-urban constituencies and had addressed the voters in a common idiom. Even in Toronto and Hamilton, the ILP spoke in a "producerist" tongue that differed from late nineteenth-century producerist ideology only in the expulsion of manufacturers from the alliance for the crime of profiteering during the war.[31] Both the ILP and UFO had an electoral interest in defining farmers and workers as equal members of a "producing" class with a common goal of wrestling the government from the hands of the "interests" and placing it in the hands of the "democratic" classes. Moreover, such language had deep roots in both the farm and labour movements and was reinforced by the liberal wartime critique of corruption and profiteering. Although the

UFO was itself divided over "broadening out" in the direction of a non-class-specific reform movement, the ILP caucus had established a *de facto* people's party by agreeing to form a cabinet led by the chief proponent of broadening out, Premier E.C. Drury. Even radicals like Arthur Mould, the 1921 federal candidate in London, aimed their fire at the unfair "principle of privilege" adopted by Parliament for the "minority class of the nation."[32] Labour and farmers were united by a common enemy.

This hardly left room for the caucus to address specifically working-class concerns, even if the ILP had had a clear conception of just what these might be. The lack of such a program allowed long-established differences free play within the party. One such issue, prohibition, was handled adroitly by the ILP leadership. While the provincial trade union federation, the Labor Educational Association, campaigned in favour of stronger beer being made available, the ILP managed to defuse the potentially divisive issue by promising to respect the referendum on the issue. Such a stand was unassailable, given the ILP's uncritical endorsement of such mechanisms of direct legislation.[33] The tariff issue was less amenable to easy solution, particularly as a post-war depression began to loom. In this debate, it soon became apparent that the disavowal of the old parties was not necessarily extended to the abandonment of old ideologies, and the debate soon saw erstwhile Conservatives defending protectionism against socialists, single taxers, and former Liberals. Although not a provincial issue, the controversy could not fail to revive buried animosities in the provincial party.

The 1920 ILP convention, after reaffirming the alliance with the UFO, managed to hammer out a tariff policy favouring the "gradual elimination of import duties on all necessities of life." The *Industrial Banner* explained that the tenor of the convention revealed that "in the opinion of the delegates there were reconstruction problems that overshadowed the tariff altogether."[34] Thomas Tooms suggested that the tariff question was "a twaddle," for workers suffer the same destitution and poverty in high-tariff countries as they do in low-tariff ones. A Hamilton ILP delegate to the convention, Labour Minister Walter Rollo, however, told the delegates to "quit dreaming" and predicted, "Not one of our labor candidates could run on a free trade platform and have a chance to win a single seat in Ontario." Given the large number of American branch plants in Hamilton, whose existence was due to the tariff barrier with the United States, it is hardly surprising that the Hamilton ILP was firmly committed to protectionism. It dismissed the ILP convention as "none too representative" and, with the support of both Hamilton labour papers, the *Labor News* and the *New Democracy*, campaigned to have the party reverse its decision. The Hamilton ILP did not, in fact, deny that the tariff had been misused to enrich the few and, as democrats, they opposed this. The solution, as they saw it, was to establish a "non-partisan, non-political commission" that would set the tariff "scientifically." They were convinced that such a body could devise a tariff structure "which would prove acceptable to the farmers, manufacturers and workers." In short, democracy and reason could solve the problem; no fundamental social cleavage stood in the way of obtaining a "happy medium."[35]

The potential for disaster began to present itself, for an issue had arisen in which Hamilton workers apparently felt that they had more in common with their own protected employers than with the Ontario ILP. Obviously this did not augur well for the future of independent working-class political action or for the continued development of the class solidarity that had spawned it. Hamilton's labourists, effectively unchallenged by local socialists, could not accept Simpson's view that the tariff was "a bogey issue" which diverted workers from "the real source of economic servitude [which] lies in the private ownership of natural resources and the machinery of production and distribution."[36] The Hamilton ILP demanded, and got, a special provincial convention, which reversed the decision before the 1921 federal election.[37]

The prohibition and tariff issues revealed persistent, and deepening, differences in the party. The meteoric rise of the ILP had overshadowed such problems, and major political gains could continue to do so. But the ILP was stalemated by its position in the legislature. The UFO-dominated government refused to grant the eight-hour day, paid its labourers some of the lowest wages for male workers in the province, shelved the Hydro Radial project by means of a legislative commission, and generally ignored the labour caucus. Although improvements were made in the Workmen's Compensation Act, and labour-supported protective legislation for women was adopted, working-class voters who had foreseen the arrival of a producers' democracy could hardly feel inspired by the few gains the ILP caucus had made.[38] The ILP's two cabinet ministers held portfolios that were less significant to labour than had been immediately apparent. The Ministry of Labour, under Walter Rollo, had until recently been subsumed under Public Works, and it remained small and insignificant compared to the latter. Harry Mill's Mines portfolio had also been established only recently. Rather than allow for ILP influence on government policy, Rollo and Mills generally found themselves selling UFO actions — or inaction — to the caucus and the party.

Under these circumstances, as the ILP's performance was falling far short of its promise, MacBride's apostasy was particularly damaging. The two Niagara region Labor MPPs, Charles Swayze and Frank Greenlaw, stated publicly that they agreed with MacBride's criticism of the accord with the farmers, and a Hamilton MPP, George Halcrow, declared that Labor ought to have received the important Public Works portfolio. With the support of the Hamilton party, Halcrow continued to stand as the representative of undiluted labourism at Queen's Park. Rather than succumb to the tendency to subordinate working-class interests to a reform movement dominated by farmers, Halcrow argued that ILP support of the Drury government was conditional. To demand that ILP MPPs submit to party discipline, resigning themselves to an ineffective reform government that was deaf to the working class, could only lead to the re-entry of partyism through a back door.[39] Halcrow's commitment to labourist principles, growing differences over the tariff in party ranks, and MacBride's willingness to exacerbate rifts in the caucus and the party in the interests of cultivating his own political base all combined to threaten the unity of the labour forces that had propelled the ILP to Queen's Park.

The ineffectiveness of the labour caucus was revealed by a major strike of workers employed on the Hydro Commission's huge canal project at Chippewa in the summer of 1920. After some success the previous season, the powerful Niagara District Trades Federation, which united the workers on the Hydro and Welland Canal projects, was determined to win the elusive eight-hour day. As the two thousand Hydro workers threatened to quit work, the region's two labour MPPs, as well as MacBride, rushed to Niagara Falls and persuaded the federation to leave the matter in their hands. The caucus soon discovered how little influence it had over Adam Beck and the Hydro Commission, and had to content itself with the establishment of a legislative committee to investigate conditions on the project. In that forum, the powerlessness of the caucus was displayed publicly. The inquiry rejected the workers' claims, recognizing "the basic principle" of the eight-hour day but recommending that a ten-hour day was needed to finish the project on schedule. A dissenting statement by a United Farmers MPP, W.H. Casselman, rejecting the eight-hour day as "a vicious principle" added little to the ILP's credibility in its pursuit of an alliance with the farmers.[40] Although the *Industrial Banner* tried to focus workers' animosity on Beck, the bitterness of a futile strike during which Hydro employees were evicted from housing owned by the commission shattered illusions in the ILP caucus, and, by extension, in the party.[41] For a large group of Ontario's unionized workers, the "political" front had collapsed at a crucial juncture.

By autumn, the ILP's provincial executive was moved to act to save the reputation of the party. A well-publicized meeting with the caucus apparently proceeded smoothly, but immediately afterwards MacBride attacked the provincial secretary for giving allegedly inaccurate details of the meeting to the press and announced he would cross to the opposition benches.[42] A subsequent meeting, without MacBride, was the first and only major attempt to rethink the functioning of the caucus. A resolution was adopted that, while maintaining the alliance with the farmers, the ILP would "emphasize its distinction as a separate political unit in the Legislature." To demonstrate its independence from the cabinet, the caucus replaced Rollo with Halcrow as house leader. The meeting also established, again for the first time, a clear list of demands that it would make upon the Drury government; unemployment relief, old age pensions and improvements in the Mothers' Allowance Act were to be dealt with in the coming session. Finally, in a move that reflected both a growing red scare and the ILP's vulnerability to rising discontent within its ranks, the meeting resolved that "extremists" — referring to a minority of revolutionary socialists — should "decline nomination to executive positions within the party."[43] Such actions on the part of the ILP leadership revealed that a socialist critique of the ILP and of labourism was gaining support within the ranks of the party.

For the moment, the ILP provincial executive's immediate problem, however, continued to be M.M. MacBride. His departure to the cross-benches, and his alliance with Joseph McNamara, who had been elected as an independent returned soldier, brought the differences onto the floor of the house. In February 1921, they introduced an eight-hour bill in the house in an effort to embarrass an ILP caucus still tied to the United Farmers.[44] Moreover, MacBride was still a member of the party until he was expelled *in absentia* at the provincial convention in April. The Brantford ILP, however, refused to recognize the expulsion and defended MacBride's actions in the legislature. The local focus of the provincial labour movement had returned to haunt the ILP. The Brantford members' loyalty was to their own representative rather than to the provincial movement. In an unpleasant and futile ritual, the ILP executive trekked to Brantford in an effort to persuade a meeting of MacBride loyalists to expel the errant MPP on pain of losing their charter.[45]

The conflict with MacBride was only the most public manifestation of a party in crisis. The 1922 municipal elections went poorly for the ILP. Even in the stronghold of Hamilton the ILP suffered setbacks as both controllers were defeated and only two aldermen elected.[46] Not surprisingly, some of those who prized their political careers above the party's declining fortunes began to rethink their political commitments, and local trades councils or labour parties effectively lost control of their nominees on municipal councils. In London, for instance, aldermen endorsed by the TLC were regularly called on the carpet for their disavowal of labour. In 1915, a labour alderman shocked unionists by expressing his support of property qualifications for municipal office, and in 1920 the "soldier-labor" alderman, Cameron Wilson, refused to support local street railway workers in their demands and severed his ties with the labour movement. The following year Aldermen Watkinson and Ashton were refused the support of the Labour Party for opposing increased property taxes for businesses and supporting municipal wage cuts. In Hamilton, the Hydro Commissioner, Gordon Nelson, quit the ILP to run as an independent; as a conservative labour paper commented, the ILP endorsement was becoming meaningless for a candidate's success. In 1923, three Hamilton ex-party members ran for municipal office, although all were defeated.[47] In the legislature, Halcrow's trajectory away from the caucus was speeded by the Drury government's continued wage cuts. His expressed view that the UFO government was little better for workers than past Tory or Grit governments finally prompted other members of the ILP caucus to demand that he be dropped as house leader.[48] At the party's 1922 provincial convention, any illusion that the party controlled its MPPs finally collapsed. Karl Homuth, Swayze, and Tooms were all censured for their record in the legislature; none, however, bothered to attend to answer the charges.[49] In the 1923 provincial election, the ILP was decimated. Working-class despair was reflected in the voter turnout. In twenty-two ridings contested by the ILP in 1919, 352,342 voters had gone to the polls; in 1923 the number declined to 258,174. Almost a hundred thousand voters stayed home. The ILP caucus was reduced to three, two of whom, Heenan and Homuth, soon returned to the folds of the Liberal and Conservative parties. The old order was firmly re-established.

III

The mass popularity of labourism during and immediately after the world war presented socialists with a dilemma. Did the Independent Labor Party contribute to the struggle for socialism by providing a political focus for working-class demands, or were its vague politics and implicit acceptance of capitalist social relations a hindrance to the development of a socialist consciousness? The debate raged furiously inside Ontario's largest socialist organization, the Social Democratic Party. At the outset of the war, the SDP was growing significantly as new branches were organized around the province. Already, it had over 4,000 members, more than half of whom were in Ontario; its newspaper had a circulation of 30,000. Moreover, in its stronghold of Toronto, the party had developed a regular, if tumultuous, working relation with the trades council.[50] By 1918, however, it was clear to some SDPers, particularly Jimmie Simpson, that ignoring the ILP would mean the marginalization of the Social Democratic Party. Against SDP members who viewed the ILP as the instrument of opportunists more interested in being elected to Parliament than in educating the working class, Simpson and his allies felt that there should be no "hard and fast rule" regarding the ILP as it was not yet clear where the movement was leading and an important opening for socialist ideas could be developing.[51]

To realize such an opportunity, however, proved difficult. ILP branches often listened with interest to socialist speakers, but before 1920 there was no pressing reason to question the party's electoral strategy or lack of programmatic clarity in light of its apparent success in gaining members and public attention. Moreover, the "education" of workers was the rationale behind socialist organizing before the war and socialists were still keen to find a political forum that allowed for the untrammelled presentation of socialist ideas.[52] Ironically, the generally conservative Trades and Labor Congress of Canada provided that opportunity. In 1917 the Congress adopted a resolution calling for a Canadian Labor Party based on the British "principle" of uniting "trade unionists, socialists, fabiens [sic], co-operators and farmers" into a federated party.[53] This structure appealed to trade unionists who were afraid to hand over authority to labour politicians, but it benefited socialists in much the same way, by allowing them the autonomy to function independently and in a united front with trade unionists and others.

The founding convention of the Ontario Section of the Canadian Labor Party (os/clp) was held on March 29, 1918. The debates that took place at this meeting were a good indication of the ideas prevalent among those active in the political labour movement, as well as an approximate gauge of the relationship of forces among political currents. Trade unions were accredited with 200 delegates, the ILP with 100, the SDP with 56 and the revolutionary socialist parties, the Socialist Labor Party (SLP), and the Socialist Labor Party of North America (SPNA) with 5 and 3 delegates respectively. The UFO, co-operative societies, Fabians, and Russian and Jewish socialist societies were also represented. This is, of course, only a general indication, particularly as several ILP or union delegates were also members of socialist groups. It does, however, provide evidence of a movement for working-class unity, as well as a recognition of the legitimacy of socialism within the labour movement. Nevertheless, attempts to persuade those present to adopt an explicitly socialist program did not succeed. A motion by Tom Bell of the SPNA calling for a "recognition of the class struggle," with the party having as its immediate aim the "abolition of the capitalist system" received only thirty-five votes. A further resolution based upon the British Labour Party's recently adopted policy supporting the "common ownership of the means of production" failed 129 to 69. Although some opposition to these motions arose from a fear of isolating the party and undermining working-class unity, others maintained a strong opposition to socialism. James Gunn, a former ILP candidate, did not want "state regulation in place of capitalist regulation," while Frank Barber, Toronto single-tax advocate, refused to recognize irresolvable class antagonisms. A.W. Roebuck, former ILP candidate in Temiskaming (who had run there with considerable Liberal support) was of a similar opinion.[54] Despite major differences, though, there was an obvious effort to control antagonisms and prevent open splits. The final program was adopted almost unanimously.

A provincial executive was elected with H.J. Halford of the Hamilton ILP and James Simpson of the SDP as the two dominant figures, reflecting the alliance between the two parties. Moreover, the presence of representatives of fifteen trades councils at the founding convention demonstrated its strong base in the unions.[55] The OS/CLP organized no branches, nor did it accept individual memberships. In fact, despite an auspicious inauguration, the party was inactive until 1921, and the ILP continued to dominate independent labour electoral politics. The only exception was in Toronto in the summer of 1919, when advocates of industrial unionism who had been active in that city's general strike movement took the lead in establishing a Toronto section of the OS/CLP under the presidency of a revolutionary socialist, John MacDonald, to contest the municipal election. Local branches of the ILP and the trades council participated, as well as a substantial number of local unions.[56] The effort was not particularly successful and by 1921 the conservative *Labor Leader* could mock Simpson as the sole surviving member of the Toronto CLP.

By 1921, however, the crisis in the ILP had persuaded socialists to attempt to breath life into the OS/CLP. The OS/CLP convention of that year was small and geographically less representative than the 1918 meeting. Few delegates came from outside of Toronto, Hamilton, or London; none came from the north. The convention rejected suggestions from the ILP executive officers that the OS/CLP dissolve itself and instead claimed the responsibility of organizing the federal election campaign, since it could claim to be more representative than the ILP in that it included trade unions and socialist organizations. The ILP loyalists were furious. The provincial executive publicly reiterated its position as the dominant working-class party in the province, while Hamilton ILPer Peter McCabe described the event as "the biggest 'red' meeting that [he] ever was at." The ILP legislative caucus, which had not been represented at the convention, similarly disparaged the OS/CLP's claims.[57]

Nevertheless, an alternative organization that combined the impulse towards labour political representation with an implicit critique of the faltering ILP had the potential to draw increasing numbers to its ranks. Yet, the OS/CLP had failed to adopt a clearly socialist platform in 1918, and in 1921 was still measured in its criticism of the ILP in order to avoid an open split. Events in London revealed both the earnest desire of OS/CLP leaders to maintain a united front with the ILP and the logic of its separate existence. A growing polarization in both the London trades council and the local ILP led a group of about twenty radicals, including the former secretary of the council, William Tite, to request recognition as a CLP branch. The OS/CLP executive refused, reiterating its position that the CLP was a united front of the ILP and socialist, farmer, and trade union organizations, not a party based on individual membership in competition with the ILP. Those who wished to join a labour party, they declared, must join the ILP.[58] As a compromise, the local Labor Representation Committee — an alliance of the ILP, the trades council and individual unions — dubbed itself the London Labor Party and declared its identification with the CLP. Under the presidency of John Colbert, a leader of the street railway union and a former alderman, the more radical London Labor Party soon eclipsed the demoralized London ILP and ran Arthur Mould in the 1921 federal election.[59] Although Mould generally spoke in a language similar to the ILP in the 1919 election, declaring that "those who toil can best be represented by themselves," he added that the growing threat of unemployment could only be addressed by "production for use instead of profit."[60]

The 1922 OS/CLP convention was a turning point in the organization's relationship to the ILP. While the ILP was declining, affiliation to the OS/CLP was growing, a notable achievement at a time of falling trade union membership and activity due to unemployment and wage cuts. With fifteen new affiliates, including the Kingston, Sault Ste. Marie, Twin City (Kitchener-Waterloo), and Stratford trade councils, the total affiliated membership was estimated as high as 40,000. At the urging of the London Labor Party, the convention decided to establish CLP branches based on individual membership, thereby placing the OS/CLP directly in competition with the ILP for members. The wording of the resolution, although attempting to smooth relations between the organizations, left little doubt that the two labour parties now constituted two distinct alternatives in the political labour movement: "It shall be expressly understood in the charter given (local OS/CLP branches) that they are not in conflict with local ILP's except in friendly rivalry to build up the labor movement."[61]

Around the province the debate opened. Joseph Marks, the moving spirit of the ILP, declared that the OS/CLP was unrepresentative of labour. In Hamilton, both the trades council and the central branch of the ILP stood true to their original conceptions of labourism in the face of appeals by the OS/CLP president, Harry Kerwin, and some support for affiliating from within the local ILP. In London there was little opposition from the remnants of the ILP to joining, and a second branch of the London Labor Party was formed for approximately one hundred individual members who did not already belong through their affiliated organizations. In Toronto, where socialists had always played a significant role in the ILP, the Labor Representation Political Association — a united front of the local labour council, unions, ILP locals and the Women's Labor League — emerged by late 1921 with a substantial number of socialists in its leadership. Revolutionary socialists like William Moriarty were critical of the "evasions" in its federal election manifesto and its attempt to ascribe the economic crisis to the war rather than to capitalism. Still, Moriarty and his nascent Workers' Party of Canada affiliated themselves to the association, as did upwards of thirty other organizations, including not only international unions, such as the conservative street railway workers, but the British-based Amalgamated Society of Carpenters, the Canadian Electrical Trades Union, and the Amalgamated Clothing Workers, all of which were engaged in bitter jurisdictional disputes with the American Federation of Labor unions that were represented in the local trades council.[62] The Labor Representation Political Association was a remarkable political united front under the direction of socialists like Jimmie Simpson and John MacDonald.

Only six years after the founding of the Independent Labor Party of Ontario, and less than four years after the election of the Farmer-Labor government of E.C. Drury, the province's political labour movement had undergone a startling metamorphosis. An air of doom hung over the 1923 convention of the ILP. Confronting a provincial election, the small gathering of only nineteen delegates from a mere twelve branches (even though the party still claimed sixty-six branches) reopened the bitter debate over its relationship with the United Farmers. A resolution, moved by George Keen of the re-formed Brantford branch, that the ILP participate in no government "unless the Labor Party [was] sufficiently strong to form a government" was defeated and the alliance with the UFO reconfirmed.[63] A sign of the ILP's growing isolation was the decision of the Labor Educational Association, which had sponsored the party's founding convention in 1917, to adopt the American Federation of Labor's "non-partisan" policy. A month before the 1923 election, the association produced a questionnaire for candidates and declared that it would support those who favoured eight-hour day legislation and wage improvements for workers on provincial government contracts.[64]

The 1923 convention of the Ontario Section of the Canadian Labor Party, in contrast, outlined an election platform that concentrated on the failure of the provincial government to meet working-class demands. The Drury government's failure to pay union wages, to raise the niggardly levels of women's minimum wages and mothers' allowances, and to improve the Factory Act suggest that, though not explicitly socialist, the os/CLP stood for a coherent series of reforms that it considered more important than participating in a coalition government. The most notable aspect of this meeting, however, was the affiliation of the Workers' Party of Canada to the os/CLP. The Workers' Party, which included several of the leading militants in the Toronto labour movement from the days of the 1919 general strike, had emerged as the most substantial revolutionary current in Ontario, although in the west this status was still challenged by the One Big Union.[65] The CLP now encompassed all the main socialist currents, whether revolutionary or reformist in their approach to political change. With the failure of labourism and the ILP, the banner of independent political action had clearly fallen to the socialists and to the CLP. The energies of the OS/CLP members, unlike those of the ILP, were evident over the course of the next year. Thirty-eight new affiliates — both political organizations (including eight Workers' Party branches) and unions — were gained, and over 100 delegates attended the 1924 convention. The convention's message to the provincial labour movement contrasted sharply with the language of the ILP. Whereas labourism had traced the powerlessness of the workers to their effective exclusion from the electoral process, the CLP spoke more broadly of a ruling class based on capitalist social relations and private property. "The Canadian Labor Party," the convention declared, "puts human rights before property and ownership in both industry and politics. Its test of human society is not the maintenance of special privilege for few — but of more abundant reality in life for all souls in the social order." The program of the OS/CLP, however, did not speak of a revolutionary assault on capitalist power and the participation by the communists of the Workers' Party of Canada, though substantial, was not overwhelming. Rather, this was an electoral united front of reformist socialists like Jimmie Simpson, Arthur Mould, and the Hamilton alderman, Sam Lawrence; and the revolutionary socialists of the Workers' Party. Its program, therefore, was confined largely to legislative demands. Moreover, the OS/CLP continued to model itself consciously on the British Labour Party and applauded the gains made by its British counterpart.

Electorally, the OS/CLP had few prospects, given the devastating experience of the ILP. Moreover, an explicitly left-wing political movement was unlikely to be able to recreate the unity of 1919, predicated, as it was, on the lack of a political program by the ILP. Nevertheless, independent working-class political action had come to be identified with socialists and its non-socialist form — labourism — had disappeared from the electoral landscape and from the labour movement. The distinction between labourism and the reformist social democracy represented within the CLP was effectively drawn by the paper of the Workers' Party when it counterposed the activities of James Woodsworth in the House of Commons with the provincial ILP caucus. Whereas labourism had seen industrial and political action as distinct and separate, the Workers' Party sought to fuse these two elements of working-class power. Although critical of Woodsworth, *The Worker* praised his effective use of Parliament to "focus attention on the issues of the mass struggles outside of parliament ... and so perhaps force whatever concessions possible from the capitalist class." The ILP, in contrast, had failed to direct the industrial militancy of 1919 and 1920 towards attainable political goals. The legislative caucus, argued *The Worker*, was directly responsible for the demoralization of its working-class supporters:

> One does not expect Rollo, Halcrow and their fellows,
> to have any sense of the international interests of the
> working class or of the developing social revolution,
> but, even from them, one does at least look for some
> clear-cut declaration and activity in the problems of
> unemployment, wage cuts, etc.[66]

Erstwhile ILP members and voters had foreseen a social revolution of sorts that would follow an electoral breakthrough; their assessment of the record of the ILP and its legislative caucus could not have been very much different.

Although the united front of social democrats and the Communist Party (as the Workers' Party was renamed) would not be maintained beyond 1927, when Simpson and Mould led the reformist socialists out of the CLP, there would be no return to the politics of labourism. Conservative trade unions were, once again, comfortable in the Conservative Party and had political organs in the *Canadian Labor World* in Hamilton and the *Labor Leader* in Toronto. The Communist Party and the individuals who, in the next decade, would come together to form the Co-operative Commonwealth Federation were the heirs of the sentiment that workers must rely on their own representatives in office and not trust their fate to the Liberals and Conservatives. Members of the Ontario Section of the Canadian Labor Party had come to recognize the necessity for a more rigorous understanding of political power and of the state. It would no longer suffice to elect working-class representatives and rely only on their good will and judgment. Not surprisingly, the conclusions socialists reached regarding the ability of working-class representatives to use Parliament in the interests of labour varied greatly. Nevertheless, communists and social democrats both set about trying to understand the relationship between capitalism and political power in order to avoid repeating the debacle of the Independent Labor Party.

NOTES

1   *Globe*, Toronto, Oct. 21, 1919.
2   *Industrial Banner* (hereafter *IB*), Oct. 17, Nov. 7, 1919.
3   National Archives of Canada (hereafter NAC), MG 30, A 31, Tom Moore Papers, Speeches, Memoranda and Clippings, 1918-46, "Vote for MacBride ...," 1919.
4   On the 1919 election in the context of the Progressive revolt see L.A. Wood, *A History of Farmers' Movements in Canada* (1924; Toronto: University of Toronto Press, 1975), pp. 329-34; W.L. Morton, *The Progressive Party in Canada* (Toronto: University of Toronto Press, 1950), pp. 83-86; Jean MacLeod, "The United Farmer Movement in Ontario, 1914-1943," (M.A. thesis, Queen's University,

1958); Brian D. Tennyson, "The Ontario General Election of 1919: The Beginnings of Agrarian Revolt," *Journal of Canadian Studies*, 4 (Feb. 1969), 26-36; Charles M. Johnston, *E.C. Drury: Agrarian Idealist* (Toronto: University of Toronto Press, 1986).

5   *IB*, Apr. 27, 1917.

6   University of Western Ontario, Regional Collection, London, Ontario, Trades and Labor Council Records (hereafter London TLC), Minutes, Feb. 21, 1917.

7   *IB*, July 6, 1917.

8   *IB*, June 30, 1916.

9   Canada, Department of Labour, *Labour Organization in Canada* (hereafter *LOC*), (Ottawa, 1917), pp. 40-41. For an analysis of the background and nature of labourism in Canada, see Craig Heron, "Labourism and the Canadian Working Class," *Labour/Le Travail*, 13 (Spring 1984), pp. 45-76.

10 The federal Department of Labour recorded the organization of a substantial number of new trades councils, particularly but not only in eastern Ontario, as well as their role in municipal politics. See *LOC*, 1918, pp. 110-11; 1919, pp. 58-59, 153-54; 1920, pp. 55-56, 157-58. For comment on the growing militancy of trades councils see *IB*, Mar. 7, 1919. On St. Catharines see *IB*, Jan. 30, 1914, May 17, 1918. On Brantford see Brantford *Expositor*, Jan. 6, 1917. On Berlin/Kitchener see *IB*, Jan. 2, Dec, 11, 1914; *Labour Gazette*, Feb. 1915, p. 898; *Plumbers, Gas and Steam Fitters' Journal* (Chicago), Mar. 1915, p. 23. One of Peterborough's oldest unionists, Hartley had been a member of the town council in 1889. See John McPhee, "The Labour Movement," in Ronald Borg, ed., *Peterborough, Land of Shining Waters* (Toronto: University of Toronto Press, 1967), p. 292. See also *IB*, Nov. 14, 1914, Oct. 15, Dec. 24, 1915. On Welland see *IB*, Mar. 6, 1914, Nov. 16, 1917; *Labor News* (hereafter *LN*), Nov. 23, 1917. On London see *IB*, Jan. 15, 1915; London TLC, Minutes, Jan. 20, Mar. 3, 1915.

11 See for example, London TLC, Minutes, Election Committee, Dec. 11, 1915. The election platform was dealt with separately from, and after, the selection of candidates.

12 See Heron, "Labourism," p. 54.

13 This statement was often printed. See, for example, *LN*, Aug. 3, 1917.

14 Rollo, a broom maker, had been secretary of the Hamilton trades council for thirteen years at the time of his election to the provincial legislature. Long active in labourist politics, he had come within thirty-nine votes of joining Studholme in the legislature in the 1914 provincial election. He was also editor of the *Labor News* for several months in 1919 (*IB*, Dec. 5, 1919; *LN*, May 9, Nov. 28, 1919). Halcrow, a member of the plumbers' union, was president of the Hamilton TLC for eight years. (*Canadian Parliamentary Guide* (Ottawa, 1920), p. 299; *IB*, Jan. 7, 1916, Jan. 10, 1919). For a comparison of the leadership of the Hamilton trades council and the ILP see *LN*, Aug. 9, 1918, Jan. 31, 1919. On 1919 Hamilton municipal elections see *LN*, Dec. 20, 1918, Jan. 3, 1919.

15 D. Wayne Roberts, "Studies in the Toronto Labour Movement, 1896-1914," (Ph.D. thesis, University of Toronto, 1978), pp. 362-63, 416-22.

16 *Canadian Forward* (hereafter *CF*), Dec. 2, 1916, Apr. 24, 1917.

17 *CF*, Feb. 24, 1918.

18 On Carey's connections with the Unionist Party see NAC, MG 27, II, D 13, N.W. Rowell Papers, vol. 3, file 17, Rowell to Borden, Oct. 17, 1917; *LN*, Nov. 2, Nov. 23, 1917. Bruce was a member of the Social Democratic Party (*CF*, Dec. 10, 1917).

19 *IB*, Oct. 18, 1918; Toronto *Star*, Nov. 9, 1918; Royal Commission on Industrial Relations, *Evidence*, p. 2947 (J.H.H. Ballantyne).

20 See James Naylor, "Toronto, 1919," *Historical Papers* (Canadian Historical Association, 1986), pp. 33-55.

21 *IB*, Oct. 10, 1919.

22 Brantford *Expositor*, Nov. 9, Nov. 12, 1917.
23 See for example *IB*, Dec. 4, 1914.
24 *IB*, Nov. 7, 1919.
25 *Labor News*, Sept. 6, 1919.
26 NAC, Moore Papers, Speeches, Memoranda and Clippings, 1918-46, "Vote for MacBride ...," 1919; Trades and Labor Congress of Canada (hereafter TLCC), Proceedings, 1919, p. 136.
27 J.L. Rutledge, "The Birth of the Labor Party," *Maclean's Magazine*, 33 (Jan. 1920), p. 84.
28 *IB*, July 23, 1920; *Financial Post*, Apr. 27, 1918; Brantford *Expositor*, May 5, June 3, Oct. 2, 1919, *Ontario Labor News*, May 15, 1919, *CF*, Apr. 18, 1918.
29 Rutledge, "Birth of the Labor Party," p. 23; *LN*, Sept. 16, 1920. On agreement with MacBride see *IB*, Jan. 30, 1920; *Labor Leader* (hereafter *LL*), Jan. 30, 1920.
30 NAC, MG 26, H 1, R.L. Borden Papers, RLB series, file 1690, Guelph ILP to Borden, Jan. 24, 1918.
31 On producerism see Bryan D. Palmer, *A Culture in Conflict: Skilled Workers and Industrial Capitalism in Hamilton, Ontario, 1860-1914* (Montreal: McGill-Queen's University Press, 1979), pp. 98, 101, 108-109.
32 *Herald* (London), Nov. 17, 1921. See also University of Western Ontario, Regional Collection, Arthur Mould Papers, "Reminiscences of Arthur Mould," for biographical information.
33 Gerald A. Hallowell, *Prohibition in Ontario, 1919-1923* (Ottawa: Ontario Historical Society, 1972), pp. 51-52, 66-67, 84, 148, 165; *IB*, Feb. 7, Sept. 5, Oct. 17, 1919, *Labour Gazette* (June 1919), pp. 715-16.
34 *IB*, Apr.9, 1920.
35 *LN*, Apr. 9, 1920.
36 *IB*, Sept. 9, 1921.
37 *LN*, Oct. 28, Nov. 29, 1921; *IB*, 25 Nov. 1921.
38 Labourers on provincial contracts received thirty cents an hour (*LL*, July 29, 1921). By contrast, Hamilton unskilled civic workers, at the same time, received fifty cents (*LL*, Oct. 28, 1921). On the Hydro Commission see *IB*, July 23, 1920; Queen's University Archives, Andrew Glen Papers, box 5, file 23, "Information Bulletin," Aug. 6, 1920; MacLeod, "The United Farmer Movement," p. 134. For Trades Congress President Tom Moore's comments see *LL*, July 9, 1920. Protective legislation included the Minimum Wage Act, which established a board to set minimum wages for women by industry and locality, and the Mothers' Allowance Act, which provided a pension for widows with more than one dependent child.
39 Brantford *Expositor*, Nov. 7, Nov. 12, 1919, Jan. 3, 1920; *LL*, Jan. 23, 1920, *New Democracy* (hereafter *ND*), Jan. 28, 1920.
40 Archives of Ontario, RG 3, Prime Minister's Office (Drury), box 39, Chippewa Development, Report, June 4, 1920.
41 *IB*, June 25, July 2, 1920, Nov. 25, 1921.
42 *LL*, Oct. 29, Nov. 5, 1920; Glen Papers, box 1, file 4, MacBride to Glen, Nov. 3, 1920; *LN*, Oct. 28, 1920; *Herald*, Nov. 4, 1920.
43 *LN*, Nov. 25, 1920; *LL*, Nov. 26, Dec. 17, 1920; *ND*, Dec. 16, 1920.
44 *LL*, Jan. 14, Feb. 11, 1921; NAC, MG 28, I, 230, Canadian Manufacturers' Association, Executive Council Minutes, Feb. 25, 1921, Industrial Relations Committee, "Ontario Eight-hour Day Bill."
45 *LN*, Apr. 25, 1921; *IB*, Apr. 29, 1921; *ND*, May 4, 1921.
46 *LOC*, 1921, p. 57; *LN*, Jan. 28, 1922.
47 *IB*, Feb. 15, 1915; *LL*, Sept. 20, 1920, Jan. 7, 1921, Dec. 1, 1922; London *Advertiser*, Jan. 2, 1921; *LN*, Dec. 22, 1922, Jan. 30, 1923; *ND*, Jan. 4, 1923.
48 *LL*, Sept. 30, 1921; Metropolitan Toronto Reference Library, J.W. Buckley Papers, Labour MPP's to Buckley, Feb. 1, 1922.

49 *LN*, Apr. 28, 1922; *LOC*, 1922, pp. 221-22.

50 *IB*, June 1914. New SDP branches included: Brantford, *IB*, July 17, 1914; St. Thomas, Ingersoll, Chatham, Windsor, *IB*, Aug. 28, 1914; London, *IB*, Dec. 4, 1914. On the influence of the SDP see University of Toronto Library, J.S. Woodsworth Collection, J. McA. Conner Papers, "The Canadian Socialist Movement" and Norman Penner, *The Canadian Left: A Critical Analysis* (Scarborough: Prentice-Hall, 1977), p. 52. On the relationship with the Toronto trades council see *IB*, Dec. 25, 1914; NAC, MG 28, I44, Toronto District Labor Council, (henceforth TDLC) Minutes, Mar. 18, 1915, Apr. 20, 1916.

51 For the debate in the SDP's paper see *CF*, especially Oct. 28, Dec. 2, 1916, Apr. 24, 1917, Feb. 24, Mar. 10, Mar. 24, 1918.

52 For instance, "The SDP watchword for 1914 is education, both within and without its ranks" (*IB*, Feb. 6, 1914). In this sense, various socialist currents were in agreement with the Socialist Party of Canada in believing that "socialists' main function was to educate the proletariat." A. Ross McCormack, *Reformers, Rebels, and Revolutionaries: The Western Canadian Radical Movement, 1899-1919* (Toronto: University of Toronto Press, 1977), p. 68.

53 TLCC Proceedings, 1917, pp. 43-45.

54 TLCC Proceedings, 1918, p. 46; *IB*, Apr. 5, 1918; Margaret Prang, *N.W. Rowell: Ontario Nationalist* (Toronto: University of Toronto Press, 1975), p. 223; *LN*, Apr. 5, 1918; Buckley Papers, scrapbook, vol. 7, p. 21. Roebuck considered the Liberal Party, the UFO, and the ILP as "one party." Archives of Ontario, A.W. Roebuck Papers, Roebuck to A.A. McKeldie, Nov. 19, 1919.

55 *IB*, Apr. 5, 1918.

56 TDLC, Minutes, Nov. 6, 1919; *IB*, Nov. 7, Nov. 14, Nov. 28, 1919.

57 *LL*, July 29, Aug. 19, Oct. 7, 1921. For ILP Secretary J. Marks comments to Toronto trades council see TDLC Minutes, Oct. 6, 1921.

58 TDLC, Minutes, July 6, 1922 (OS/CLP Executive Minutes).

59 London *Advertiser*, Sept. 30, 1921; London TLC, Minutes, Nov. 2, 1921.

60 *Herald*, Dec. 5, 1921.

61 *IB*, Feb. 22, 1922; *LL*, Mar. 3, 1922.

62 *LL*, Mar. 10, Mar. 17, 1922. The more radical East Hamilton ILP affiliated itself to the OS/CLP, but the main Central Branch of the party repeatedly deferred the issue despite a campaign by Bert Furey in favour of affiliation. His main opponent was the conservative single-taxer Henry George Fester. See Hamilton Public Library, Independent Labor Party, Hamilton Central Branch, Minutes, Oct. 22, 1922; *LN*, Oct. 22, 1922; *LL*, May 12, 1922; London *Advertiser*, May 8, May 13, 1922; *Workers' Guard*, Dec. 10, 1922; Glen Papers, box 2, file 9, "Affiliated with LRPA," May 1923.

63 Glen Papers, box 2, file 8, ILP Provincial Convention Proceedings, 1923; *LN*, Apr. 27, 1923.

64 *Canadian Congress Journal*, 2 (June 1923), pp. 251-52; Labor Educational Association of Ontario, *Official Annual Labor Review, 1924*, p. 41.

65 Archives of Ontario, Prime Ministers' Papers, box 34, Simpson to Drury, Feb. 27, 1923; *LL*, Mar. 2, 1923; *Worker*, Mar. 15, 1923. For the history of the Workers' Party see William Rodney, *Soldiers of the International: A History of the Communist Party of Canada, 1919-1929* (Toronto: University of Toronto Press, 1968) and Ian Angus, *Canada's Bolsheviks: The Early Years of the Communist Party of Canada* (Montreal: Vanguard, 1981).

66 *Worker*, May 15, 1922.

THE JEWISH EXPERIENCE IN ONTARIO TO 1960

Gerald Tulchinsky

"Jews cannot hold land in this province." With this curt statement the Upper Canada Executive Council in 1797 rejected the petition from a merchant, Levy Solomons, for a land grant. It was hardly a warm welcome to a Jewish communal existence in Ontario.[1] Though census returns indicated a growing Jewish population in the province in the 1860s and 1870s, total figures were tiny until in the 1880s the first major wave of immigrants more than doubled the number of Jews, to over 2,500. The 1880s and 1890s saw not only increasing numbers but also significant changes in the intensity of Jewish life in the province. In Toronto and in the new communities religious, political, social, and cultural dimensions of the Jewish experience announced the arrival in Ontario of Eastern European Jews with all their attendant "intellectual baggage." The major migrations of the eighties, and those that followed until the 1920s, transformed the social and economic structure of Ontario Jewry, notably in Toronto and Hamilton, where a Jewish working class emerged in the clothing industry that burgeoned after 1900.

The history of this minority in Ontario is only one example of the immigrant experience in a larger society that was essentially Anglo-Celtic in origin, Protestant in religion, and British in its political, legal, and social institutions. Yet the Jewish dimension demonstrates the variety and complexity of the immigrant experience within Ontario's cultural context. To be sure, Russian, Polish, and Lithuanian Jews shared much with immigrants coming from these and other countries. In Toronto "the Ward" brought Jews not uncomfortably together with Italians, Macedonians, Poles, and Chinese during the early twentieth century,[2] and the gradual move of the Jewish community into west-end wards of the city after World War I created districts of ethnic diversity including Poles, Lithuanians, and Ukrainians.[3] But there were nevertheless major differences between Jews and other non-Anglo-Celtic immigrants. While Italians and Macedonians tended to arrive as "target immigrants" or "sojourners" (the Italians often under contract to a *padrone*) to work on construction for a period of time and then return to their homeland, Jews arriving in America were overwhelmingly determined never to return to live in Eastern Europe and rarely did so.[4] Unlike the ethnic communities in which young single males predominated at the earliest stages, Jews tended to migrate as families, or to unite them shortly thereafter. As well, few Jews (barring those *in extremis*) accepted employment on construction projects in isolated areas in Northern Ontario, preferring instead jobs near home in industry, notably in clothing factories and shops. In the realm of political ideas, however, there was some convergence of Jews and other non–Anglo-Saxon immigrants, notably on the far left, where in the Social Democratic movement and other associations, Jews allied themselves with Ukrainians, Finns, and others in pursuit of the Marxist nirvana.[5]

Perhaps there was also a broad sense of the common experiences, some of them humiliating, they were undergoing as non–Anglo-Celts in an Ontario where the culture of ethnic minorities enjoyed at best second-class status. Though it would be incorrect to suggest that a unity of outlook developed among non–Anglo-Celts, they seem to have reacted sometimes in similar ways — occasionally in unison — to their social designation as "foreigners."

The Jewish experience in Ontario should also be examined in relation to Jewish immigrant life in other Anglo-Celtic countries. Explaining the adjustment, decline, and recent revival of the Jewish community in Melbourne, Australia, to the mid-1960s, Peter Medding emphasizes that "the group-strengthening factors have become predominant" as Jews have accommodated themselves to Australian society, but because of large infusions of East European immigrants since the 1920s, they have "resisted structural assimilation and not undergone a large-scale entry into its social cliques, organizations, institutional activities and general civic life culminating in intermarriage."[6] Gideon Shimoni's analysis of South African Jewry stresses the importance of the persistence of Zionism as the normative form of Jewish identity. Thus, while sharing the environment, Jewish orientation was in part extra-territorial.[7]

In those environments, therefore, Jewish identity and persistence are strong. But is America different? Is the Jewish experience in the United States — and perhaps in Canada — somewhat more complex, partly at least because of its libertarian character? In assessing the Jewish experience in the United States, the historian Henry Feingold believes that the United States "employs a centripetal force to draw its disparate elements into a national community, [creating] ... for Jews ... both a prospect and a problem" which, he later explains, "means that the Jewish community continues to delicately balance the pulls of American and Judaic culture and to reconcile them where possible."[8]

Another student of American Jewry, Arnold Eisen, stresses that as the sense of chosenness imported by Jews to America was confronted by the need and increasing opportunities for participation in ever wider spheres of American life, Jewish self-definition has undergone reexamination and reformulation.[9] These comparisons give rise to certain questions such as: How significant are "group-strengthening factors," and how strongly has the Jewish community in Ontario resisted integration into the general society? To what extent was Zionism of pivotal importance in the evolution of the Jewish community and of significance in its definition of itself? And to what extent has the American Jewish dilemma of preserving chosenness while welcoming new opportunities been characteristic of Jewish life in this province?

A comparison with the history of Quebec Jewry provides our discussion with even more significant, and equally bothersome, counterpoints. In the lower province, the Jewish community was caught between the upper and nether millstones of Anglophone-Protestant attitudes of ascendancy and Francophone-Catholic aspirations for national revival, thereby undergoing the severe pressures that marked its passage from minority to "third solitude." [10] In Ontario this kind of conflict did not dominate the provincial political and social agendas, and Jewish development presumably could proceed "normally" within the constraints imposed by Ontario's overwhelming cultural homogeneity. There is yet another point of contrast. As compared to Quebec's somewhat slower and generally undiversified economic development through most of the nineteenth and twentieth centuries, Ontario's growth in the same period was dynamic in the major fields of agriculture, manufacturing, transportation, and resource exploitation. Thus, it might be assumed that Ontario's Jewish community would perhaps share those important distinguishing features of the provincial economy. It is within such international, continental, and national environments that we must properly assess the history of Jewry in this province.

The earliest Jewish arrivals in Ontario were merchants from the Montreal group that had arrived in the wake of the British conquest of Canada in 1760. Most of them seem to have sojourned only briefly in the province. Ezekiel Solomons, in association with William Grant, enjoyed substantial interests in the fur trade at Michilimackinac and made at least one trip there as early as the 1760s.[11] In the Windsor-Detroit district Chapman Abraham, a German-born Jew from Montreal, traded in wine and brandy and supplied muskets, gunpowder, ball, and shot to the British forces until he was captured during Pontiac's uprising.[12] Other traders followed, including Moses David, who conducted a varied business career until his death in Windsor in 1814.

The evidence of Jewish migration to Ontario that is recorded in earliest censuses tells us that there were a few individuals scattered in the frontier areas of the province besides the nucleus of the group in

York. The Upper Canada census of 1842, for example, reveals that there were individuals and small groupings of Jews throughout southern Ontario, with a significant number in the western districts (see Table 1). But there is little information about them. It is likely that some — perhaps most — were pedlars, storekeepers, or traders in various commodities like cattle, grain, and timber, or that they may well have been itinerant glaziers, jewellers, tailors, cigar makers, or other tradesmen. Though we have no evidence of Jewish farmers amongst these early settlers, the possibility exists. Nor is much known about the migration of these people from place to place, their relationships with their neighbours, or their observance of Jewish family, dietary, and religious rites.[13] Sigmund Samuel's reminiscences reveal, however, that before his father arrived in Toronto in 1855, these were honoured more in the breach than in the observance.[14]

Although before 1870 Ontario's Jewish population grew slowly, it began to take on some characteristics as a community. By 1861 Toronto had a Jewish population of 153 and Hamilton 77, whereas there were still only a handful each in Ottawa, London, and Kingston. But, as Stephen Speisman points out, in Toronto in 1849 rudiments of communal organization had been established with the purchase of land for a cemetery and the beginnings of a congregation.[15] Here, a small group of Germans like the Rossins and the Nordheimers had settled and begun to merge with the few English Jews who had arrived earlier.

The 1850s and 1860s witnessed the beginnings of communities elsewhere in the province. The Hebrew Benevolent Society, *Anshe Shalom* (People of Peace), was established by German Jews in Hamilton in 1853, and a few years later a nucleus of pedlars and storekeepers was forming in the village of Lancaster near Cornwall.[16] By 1871 London and Ottawa had Jewish populations of 25 and 35 respectively, though permanent congregational institutions — *minyanim* for regular prayer, and cemeteries — were not acquired until the end of the 1880s, by which time London's community numbered 144 and Ottawa's 46.

Though little is known about the tiny Jewish enclaves in most Ontario towns and villages in the late nineteenth and early twentieth century, there is some information about a fascinating group of Jews located in and around the village of Lancaster in rural Glengarry County, a few miles northeast of Cornwall. This tiny Jewish community was founded by Noah Friedman shortly after he immigrated to Canada from Poland in 1857.[17] He was followed by Harris Kellert, his brother-in-law, ten years later.[18] They and their families probably constituted the majority of the Jewish population of ten persons in Glengarry County in 1861 but they were followed by many others, including Abraham Jacobs and his large family.[19]

By 1871 the community numbered thirty-nine, while in nearby villages of Stormont County there were nineteen and in the town of

Table 1
Ontario's Jewish Population by Religion, 1842-1961

1842	1,105 [a]
1848	130
1851	106
1861	614
1871	518 [b]
1881	1,193
1891	2,501
1901	5,321
1911	27,015
1921	47,458
1931	62,094
1941	69,217
1951	85,467
1961	109,344

a   This census includes the following Jewish population in Upper Canada's countries and districts: Wellington (913), Home (68), Western (43), Prince Edward (42), Midland (18), London (6), Niagara (5), Johnstown (5), Dalhousie (3), Talbot (1). The figure for Wellington is so large that it must be an error. According to the census of 1848, there were no Jews in Wellington; none in the 1851-52 census; and only eight in 1860-61.

b   This census lists 235 Jews in Oxford County, a number which is probally an error.

Source: *Census of Canada*, 1871-1961

Table 2
Jewish Population by Religion in Ontario Urban Centres, 1848-1871

	1848	1851	1861	1871
Toronto	27	20	153	157
Hamilton	–	4	77	131
London	–	7	3	35
Ottawa	–	–	4	25
Cornwall	–	–	–	26
Kingston	–	–	5	12
Oil Springs				7
Brantford	–	–	–	1
Chatham				2

Source: *Census of Canada*, 1870-71 (Ottawa: 1876), Vol. 4, 134-35, 164-65, 180-81; Vol. 1, 86-143.

Cornwall twenty-six Jews. This Glengarry-Stormont-Cornwall group continued to exist for the next twenty years, although their numbers declined slowly. While in Glengarry, Jews were essentially pedlars and general store owners, or both. However, many of the original settlers moved to Montreal (and in some cases to nearby Cornwall), where family connections, Jewish educational and religious facilities, and more opportunities for business — notably in that city's burgeoning wholesale clothing business — were available. (Kellert and Friedman formed a fancy goods wholesale business before becoming clothing manufacturers.) [20] The Glengarry experience foreshadowed the fate of many small Jewish communities: initial settlement, followed by growth over a decade or two, and then decline, as the younger generation moved to cities to follow other business or professional careers.

By the 1880s Toronto was already becoming well endowed with the elements of Jewish communal existence. Not only was the Holy Blossom synagogue's new building on Bond Street under construction but the congregation also had acquired as its spiritual leader an English-speaking "minister," the Rev. Barnet E. Elzas, a graduate of Jews College in London. In fact two new congregations had emerged, *B'Nai Shalom* (Sons of Peace), a fragment of the Holy Blossom, and the *Goel Tzedec* (Righteous Redeemer), formed by recent Lithuanian immigrants. Mutual aid societies had also been formed, indicating the existence of a flourishing community life. By 1890 Hamilton had two synagogues: the *Anshe Shalom* congregation, which was housed in an impressive structure erected in 1880, and the *Beth Jacob* (House of Jacob) in 1888. There were also several mutual aid and philanthropic organizations. [21]

The 1880s and 1890s were critical decades not only for growth but also for the spread of Ontario's Jews across the province. Thus, while the principal communities in Toronto and Hamilton increased both in size and diversity, and secondary cities such as Ottawa and London now had organized religious institutions, sizeable communities also existed in cities where the Jewish presence had hitherto been transitory, or very small. Such was the case in Cornwall, where fifteen families constituted themselves a congregation by purchasing a cemetery plot in 1898; in Windsor, where fourteen families did the same in 1893; and in Kingston in 1891. [22] As well, during the 1890s, many other smaller cities — St. Catharines and Welland in the Niagara Peninsula; Brantford, Galt, Hespeler, Guelph, and Berlin in the Grand River Valley; Belleville and Peterborough in the south-central part of the province; Sault Ste. Marie, North Bay, Sudbury, Fort William, and Port Arthur in the north — attracted small numbers of Jews. These formed the nuclei of the organized communities that came into being after the turn of the century, when further waves of immigrants boosted the province's Jewish population to over 27,000 by 1910. Indeed, smaller numbers were also migrating to Ontario's smaller towns like Woodstock, Midland, Almonte, Mattawa, Goderich, Wingham, Eganville, Alliston, Lanark, and Merrickville.[23]

Generalizations about the evolution of these small communities are, of course, risky. But it seems that, on the basis of surveys conducted by the Canadian Jewish Congress in the 1950s, they followed a common pattern of development.[24] In each of these towns or small cities, the first Jews to decide on permanent settlement usually undertook to buy a piece of land for a cemetery, following the tradition established by Abraham, whose first endeavour after settling in Hebron was to purchase a separate burial plot for himself and his descendants. At the same time, they constituted themselves a *chevra kadisha* (a holy society) to bury the dead. And they assembled with fellow Jews for prayer, first in a home, then in a hall rented from the lodges of Oddfellows, Orangemen, Foresters, Elks, or Moose. A few years later a campaign would be mounted to raise funds to buy a house or large shed for conversion to a synagogue, or to erect a new building. At about the same time arrangements would be made to employ a *melamed*, a man who, besides organizing religious services, was responsible for teaching children the rudiments of the subjects required for the observance of *bar mitzvah*, in organized classes known as *cheder*. This individual usually served also as cantor and *shochet* (ritual slaughterer).[25]

Once acquired, a synagogue was usually the focal point of the small-town Jewish community. In the sanctuary religious rites and holidays were observed, the most well-attended — the high holy days of *Rosh Hashanah* and *Yom Kippur* in the autumn — attracting many Jews from outlying small towns and villages. As well, *cheder* (classes for children) and meetings of the synagogue ladies' auxiliary, or other separate associations of men, women, and young people took place. By far the most active and important of these groups were those formed by the women. From their kitchen, the ladies' auxiliary took care of the vitally important culinary dimensions of communal life, providing *shnaps*, wine, herring, honey cake, and other delicacies for the men and boys who attended Sabbath services on Saturday mornings and banquets of broiled chicken, brisket, *knishes, kashe, tsimmes, verenikes, holupzes* for holidays, weddings, bar mitzvahs, circumcision celebrations, and other communal occasions. These women, through their auxiliary and through *Hadassah*, were among the community's most important and influential members.

While absorbed with the reconstitution of their own lives in Canada, the immigrants were also sending aid to their families who were still in Europe or attempting to bring loved ones over to Canada, and to help the communities from which they came. And they were involved in the world-wide efforts to establish a Jewish national home in Palestine. Although the return to the land of Israel was an important aspect of the messianic dream embedded in Judaism since biblical days, only with the emergence of modern political Zionism in the 1890s were sustained, organized efforts made to build Jewish life anew in what was then a tiny, impoverished corner of the Turkish empire. Zionism took immediate root in Canada. In 1899 Clarence de Sola of Montreal established the Federation of Zionist Societies of Canada (renamed the Zionist Organization of Canada in 1921). The movement spread across the Dominion and developed many branches in Ontario, from Fort William to Kingston.[26] In Toronto the early Zionist movement was especially active and took on an élan that characterized it and its numerous distinguished leaders for many years. For the next sixty years the movement in Ontario was led by Lillian and Archie Frieman of Ottawa and Rose Dunkleman and Samuel Zacks of Toronto, who laboured in small communities and large to provide as much material, moral, and political assistance as possible for the fulfilment of the Zionist dream.

Zionist activity provided much of the organizational focus of Jewish life in the typical small Ontario Jewish community. While men formed a Zionist society for educational and fund-raising purposes, women formed themselves into a chapter of the *Hadassah* organization, which was established in Canada in 1917 for the amelioration of the health and welfare of women and children in Palestine.[27] With almost religious zeal, these women raised funds for their special projects, the most important of which was Youth Aliyah (the rescue of children from Nazi Europe). Bazaars, bake sales, tag days, and appeals kept the Jewish community throbbing with what seemed like constant activity.

The Jewish youth in small towns usually belonged to Young Judaea clubs, which were affiliated with a national organization whose provincial headquarters were located in Toronto. Like *Hadassah*, Young Judaea was established in 1917 in the midst of enthusiasm for the achievement of a "Jewish national home" in Palestine as promised by the Balfour Declaration of November that year. The organization was intended to provide a stimulus and a focus for support from Canadian Jewish youth for this national endeavour.[28] It became a school for Jewish-Canadian citizenship, raising the consciousness and pride of Jewish youth, whose Canadianness in a multi-ethnic society was enhanced by their association with the revival of a Jewish national home in Eretz Israel. Besides modest efforts at fundraising — mainly for the Jewish National Fund, which was devoted to the purchase and reforestation of land in Israel — Young Judaea club members (with all the fervour of teenage true believers) taught themselves modern Jewish history from the Zionist perspective, celebrated holidays as they were observed on *kibbutzim* (collective farms) in Israel, and foregathered at regional assemblies attended by Zionist leaders from Canada and Israel. Some even planned to make *aliyah* (to emigrate) to the new state.[29]

From the 1940s on many young Jews attended Camps Shalom at Gravenhurst and Hagshama (Fulfilment) at Sharbot Lake, later Perth, the provincial Young Judaea summer camps for Ontario and Quebec. Here more intensive Zionist education was undertaken by the movement's leaders, often assisted by visitors from Israel.

The organizational activity of small-town Jewish men was usually limited to the *B'nai Brith* (Sons of the Covenant) lodge, a Jewish fraternal order devoted to a variety of public service endeavours and — through the Anti-Defamation League — to combating anti-Semitism and race prejudice.[30] The management of synagogue business and religious affairs was left entirely to the men. They hired the man who served as *melamed, shoichet,* and cantor, usually after a process of interviews, auditions, and teaching demonstrations.[31] Then, having hired this important person, who was often highly learned and deeply dedicated — perhaps even a scholar — the synagogue executive set about trying to amass the funds to pay his salary and to meet other communal expenses. Like missionaries, these "rabbis" served scattered and tiny communities, some of them distant from major Jewish centres that possessed important amenities like *mikveh* (ritual immersion) and ready access to kosher food as well as contacts with centres of learning. It is no exaggeration to say that without these "rabbis," small-town Jewish communities would not have survived.

The men also organized the annual campaign for funds to assist a variety of Jewish charities in Canada and Europe and for Zionist activities in Palestine. These campaigns, co-ordinated from Montreal and Toronto, often featured visiting speakers who informed the entire community of the desperate need for funds in Palestine. One visitor coming from Palestine in 1938 to solicit funds, however, was moved and depressed by the weak economic position of the Jews in Canada. After visiting some Ontario communities, he reported, "The Jews are mostly middle-class elements, the majority have to struggle for a living. There are many poverty-stricken. Thousands are getting Government Relief and help from Charitable Institutions."[32]

Small communities were also affiliated with the Canadian Jewish Congress, whose central region included all of Ontario. In 1915 efforts were begun to establish a democratic representative body for Canadian Jewry and to protest the atrocities against Jews in Poland and the Ukraine; the contribution by Ontario Jewry was substantial.[33] When the Congress was formed in 1919, it was intended to have a component representative of small-town Jewry, an element that was reintroduced when the Congress was re-established in the mid-1930s with Ontario as one of its distinct features. At periodic conventions of the Central Region, the delegates from small towns were able not only to voice their concerns about large issues like the growing threats to Jews in Europe and Canada's highly restrictive immigration policy, but also increas-

ingly to draw aid and advice from Congress officials on a variety of local
matters, such as the content of education programs and the recruitment
of adequately trained teachers for the congregational schools. Officers
of Congress kept community representatives informed of events of
general Jewish interest, in particular the progress of their work for
improved public relations, tolerance, and understanding as well as a
variety of matters — like the teaching of religion in Ontario's public
schools — that affected the welfare of Jews in the province.

They were special people, these small-town Jews. Without benefit
of the rich Jewish cultural life of the big cities and, without the comforts
of large numbers, exposed to the sometimes harsh and bewildering
cultural environment in which they lived, they attempted — and
largely succeeded — to sustain their communal customs and traditions
and to pass them on to their children.

The great wave of immigration to Canada at the end of the nineteenth
century and in the first decade of the twentieth raised Ontario's Jewish
population by a factor of five, from 5,321 to 27,015 by 1911.[34] But, as
Table 3 demonstrates, Toronto Jewry grew by almost 600 per cent while
Ottawa's rose by approximately 400 per cent, the Jewish population of
Kitchener/Waterloo however, rose from 20 to 239, Owen Sound from
18 to 65, Brantford from 2 to 154, and Guelph from 13 to 86. Just as
significant was the emergence in that decade of new communities in the
north of the province: Englehart, Cochrane, and North Bay for example,
by 1911, suddenly gained communities of 126, 87, and 35 Jews respectively. Kenora went from 5 to 34 in that decade, Fort William–Port
Arthur from 13 to 267, and Sault Ste. Marie from 8 to 80, indicating the
emergence of Jewish communal life in "New Ontario," where towns
with resource-based economies had emerged in the early 1900s. In
response to inquiries from the Industrial Removal Office in New York
concerning the possible placement of poverty-stricken Jewish immigrants in Canadian cities in 1912, G. Weissman sent news about the need
for freight handlers, skilled tradesmen, and day labourers at local
railway yards, grain elevators, and dredging and construction sites,
and in factories.[35]

As Table 4 indicates, many of these northern communities thrived
through the twenties, thirties, and forties. Synagogues and communal
societies were established, and these towns were tied into the national
and provincial Jewish organizational networks, although the largest of
them, Fort William–Port Arthur, was oriented to Winnipeg. By the
1950s the Jewish population in these northern Ontario cities and towns
began to decline; economic fluctuations discouraged permanence as
did the absence of opportunities for advanced education and Jewish
social life for the youth. As the Jewish population left, the synagogues
gradually emptied while a few stalwarts held on; then the buildings and

Table 3

Jewish Population by Religion in Ontario Urban Centres, 1881-1961

	1881	1891	1910	1911	1921	1931	1941	1951	1961
Toronto	543	1,425	1,610	18,237	34,377	45,205	48,744	66,273	87,517
Hamilton	177	316	1,661	1,671	2,548	2,609	2,562	3,158	3,318
Ottawa	20	46	398	1,743	2,796	3,294	3,788	4,484	5,036
London	47	144	206	571	696	679	710	871	1,301
Windsor	4	16	171	305	979	2,209	2,224	2,330	1,653
Kitchener-Waterloo	0	6	20	239	298	411	429	434	641
Brantford	9	5	2	154	241	206	214	228	303
St. Catharines	24	15	30	109	224	314	378	512	582
Kingston	22	39	128	234	320	235	290	302	366
Cornwall	24	52	50	104	89	210	186	183	220
Oshawa-Whitby	14	9	9	85	147	193	307	374	462
Sudbury	–	11	71	87	126	190	232	184	222
Fort William–Port Arthur	–	–	13	267	368	362	391	316	301
Sarnia	26	38	4	45	57	106	104	185	201
Chatham	22	23	10	–	–	–	85	147	131
Belleville	17	26	32	32	61	89	99	130	128
St. Thomas	6	8	19	41	74	55	62	87	30
Sault Ste. Marie	–	10	8	80	115	85	101	116	142
Brockville	–	9	24	–	46	39	59	56	63
Peterborough	1	19	8	39	136	139	175	232	243
Timmins	–	–	–	–	95	206	313	202	142
Guelph	–	11	13	–	87	–	165	198	250
Owen Sound	–	–	18	65	72	55	86	–	64
North Bay	–	–	–	–	66	151	125	105	119
Welland	–	–	–	–	207	15	81	107	129

Source: *Census of Canada*, 1881-1961

Table 4

Jewish Population by Religion in Northern Ontario, 1891-1951

	1891	1901	1911	1921	1931	1941	1951
Sault Ste. Marie	10	8	80	115	85	101	116
Mattawa	9	20	5	4	1	7	18
Nipissing	1	48	175	12	33	20	24
Sudbury	11	71	87	126	110	232	184
Lakehead	–	13	267	368	362	391	316
Algoma	5	35	75	56	7	48	17
North Bay	–	–	35	66	151	125	105
Timmins	–	–	–	95	206	313	202
Kenora	–	–	–	64	73	79	62
Muskoka and	–	–	61	42	43	36	41
Parry Sound	20	20	41	29	6	19	12
Porcupine	–	–	67				
Cobalt	–	–	80	49	39	20	7
Cochrane	–	–	87	21	38	11	13
Calvert					99		36
Englehart	–	–	126	9	24	51	34
Teck (Kirkland Lake)	–	–	–	7	134	308	169
Tisdale	–	–	–	–	44	65	30
Haileybury	–	–	19	1	3	–	–

Source: *Census of Canada*, 1891-1961

furnishings were sold — though torah scrolls were preserved — as the last survivors also left or died off, although the bitter-sweet memory of these little Jewish communities — and the vivid "characters" who lived in them — will remain forever alive in Morley Torgov's novel, *A Good Place to Come From*.[36]

Ontario's immigrant Jews came from many lands. But the numbers of Hungarians, Germans, Czechoslovakians, French, Dutch, Scandinavians, and Belgians were tiny in comparison to the vast tide of people entering from Russia, Lithuania, and Poland. By 1931, of the nearly 54 per cent of Ontario's foreign-born Jewish population, nearly half came from Russia and Poland and an additional 2.46 and 3.12 per cent from the United States and Romania respectively.[37] Russians and Poles settled in varying proportions in Ontario's cities, according to Rosenberg's excellent data, but only in Toronto did Poles outnumber Russians among the foreign-born Jews.[38] While this fact may have made little difference to the overall character of Jewish communities in those cities — since differences between Russian and Polish Jews were not substantive — Toronto's large Polish contingent supplied the community with a Polish-Jewish face. Many of its mutual aid societies carried the names of Polish towns and cities, such as Lodz and Ostrovche, while several of its prominent rabbis like Rosenberg, Graubart and, much later, Felder, were recruited from Polish *yeshivas* (talmudic academies).[39]

Small-town Jewish economic life began humbly. In these places, most Jews followed a variety of commercial pursuits from the very earliest times. During the era of greatest growth, these activities tended to be concentrated in small-scale retail trade (often beginning as peddling and, later, as proprietorships of women's and men's apparel or furniture stores) or in scrap metals. Though these enterprises started from humble beginnings, they were sometimes the foundations for substantial commercial and industrial enterprises. In Hamilton, for example, in the early 1900s Jacob Goldblatt began a scrap business that developed into a gigantic enterprise of supplying metals for smelting in the furnaces of Stelco; the Levy family created a similar large firm supplying scrap to Dofasco.[40] These operations — and several located in Toronto, like that of the Frankels, begun in the 1880s — had widespread links to central and western Ontario, where local and regional scrap metal dealers bought their supplies from independent collectors and dispatched huge tonnages by train or truck to the Hamilton and Toronto brokers, who in turn transported these materials to the smelters.

Jewish economic pursuits in Toronto — and to a lesser extent in Hamilton — were considerably more varied. In those places significant numbers of Jews were wage-earners employed by commercial and industrial businesses, the clothing industry in particular. Here the manufacture of ready-made clothing in factories and shops had become the "great Jewish metier" by the early 1900s, and this vast, growing, and varied industry attracted the overwhelming majority of wage-earning Jewish men and women. As well, the industry — somewhat poignantly referred to by Jews as the *shmatte* (rag) trade — served as an avenue of business opportunity for many Jews who, with daring, an eye for style, and a bit of *mazel* (luck) succeeded in becoming successful manufacturers.[41] But, from the perspective of internal communal class structure, Daniel Hiebert has demonstrated that the emergence of the Jewish presence in major branches of the clothing industry served to separate and polarize, geographically and intellectually, large elements of the Toronto Jewish community.[42] Employees, hired usually for short periods by small-scale manufacturers or contractors who produced finished goods from materials supplied by manufacturers, became increasingly radicalized as their frustration turned to protest against the sweatshop conditions that existed in this highly competitive and volatile industry.

The Jewish presence in Toronto's clothing industry attracted considerable notice during two federal royal commissions that investigated the sweating system in the late 1890s. A.W. Wright, who relied heavily on evidence supplied by Louis Gurofsky — a former clothing contractor — noted in his report of 1896 that conditions in contractors' shops were deplorable. The investigation by William Lyon Mackenzie King two years later collected further details — some of which he published in articles for the *Mail and Empire* — of the misery endured by Jewish workers in Toronto sweatshops.[43]

Conditions were so bad that the health and general welfare of workers, including large proportions of women and children, were seriously threatened. Although conditions under which contracts for the manufacture of government uniforms may have improved as a result of King's startling revelations, the well-being of this industry's workers — an increasing proportion of whom were Jews — remained essentially unchanged until the 1930s. An industry characterized by small fixed capital requirements and extreme volatility (because of management practices and sudden style changes) was tailor-made for serious conflict between labour and management. In a major new work, Ruth Frager points out that as the Jewish component of both the entrepreneurs and the workers increased after 1900, the strikes, lockouts, and attendant violence impinged significantly on the Toronto Jewish social scene.[44] Women as well as men actively protested against low pay, seasonal layoffs, piecework rates, unsanitary shops, and employers' aggressive union-busting tactics.

Radicalization was produced not only by the conditions in a brutally competitive industry in which both workers and small-scale employers were exploited, but by the left-wing radical ideas that formed part of the intellectual baggage of many Eastern European immigrants to Canada; Jews were no exception.[45] When the Communist Party of Canada was established in 1919, separate sections were formed by supporters in specific ethnic groups, notably Finns, Jews, and Ukrainians. In Toronto the activities of Jewish left-wing intellectuals and workers who were concentrated in the clothing trades unions effectively mobilized support for garment-trade strikes and other collective measures like boycotts.[46] Although the majority of Toronto's Jewish clothing workers appear to have favoured more moderate action through unions affiliated with American internationals like the Amalgamated Clothing Workers and the International Ladies Garment Workers unions, both the Amalgamated and the ILGWU fought many bitter strikes against employers during the 1920s and 1930s for better wages and working conditions. What helped to mobilize many and what characterized their stated aims were the ideals of social justice, humanism, and reform that they brought with them from Europe.[47]

These and other elements of Jewish intellectual life found expression in literature as well as in political organization and debate. Much of this took place in Yiddish, the native language of the immigrants and the medium of expression in homes, workshops and factories, clubrooms and synagogues.[48] Newspapers from Europe and other American and Canadian Jewish centres like New York and Montreal circulated in Toronto. In 1910, the *Yiddisher Zhurnal* (Jewish Journal) was founded in Toronto as a communal medium and forum devoted heavily to reporting and commenting on events in the "Jewish world" abroad and at home. Edited for many years by Abraham Rhinewine, a fine Yiddish essayist himself, the *Zhurnal* became a focus for, and a stimulus to, local Yiddish writers like L. Rosenberg, S. Nepom, and P. Matenko, all of whom contributed to an important book published in Toronto in 1919 and suggestively entitled *Kanada: A Zamelbuch* (Canada: an Anthology).[49] Here, in poetry, short stories, and essays appeared the anguish and hopes of the Jewish immigrant in a country celebrated by J.I. Segal in his poems entitled "Oif Frieye Vegn" (On Free Roads). Of Toronto's Yiddish poets, Nepom was the most renowned. A streetcar conductor, he wrote prolifically, though he published only three slim volumes of poetry, the last of which was entitled *Tramvai Lider* (streetcar poems). In the opinion of Adam Fuerstenberg, a student of the proletarian tradition in Canadian Yiddish literature, these poems possess the "raw immediacy [and] honesty that redeems them as authentic poetic testimonials to the hardships faced by Jewish immigrants to Canada."[50] Yiddish culture thrived also in the smaller centres. In London, for example, Dr. Isidore Goldstick, a high school language teacher, published translations of Yiddish literature in English and Melech Grafstein published various Yiddish works and two major English anthologies devoted to the Yiddish writers, J.L. Peretz and Sholem Aleichem.[51]

After 1922, Toronto and Ontario were also served by an English-language weekly, The *Canadian Jewish Review*, edited by Rabbi Barnet Brickner of Holy Blossom synagogue. A few years later The *Jewish Standard* was started to combat the *Review's* anti-Zionist influence; under the editorship of the feisty Meyer Weisgal, it offered an outlet for budding literati along with articles reflecting its decidedly pro-Zionist views.[52] The *Vochenblatt*, a leftist weekly, also began publication in Toronto in the 1920s.

Orthodox Jews, whose lives were largely governed by the laws of the *Torah* and who devoted at least some of their time to its study, enjoyed a separate life of the mind that was exercised in the synagogue, school, and home. Yet it was no less lively for that. Among its rabbinical leaders — Rosenberg, Yehuda Leib Graubart, Jacob Gordon, Jacob Price, and Gedaliah Felder among others — was a tradition of learning and teaching that produced numerous scholarly treatises as well as several Toronto *yeshivot* (seminaries) with several hundred students.[53]

Ontario's rabbinical leaders included both learned Orthodox clerics like these, and Reform and Conservative rabbis. Reform rabbis, all of them recruited from the United States and trained at Hebrew Union College in Cincinnati, where Social Gospel ideas were influential, were active in a variety of social causes in Toronto from the 1920s onwards. Maurice Eisendrath, rabbi of Holy Blossom, was a leading peace activist in Toronto during the 1930s, as was his wife.[54] He began a tradition that was pursued by his successors in that pulpit, Abraham Feinberg and Gunther Plaut, as well as by Rabbi Samuel Sachs of the Conservative synagogue, *Goel Tsedec*.[55] Reuben Slonim, appointed rabbi of McCaul Street *Beth Medresh Hagadol* in 1937, participated enthusiastically in Jewish-Christian dialogue as well as the Zionist movement during his lengthy tenure.[56]

Socialist ideals, with admixtures of Jewish religious universalism, were translated into vigorous left-wing educational and cultural activities in the Toronto Jewish community. Of these, there was considerable variety because left-wing opinion ranged all the way from the Moscow-oriented United Jewish People's Order to the Bundist Workmen's Circle (a non-Zionist group favouring Jewish cultural autonomy) to the sometimes overlapping left-Zionist organizations (Poale Zion-right, Poale Zion-left, Farband, and the Histadruth), which supported various forms of workers' collectives, trade unions, and *kibbutzim* in Palestine.[57] Each of these three main groupings (Communist, Bundist, and Zionist) formed its own cultural institutions, centred on its specific ideology. Each formed its own schools to teach children the fundamentals of Jewish identity, language, history, customs, and traditions from its specific perspective. Thus might the young be taught to emulate, and possibly fulfil, the ideals of the elders. Though some of these institutions did not survive beyond a few years, those that did contributed enormously to sustaining a Jewish ethnic identity seen through the prism of Jewish, leftist, secular, humanistic, and universalist values. Zionism stressed the attainment of the peoplehood of Israel in the land of Israel by reconstituting Jewish life through physical labour, co-operative institutions, and the reformulation of national life. Moreover, these organizations enabled masses to enter Jewish civil society and created mechanisms for the emergence of leadership as well as a multiplicity of forms of cultural expression.

Although such schools became the pivotal points in their respective supporters' communities and the site of much of their cultural lives, they constituted only one segment of Jewish education in Toronto. Speisman notes the significance of the *Talmud Torah* as an institution of central importance in the community from its inception in 1904.[58] Pursuing an essentially religious curriculum that emphasized Bible, Talmud, Hebrew traditions, and history, this institution schooled its pupils in mainstream Orthodox Judaism without the modern overlay of secularism and political ideologies that were standard fare in the other schools. Besides these, there were also many synagogue schools. Here — after attending public school all day — both boys and girls were provided with the elements of Jewish education and boys with the preparation for their *bar mitzvah*. But in spite of all these institutions (and private lessons provided by impecunious rabbis and teachers to special students), there was serious alarm about the large proportion of the community's youth who were receiving little or no Jewish education whatsoever. This problem, one of the factors that had prompted communal leaders to found the *Talmud Torah*, was perennial, and throughout the pre-war and postwar years, rabbis and newspaper columnists voiced profound concern for the continuance of Jewish awareness and religious observance by the younger generation.

Without doubt, there was cause for concern. Among a people whose survival was largely attributable to its devotion to learning and the preservation of its religious beliefs and tradition despite persecution, it was the supreme irony that in a libertarian society such as Canada's, cultural survival would appear to be threatened by Canadian-born Jews' mounting neglect and ignorance of their religious traditions, culture, and history.

Libertarian? Surely the Canadian framework of British liberties promised and delivered immense freedom for Jews and other immigrants in the somewhat raw "Dominion of the North" linked by law, tradition, culture, and family ties to the home of the mother of parliaments, the common law, and individual freedom. Yet, while the formal structure of liberty allowed no state oppression of Jews, there was considerable anti-Semitism in Ontario. The remark directed at one prospective Jewish settler in the 1780s indicated what was to become a considerable force a century later. Early manifestations of anti-Semitism in Ontario seem to have had no organized political *raison d'être* or cultural focus, although as Bryan Palmer points out, anti-Semitism could activate the mob spirit of the charivari in Upper Canada.[59] The radical reformer William Lyon Mackenzie wrote to himself of Sir Francis Bond Head's Jewish ancestry that "Sir Francis has the blood of the Asian desert in his veins."[60] It was more a form of jocular contempt that found expression in Sir John A. Macdonald's description of a Jewish emigration scheme of the 1880s as "the Old Clo' move," a reference to Jewish itinerant second-hand clothes pedlars who went about the streets shouting out "old clo'."[61] Or the case of Joel Miller who enlisted in the Toronto Rifles, a militia regiment, and who, after active service during the North-West Rebellion of 1885 and years of devoted attendance to regimental duties, was denied both his medal and promotion to sergeant, on the grounds, he alleged, that he was a Jew.[62]

But these views of Jews as a suspicious minority that pursued lowly occupations and was unworthy of recognition in Canada's proud fighting tradition were not limited in their appeal. Goldwin Smith, Toronto's leading intellectual at the end of the nineteenth century, published anti-Semitic articles in his newspapers, The *Bystander* and the *Weekly Sun*, and Jews were also reviled in some Christian publications for the "crime" of deicide.[63] Claude Bissell points out, in his biography of Vincent Massey, that in the early 1900s students at the University of Toronto were exposed to the virulent anti-Semitism of instructors like Maurice Hutton.[64] William Lyon Mackenzie King, a University of Toronto graduate, as royal commissioner investigating the sweating system and feature writer for the *Mail and Empire*, drew attention to the Jewish exploitation of labour (usually their own) in the garment trades.[65] The fact that both Massey and King during the 1930s and 1940s tried to prevent Jewish refugees from reaching Canada is probably at least partly attributable to their early exposure to Hutton's and other anti-Semitic sentiments that were current in late nineteenth century Ontario.[66]

However, Jews probably fared no worse at the hands of newspaper reporters — especially those writing for the Toronto *Telegram* — than Italian, Chinese, Ukrainians, and other ethnic minorities who were more or less conspicuous by reason of accent, appearance, name, clothing, or address. Conformity with general norms, especially by the youth, did result in a degree of acceptance. In sports, a few Jewish boxers and hockey and baseball players (Alex Levinsky, Sammy Luftspring, "Goody" Rosen) made it into the professional ranks, while amateur Jewish baseball and basketball teams in Toronto took their places on the local sports scene during the 1930s and 1940s. Yet some of these baseball games sparked several nasty anti-Semitic manifestations during the summer of 1933 in the Beaches district of Toronto, and a serious riot at Christie Pits, indicating that the brotherly spirit in sports had certain limitations.[67] And Sammy Luftspring, a professional wel-terweight boxer, encountered considerable anti-Semitism during his career in the ring during the 1930s.[68]

More damaging, however, was the existence of serious discrimina-tion against Jews during the inter-war years in recreation, employment, housing, and education. In a useful review of this subject, Irving Abella points out that Jews were excluded from many summer resorts and residential districts.[69] Jews simply could not find employment in certain fields such as banking, insurance, or finance. Newspaper advertise-ments for jobs and housing frequently included the warning "Chris-tians Only Need Apply." Very few managed to find jobs as primary and secondary school teachers, and Jews in university professorial and research positions were extremely rare.[70] In certain professions like engineering and architecture, there were practically no Jews. Though medicine, law, dentistry, and pharmacy were far more open profes-sions where the Jewish proportion was larger than their share of Ontario's population, informal quotas existed at medical schools like the University of Toronto, where Jewish applicants required substan-tially higher grades than non-Jews to gain entry and where Jews, in Michael Bliss's words, "could not hope for a career in an institution permeated with genteel anti-Semitism."[71] Anti-Semitism surfaced at Queen's University in 1943 when its board of trustees learned that because of a recent and sudden increase in Jewish enrolments, Jews now constituted about 7 per cent of the undergraduate student body, 15.1 per cent in arts, 13.4 in medicine, and 2.8 in engineering.[72] Jews were not admitted to university fraternities or sororities, and for those Jewish medical graduates seeking internships or residencies at certain hospi-tals such as the Toronto General, the cause was totally hopeless.[73] Even employment as clerks in large department stores like Eaton's was barred to Jews, although many worked in that company's clothing factories nearby. Young Jews growing up in Toronto during the thirties and forties believed that they faced even higher obstacles than others in getting a job during that dark decade.

They were confronted also by overt and organized anti-Semitism, especially in Toronto, where the Swastika clubs in the city's over-whelmingly Anglo-Celtic Protestant east end wore Nazi emblems, posted anti-Jewish slogans, and harassed Jews along the beaches.[74] Anti-Semitic activities in Ontario continued through the 1930s with the encouragement of Adrien Arcand, the notorious Quebec fascist leader, as well as with the support of the German National Socialists. Nazi sympathizers succeeded in eliciting pro-Nazi sentiments among some Canadians of German origins who organized branches of the *Deutscher Bund* in Toronto, Kitchener, Ottawa, St. Catharines, and Windsor.[75]

The Nazi horrors in Germany and the rest of Europe during World War II galvanized the Jewish community into exerting pressure on the federal government to admit Jewish refugees into Canada. The Canadian Jewish press, both Yiddish and English, carried enough stories of the atrocities against Jews during the thirties that there was no doubt of the murderous intent of the Nazis. What was unknown until early 1943 was the extent of their mass murders in Russia and Poland. Thus the rescue of their people from those countries was of the utmost importance, and, as historians Abella and Troper have so effectively explained, several organizations sprang into action.[76] The Canadian Jewish Congress, the Jewish Immigrant Aid Society, and the Canadian Jewish Committee for Refugees, with the support of Jewish and other Members of Parliament, all sought to persuade the government to relax its rigid exclusionist policies against Jews. Some Ontario newspapers like the *Toronto Star* carried strongly supportive editorials and the Canadian National Committee on Refugees and Victims of Political Persecution, a non-Jewish organization, campaigned actively for the admission of Jewish refugees to Canada. All of this — as Abella and Troper recount — was to no avail.

The effect of the Holocaust on Canada's Jews, once its fullest extent became known in 1945, was one of incalculable, stunned, and wrenching horror. Long into the night in many homes, tears were shed for the lost families whose faces stared out from faded photographs. Possible family survivors were sought with desperate but rapidly fading hope. A letter might arrive in 1946 or 1947 from Poland, Romania, or Israel from a distant relation who had survived, telling the story of what had happened in the town or village to the rest of the family. Murdered, all of them murdered. How could it have happened? How could it have happened? Grief erupted again, many times, long into the night. Where was God? Where was man?

In the post–World War II years, notably since the gradual liberalization of Canada's immigration policy toward Jews after 1947, a considerable flow of survivors migrated to Ontario, many of them to Toronto. Under the auspices of various organizations like the Canadian Jewish Congress and the Jewish Immigrant Aid Services, over 35,000 Jewish immigrants arrived in Canada between 1947 and 1961, most of them from Europe, along with a number of *Yordim* (those who go down, or leave) from Israel, and a small number from other Middle Eastern countries.[77] Ontario's Jewry thus received an important new infusion of population that contributed enormously to the cultural life of the community. Religious life was strengthened by the fact that a number of new orthodox congregations — mainly in Toronto — were formed, and older ones were reinforced by the new arrivals. The immigrants strengthened Jewish life by reforging the bonds between Jews in Ontario — many of second and third generation by this time — and the East European Jewish tradition. Not only were most of the new arrivals survivors in a literal sense, they also conveyed to Ontario a renewal — tragically, the last from these countries — of the vibrant religious, political, and literary expressions of a Jewish world now in ruins, the last of the resonances from what had been for centuries the heartland of European Jewish culture.

Renewal, hope, and commitment also came to Ontario's Jews from the Land of Israel. Ben Dunkleman, barely home from active service as an officer with the Queen's Own Rifles, along with several hundred other Canadians, rushed to Palestine in 1947 and 1948 to join the armed forces defending Israel.[78] As David Bercuson explains, in Toronto and other Canadian cities the fundraisers, led by Samuel Zacks of Toronto, swung into even more vigorous action. They performed marvels in the mobilization of money and material, while efforts were also underway to secure official Canadian recognition for the State of Israel.[79] From 1948 onward the attachments between Ontario's Jews and Israel grew enormously. The bonds of unity solidified as each of Israel's major crises developed.

Over nearly a century and a half, the Jewish experience in Ontario has been highly varied. At first, Jews spread themselves so widely across the province that, by the early 1920s, a community existed in every city, and few places of any size were without a Jewish family or two, usually engaged in some kind of commerce. But Jewish permanent communal existence took form mainly in the metropolis of Toronto, in large cities like Ottawa, Hamilton, and London, and in numerous small cities and towns from Cornwall to Windsor to Timmins and Fort William. This spread created both diversity of experience — in exposure to surrounding assimilationist influence and in institutional Jewish life — as well as unity and cohesion through institutions like *Hadassah*, the Zionist Organization of Canada, Young Judaea, and the Canadian Jewish Congress, all of which served as vehicles to express the commonality of the Jewish people through arrival, adjustment, disaster, and revival. These organizations also offered an opportunity for the emergence of rank-and-file women, youth, and men into Jewish civil society, into the status that went with elected positions of leadership, and into some sense of ethnic pride in an Ontario society that was monolithically Anglo-Celtic. This diversity of experience was also evident in Jewish economic and occupational pursuits, depending on time and location. Between 1931 and 1961 the Jewish occupational pattern, according to John Porter, approached more closely to the Canadian norm as more Jews entered professions and as general trends moved towards service occupations and, in proportional terms, away from agriculture and primary and manufacturing sectors.[80] As the Jewish working class in the Toronto clothing industry slowly disappeared following World War II, the community became even more middle-class and white-collar occupationally than it had been between the wars.

These transformations helped to create a more self-assured Jewish community in Ontario. Economic upward mobility, the decline, though not the disappearance, of overt anti-Semitism, and the emergence of Israel as the increasingly significant focus of Jewish attention were all of great importance. The loss of much of this diversity has changed and perhaps lessened the cultural life of the community by greatly reducing or eliminating the ideological and political range of expressions that were current a generation earlier. By the late 1950s the once-vibrant Toronto Jewish Labour Lyceum on Spadina was but an empty shell,[81] while the Jewish influence in the clothing unions was clearly waning as sons and daughters did not follow their fathers and mothers as workers in the clothing factories, but chose professions or business instead.

But while conformity, adaptation, even assimilation to Canadian norms were emerging and some degree of acceptance was evident as well, it would be wrong to conclude that Jewish identity was disappearing. In some respects it was undergoing substantial strengthening as a result of the experiences of the State of Israel. From 1948, through 1956 to 1967, Israel's military crises sharpened the Jewish identity while creating an unprecedented degree of communal unity in Canadian Jewry and strengthening a lengthy tradition of Zionism as a normative form of identity. By the 1950s old intracommunal tensions between Zionists and their opponents, and those who were indifferent, were fading because the Holocaust and mounting solidarity with the battle for Israel's very survival made such debates hollow. There was also among Jews a growing sense of the immensity of the loss experienced through the Holocaust in the murder of families and communities and in the eradication of the East European cultural tradition that had always provided Canadian Jewry with sustenance, renewal, and personal linkages. Though the shock of such a loss was too immense to absorb immediately, divisions between Zionist and non-Zionist became irrelevant as a broad consensus emerged within the community that Israel had become a focus of Jewish identity and a new source for cultural renewal. By the 1960s, therefore, there was a curious ambivalence within Ontario's Jewry. It was produced by increasing adjustment to their local milieu — with a concomitant loss of insularity and peculiarity — along with the emergence of a reinforced trans-oceanic persuasion that linked them by sentiment and family ties to Israel, an old-new land with whose fate in some ways, they clearly believed themselves to be inextricably connected. At the same time it was increasingly apparent that to be Jewish was not incompatible with being Canadian. The post-war world saw Jewish achievements and contributions to all the principal activities of mainstream Canadian life. Large Jewish corporations in many business sectors joined with other ethnic groups to challenge and complement Anglo-Saxon dominance in Ontario's commercial manufacturing, finance, and real estate developments. Jewish contributions to philanthropy were particularly noteworthy, as were achievements in the performing arts and scholarship.

In conclusion, therefore, we might observe that Ontario shared certain of the characteristics of similar societies. Like Australia's state of Victoria, Ontario's culture was shaped by the Anglo-Celtic values and political traditions of that charter group, which formed the overwhelming majority of its population, as well as by the experience produced by a continuing relationship with the Mother Country and the openness and opportunity in a new society where constraints were honoured in the breach as well as in the observance. In ways similar to South Africa, which was scarred by both national rivalry and a race conflict, Ontario's history was in part shaped by the rivalries in this nation between two cultures, two nationalities and two religious traditions. And like the United States, Ontario was in part moulded in the North American spirit of opportunity and optimism that tempted, promised, and forced a certain cultural conformity, individual liberty, and intra-communal toleration. Thus, Ontario's Jewish experience bore many similarities to the adjustment of Jews in Australia, South Africa, and North America. Yet it was also in some ways unique. The history of Ontario and its Jewish community reflects the emergence of an intense pride and ascendancy in a province whose special Britishness, large population, and burgeoning economic prosperity made it in many ways Canada's vital centre. Here Jewish life could expand and prosper without the kind of social tensions and political conflict that Jewish existence elicited in Quebec. More comfortable, more diverse, and more geographically dispersed, the Jewish experience in Ontario reflected the society in which it had emerged, as well as the enduring features of Jewish culture and the momentous transformations in modern Jewish history.

NOTES

1   *Report of Public Records and Archives of Ontario* (Toronto: 1931), p. 109. (I am indebted to Professor Keith Johnson of Carleton University for this reference.) Levy Solomons was probably a relation of Lucius Levy Solomons, a Montreal merchant who died in 1792. See Benjamin G. Sack, *History of the Jews in Canada* (Montreal: Harvest House: 1965).

2   See Robert F. Harney and Harold Troper, *Immigrants: A Portrait of the Urban Experience, 1890-1930* (Toronto: Van Nostrand, 1975).

3   Zofa Shahrodi, "The Polish Community in Toronto in the Early Twentieth Century," in Robert F. Harney, ed., *Gathering Place: Peoples and Neighbourhoods of Toronto, 1834-1945* (Toronto: Multicultural History Society of Ontario, 1985), pp. 243-55, p. 251; Zordiana Yaworsky Sokolsky, "The Beginnings of Ukrainian Settlement in Toronto, 1891-1939," ibid., pp. 279-302, passim.

4   See Lillian Petroff, "Sojourner and Settlers: the Macedonian Presence in the City, 1903-1940," ibid., pp. 177-203, p. 178.

5   Tim Buck, *Yours in the Struggle: Reminiscences of Tim Buck* (Toronto: NC Press, 1977), pp. 40, 43, 45, 84.

6   Peter Medding, *From Assimilation to Group Survival: A Political and Sociological Study of an Australian Jewish Community* (New York: Hart, 1969), p. 269.

7   Gideon Shimoni, *Jews and Zionism: The South African Experience, 1910-1967* (Cape Town: Oxford University Press, 1980), Chap. 2.

8   Feingold, *Zion in America: The Jewish Experience in America From Colonial Times to the Present* (New York: Hippocrene Books, 1981), Introduction and p. 331.

9   Arnold Eisen, *The Chosen People in America: A Study in Jewish Religious Ideology* (Bloomington: Indiana University Press, 1983), Introduction.

10   Gerald Tulchinsky, "The Third Solitude: A.M. Klein's Jewish Montreal, 1910-1950," *Journal of Canadian Studies* (1984), 19, No. 2, pp. 96-113.

11   See Joanne Burgess, "William Grant," *Dictionary of Canadian Biography*, Vol. 5, pp. 376-77, p. 376, and Walter S. Dunn Jr. "Lucius Levy Solomons," *Dictionary of Canadian Biography* Vol. 4, pp. 718-19.

12   Robert A. Rockway, *The Jews of Detroit: From the Beginning, 1762-1914* (Detroit: Wayne State University Press, 1986), pp. 3-4.

13   A few converted from Judaism to Christianity, the most noted of whom was Isaac Hellmuth, a Polish Jew who was ordained an Anglican priest and became Bishop of the Diocese of Huron. See *The Canadian Church Magazine*, 3, No. 32 (Feb. 1889) pp. 1-2. I am grateful to Professor Fred Armstrong of the University of Western Ontario for this source.

14   Sigmund Samuel, in *Return, the Autobiography of Sigmund Samuel* (Toronto: University of Toronto Press, 1963), pp. 10-11.

15   Stephen A. Speisman, *The Jews of Toronto: A History to 1937* (Toronto: McClelland and Stewart, 1979), p. 16.

16   Louis A. Kurman, "The Hamilton Jewish Community," *Wentworth Bygones*, 8 (1969), 8-12.

17   Arthur D. Hart, ed., *The Jew in Canada: A Complete Record of Canadian Jewry From the Days of the French Regime to the Present Time* (Montreal: Jewish Publications, 1924), p. 96.

18   Ibid., p. 102.

19   Ibid., p. 98. Solomon Levinson and Jacob Cohen (in 1869) and Harris Vineberg (ibid., 342).

20   National Archives of Canada [hereafter NAC], R.G. Dun and Company, Credit Registers, Montreal 1841-1876, no. 4076.

21   Kurman, "Hamilton Jewish Community", pp. 8-9.

22   Gottesman, ed., *Canadian Jewish Reference Book and Directory* (Toronto, 1961), pp. 350, 356. One of the best available studies of social and religious life in a small Ontario Jewish community is Marion E. Meyer's *The Jews of Kingston: A Microcosm of Canadian Jewry* (Kingston: Limestone Press, 1983).

23   Louis Rosenberg, *Canada's Jews: A Social and Economic Study of the Jews in Canada* (Montreal: Bureau of Social and Economic Research, Canadian Jewish Congress, 1939).

24   Canadian Jewish Congress, Central Region, Archives. I am greatly indebted to Dr. Stephen Speisman, Archives Director, for drawing my attention to this material and for making it easily accessible.

25   In the latter role — in the uncharitable minds of boys under his occasionally rough-handed tutelage —his performance seemed indistinguishable from his behaviour in the classroom.

26   See Gerald Tulchinsky, "Clarence de Sola and Early Zionism in Canada," in Moses Rischin, ed., *The Jews of North America* (Detroit: Wayne State University Press, 1987), pp. 174-94.

27   See L.M. Gelber, "The Zionist Movement in Canada" and "Hadassah in Toronto," in L. Raminsky, ed., *Hadassah Jubilee: Tenth Anniversary Toronto* (Toronto: Hadassah Council, 1927), pp. 83-87, 149-73.

28   Ibid., pp. 174-83.

29   See *The Judaean*, 11, No. 8 (Oct. 1942), p. 1, and No. 9 (Jan. 1943), p. 110.

30   Robert Shosteck, *Small-Town Jewry Tell Their Story: A Survey of B'nai B'rith Membership in Small Communities in the United States and Canda* (Washington: B'nai B'rith Vocational Service Bureau, 1953) pp. 35-36.

31   These occasions, I am informed by an impeccable authority, provided much amusement for the small boys who, being forced to act the role of model pupils for these displays of pedagogical prodigies, often shamelessly tried to use the occasions for as much hilarity as they could get away with.

32   Central Zionist Archives, Jerusalem, KKL 5/1137, Leib Yaffe (Montreal) to Keren Hayesod (Jerusalem), June 28, 1938.

33   David Rome, *Early Documents on the Canadian Jewish Congress, 1914-1921* (Canadian Jewish Congress, Montreal, National Archives, New Series, no. 1, 1974); NAC, MG 26H, Borden Papers, vol. 157, microfilm, reel C4367, pp. 84481, 84488, 84495; vols. 81-83 (C 4321) passim.

34   Though in relation to other provinces, Ontario's share of the Canadian Jewish population actually fell from 45.5 to 40.41 per cent between 1901 and 1911, and further to 38.02 by 1921 as percentages in western provinces rose dramatically. (Rosenberg, *Canada's Jews*, p. 19).

35   American Jewish Historical Society Archives, Brandeis University, Waltham Mass., I-91, Industrial Removal Office Papers, box 70, G. Weissman to Philip L. Seman, Feb. 29, 1912.

36   See also the poignant story by Norman Levine, "By a Frozen River," *Saturday Night*, Dec. 1976, pp. 49-52.

37   Rosenberg, *Canada's Jews*, pp. 78-80.

38   Ibid., p. 80.

39   Hart, p. 130; Leah Rosenberg, *The Errand Runner: Reflections of a Rabbi's Daughter* (Toronto: John Wiley and Sons, 1981).

40   See Louis Kurman, "History of the Jewish Community of Hamilton," in Eli Gottesman, *Canadian Jewish Reference Book and Directory* (Montreal: Jewish Institute of Higher Research, 1963), p. 346.

41   See Ben Dunkleman, *Dual Allegiance: An Autobiography* (Toronto: Macmillan-Signet, 1976), Chap. 2. Hart, *The Jew in Canada*, pp. 133, 135, 162, 173, 225, 319, 347, 362.

42   Daniel J. Hiebert, "The Geography of Jewish Immigrants and the Garment Industry in Toronto, 1901-1931: A Study in Ethnic and Class Relations" (Ph.D. thesis, University of Toronto, 1987).

43   *Report to the Honourable the Postmaster-General on the Methods Adopted in the Carrying Out of Government Clothing Contracts by W.L. Mackenzie King, M.A., LL.B.* (Ottawa: Government Printing Bureau, 1898).

44   Ruth A. Frager, "Uncloaking Vested Interests: Class, Ethnicity, and Gender in the Jewish Labour Movement of Toronto, 1900-1939" (Ph.D.thesis, York University, 1986).

45   See note 5.

46   For a nostalgic view of the Jewish "left" in Toronto in the interwar period, see Erna Paris, *Jews: An Account of Their Experience in Canada* (Toronto: Macmillan, 1980) pp. 117- 210.

47   See Jonathan Frankel, *Prophecy and Politics: Socialism, Nationalism, and the Russian Jews, 1862-1917* (Cambridge: Cambridge University Press, 1984).

48   See Melech Ravitch, "Yiddish Culture in Canada," Gottesman, *Canadian Jewish Reference Book*, pp. 75-80.

49   L. Rosenberg, ed., *Kanada: A Zamelbuch* (Toronto: Farlag "Vissen," 1919). Rhinewine wrote a useful account of Jewish political emancipation in Canada that was translated into English by the London intellectual, Isidore Goldstick. See Rhinewine, *Looking Back a Century on the Centennial of Jewish Political Equality in Canada* (Toronto: Kraft Press, 1932).

50   Adam G. Fuerstenberg, "Faithful to a Dream: The Proletarian Tradition in Canadian Yiddish Poetry," paper delivered to American Association of Professors of Yiddish, Modern Language Association Annual Conference, Washington, Dec. 27, 1984).

51   Ravitch, "Yiddish Culture in Canada," Gottesman, *Canadian Jewish Reference Book*, pp. 78-79.

52   See Meyer Weisgal, *So Far: An Autobiography* (Jerusalem: Weidenfeld and Nicholson: 1971), pp. 92-94, 105-106.

53   Graubart was the author of numerous scholarly works; *Encyclopedia Judaica*, Vol. 8, 862.

54   Thomas Socknat, *Witness Against War* (Toronto: University of Toronto Press, 1987), pp. 125-27, 164. See also Maurice N. Eisendrath, *The Never Failing Stream* (Toronto: Macmillan, 1939), a collection of Eisendrath's speeches, for evidence of the passion with which Reform rabbis embraced the Social Gospel.

55   Socknat, *Witness Against War*, p. 127.

56   See Reuben Slonim, *To Kill a Rabbi* (Toronto: ECW Press, 1987).

57   Irving Abella, "Portrait of a Jewish Professional Revolutionary: The Recollections of Joshua Gershman," *Labour/Le Travailleur*, 2, No. 2 (1977), 185-213.

58   Speisman, *Jews of Toronto*, p. 171.

59   Bryan Palmer, "Discordant Music: Charivaris and Whitecapping in Nineteenth Century North America," *Labour/Le Travailleur*, 3 (1978), 5-62, p. 30. The Belleville newspaper owner, George Benjamin, who was not a Jew, was hung in effigy by a mob in April of 1837. Susanna Moodie, among many others in Belleville, believed that, despite his protestations to the contrary, Benjamin was indeed a Jew. See Carl Balstadt, Elisabeth Hopkins, and Michael Peterman, *Susanna Moodie: Letters of a Lifetime* (Toronto: University of Toronto Press, 1985), pp. 88-89, 147.

60   Quoted in S.F. Wise, ed., *Sir Francis Bond Head: A Narrative* (Toronto: McClelland and Stewart, 1969), Carleton Library, No. 43, p. xv.

61   Henry Trachtenberg, "Opportunism, Humanitarianism, and Revulsion: 'The Old Clo' Move Comes to Winnipeg, 1882-83," paper presented to Canadian Historical Association, Winnipeg, 1986.

62   NAC, RG 9, II, A 1, vol. 231, Deputy Minister Docket A 9477. I am grateful to Barbara Wilson for this reference.

63   B.G. Sack, *History of the Jews in Canada* (Montreal: Harvest House, 1965), pp. 235-6, 252. William H. Elgee, *The Social Teachings of the Christian Churches, The Early Period, Before 1850* (Toronto: Ryerson, 1964), pp. 113-14.

64   Claude T. Bissell, *The Young Vincent Massey* (Toronto: University of Toronto Press, 1981), pp. 35-36. Edmund W. Bradwin, the worker-instructor of Frontier College, wrote favourably of Jewish workers. See Edmund W. Bradwin, *The Bunkhouse Man* (Toronto: University of Toronto Press, 1972), pp. 108-9.

65   *Royal Commission 1898.*

66   Bissell, *Young Vincent Massey*, p. 36.

67   See Cyril H. Levitt and William Shaffir, *The Riot at Christie Pits* (Toronto: Lester and Orpen Dennys, 1987).

68   Sammy Luftspring with Brian Swarbrick, *Call Me Sammy* (Scarborough: Prentice Hall 1975). As well as being a fascinating account of a boxer's career, this book provides a rare look at Toronto's Jewish "underside" of gamblers, street toughs, and bootleggers in the 1930s.

69   Irving Abella, "Anti-Semitism in Canada in the Interwar Years," in Moses Rischin, ed., *The Jews of North America* (Detroit: Wayne State University Press, 1987), pp. 235-46, p. 237. See also Dunkleman, *Dual Allegiance*, p. 10, and Dennis H. Wrong, "Ontario's Jews in the Larger Community," Albert Rose, *A People and Its Faith: Essays on Jews and Reform Judaism in a Changing Canada* (Toronto:

University of Toronto Press, 1959), pp. 45-59, p. 53. "I remember seeing such signs ["Christians Only Need Apply"] myself on Toronto Island and at Lake Ontario resorts east of Toronto in the late 1930s and early 1940s, some of them far more direct — simply asserting "No Jews Wanted" — than similar notices displayed in the eastern United States during the same period."

70   Rosenberg, *Canada's Jews*, p. 192; see memoir of Ray Rothbart, *From Our Lives: By Members of the Baycrest Terrace Memoirs Group*, pp. 160-168.

71   Michael Bliss, *Banting: A Biography* (Toronto: McClelland and Stewart, 1985), p. 177. See also p. 179.

72   Frederick W. Gibson, *Queen's University* , Vol. 2, *1917- 1961: To Serve and Yet Be Free* (Montreal: McGill-Queen's University Press, 1983), pp. 199-202. Most of the increase in the Jewish student body came from Quebec, where, it was discovered, their marks were not high enough to gain them entry into McGill. The Queen's Faculty of Arts then simply decided "on quite different grounds to raise its admission requirements to full senior matriculation." Gibson, *To Serve*, p. 202. Queen's had always been considered hospitable to Jews. Even though under its revised charter of 1912 "the University shall continue distinctively Christian and the trustees shall satisfy themselves of the Christian character of those appointed to the teaching staff," Jews have been members of the university faculty since 1937. Hilda Neatby, *Queen's University*, Vol. 1,*1841-1917: And Not To Yield*, ed. Frederick W. Gibson and Roger Graham (Montreal: McGill-Queen's University Press, 1978), p. 265.

73   Jews at the University of Toronto formed their own fraternities. The Alpha Omega Fraternity, which was founded in Philadelphia in 1907 as "the result ... of ... the need for the Jewish student in the dental schools to seek mutual assistance, to foster self-improvement and to repel the undemocratic policies allowed to exist at their schools of higher learning," established a branch in Toronto in 1921. Walter I. Levine, *Fifty Year History of Alpha Omega Fraternity* (Philadelphia, 1957), pp. 5, 12.

74   Lita-Rose Betcherman, *The Swastika and the Maple Leaf: Fascist Movements in Canada in the Thirties* (Toronto: Fitzhenry and Whiteside, 1975), pp. 45-60.

75   Jonathan F. Wagner, *Brothers Beyond the Sea: National Socialism in Canada* (Waterloo: Wilfrid Laurier University Press, 1981), pp. 68, 79-80, 90-91.

76   Irving Abella and Harold Troper, *None Is Too Many: Canada and the Jews of Europe, 1933-1948* (Toronto: Lester and Orpen Denys, 1982).

77   Joseph Kage, *With Faith and Thanksgiving: The Story of Two Hundred Years of Jewish Immigration and Immigrant Aid Effort in Canada (1760-1960)* (Montreal: Eagle, 1962), pp. 129, 153.

78   Ben Dunkleman, *Dual Allegiance: An Autobiography* (Scarborough: Macmillan-New American Library, 1976), pp. 131-32.

79   David Bercuson, *The Secret Army* (Toronto: Lester and Orpen Denys, 1983), p. 47.

80   John Porter, *The Vertical Mosaic: An Analysis of Social Class and Power in Canada* (Toronto: University of Toronto Press, 1965), p. 562.

81   See Ben Lappin, "May Day in Toronto; Yesterday and Now," *Commentary*, 19, No. 5 (May 1955), 476-79 for a nostalgic look back to the "old days" when thousands of Jewish clothing workers and their families marched on Spadina every May first.

THE BATTLE FOR WILDERNESS IN ONTARIO: SAVING QUETICO-SUPERIOR, 1927 TO 1960

Gerald Killan & George Warecki

On April 12, 1960, a remarkable thirty-three year environmental battle came to a successful conclusion with a diplomatic exchange of letters between Ontario and the United States. The purpose of the exchange was to protect the primitive character of Quetico Provincial Park and the adjacent Boundary Waters Canoe Area of the Superior National Forest in Minnesota. The campaign had been led by a small group of conservationists known in the United States as the Quetico-Superior Council (formed in 1928), and in Ontario as the Canadian Quetico-Superior Committee (formed in 1949), reorganized as the Quetico Foundation in 1954. Originally, these groups had aspired to a greater goal — a Canadian-American treaty to set aside the entire Rainy Lake watershed, a region five times larger than the area affected by the exchange of letters. Over the years, however, a complex array of local, dominion-provincial, federal-state, and international considerations combined to recast the initial program of the Quetico-Superior Council into the less grandiose but politically palatable scheme adopted in 1960. The lengthy battle to defend "the Quetico" against industrial and commercial exploitation is an important chapter in Ontario conservation history. It was the first organized effort to protect the wilderness in the province, and as such, it laid a foundation for the subsequent efforts of Ontario's wilderness preservation movement of the late 1960s and 1970s.

Unlike historians in the United States, Ontario scholars have neglected the Quetico-Superior story. The only historian who has attempted to unravel the Ontario phase of the conservationist campaign is R. Newell Searle of Minnesota in his comprehensive study *Saving Quetico-Superior: A Land Set Apart*. Searle's interpretation is written from the perspective of the leading American conservationists, and his view of Ontario events and personalities is largely shaped by their assumptions and biases. He draws a picture of a struggle between

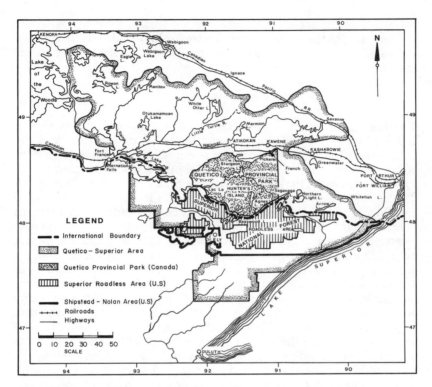

The Quetico-Superior area and Rainy Lake watershed. (Map by Sandy Soga Sparks, Oakridge Drafting.)

indomitable wilderness "warriors" and successive provincial governments ostensibly dominated by timber interests and generally unsympathetic towards the conservationists' cause.[1]

This interpretation, however, is one-sided and simplistic. The wilderness proponents did not possess a monopoly on either virtue or advanced conservationist thinking, and at no time did the Ontario government oppose all the features of the Quetico-Superior program. From the outset senior provincial officials and politicians favoured the idea of managing the Quetico Provincial Park portion of the Rainy Lake watershed in accordance with multiple-use principles that emphasized the recreational and scenic values of the land. The provincial government's reluctance to engage in negotiations for the creation of an international wilderness area embracing the entire watershed stemmed from the traditional fear that it might lose its right to manage the natural resources of the region. Ontario officials parted company with the wilderness groups mainly over the treaty proposal, which entailed federal involvement and the loss of provincial sovereignty over an immense piece of Crown land.

I

The Rainy Lake watershed, a vast region embracing some 14,500 square miles of lake-spangled and forested land, lies on both sides of the international border between Ontario and Minnesota. It stretches from Rainy Lake on the west to Lake Superior on the east and includes both Quetico Provincial Park and the Superior National Forest. During the 1920s, this region became the subject of an intense debate between developmental and conservationist forces. The latter were alarmed when Edward W. Backus, the imperious Minnesota timber baron who controlled much of the forest products industries in the watershed, unveiled a huge industrial scheme to construct a series of dams in the boundary waters region from Fort Frances to the eastern boundary of Quetico Park. If completed, the dams would raise water levels in the border lakes by at least fifteen feet, and as much as eighty feet, with incalculable damage to the scenic and recreational qualities of the area.

Backus's industrial vision for Quetico-Superior aroused the ire of conservationists in the United States, where a so-called "wilderness cult" had flourished since the turn of the century and where wilderness protection had already emerged as a national political issue.[2] To wild-country enthusiasts in the American Midwest, Quetico-Superior had great symbolic value as "the last of the North Woods," the only nationally owned lake country of its kind, and a place unrivalled for canoeing in primitive surroundings. Those who appreciated the significance of the region resolved to block Backus at every turn and to argue their case before the International Joint Commission (IJC), which began public hearings on the Backus plan — the Rainy Lake Reference — in 1925. Confidence surged in conservationist ranks in 1926 when, after a bitter struggle against other development interests, three roadless areas encompassing some one thousand square miles of exceptional canoe country were set aside in the Superior National Forest with logging prohibited in shoreline reserves along all waterways and portages.[3]

The conservationists realized that to defeat Backus they would have to fashion an alternative plan for the Rainy Lake watershed. This task fell largely upon Ernest C. Oberholtzer (1884-1977), a Harvard-trained landscape architect, self-educated naturalist, and woodsman who lived on an island in Rainy Lake. He received advice and encouragement from a small group of wildland enthusiasts, including Sewell T. Tyng, an influential Wall Street lawyer, officials of the Izaak Walton League in Chicago, and a dozen young Minneapolis professionals, mainly lawyers, such as Frank Hubachek, Charles S. Kelly, and Fred Winston. In June 1927 the sole Ontarian joined the group in the person of Arthur Hawkes of Toronto, the one-time publicity agent for the Canadian Northern Railway, who in 1909 had been instrumental in the establishment of the Quetico Forest Reserve. No stranger to the techniques of publicity campaigns, Hawkes advised the American conservationists to emphasize the history of the voyageurs and to reconstruct, in speech, print, and motion picture, the pageantry of the Northwest Company and the great fur trade depots at Fort William, Grand Portage, and Rainy Lake. Oberholtzer thought Hawkes's ideas were inspired, and from this point on, the historical theme figured conspicuously in the literature of the QSC campaign.[4]

In November 1927 Oberholtzer completed his plan for the Rainy Lake watershed. He proposed a multiple-use program with the primary emphasis on wilderness recreation and scenic preservation: "The key note of the plan [was] a treaty between the Dominion of Canada and the United States," that would secure four main objectives throughout the watershed: (1) that all shorelines be reserved from logging, flooding, or other form of exploitation; (2) "that all the hinterlands" beyond the shoreline reserves "be devoted to practical forestry for economic purposes"; (3) "that all fish and game be regulated for maximum productivity"; and (4) that the watershed be administered by an international commission made up of Canadian and American forestry, park, and wildlife officials. Oberholtzer considered that these four objectives had to be entrenched in a treaty to ensure that the protection was permanent.[5]

On January 27, 1928, the conservationists founded the Quetico-Superior Council (QSC), "an international organization associated with the Izaak Walton League of America for the sole purpose of obtaining, with the consent of the Province of Ontario, a treaty ... to protect ... the Rainy Lake watershed...."[6] Ernest Oberholtzer became president of the council; the executive committee comprised largely businessmen and professionals from Minneapolis-St. Paul, and two Canadians — Arthur Hawkes and Jules Preudhomme, the solicitor for the City of Winnipeg who had appeared before the IJC to oppose the Backus scheme.

When first presented with the QSC plan in November 1927, the Ontario Minister of Lands and Forests, William Finlayson, promised to co-operate with American federal and state authorities to harmonize management policies in the watershed. An ardent proponent of scientific forestry and an especially capable and enlightened administrator, Finlayson was intrigued by the conservationists' program because the QSC's ideas on land-use planning ran parallel to his own. During his first year in the lands and forests portfolio, for instance, Finlayson had moved swiftly to introduce the Forestry Act (1927) in order to expand the policy of classifying agricultural and forest land. He later built upon this Act with further legislation that encouraged the pulp and paper industry to operate on a permanent sustained-yield basis, and expanded the provincial forest reserve system.[7]

Although Finlayson saw much merit in the QSC proposal for the Rainy Lake watershed, there were two aspects of the program that he found unacceptable. He rejected both the treaty aspect of the Oberholtzer scheme and the idea of an international commission to administer the region. For Ontario politicians, these proposals raised the spectre of control by the federal government of a vast, resource-rich expanse of provincially owned Crown land. As Christopher Armstrong has argued in *The Politics of Federalism: Ontario's Relations with the Federal Government, 1867-1942*, all Ontario governments since Confederation had "sought the widest possible sphere of independence in shaping policies designed to promote the economic growth of the province, particularly through the development of natural resources, where ownership of lands, forests, and minerals gave the provincial government great authority."[8] Unfamiliar with dominion-provincial relations in Canada, and influenced by American centralist biases, the QSC leaders failed to plumb the depths of the Ontario government's hostility to the idea of a treaty. As a result, Oberholtzer naively proceeded in February 1928 to invite the province to commence negotiations with the American and dominion governments for a watershed agreement. The invitation was brusquely dismissed.[9]

Even though the QSC program had been rebuffed by Ontario on the treaty question, in the United States it received an enthusiastic public reception, which climaxed in 1930 with the passage through Congress of the Shipstead-Nolan Act. This legislation placed huge obstacles before the Backus scheme by establishing a 400-foot shoreline reserve policy on all federally owned property in the boundary waters area and by requiring Congressional approval for each dam project.[10]

Significantly, Ontario Lands and Forests Minister Finlayson demonstrated in 1930 that he intended to keep his promise of "friendship and co-operation" with the Americans in managing Quetico-Superior "so that the services on both sides of the international line [might] be correlated as much as possible." Notified by the Prairie Club of Chicago that scenic destruction was being perpetrated by timber companies along the border lakes in Quetico Provincial Park, he moved with alacrity to regulate the loggers. Acting on the advice of the Prairie Club directors, who had been primed with information by the wilderness author and ecologist, Sigurd Olson, Finlayson issued instructions for the establishment of shoreline reserves on eight major canoe routes along the international border.[11]

Meanwhile, Edward Backus's industrial empire fell victim to the Depression, and in November 1931 his Minnesota and Ontario Paper Company went into receivership. Much to the chagrin of the conservationists, the receivers pursued a modified version of Backus's original development scheme. The issue was not resolved until 1934, when the International Joint Commission concluded its deliberations on the Rainy Lake Reference by ruling against the plan to dam the waterways along the border.[12] Other successes soon followed. In June 1934 President Franklin D. Roosevelt appointed a Quetico-Superior Committee to pursue the idea of creating an international "wilderness sanctuary." Three members of the QSC were appointed to the committee — Oberholtzer, Sewell Tyng, and Charles S. Kelly— along with one representative each from the departments of Agriculture and the Interior. Two years later the President expanded the Superior National Forest by 1,250,000 acres, thereby consolidating what had been three separate pieces of land.

These notable achievements were attributable to the extensive public support that the QSC leaders enjoyed in the United States. It was frustrating for the conservationists that Ontarians took so little interest in their cause. Few newspapers covered the QSC story, a situation that Oberholtzer attributed to "a conspiracy of silence."[13] Actually, Ontario's apathy was due, not to a Backus-inspired conspiracy, but rather to a general lack of knowledge about the remote Rainy Lake watershed. Few southern Ontarians visited distant Quetico Provincial Park, since there were no cottages, camps, or resorts to attract them. Access remained difficult. Until 1954 no highway existed north of the park, and the Canadian National Railway provided only infrequent service to the isolated station at Kawene, some eight miles by logging road from the park headquarters at French Lake. For these reasons most visitors to Quetico were Americans, who entered the park from Minnesota. Of the 1,234 recorded visitors in 1930, a mere half dozen identified themselves as Canadians. The journalist and outdoorsman Gregory Clark of the Toronto *Daily Star* added another reason for the public's indifference to the QSC program. "You cannot expect from the Canadian public," he wrote to Oberholtzer, "anything like the response ... in the United States because ... you have suffered and lost so much of your wilderness and we are merely in the process of losing it."[14]

Unable to make an impression on the Ontario public and politicians, the QSC understandably concentrated its efforts in the United States. Only after the IJC had ruled on the Rainy Lake Reference in 1934 did the wilderness forces again direct their attention to Ontario. Their timing was in part shaped by the changed political climate in the province following the election of Mitch Hepburn and the Liberals in June 1934. This time the QSC found a willing ally in Ontario — the noted historian and civil servant Lawrence J. Burpee, who, among other things, was the first Canadian secretary of the International Joint Commission. In an extraordinary burst of activity, Burpee arranged a string of endorsements for the QSC program and persuaded a variety of distinguished Canadians to serve as members of a proposed Canadian advisory board.[15] Most encouraging of all, two of Burpee's politically connected friends —Vincent Massey, who had been the first Canadian Minister to Washington from 1926 to 1930, and Duncan McArthur, the Ontario Deputy Minister of Education — seemed to offer easy access to Premier Hepburn. At the Department of External Affairs in Ottawa, John Read informed Burpee that he did "not see any very serious difficulties in the way of a treaty."[16] In Minnesota, Ernest Oberholtzer was ecstatic. "It is simply a matter now," he declared in October 1935, "of approaching the Ontario officials, giving publicity to the whole thing on both sides, and then setting our Canadian friends to work to bring about whatever measures are necessary."[17]

Oberholtzer was sorely mistaken in his optimistic assessment of the Ontario situation. The board of advisors never met because Vincent Massey requested that the names of its members be withheld until he had explained the QSC objectives to Hepburn, something he apparently failed to do. Duncan McArthur proved more reliable, but when he raised the topic with Hepburn, it was waved aside on at least two occasions: "the P.M.'s mind was on other matters."[18]

In spite of his yeoman service, Burpee did not succeed in changing the views of Ontario officials on the matter of a treaty to entrench the QSC program. As the celebrated feud between Premier Hepburn and Prime Minister Mackenzie King heated up after 1936 and soured dominion-provincial relations, any prospects that the Premier might agree to the QSC treaty proposal flickered out completely. In addition to these considerations, lands and forests officials harboured deep suspicions about the intentions of the American government. Nearly one million acres of land in the Superior National Forest were still privately owned. Before any treaty could be struck, these properties would have to be acquired at great expense. Doubting that this would be possible in the middle of the Depression, the Minister of Lands and Forests, Peter Heenan, informed Oberholtzer in December 1936 that he wished to hear no more about negotiating a treaty "until the United States [had] completed ownership on the Minnesota side."[19] When the American government made diplomatic overtures to Ontario in 1938 and sought a commitment to discuss a treaty in the event that Washington resolved the ownership issue, the province again turned a deaf ear. After eighteen months of silence and repeated requests for an answer by the Canadian Secretary of State's office, the Ontario government decided that, owing to the outbreak of World War II, the matter was not important enough to discuss.[20]

A bitterly disappointed Ernest Oberholtzer blamed the Ontario Deputy Minister of Lands and Forests, Walter Cain, the official who for years had stood between the conservationists and the Minister and the Premier, for the failure to obtain a treaty. In a fit of anger, Oberholtzer excoriated Cain as "an old type of beaurocrat [*sic*] who is in closest confidence with the lumbermen and lower people."[21] More recently, Newell Searle, who relied heavily on the Oberholtzer papers, also identified Deputy Minister Cain as the villain of the piece and attributed Ontario's lack of enthusiasm for a treaty to governments "still dominated by lumbermen."[22] But this interpretation is not convincing. The provincial response to the QSC program was conditioned neither by a reactionary deputy minister nor by nefarious timber interests, but by traditional concerns about provincial rights and the ownership and control of the natural resources in the Rainy Lake watershed. As early as 1929, the Winnipeg lawyer Jules Preudhomme had tried in vain to explain to Oberholtzer that Ontario's hostility to the treaty should not be equated with a general antagonism to all the QSC objectives. "It simply reflects," Preudhomme wrote, "the jealousy with which provincial rights and control of natural resources have always been watched in that Province."[23] Regrettably, his explanation fell on deaf ears.

If Oberholtzer had been less self-righteous, he might have been able to appreciate that Ontario officials shared many of his views on managing the Quetico wilderness. In 1937 for instance, George Delahey, district forester at Fort Frances, with the blessing of the unfairly maligned Deputy Minister Cain, inserted clauses in four new timber licences to protect some 106 miles of shoreline along canoe routes in the section of Quetico Provincial Park contiguous to the Shipstead-Nolan area.[24] In this regard, Delahey and Cain were expanding to Quetico Park some of the multiple-land use policies already operating in Algonquin Provincial Park. Since 1931 the superintendent of Algonquin, Frank A. MacDougall, had vigorously applied management policies in his park every bit as progressive as those being pursued by the QSC for Quetico-Superior. To minimize conflicts between recreation and logging, he maintained a roadless and lease-free wilderness interior in Algonquin and created no-cut scenic reserves along shorelines and portages. He also established the first nature reserves and introduced scientific fish and wildlife management.[25]

The steely-eyed, craggy-faced MacDougall was the first professional, university-trained forester to hold the position of superintendent in Algonquin. After graduating from the University of Toronto School of Forestry in 1923, he had joined the Ontario Department of Lands and Forests, where he had quickly distinguished himself as a first-rate administrator. In his capacity as district forester in Sault Ste. Marie, he impressed his superiors by promoting reforestation on a large scale near Thessalon, in what became the Kirkwood Forest Management Unit. William Finlayson, convinced that the traditionally ill-trained and politically appointed provincial park superintendents of bygone years had to be replaced by professional foresters and resource managers, personally selected MacDougall for the Algonquin post.

During his decade in the park, MacDougall introduced the philosophy of "multiple-use" to Ontario and thereby established himself as one of the most creative people in the annals of the Department of Lands and Forests.

When Frank MacDougall replaced Walter Cain as deputy minister in 1941, he soon resolved to extend to Quetico Park the management policies he had pioneered in Algonquin. He made this decision in October 1941 after the Izaak Walton League petitioned against the plans of the J.A. Mathieu Lumber Company to cut in the vicinity of Crooked Lake along the international boundary. The Waltonians urged the department to withdraw from timber harvesting a 400-foot shoreline reserve on the lake, as had been done in similar zones across the border in the Shipstead-Nolan area.[26] Instead, MacDougall stunned everyone concerned by abruptly ending the *ad hoc* creation of shoreline reserves and instituting a uniform 300-foot-wide reserve policy along all canoe routes in Quetico Park.[27] A year later, the results of MacDougall's dramatic policy were evident. Ernest Oberholtzer paddled Crooked Lake and complimented the Ontarians "on the improvement over previous operations anywhere in Quetico Park. I saw no logging dams or flooded shores. I saw no islands that had been logged ... [T]here was a real effort to protect shore-line timber and usually with much success."[28]

Not surprisingly, the Quetico-Superior Council thought it had found a kindred spirit in Frank MacDougall. Perhaps here was the Ontario official who would support their campaign to protect the recreational and scenic qualities of the Rainy Lake Region under international treaty. But meetings with MacDougall and Lands and Forests Minister N.O. Hipel disabused the American conservationists of this notion. MacDougall and Hipel were no more interested in negotiating a treaty than their predecessors had been. Still, the Americans were encouraged by the "friendly and cooperative" reception they received in Toronto. Kenneth Reid of the Izaak Walton League found that the QSC and the Ontario officials agreed "in all essentials of management policies ... for both sides of the border."[29] Lands and Forests Minister Hipel concluded the discussions with the Americans in January 1942 by instructing the regional forester, W.D. Cram, to meet twice a year with his counterpart in the U.S. Forest Service, Jay H. Price, in order to co-ordinate the management policies in Quetico Provincial Park and the Superior National Forest. For all intents and purposes, the basis of the formal agreement eventually signed in 1960 had been reached.

(Upper left) *Lawrence J. Burpee (on the left), first Canadian secretary of the International Joint Commission, with W. Stewart Wallace in 1927. (Courtesy Archives of Ontario.)*

(Top) *Harold C. Walker, a member of the Canadian Quetico-Superior Committee, and first chairman of the Quetico Foundation. (Courtesy Minnesota Historical Society.)*

(Left) *Ernest Oberholtzer, holding his young friend Bob Hilke, at his island residence, Rainy Lake, in the 1930s. (Courtesy Quetico Park Archives.)*

(Upper left) *Frank A. MacDougall, Ontario Deputy Minister of Lands and Forests. (Courtesy Archives of Ontario.)*

(Top) *Sigurd F. Olson about 1962. (Courtesy Bruce M. Litteljohn.)*

(Left) *Charles S. Kelly about 1940. (Courtesy Minnesota Historical Society.)*

(Upper left) *Edward W. Backus in the 1920s. (Courtesy Minnesota Historical Society.)*

(Top) *Frank B. Hubachek on Basswood Lake in the 1920s. (Courtesy Minnesota Historical Society.)*

(Left) *Chester S. Wilson, Minnesota Commissioner of Conservation in the 1940s. (Courtesy Minnesota Historical Society.)*

(Upper left) *M.S. "Pop" Fothering-ham, president of Steep Rock Iron Mines Ltd., and a founder of the Canadian Quetico-Superior Committee 1949. (Courtesy Shirley Peruniak, Quetico Park Archives.)*

(Top) *Donald P. O'Hearn, executive secretary of the Canadian Quetico-Superior Committee, in Quetico Park during the early 1950s. (Courtesy Shirley Peruniak, Quetico Park Archives.)*

(Left) *Two men who shaped the provincial park policy of Ontario — Leslie M. Frost and Frank A. MacDougall in Lindsay, Ontario, in 1969. (Courtesy Archives of Ontario.)*

II

During World War II, Ontario's park officials and politicians discovered that, when it came to assessing the QSC program, they had much in common with their counterparts in Minnesota. Before 1943 there had been little communication between the two governments on the subject, but this changed with the appointment that year of Chester S. Wilson as Minnesota's Commissioner of Conservation. Wilson subjected the QSC scheme to critical scrutiny and launched a personal crusade to recast it into a more politically acceptable form. In 1944 he communicated his views to the Ontario government, explaining that Minnesota, no less than Ontario, rejected the centralist-federalist bias of the QSC program. Taking a firm states-rights position, Wilson refused to accept the idea that Minnesota should hand over title to the extensive state forest lands in the Shipstead-Nolan area and other parts of the watershed. And, for the same reasons as Ontario, he opposed the notion of a Canadian-American treaty to protect the watershed, since it would require undue federal interference in state lands. The very idea of setting apart the entire Rainy Lake region, Wilson explained to the Ontario Department of Land and Forests, was also impracticable.[30]

By challenging the QSC objectives, Chester Wilson angered Ernest Oberholtzer, who denounced him in 1944 as a tool of the hydro and timber interests. The charge was unfounded: Wilson himself sought to create an international wilderness zone in the border lakes region, a place that would be free of "roads, tourist resorts, commercial airplane traffic, or other developments inconsistent with preservation of wilderness values."[31] But he believed that this wilderness zone should be restricted to a tract of land about one-fifth the size of the Rainy Lake watershed. It would only encompass the federally owned roadless areas of the Superior National Forest, and the Hunter's Island portion of Quetico Provincial Park (the section bounded by the international border, Lakes Saganaga and Kawnipi, and the Maligne River).

At war's end, Wilson argued that conservationists and government agencies on the American side should give urgent priority to the acquisition of the 137,000 acres of private lands scattered throughout the Superior roadless areas. Resorts on these lands were growing in popularity, and they posed an enormous threat to the solitude of the wilderness canoe country. By 1945 some two dozen aircraft were droning incessantly back and forth across Quetico-Superior, carrying passengers and supplies to forty interior resorts, nineteen of which were located in the roadless areas. Since Minnesota had determined to prevent the federal government from gobbling up the state forest lands and adding them to the Superior National Forest in keeping with the QSC scheme, the conservationist groups and the U.S. Forest Service had little choice but to concentrate on purging the roadless areas of the resorts.

Ernest Oberholtzer, blinded by his resentment of Wilson, resisted the change in emphasis. All the same, during 1945 the Minnesota Conservation Department, the U.S. Forest Service, and the conservationist groups finally reached a consensus that the federal government must attempt both to acquire the private holdings in the roadless areas of the Superior National Forest and to seek an aircraft ban for the border lakes. Subsequently they combined to draft a federal acquisition bill to enable the American Secretary of Agriculture to purchase the resorts in the roadless areas that would impair the wilderness character of the canoe country.[32]

Wilson eventually received Ontario's support for his modified version of the QSC program, but not without having to overcome serious opposition. In Fort Frances, the acting district forester, J.M. Whalen, proved to be a formidable opponent. He was of the opinion that Quetico Park should be abandoned because it ran annual operating deficits and few Ontarians used it.[33] In 1944, just as the Americans were beginning to consolidate the roadless areas, Whalen approved the applications of two American fly-in resort operators to lease land in the Hunter's Island portion of the park. H.W. Crosbie, chief of the Division of Land and Recreational Areas, agreed that the commercial leases should be granted and advised Deputy Minister MacDougall that "no advantages [would] be gained by Ontario" in acceding to the American proposal for co-operation in creating an international wilderness region, even on the limited scale proposed by Chester Wilson. The sole beneficiaries of such a scheme, Crosbie believed, would be the tourist operators in Minnesota. He thought that the Americans wanted Ontario to maintain Quetico Park in a wilderness state for the benefit of the resort owners in the Superior National Forest. Since the Forest Service proposed only to remove the nineteen resorts in the roadless areas, the remaining operators in the national forest would be ideally located to exploit Quetico Park. After studying the matter, Premier George Drew also concluded that the American joint wilderness scheme smacked of a conspiracy. "It seemed to me," Drew

Clifford Sifton, of the Canadian Quetico-Superior Committee. (Courtesy Michael C. Sifton, Toronto.)

recalled, "that under the guise of an appeal to preserve and protect the [Quetico] Park area, this actually was an attempt to continue an exclusive resort playground" for a group of Chicago millionaires.[34]

As luck would have it, local business interests in Fort Frances entered the debate and tipped the scales in favour of leaving the Quetico interior free of resorts, at least for the time being. Both the chamber of commerce and the Canadian Legion vigorously opposed the prospect of American businessmen gaining a foothold in Quetico Provincial Park. The Fort Frances interests demanded a moratorium on resort leases until after the war, when a highway would probably be built from Port Arthur; then the future of the park could be carefully planned and developed by and for Ontario citizens! The chamber of commerce also requested that the decision on the international wilderness zones be deferred until the question of highway access had been resolved. Under this intense local pressure acting district forester Whalen wilted and in September 1944 withdrew his recommendation on the granting of leases to the American resort operators.[35]

With this threat neutralized, Chester Wilson set out to promote his wilderness concept in Ontario. In March 1946 he led a delegation to Toronto and outlined the American plan to set up a revolving fund to acquire private lands in the roadless areas.[36] In June, Wilson and Galen Pike, Supervisor of the Superior National Forest, addressed the Port Arthur Convention of the Northwestern Ontario Associated Chambers of Commerce before moving on to Kenora and Fort Frances for talks with local business and political interests. "We made it clear," Wilson explained, "that we were not fronting for any program of federal or international control of the whole Rainy Lake watershed, and that our aim was simply to get the existing authorities ... to co-operate in protecting ... the wilderness canoe country along the boundary on both sides." As Wilson and Pike undertook their public relations tour, the distrust of American intentions began to dissipate. The northwestern Ontario businessmen responded warmly to Wilson's statement that he fully endorsed the construction of a Fort Frances–Port Arthur highway to the north of Quetico Park. That road, he hoped, would stimulate a local tourist industry that would chiefly benefit Ontario merchants, tourist outfitters, and resort owners. "Our plan is not to isolate this territory," he insisted, "but to protect wilderness zones of reasonable size and make them accessible to the public by encouraging construction of roads, resorts, and summer homes around the margin."[37]

Following these productive meetings, Governor Edward J. Thye of Minnesota, in conjunction with the Izaak Walton League, requested the Ontario government to declare a temporary suspension of land disposition in Quetico Park, while the American conservationists ushered through Congress their acquisition bill to eliminate the private holdings in the Superior roadless areas. "Naturally, our whole purchase program would be futile, and would have to be dropped if those we bought out on the American side merely hopped across on your side," explained Kenneth Reid of the Izaak Walton League.[38] After conferring with the chamber of commerce and the Conservative Party Association in Fort Frances, the Ontario government agreed to the request.[39] Clearly, Chester Wilson's work had paid dividends; his public relations efforts had been the critical element in winning over the regional economic and political power brokers in northwestern Ontario, and ultimately the Drew cabinet. A year later, in May 1948, the Land and Recreational Areas chief, Wilson Cram, confided to Sigurd Olson of the Quetico-Superior Council that the suspension on leases "would be extended indefinitely." Olson wrote excitedly to his colleagues: "It is a set policy, and will be continued [until] such time as we give up the fight on our side."[40] However, there was little chance of the American conservationists "giving up the fight"; indeed, the assault on commercialism in the Superior roadless areas intensified in December 1949, when President Harry S. Truman signed a precedent-setting executive order establishing an airspace reservation above the roadless areas. The order also specified that, beginning on January 1, 1952, the owners of private land in the roadless areas would be prohibited from using aircraft to reach their properties.[41]

In the postwar era, as Chester Wilson and others modified the original Quetico-Superior Council scheme, the QSC did not abandon its goal of protecting the entire Rainy Lake watershed by formal treaty between Canada and the United States. With the help of several influential Canadians — Clifford Sifton, who controlled a string of newspapers and radio stations, Harold C. Walker, a prominent Toronto lawyer, and Vincent Massey — the American conservationists finally succeeded in establishing a Canadian Quetico-Superior Committee, the first organization formed in Ontario dedicated to wilderness protection. In March 1949, no less a patron than General Dwight D. Eisenhower had written in his capacity as President of Columbia University to Vincent Massey, Chancellor of the University of Toronto, endorsing Ernest Oberholtzer's 1927 scheme for Quetico-Superior. With Eisenhower's letter in hand, Massey organized a luncheon for a group of eminent Ontarians who had shown an interest in the QSC cause. Evidently Eisenhower's endorsation, combined with Massey's personal suasion, did the trick, for all the luncheon guests agreed to form the Canadian Quetico-Superior Committee.[42]

Encouraged by the momentum building in Ontario, the American conservationists rushed precipitately into action in late 1949 and prepared a draft "Treaty for the Establishment of an International Peace Forest in the Quetico-Superior Area."[43] Written largely by Ernest Oberholtzer and reworked by the American State Department, the document reached the Ontario government in January 1950. It called for the joint management of the Rainy Lake and Pigeon River watersheds "to protect the rare natural values" of the area and "to perpetuate the wilderness character of the region in the form of an international memorial forest." Its many virtues notwithstanding, the draft treaty had no chance of being accepted by Ontario. Article eleven sealed its fate by proposing to obligate the Canadian and American governments to establish an international advisory committee as the mechanism for implementing joint management of the region. The QSC bungled by specifying that the dominion cabinet would appoint the three Canadian representatives, a proposal certain to anger provincial authorities. Harold Walker tried gamely to argue that the treaty would "not involve the surrender of sovereignty, management or jurisdiction," but Ontario officials found his logic confusing and unconvincing.[44] Walker and the other members of the Canadian Quetico-Superior Committee remained remarkably insensitive to dominion-provincial relations and greatly overestimated their capacity to influence public policy behind the scenes. Some eighteen years later, in 1967, Walker confessed how politically naive he had been at this time, and "how very little" he had known "about finding the ropes to be pulled, let alone *how* they could be pulled when found. It wasn't obvious to me that even a polite request from Ottawa might cause Queen's Park to condemn the whole project from the beginning."[45]

The draft treaty also came under scathing attack from the Northwestern Ontario Associated Chambers of Commerce, whose members petitioned both the federal and provincial governments "not to surrender Quetico Park to an International authority." So, too, did the Northern Ontario Outfitters' Association.[46] Both groups feared that international control under a treaty would jeopardize the construction of a highway from the head of Lake Superior to Fort Frances. Their opposition was not a case of businessmen versus wilderness, for the associated chambers of commerce had already approved of Chester Wilson's zoning proposals, which blended wilderness protection for the canoe country with resort development along a Fort Frances–Port Arthur highway. Moreover, the business organizations were not far off the mark in harbouring suspicions of the intentions of the more inflexible wilderness proponents. Ernest Oberholtzer, for one, did not relish the thought of a development road cutting through the centre of the Rainy Lake region.

With the treaty proposal in tatters, the Canadian Quetico-Superior Committee had perforce to review its plans. It fell to Donald P. O'Hearn, hired as executive secretary of the committee in August 1950, to assess the status of the group. A highly regarded member of the parliamentary press gallery, O'Hearn enjoyed open-door privileges in the office of Premier Leslie Frost. Through his ties with the Premier, O'Hearn obtained access, in September 1950, to the Department of Lands and

Forests file on Quetico Park. As O'Hearn perused the documents, he realized that "the project had been very badly handled from the start" by his American colleagues. "The initial suggestion ... that the Dominion should take over the land," he reported, seemed "in the light of practical politics ... absolutely fantastic." O'Hearn was also struck by the weight given to the opinions of business and political interests in Fort Frances. Unless the local people could be won over, he concluded, the QSC did not stand a chance of realizing its objectives. Nowhere in the Ontario government could O'Hearn find sympathy for the concept of a Canadian-American treaty. Later, in private discussions with the Premier, he discovered that Frost had "made up his mind that the [QSC] project, particularly the treaty aspect, wasn't feasible." On more than one occasion, Frost told O'Hearn that "the province would do 'acre for acre' what the U.S. did," but "that 'Old Man Ontario would not give away control of his land.'"[47]

Subsequently, O'Hearn recommended a "practical politics" strategy for the Canadian Quetico-Superior Committee, one that placed him closer to Minnesota's Chester Wilson than to Ernest Oberholtzer. "If the prime purpose of the committee is early implementation of the treaty," he wrote, "I would recommend its discontinuance." Retain the treaty idea simply "as an ultimate objective without any real expectation of seeing it for many years," urged O'Hearn. The first priority of the committee must be the cultivation of "sympathetic opinion in the Rainy River and Lakehead districts," and to accomplish that the committee "should heartily endorse [the Fort Frances–Port Arthur] road" to be built to the north of Quetico Park. Every effort must be made to promote tourist resorts and outfitters along this transportation corridor to match the long-established American tourist industry based on the recreational use of the wilderness canoe country. Then, perhaps, the province might "look on the treaty in an entirely different light."

O'Hearn's report fuelled an intense debate within the QSC movement. Eventually, in the light of the certainty that a highway would be built between Atikokan and Fort William, the voices of moderation sided with O'Hearn over the opposition of Ernest Oberholtzer. In 1952 the Canadian QSC declared in favour of the highway and called for a co-operative effort among all interest groups and the government to fashion a management plan for the highway corridor. On cue, the Northwestern Ontario Associated Chambers of Commerce resolved to assume this planning challenge, and in September 1952 they struck the "Quetico Committee of Northwestern Ontario," with M.S. "Pop" Fotheringham as chairman.[48] The establishment of this committee had been engineered in part by the conservationists, particularly through the influence of Fotheringham, the president of Steep Rock Mine in Atikokan and a founding member of the Canadian QSC. In the spring of 1954 Fotheringham's planning group completed its task and submitted a report to the Department of Lands and Forests. The committee's recommendations became the basis of the government's policy for Quetico announced by the Minister of Lands and Forests, Clare Mapledoram, the member for Fort William, at the official opening of the Fort William–Atikokan highway in August of that year.

In his statement, Mapledoram confirmed that cottages and resort leases would continue to be banned in the park. Provision for cottage and resort development would be made on lakes contiguous to the new highway. Access roads from the new highway would not be permitted to penetrate the interior of the park. Shoreline reserve clauses to protect "all lakes and streams, islands and portages" would be inserted in future timber licences, a policy that seemed academic at the time since the timbermen had all left the park in 1946. (They did not resume bush operations until 1961.) In two major respects, the 1954 policy for Quetico fell short of the original QSC objectives. Like all his predecessors, Mapledoram rejected the idea of a wilderness treaty. "This great natural park will be controlled and operated by the province of Ontario," thundered Mapledoram. "It will not be an international proposition."[49] The Quetico policy also deviated from the QSC program in that its protectionist features were restricted to the park and did not apply to the rest of the Ontario portion of the Rainy Lake watershed. None of this came as a surprise to the QSC leaders who had been active in the policy making. Theoretically, they were still committed to the treaty concept, and they raised it again in the future; but political realities had led the conservationists to adopt an incremental strategy for the time being.

In October 1954 the wilderness supporters capped their success by receiving a charter for the Quetico Foundation, a "non-profit organization ... to encourage financially and otherwise, educational and scientific projects" to "increase public awareness" about the Quetico area. Its board of directors comprised members of the Canadian QSC and the Quetico Committee of Northwestern Ontario. The foundation quickly earned the respect of Ontario officials by funding research projects on the archaeology and geology of Quetico and by instituting a program of publicity and education that included the publication of books, magazine articles, and the Quetico *Newsletter*, and the production and distribution of Christopher Chapman's award-winning film *Quetico* in 1958. Impressed by the foundation's accomplishments, Clare Mapledoram invited the group in 1956 to expand its mandate to include other wilderness parks like Algonquin and Lake Superior. Consequently, in 1958 the Quetico Foundation amended its letters patent to widen its role as Ontario's quasi-official watchdog over wilderness.[50]

Even the foundation's American ally, the President's Quetico-Superior Committee, convinced provincial officials of its good intentions. Beginning with a meeting at Basswood Lake in 1955, Charles Kelly, chairman of the President's QSC, greatly influenced lands and

*Aerial view of Lac La Croix, Boundary Waters Canoe Area, 1940.
(Courtesy Shirley Peruniak, Quetico Park Archives, copy of U.S. Forest
Service photo by L.J. Prater.)*

*Scenery typical of "the Quetico" : Fifth portage, Twin Falls, Maligne River.
(Courtesy Shirley Peruniak, Quetico Park Archives.)*

forests personnel by mapping out the progress made by the American government in reclaiming the alienated lands within the roadless areas of the Superior National Forest. Private holdings had been reduced from 350,000 acres to 55,000 acres since the late 1940s. After the meeting, Ben Greenwood, chief of the Parks Division, reported that he saw "no reason why this U.S. Committee should be looked upon with suspicion."[51] By 1957, the middle of the Eisenhower administration, all but 2 per cent (30,000 acres) of the roadless areas lay in the public domain. So impressed were Ontario officials with the progress of the acquisition program that they willingly co-operated with the Americans when

Pickerel Lake, Quetico Provincial Park. (Courtesy Bruce M. Litteljohn.)

problems arose. In 1957, for instance, the province suspended Crown land sales on the Canadian side of the international border, on Saganaga Lake to the east of Quetico park, and Lac La Croix to the west, when it was learned that American resort owners were attempting to relocate on the Ontario shore of these lakes that stretched along the northern boundaries of the roadless areas.[52]

Basking in the glow of the close relationship with Ontario officials, the conservationists decided it was an opportune time to resurrect the proposal for a Canadian-American treaty to perpetuate the Quetico-Superior wilderness. They pinned their hopes on obtaining the support of the major interest groups in Northwestern Ontario. Accordingly, the conservationists presented various regional organizations with a harm-less-sounding resolution that called for an "international agreement" to protect "for all time the finest canoe country in the world." Their campaign collapsed at the Port Arthur annual meeting of the North-west Ontario Municipal Association, where the Minister of Lands and Forests, Clare Mapledoram, attacked the resolution and forced its withdrawal without a vote. He saw through the QSC strategy. The term "international agreement" was simply a euphemism for "treaty," and a treaty of any kind threatened to compromise provincial sovereignty over the Rainy Lake watershed, something no Ontario politician would condone.[53]

It was in the wake of this defeat in late 1957 that the conservationists proposed an alternative to a treaty — a diplomatic exchange of letters between the Ontario and American governments committing each jurisdiction to co-operate in working out, informally, through biannual meetings of a joint advisory committee, common management policies for the wilderness preserves on both sides of the border. Here was a pragmatic proposal that found instant favour among all concerned.[54] Subsequently, negotiations for the exchange of letters with the Ameri-can State Department were conducted though the office of the Hon. Howard C. Green, the Canadian Secretary of State for External Affairs. The announcement of the exchange took place simultaneously in Washington and at Queen's Park, Toronto, on April 12, 1960. "Now our sole obligation is this," emphasized Premier Frost, "that if we change policy at any time, we give notification of that to the American commit-tee, so that we are not doing things which are running counter to what they are attempting to do on their side. Likewise, they would give us notice of any changes that would apply on their side." Through "friendly co-operation," he concluded, "we can work out policies which will be of benefit to both sides of the line."[55] His optimism was shared by Charles Kelly, who believed that Frost had committed his government to the protection of wilderness "almost as fully as if we had obtained the treaty."[56]

Actually, Frost had simply confirmed the long-standing practice of previous governments. Since 1927, Ontario's politicians and civil servants had shown by word and deed that they would act in conjunction with the Americans in managing Quetico-Superior. With their blinders on and their eyes glued on the ultimate objective of a formal treaty to protect the Rainy Lake watershed, the American conservationists repeatedly antagonized provincial officials who otherwise supported their goals. As misunderstandings deepened on both sides, some QSC leaders occasionally lost sight of the fact that the Ontarians sympathized with major elements of their program. For too long, tactical errors, excessive pride, self-righteousness, and ignorance of dominion-provincial relations (a sin of which the members of the Canadian QSC were also surprisingly guilty), prevented the conservationists from reaching an agreement with Ontario well before the 1960 diplomatic exchange of letters. In 1928, for instance, William Finlayson had wanted to work with the Americans to harmonize management policies on both sides of the border. His discussions with the QSC leaders came to nothing because the conservationists insisted on raising the treaty proposition. The same situation obtained in 1941-42, when Frank MacDougall and N.O. Hipel met with the QSC leaders. Although no firm agreement was reached before 1960, from the outset of the QSC campaign Ontario modified its management policies in Quetico Provincial Park to keep in lockstep with developments across the border. Nevertheless, three decades slipped by before the conservationists recognized that their disagreements with the province did not involve the question of whether or not to protect the wilderness; the quarrel essentially revolved around the treaty or sovereignty issue. Thus one of the biggest obstacles faced by the wilderness warriors was of their own making. When they de-emphasized the treaty proposition, and then jettisoned it, Leslie Frost's "Old Man Ontario" gave them a warm reception.

Postscript

After 1960 the issue of wilderness preservation in Ontario took an entirely new direction. In 1961, after a fifteen-year hiatus, commercial logging resumed in Quetico Park. By this time, technological and market changes in the forest industries had brought about a transformation in logging practices. Gone were the days of the teamster, winter camp, and spring drive. Now the timber operators, facing problems of labour costs and dwindling stocks, sought a highly mechanized and automated year-round operation. Technological advances in equipment, particularly in the form of chain saws, wheeled tractors, and skidders, allowed for the harvesting of trees previously considered uneconomic. Logging sites reverberated with the scream of chain saws and the roar of engines. Timber companies also required wide, permanent, and ballasted gravel roads through formerly inaccessible areas to accommodate the massive trucks needed to haul the logs to the mills. As this technological revolution was taking place in the forests of Quetico, the ranks of wilderness canoeists swelled to unanticipated numbers, setting the stage for a dramatic clash between logger and recreationist. With the emergence of broad-based environmental and wilderness preservation movements in Ontario, the final element was added for an explosive political mix.

Represented by such groups as the Algonquin Wildlands League, the National and Provincial Parks Association of Canada, and the Coalition for Wilderness, a new generation of wilderness advocates spurned the multiple-use philosophy espoused earlier by the Quetico-Superior Council and the Quetico Foundation. The preservationists looked for more than the protection of the recreational and scenic qualities of the wilderness; they were primarily interested in setting aside large tracts of Crown land for ecological reasons. From the ecological perspective, the shoreline reserve policy that permitted commercial logging beyond the waterways created only a sham, cosmetic wilderness; the preservation of natural areas and ecosystems was not compatible with commercial logging. In 1969 the Algonquin Wildlands League launched the most recent phase in the battle for wilderness in Quetico Park, which resulted in a ban on logging in 1971 and the designation of Quetico as a wilderness class park two years later. The preservationists also lobbied successfully for a provincial parks policy, adopted in 1978, that committed the Government of Ontario to establishing a system of wilderness parks in all regions of the province.

NOTES

1   The best and most detailed analysis of the conservationist campaign is to be found in R. Newell Searle, *Saving Quetico-Superior: A Land Set Apart* (Minnesota Historical Society Press, 1977). For the Quetico-Superior story in a wider context see also Craig W. Allin, *The Politics of Wilderness Preservation*, Contributions in Political Science, No. 64 (Westport, Conn.: Greenwood, 1982); Donald N. Baldwin, *The Quiet Revolution: Grass Roots of Today's Wilderness Preservation Movement* (Boulder, Colo.: Pruett, 1972); and Roderick Nash, *Wilderness and the American Mind*, rev. ed. (New Haven: Yale University Press, 1973). In Canada, only Richard Lambert and Paul Pross have examined the Quetico-Superior story, albeit very briefly, in *Renewing Nature's Wealth: A Centennial History of the Public Management of Lands, Forests and Wildlife in Ontario 1763-1967*(Ontario Department of Lands and Forests, 1967), pp. 479-81. For a recent but unpublished analysis see George Michael Warecki, "The Quetico-Superior Council and the Battle for Wilderness in Quetico Provincial Park, 1909-1960" (M.A. thesis, University of Western Ontario, 1983).

2   For "the wilderness cult" see Nash, *Wilderness and the American Mind*, Chap. 9. Wilderness protection first became a national *cause célèbre* in the United States from 1908-1913, when conservationists fought unsuccessfully to prevent the damming of the Hetch Hetchy valley as a water reservoir for the city of San Francisco. See ibid., Chap. 10.

3   For the roadless areas controversy see Baldwin, *Quiet Revolution*, pp. 100, 128-51, and Searle, *Saving Quetico-Superior*, Chap. 2.

4   Minnesota Historical Society, St. Paul, Minn., Quetico-Superior Council Records, (herafter QSC), Arthur Hawkes papers, P 34, box 25, Oberholtzer to Hawkes, June 13, 1927; Hawkes to Oberholtzer, June 28, 1927; Oberholtzer to Hawkes, July 4, 1927. For the origins of Quetico Provincial Park see Lambert and Pross, *Renewing Nature's Wealth*, pp. 284-85.

5   Ontario Ministry of Natural Resources, Records Branch, Whitney Block, Queen's Park, Toronto, Land Records (hereafter LR), file 116062, Oberholtzer to Finlayson, Nov. 2, 1927.

6   LR, file 116062, Oberholtzer to Finlayson, Feb. 16, 1928.

7   For Finlayson's legislation see Peter Oliver, *G. Howard Ferguson: Ontario Tory*, Ontario Historical Studies Series (Toronto: University of Toronto Press, 1977), pp. 342-43.

8   Christopher Armstrong, *The Politics of Federalism: Ontario's Relations with the Federal Government, 1867-1942*, Ontario Historical Studies Series (Toronto: University of Toronto Press, 1981), p. 233.

9   QSC, William Finlayson folder, P 34, box 21, Finlayson to Oberholtzer, Nov. 9, 1927; LR, file 116062, Finlayson to W.G. Dorr, Nov. 14, 1927; Oberholtzer to Finlayson, Feb. 16, 1928; Finlayson to Oberholtzer, Feb. 20, 1928.

10   Searle, *Saving Quetico-Superior*, pp. 70-74, 89.

11   LR, file 116062, Finlayson to W.G. Robertson, Gen. Mgr., Ontario Motor League, Aug. 29, 1930. LR, file 74226, T.W. Allinson, Prairie Club of Chicago, to Hon. W.L. Mackenzie King, Sept. 24, 1929; W.C. Cain to Mr. Houser, Feb. 6, 1930; Cain to Supt. John Jamieson, Feb. 6, 1930. For Olson's influence see QSC, Sigurd Olson papers, P 34, box 47, Olson to Oberholtzer, Jan. 28, 1931.

12   *Final Report of the International Joint Commission on the Rainy Lake Reference, Washington-Ottawa 1934* (Ottawa: J.O. Patenaude, 1934), pp. 48-49.

13   QSC, J.W. Dafoe papers, P 34, box 16, Oberholtzer to Dafoe, Oct. 28, 1929.

14   QSC, Toronto *Star* papers, P 34, box 55, Gregory Clark to Oberholtzer, Apr. 20, 1929. For user statistics see Quetico Provincial Park Archives (hereafter QPP), historical file (1940s), W.D. Cram to F.A. MacDougall, May 3, 1944.

15   QSC, Canadian Advisory Board folder, P 34, box 12.

16   QSC, Lawrence J. Burpee folder, P 34, box 10, Burpee to Oberholtzer, Jan. 29, 1935.

17   QSC, C3207CC—In Re Quetico-Superior/Re Canada—25.G.6.3B, Oberholtzer to Sigurd Olson, Oct. 26, 1935.

18   QSC, Larence J. Burpee folder, P 34, box 10, Oberholtzer to Burpee, Dec. 17, 1936.

19   Ibid.

20   LR, file 116062, E.H. Coleman, Under Secretary of State to Hon. A. Mathews, Lt.-Gov. of Ont., Aug. 4, 1939, and W.C. Cain to F.V. Johns, Assist. Prov. Sec. of Ont., Nov. 1, 1939.

21   QSC, C3207CC—In Re Quetico-Superior/Re Canada—25.G.6.3B, Oberholtzer to William Zimmerman, Jr., Oct. 1, 1939.

22   Searle, Saving *Quetico-Superior*, pp. 108, 121, 123.

23   QSC, Jules Preudhomme folder, P 34, box 48, Preudhomme to Oberholtzer, Nov. 28, 1929.

24 LR, file 81996, J.F. Sharpe to Delahey, Aug. 18, 1937, and Delahey to Cain, Aug. 23, 1937.

25 MacDougall's contributions have been analysed in Gerald Killan, "A Legend in His Own Time: Frank A. MacDougall, The Flying Superintendent of Algonquin Park," paper delivered to the annual conference of the Ontario Historical Society, Huntsville, June 14, 1986. This paper will be included in the author's forthcoming history of Ontario's provincial park system.

26 QSC, C3207CC—In Re Quetico-Superior/Re Canada—25.G.6.3B, Kenneth Reid to Charles S. Kelly, Nov. 27, 1941. LR, file 116062, Reid to Hon. Mitchell Hepburn, Aug. 21, 1941.

27 QPP, historical file (1940s), W.D. Cram to J.M. Whalen, Oct. 15,1941; Cram to MacDougall, Oct, 22, 1941; Cram to J.F. Sharpe, Feb. 14, 1942.

28 QSC, W.D. Cram papers, P 34, box 16, Oberholtzer to Cram, Sept. 14, 1942.

29 QSC, C3207CC—In Re Quetico-Superior/Re Canada—25.G.6.3B, Kenneth Reid to Charles S. Kelly, Nov. 27, 1941.

30 QPP, historical file (1940s), Chester Wilson to DLF, Mar. 14, 1944.

31 Ibid., Chester Wilson to W.G. Thompson, Apr. 27, 1944. For Oberholtzer's views on Wilson see Searle, *Saving Quetico-Superior*, p. 140.

32 See Chester S. Wilson, "Last Chance to Save the Quetico-Superior Wilderness," *The Conservation Volunteer*, 9, No. 52 (May-June 1946); Warecki, "Battle for Wilderness," pp. 91-95; Searle, *Saving Quetico-Superior*, pp. 149-52.

33 LR, file 123616, Whalen to H.W. Crosbie, June 13, 1944.

34 LR, file 116062, Crosbie to F.A. MacDougall, July 26, 1945; and Premier George A. Drew to Harold Scott, Apr. 13, 1948.

35 LR, file 123616, Whalen to Crosbie, Sept. 16, 1944.

36 QPP, historical file (1940s), Memo. by W.D. Cram "Re: Meeting—Minister's Office, 14th March, 1946."

37 LR, file 116062, Chester Wilson to H.W. Crosbie, Aug. 31, 1946.

38 Ibid., Kenneth Reid to W.G. Thompson, Aug. 10, 1946; Gov. Edward J. Thye to Premier George Drew, Oct. 21, 1946.

39 Ibid., Crosbie to John McVey, Pres., Fort Frances Conservative Association, Sept. 26, 1946; H.R. Scott to Chester Wilson, Apr. 25, 1947.

40 QSC, C3207CC—In Re Quetico-Superior/Re Canada—25.G.6.4F, "Report of Conferences in Toronto," by Sigurd Olson, May 6, 1948, and "Toronto Report III," May 7, 1948.

41 For airspace reservation see Searle, *Saving Quetico-Superior*, Chap. 8.

42 Searle, *Saving Quetico-Superior*, p. 199, and Warecki, "Battle for Wilderness," p. 108. Thirty-one people joined the committee. Vincent Massey agreed to serve as chairman, with Harold Walker as vice-chairman, and the former Ontario Minister of Lands and Forests, William Finlayson, as executive-secretary. Other members were Abitibi Pulp and Paper Company president, D.W. Ambridge; Toronto public relations executive James A. Cowan; General H.D.G. Crerar; *Globe and Mail* editor Oakley Dalgleish; Massey-Harris chairman, James S. Duncan; University of Toronto biology professor J.R. Dymond; Steep Rock Mine president Donald M. Hogarth, and his successor M.S. "Pop" Fotheringham; conservationists John C. Irwin and Aubrey Walkinshaw; *Saturday Night* editor B.K. Sandwell; Clifford Sifton; and industrialist-financier E.P. Taylor. According to Dr. Omand Solandt, considerable pressure had been brought to bear on some people to support the QSC (personal interview, Jan. 12, 1988). Harold Walker's involvement came about as the result of the influence of Brookes Hubachek (son of QSC leader Frank Hubachek), a principal shareholder in the Household Finance Company. Hubachek strongly recommended to Walker, a lawyer for the company, that Walker become active in the QSC campaign.

43   QPP, historical file (1940s), "Treaty for the Establishment of an International Peace Memorial Forest in the Quetico-Superior Area," draft 12-29-49.

44   LR, file 116062, "A Wilderness Conservation Clinic—A Plan to Establish an International Peace Memorial Forest in the Quetico-Superior Canoe Country," from H.C. Walker, to the Premier and MPPs and to the Chairman and Members of Fish and Game Committee, Mar. 21, 1950.

45   Quetico Foundation Office records, Toronto, Harold Walker file, Walker to John Ridley, June 14, 1967.

46   LR, file 116062, Northwestern Ontario Associated Chambers of Commerce, 14th Annual Convention (Sept. 26-27, 1949), "Quetico Park Resolution No. 6"; and Memo from W.D. Cram to Keith Denis, Chairman, Zone I, Ontario Federation of Anglers and Hunters, Aug. 2, 1951.

47   QSC, C3207CC—In Re Quetico-Superior/Re Canada—25.G.6.4F, "Report to the Quetico-Superior Canadian Committee," by Donald O'Hearn, Exec. Sec. (Sept. 1951).

48   Fort William *Times-Journal*, Feb. 9, 1953. Copy available in LR, file 116062.

49   QPP, historical files (1950s), clipping of *Steep Rock Echo*, Sept. 1954. Archives of Ontario (hereafter AO), RG 1, BA, Draft Circulars Book No. 1 (1945-56), Parks Circular No. 1, "Policy on Quetico Provincial Park," Oct. 1, 1954.

50   QSC, C3207CC—In Re Quetico-Superior/Re Canada—25.G.6.4F, "Quetico Superior Activity in Canada," Feb. 1955, by D. O'Hearn. AO, RG 1, IA 7, box 10, file 27-0403, E.T. Kelsey, "Notes on the Quetico-Superior Movement in Canada," Sept. 13, 1966; Quetico *Newsletter*, 2, No. 1, Mar. 27, 1956, and 2, No. 2, Sept. 15, 1956.

51   AO, RG 1, IA 7, box 9, file 27-0403, Greenwood to Mapledoram, June 30, 1955. See also Searle, *Saving Quetico-Superior*, pp. 209-10.

52   AO, RG 1, IA 7, box 12, file 27-0403-4, Arthur W. Greeley to Mapledoram, Mar. 19, 1957; LR, file 161516, "Analysis of letter dated March 19th, 1957 to ... Mapledoram ... from ... Greeley."

53   Searle, *Saving Quetico-Superior*, pp. 210-13. Searle's interpretation of the last "treaty" episode is coloured by the wishful thinking of the American conservationists. He writes of "widespread public support" in Northwestern Ontario for the treaty idea. The evidence does not support this contention. His assertions that Frost did not make up his mind against the treaty until September 1957, that Greenwood was "sympathetic to the treaty," and that Mapledoram and MacDougall "quite possibly" could have been made to accept the treaty had they been able to attend the 1956 Basswood Lake meeting, are all erroneous.

54   For the negotiations leading up to the diplomatic exchange of letters, and copies of the letters, see Ontario Ministry of Natural Resources, Parks and Recreational Areas Branch, Whitney Block, Queen's Park, Toronto, Quetico-Superior Advisory Committee file.

55   Legislative Assembly of Ontario, Hansard, Apr. 12, 1960. The advisory committee worked effectively for seventeen years until disbanded by President Jimmy Carter in 1977. Since then field staff of the Ontario Ministry of Natural Resources and the United States Forest Service have co-ordinated management policies.

56   Quoted in Searle, *Saving Quetico-Superior*, p. 214.

THE CHILDREN'S WAR: THE MOBILIZATION OF ONTARIO YOUTH DURING THE SECOND WORLD WAR

Charles M. Johnston

In early September 1942, the third anniversary of the outbreak of the Second World War, an official of the Toronto Board of Education composed a sombre "Message to Students" for the *Canadian High News*. It began by quoting a letter written by a Royal Air Force pilot to his mother:

> For all that can be said to the contrary, I still maintain that this war is a very good thing; every individual is having a chance to give and to dare all for his principles, like the martyrs of old.... I have no fear of death, only a queer elation. I would have it no other way. The universe is so vast, so ageless, that the life of one man can only be justified by the measure of his sacrifice.... Those who just eat, sleep, prosper, and procreate are no better than animals if all their lives they are at peace.... But with the final test of war I consider my character fully developed [and] at my early age, with my earthly mission already fulfilled, I am prepared to die.

To his high school readers the official heartily commended the writer's sentiments "for careful study".[1]

Though certainly not as bloodthirsty or self-serving as the war lover's in John Hersey's novel, those sentiments nonetheless exalted the mystique of war in a fashion that would have been unthinkable before the conflict started. That they should be given so much prominence at the start of the 1942 school year may be explained in part by the heart-stopping stage the war had then reached. On the Russian front the titanic Battle of Stalingrad was well underway, and that of El Alamein was about to be fought in the Western Desert, two confrontations that could decide its outcome. In the Far East, Japan, in spite of a setback at

Midway, was still very much in the ascendant, capitalizing on her strike at Pearl Harbor and earlier victories in southeast Asia. And closer to home, a few days before the Toronto official sat down to compose his message for the high schools, Canada's own soldiers had received a bloody drubbing in the ill-fated raid on Dieppe. It is not surprising perhaps, at this highly uncertain stage of the war, that dramatic appeals for devotion and sacrifice should come from those anxious to alert the nation's youth and prepare them for the challenge to which others had already responded. They could have taken their cue from an English scouting magazine that had recently urged a "training in hardness" to counteract the "coddling methods" of schools, churches, and youth organizations that it blamed for the United Kingdom's unpreparedness for war.[2]

The approach seemed to depart dramatically from the comparatively tame sentiments expressed in 1940, even while the Battle of France still hung in the balance and only a matter of hours before the evacuation began of the battered British Expeditionary Force at Dunkirk. "In these troubled days," remarked the chairman of the Toronto Board of Education, "may the boys and girls in our schools learn the lessons of true patriotism and thus prepare themselves to champion loyalty, fair play, and truth."[3] What he meant by true patriotism was not clearly spelled out, even in those dark hours.

A Farmerette amidst the grape vines. (Photo from Vulcan, *1941-45, courtesy Records, Archives and Museum, Toronto Board of Education.)*

Indeed students such as those at Central Technical School were given no fiery message at all in 1940, but merely admonished to do their bit by maintaining their health, doing a good day's work at school, and practising in their daily life "those ideals that [were] typically British" — fair play and consideration for other people. Finally, students were even enjoined to emulate Queen Victoria's custom of going to the Bible for guidance in times of trouble, and to participate in a prayer day for seeking God's blessing on the cause for which Great Britain was fighting.[4] If such admonitions seem to lack the sharp cutting edge of a true call to arms, educators were probably seeking to preserve the semblance of business-as-usual and the less than militaristic spirit of the 1930s, a legacy of the massive slaughter and destruction of the Great War of 1914-18.

All the same, both public school pronouncements and denominational magazines were agreed on some basics at the outset. Before the day of victory dawned, years of sacrifice would have to be endured to rid the Western world of the greatest threat to its civilization. As well, every step imaginable would have to be taken to champion the ideals of the British Empire-Commonwealth, which had helped to nurture that civilization. "Empire Day," instituted in the heyday of the late Victorian epoch,[5] was still very much a national institution. Its ceremonies were seldom taken lightly, and certainly not in its birthplace, the city of Hamilton, whose board of education wanted a special wartime pageant featuring "Youth of Canada dedicating Itself to Empire."[6] But those who produced religious publications attached an almost spiritual significance to the day and urged their young readers to offer a balanced prayer that "all that is best in the history of our Empire may be preserved and all that is base destroyed."[7]

The commemoration of the Empire-Commonwealth had been given an enormous boost on the very eve of the war by the politically strategic royal visit of George VI and Queen Elizabeth. The mass display of calisthenics put on for the occasion by Hamilton high school students not only typified Ontario's enthusiastic welcome to the Empire's sovereign but the military orientation already given to physical education.[8] The turnout and deportment of students elsewhere in the "Loyalist Province" were no less patriotic as the King and Queen made their appearance. Exuberant Toronto youngsters did not have to be told (as they were by fidgety school authorities) to wave their handkerchiefs if they were unlucky enough to lack Union Jacks when their majesties' cavalcade rolled by.[9]

In the early stages of the war, Empire Day was relatively unstructured. But by 1942, the critical year that prompted the soul-searching message in the *Canadian High News*, the Department of Education was drafting more elaborate guidelines for its celebration in the schools. Made up of recitations, narrations, and appropriate hymn-singing ("O

Student aircraftsmen at work. (Photo from Vulcan, *1941-45, courtesy Records, Archives and Museum, Toronto Board of Education.)*

God Our Help in Ages Past" was the front runner), all to be rendered by the pupils, they underscored Great Britain's legacy of peace, freedom, and order. In the process the program gave an understandably laundered version of the history of her people: "They are ... peace-loving, going their way with no wish to quarrel with their neighbours. They have been forced to fight in many wars but they hate war." And then a pupil was supposed to portray Winston Churchill, Britain's wartime leader, and utter the following lines: "Sir, we did not make this war. We did not seek it. We did all we could to avoid it. We did too much to avoid it. We went so far in trying to avoid it as to be almost destroyed by it when it broke upon us."[10] Predictably the enemy was pictured in less than complimentary terms: "The dull brute mass of the ordinary German Army and German people," read one Empire Day leaflet, "is always so ready to be led to the trampling down in other lands of liberties ... which they have never known in their own."[11]

The program's veiled reference to the so-called appeasement policy, against which an angry Churchill had railed in the late thirties, was followed by a brief history of how the dominions had rallied to the mother country's side and of the dramatic events that had led to the fall

Aircraft models for the RCAF. (Photo fron Vulcan, 1941-45, courtesy Records, Archives and Museum, Toronto Board of Education.)

of France. Insinuated into the story line was the defeatism that had overtaken Britain's ally: "It is the end," a pupil playing a dispirited French soldier moaned, "France is lost. England, too, must surrender," a Gallic mood of despair that was pointedly contrasted with Britain's noble intention to carry on her back-to-the-wall fight.[12] Indeed defeat was turned into a kind of victory when Dunkirk became a symbol of heroic survival and moral perseverance in the face of wickedness and injustice. In the spring of 1941 the 1st of June was duly marked in Toronto schools in commemoration of the BEF's involuntary departure from the Continent. For good measure, past Britannic victories were also to be observed for the children's benefit, including Trafalgar and Waterloo (as if France was once again to be reviled as an enemy in the wake of the notorious Vichy regime.) And the visceral verse and prose of Rudyard Kipling, the "Banjo-Bard of Empire" who had fallen out of public favour in the jaded interwar years, were vigorously revived to stimulate wartime commitment. In this barrage of patriotic rhetoric, few schoolchildren could have been left unaware that the fate of the world hinged on the preservation of the Empire. Clearly this was the experience of youngsters in a large public school in Hamilton, whose bombastic principal constantly reminded them in daily assembly that they were "Britishers, first, last, and all the time."[13] But the message of inspiration was not totally Imperial. Events dear to the heart of the budding Canadian nationalist were summoned up for special observances; the favourite was Vimy Ridge, the engagement of the Great War that had owed so much to Canadian daring and management in 1917.

Political considerations surfaced at one point when pupils were told that Ottawa was much less zealous in these matters than the Province of Ontario, which, after all, had long regarded itself as the principal guardian of the Empire's and the nation's values.[14] And one source of those values was not neglected by those who sought to acquaint the province's schoolchildren with their heritage. Magna Carta came in for a good deal of attention, not only on June 15, the day it was honoured in the schools, but at the Empire Youth Rallies staged annually in Toronto, and always on a Sunday. A notable page of constitutional history was twinned with a religious exercise when the clergy of all denominations were urged to mark the day as a demonstration of Canadian youth's "unity of spirit with the rest of the Empire-Commonwealth."[15] In keeping with this mood, *The Teachers' Quarterly*, a Baptist publication for Sunday school instructors, urged the mobilization of such youth movements as a means of consolidating Christian ideals in peacetime and wartime alike.[16]

Although school authorities readily conceded that the Empire's youth should be indoctrinated in goodness, just as young Germans had been steeped in evil, many principals opposed the youth rallies on the ostensible grounds that the schools should not be helping to organize education on the Sabbath.[17] On the other hand, they may have been offended by excessively patriotic exercises that threatened to do their pupils emotional harm. Moreover, those exercises often went far beyond the special school events over which hard-worked principals already had to preside. They also reflected the intrusive presence of the Imperial metropolis. Thus there were any number of patriotic poster competitions like the one sponsored by a British Board of Trade anxious to promote greater intra-Empire commerce in wartime. Another popular device was the collecting of pupils' signatures for a statement on "Strengthening the Bonds of Empire," which was prepared from material forwarded by Britain's zealous Ministry of Information and ultimately bound and despatched to a presumably grateful King and Queen. And reminiscent of ambitious schemes hatched in London at the turn of the century to bring children of the far-flung Empire closer together, pen pal clubs were formed that enabled Ontario youngsters to exchange letters and mementos with their distant mates in wartorn Britain.[18] Even if some principals were hard pressed to keep up, at least the province's link in the Imperial connection had never shone so brightly.

Church publications for their part usually shunned appeals to a strident patriotism[19] and concentrated instead on how Britain's citizens were soldiering on through the Blitz and setting a brave example for the rest of the Empire. This took the form of both articles and stories that at times assumed the air of *Chums* or the *Boys' Own Annual*, long the staple of juvenile literature in Canada as well as in Britain. These ranged all the way from a serial called "A Suburb in Wartime" through "Young Britain is Ready" to "Adventures in an Air Raid."[20] Nor was this treatment reserved for teenagers or those in the senior years of the elementary schools. "Little ones" too were presented with poetry and prose that had a distinctive wartime flavour, even if the effort may have gone for naught given recent findings that children under seven are unable to grasp such concepts.[21] At any rate, in 1941 a poem entitled "The Blitz-Feeling" presented these lines for its tender readers in terms which seemed, on the face of it, appropriate and understandable enough:

> Said the lion cubs at the London Zoo,
> "The blitzkrieg feeling has got us too;
> With bangings and bombings to left and to right,
> Not a wink of sleep do we get at night.
>
> It's just as bad when the sun is high,
> For the sirens wail ere we close an eye.
> We wish those 'birds' with the horrible sounds
> Would find themselves other hunting grounds.
>
> When we yawned in the face of our keeper, he
> Said, 'Missing your shut-eye same as me?' "
> Very bewildered and sleepy too
> Are the lion cubs at the London Zoo.[22]

There were virtually endless stories too of the lives led by English evacuees, those city children, many from the less privileged social classes, who were removed to the safety of the countryside or to North America so they might be spared the horrors of bombing raids. Articles in denominational magazines told of Ontario girls who earmarked some of their summer earnings to help pay evacuees' expenses in Canada. Still other young people apparently took over the care of such children altogether when the latters' relatives could not cope. By doing so, the girls were assured that they were making a signal contribution to the "vast world struggle" even if they were "hurt" by being denied a more active role.[23] In any case, elementary and high school classes soon grew accustomed to the British "war guests" in their midst and were pumping them about their wartime experiences and becoming adjusted to unfamiliar accents and ways of doing things.[24]

The Aluminum Man goes to war. (Courtesy Archives of Ontario, Acc. 6863.)

Ontario girls were also told they had a role to play as "Canada's Teen-Aged Home Front Soldiers," particularly the ones who shouldered the burden of household chores in the absence of working mothers who had taken jobs vacated by men off at war. To ease the task of making do with wartime rationing, magazines periodically published "Victory Recipes" advising young homemakers how to overcome "Meatless Tuesdays" by making more imaginative use of vegetables, cheese, and eggs when preparing meals and packing lunch buckets. They were also urged to observe the Canada Official Food Rules, which recommended the weekly serving of liver, or steak and kidney pie as a means of promoting the consumption of vitamin A, the so-called blackout vitamin.[25]

Young readers were also acquainted with the "man on the farm", that is, the girl who took over the direction of the family acres after dad departed for the navy and a brother for the army.[26] Such accounts doubtless helped to attract recruits for the Farm Service, which enrolled girls and boys for harvesting and fruit picking on the farms and orchards of Ontario. The girls, dubbed farmerettes, played a summertime role that some of their mothers had as National Service Girls during the Great War.[27] The success of that earlier venture and reports of the work being done by Britain's female Land Army helped inspire the campaign to recruit Ontario girls for farm service after 1940. The farmerettes were made to feel that they were making a vital contribution to the nations's war effort and releasing military-age men for the fighting front. They were also advised, however, that the work had to

A child's V-E Day, 1945. (Courtesy Hamilton Public Library, Special Picture Collection, Morris Photographic Collection.)

be directly connected with farming. No other employment would be sanctioned, simply because they had been released from school at Eastertime (provided they attained at least 50 per cent on their examinations) without losing their year, on the clear understanding that they were headed for farm jobs.

After formally applying, those girls accepted for the service were settled in camps where farmers collected and then returned them after the day's work, which could last up to ten hours in field or orchard. The farmerettes, who were assigned to individual farmers by the camp authorities, had little or no control over their postings. By the closing years of the war some 35,000 Ontario students were enrolled in the program and stationed in sixty locations scattered around the province.[28] And included in this contingent were those members of the Canadian Girls in Training (CGIT), whose summer camps were combined with the farmerettes'.

According to a typical account, there was a military flavour to the whole operation, for the girls were housed in highly secure barrack-like accommodations under the general supervision of a house mother who ensured that her charges were properly fed, paid, and otherwise cared for while engaged in the service. (Out of their wages, money was held back to cover board.) The supervision required the laying on of properly regulated entertainment, including chaperoned dances either in the camp or the local community. As in the army or a boarding school, girls from different walks of life and with markedly varied dispositions had to learn to live together in close and unfamiliar quarters.[29]

But if they expected their farmer-employer to be volubly apprecia-
tive of their patriotic contributions, many were bound to be disappointed. Apart from casual supervision and the journey to and from the
farms, there was little contact between Ontario's "soldiers of the soil"
and the farm family that employed them. All the same, the experience
and the associations proved rewarding for many of those involved,
who came out of the experience blistered, weary, and footsore, to be
sure, but also endowed with "deep sun tans" and the "great satisfaction
that came from doing a real job."[30] Nevertheless school authorities periodically expressed disquiet about how the system interfered with the
regular academic schedule. This happened when students, in response
to appeals from the Department of Education, stayed on to help with
heavy harvesting chores in September. In the end though, the schools
reopened on time, and most, like the Paris District High School, fully co-
operated with Queen's Park and made allowances for those students
who sought deferments for farm work.[31]

Toward the end of the war, observers noted that far fewer boys than
girls were engaged in the farm service and put this down to the boys'
tendency to seek more meaningful and lucrative summer positions
elsewhere in the expanding wartime economy. Moreover, technical
school students benefited as early as 1940 from special war emergency
classes that trained them in such vital crafts as instrument making and
emergency aircraft work, and in the process opened up opportunities
for their productive employment in war industries. A related Youth
Training Program instructed students in the basics of drafting, welding,
machine shop practice, and pattern making, which paved the way for
their ready absorption into the wartime work force.[32]

While all this was hailed as worthy of Ontario's response to
wartime needs, some critics complained that the emphasis on the
immediate and the practical was encouraging too many young people
to skip classes or forsake formal schooling altogether in favour of any
kind of job with an inflated wartime wage. Evidence began to mount in
Toronto and other cities that some 15 per cent of the school population
under fourteen was, thanks in part to unscrupulous employers, working into the late night hours at theatres, restaurants, bingo halls, and
that object of middle-class and puritanical loathing, the pool parlour.[33]
Small wonder that church literature pleaded with the young to stay
with their school books as long as possible so that they might keep their
purity intact and become equipped to deal with the postwar challenges
that lay ahead.

To make matters worse for the squeamish, many of these same
young people, with "too much money to spend," were supposedly
making a mockery of the taboos and standards that had hitherto
governed their conduct. The war, in effect, was producing an unsa-
voury and unstructured climate on the home front that threatened the

health, education, and morals of impressionable teenagers.[34] Truancy
and delinquency were often traced to such factors as a father in the
armed forces, a mother in the workplace, or a marital breakdown,
phenomena that had been virtually unknown, or at least less visible, in
the peacetime thirties.[35] All the more reason then for the critics to be
gratified when more war-oriented activity was organized, formal religious training introduced in the schools, and day-care centres established for such miscreants in the hope that their time and energy would
be more suitably deployed under the proper supervision.[36] The call to
patriotism was thus conveniently aligned with secular and religious
exercises in what passed for social control.

There was as well the problem of the relations between the sexes to
ponder. The apparent erosion of moral standards by the frenzied
atmosphere of wartime brought forth denunciations of the all too
prevalent "necking party" and lamentations over the spread of venereal disease. The frequency of ill-considered wartime engagements and
marriages, not to mention (and it was almost unmentionable at the
time) the allegedly soaring number of unwed mothers, also came under
the gun. "Now girls have so many contacts with men," lamented a
Baptist magazine in 1943, "that they have to master the technique of a
more mature attitude instead of thinking only of themselves in relation
to boys." It then lectured young women on the need to maintain the
proper bearing in the event they ventured into what it called professional war work.[37]

There was too the age-old problem of "booze" to consider. Not
surprisingly, some church publications took a cataclysmic view of it.
One approvingly passed on to its young readers what a Canadian army
officer was supposed to have said: "We have two terrible forces to fight,
Alcohol and the Axis, and I don't see how we can ever be strong enough
to deal with the second until we knock out the first."[38] Then even more
implausibly, the fighting words of Winston Churchill, a dedicated non-
teetotaller if ever there was one, were evoked to give point to the
argument. In any case, the reported increase in drinking was, like the
other so-called aberrations of the time, firmly attributed to the unhealthy social environment the war had fashioned.

Some alarmists even took exception to the dance and music crazes
of the day. At times the world for many young people was populated
not so much by highly publicized political and military worthies as it
was by the folk heroes who inspired the big bands of that generation.
There were moments when Count Basie and Duke Ellington counted
for more than King George and the Duke of Kent and when jitterbug-
ging to "Boogie-Woogie," "American Patrol," or "The One O'Clock
Jump" was preferred to the more staid dance forms of yesteryear.
Typically, one high school in Hamilton produced its own popular
swing band and tried to ape Glenn Miller, Harry James, and Tommy

Dorsey, three American orchestra leaders who were among the household names that peppered the wartime vocabulary of many an Ontario teenager.[39]

All the same, there was still a war on, and young people were relentlessly reminded of the values and commitments they were supposed to embrace in a time of crisis. In some schools war service clubs were formed to organize charity drives for the stricken overseas. They were also called upon to collect such random items as scrap metal, magazines, newspapers, and "clean" baskets for what everyone called the war effort.[40] To spur on that effort, those youngsters collecting strips of vital aluminum in Toronto were rewarded with free and "attractive" movies by the Aluminum Victory Campaign, a joint undertaking by Ottawa and the Canadian Red Cross.[41] The latter was also permitted to organize branches in some urban schools to help facilitate the collection of clothing and other necessities for bombed-out victims in Britain, even if at least one rural jurisdiction frowned upon the move as an improper intrusion on instruction time.[42]

In Hamilton a scheme known as Co-ordinated Aid To Britain was fuelled by salvage collections and by concerts staged by teachers and school children, who used the proceeds to put clothes on the backs of their British opposite numbers.[43] Soon stories were circulating elsewhere about the prodigious fund-raising feats of Boy Scouts and Girl Guides, about the crowning triumph of "one Ontario lad" who singlehandedly gathered up three tons of marketable scrap, and about the preparatory school near Toronto that raised $10,000 in aid in a little over a year.[44] In one rural school a teacher received a note from a pupil announcing the donation of her prized toy horse and jester doll to the local war service association.[45] Even Hallowe'en went to war in 1943, when youngsters agreed to suspend the traditional tricks and treats in favour of collecting money to buy milk for their "young allies" overseas. And in every community the purchase of War Savings Stamps was, with varying degrees of enthusiasm, encouraged in the schools to inculcate the virtue of thrift and to give youngsters another stake in the nation's war effort.[46]

For their part, vocational students produced thousands of model enemy warplanes for the schools of the British Commonwealth Air Training Plan. Some of these, together with appropriate slides, were used in high schools for special classes in aircraft recognition. These and related offerings were brought in under the aegis of the obligatory Course in Defence Training, Health, and Physical Education pointedly established by Queen's Park in 1942 as a more fitting educational alternative to the compulsory cadet program fancied by federal authorities.[47] In Hamilton the new course was taken very much to heart. One school, Delta Collegiate Institute, led the way by adjusting its schedule to allow teachers time to contribute in their regular hours of instruction.[48]

In the process a whole generation of students who were too young for the war grew up knowing intimate details of the Messerschmitt 109 or the Junkers 88, neither of which incidentally had the range to strike Ontario from its European bases. In the same spirit students in other high schools were taught the rudiments of camouflage in the unlikely event the Luftwaffe paid a visit. But strategic facts of life mattered little to those who lobbied to have a course in air-raid precautions incorporated into the syllabus and for the construction of air-raid shelters on school premises. Though unsuccessful, they were somewhat pacified when an alternative arrangement was devised under the name Civilian Defence Programme, which would involve the use of Boy Scouts as air-raid wardens and of girl volunteers as nurses' aids if ever the need arose.[49]

In the meantime, to serve the recreational and morale-building needs of servicemen, vocational students also manufactured ping pong tables and checker boards for a body known as the Sports Committee for Troops in Training.[50] And years later many would recall how nearly all students had dutifully gathered milkweed pods as a substitute for the rarer material ordinarily used in the bulky life preservers that sailors and airmen had to depend upon in time of peril. "They also served who merely filled Mae Wests" (after their remarkable resemblance to the proportions of the buxom movie queen) could have been the comforting slogan for this particular campaign.

The varied steps in the mobilization of patriotic fervour were given an added bounce by the electronic marvel that had been dominating the Ontario juvenile scene for over a decade. Admittedly, radio broadcasting had long been the bane of educators, who were convinced of its sinister influences on those young people who sacrificed their homework to such dubious fare as the "Green Hornet" and "The Shadow." Parents doubtless shared the observations of a pre-war American study that "the intruder" known as radio could not be locked out "because it [had] gained an invincible hold over ... children."[51] That hold, it was noted, owed much to the way radio cultivated, much more so than the moving picture, the imaginative powers of the addict.

In any case, by the fall of 1942 the Toronto board, among others, was prepared to make use of the intruder for loftier purposes in wartime, notably the inculcation in youth of "worthy life ideals." Accordingly, the Department of Education in collaboration with the CBC was soon preparing special broadcasts for elementary and junior high schools from grades six to ten. Along with the predictable stories of wartime daring and courage, the programs emphasized the pluck, social responsibility, resourcefulness, and unrelenting sacrifice that had characterized pioneering Ontario, qualities still in great demand. Thus school children were treated to such epic themes as "With Axe and Flail — A Story of the United Empire Loyalists" or "With Pack and Pick — A Story of Northern Ontario Pioneers." All of this was shrewdly tied in with the unflagging call to support the mother country:

> And build ye a race, toil-bred sons of the Northland,
> As your stately pines straight, as your granite hills strong,
> Thew-knit, supple-sinewed, soul and body puissant,
> Britain's vanguard in right and her bulwark 'gainst wrong.[52]

If this sort of exposure failed to compete with radio thrillers like "Fu Manchu," then that other popular medium of juvenile entertainment, the comic book, could be recruited for the cause. After D-Day in 1944, the battlefield adventures of Canadian soldiers were colourfully portrayed in those larger-than-life proportions normally reserved for Superman. Young readers were told how such soldiers, through bravery and inventiveness that far exceeded the call of duty (and with the help of the French Resistance), bagged impressive numbers of bewildered German prisoners.[53] This was clearly the stuff of which heroes were made and was graphically woven into the fabric of patriotic juvenile literature. It doubtless provided heavy competition for the illustrated war stories periodically featured in denominational magazines. One that appeared in *Boys of Canada* related how a bright and enterprising Ontario teenager was responsible for recapturing a German prisoner of war before he could flee into what was then the neutral United States. Others sought to keep their readership by recounting the exciting adventures of youthful underground movements in various parts of Nazi-occupied Europe.[54]

The same kind of patriotic message was flashed to high school students who, for the most part, eagerly enrolled in the varied cadet corps that were greatly expanded after war broke out. Such youngsters were also advised that, like their counterparts in the United Kingdom, they could expect in due course to be recruited into the regular armed forces. Scouting too was affected by these wartime exigencies. Though the Scout movement had always distanced itself from the military, right down to discouraging the drill-ground style of salute, many a Scout ended up in the ranks of school cadet corps and learned the rudiments of military regimen.

Although at the outset cadet service was generally voluntary, it was, over the protests of some school officials and community groups, made obligatory for the upper grades of Toronto high schools in 1939. During the first year of the war, over 4,000 city students participated in cadet training, the majority of whom were between fifteen and seventeen years, the threshold of military age. Then in the fateful summer of 1940 the program was abruptly broadened as the bad news flooded in from the battlefronts in France. The number of students enrolled in Toronto virtually doubled in the academic year 1940-41, with an almost 100 per cent turnout from the ranks of boys in grades ten to thirteen.[55] By the fall of 1941, much to the gratification of local militia units, high school cadet corps were allowed to affiliate with such units, provided they were not required to drill regularly.

Some miles away, a typical county board decided in the early fall of 1940 to start a volunteer cadet corps of its own. To prove that it meant business, it set about ordering the required number of wooden rifles, a decision that must have been welcomed not only by students keen to enrol but by a local carpentry firm. Meanwhile a high school board in Milton allowed a militia unit, the Lorne Scots, to use the school grounds for parade and physical education, presumably as a spur to the institution's cadet corps.[56]

Although the attempt was made to insulate conventional academic fare as much as possible from the war's pervasive influence and the military presence, it was at times an uphill battle. Even the soberly accurate material that Queen's Park prepared for the regular syllabus on the origins and course of the war could be seen as a curricular equivalent to the cadet exercises unfolding on school grounds across the province.[57] And in one Hamilton high school those exercises revolved around the organization of nothing less than an anti-aircraft battery, complete with Bofors guns, a top-of-the-line weapon. Graduates of the exacting program may have been either relieved or distressed when they learned that they were eligible for promotion once they enlisted in the armed forces.[58]

Service in the cadets, which on Ottawa's orders finally became compulsory in the manpower crisis of 1944, had not been confined to army training. Early on those boys captivated by the glamour of the air force had their wishes fulfilled when branches of the Air Cadet League of Canada were established in the province's high schools. Toronto was quick to respond and speedily planned for an aircraft instruction building at Central Technical School.[59] So rapid was the expansion of the air cadet movement at some institutions in the city that it spilled over into special portables at nearby schools whose needs were not so pressing. Nor was the response confined to the big city schools. In Paris, for example, more attention appeared to be paid to the organization of the high school's air cadets than to the regular cadet unit. The process was stimulated by the RCAF's understandable zeal in cultivating a responsive constituency brought up on tales of aerial derring-do. In the late winter of 1941, the Air Force was already anxious to preach its virtues and broadcast the procedures whereby secondary school students could become active service recruits.

At this point, however, the Toronto board put its foot down, fearing that the school system was in danger of being turned into a recruiting station. It solemnly informed Air Force representatives that they were to pass on information only, and not indulge in any blatant drive to line up hopefuls.[60] But this also meant that the board felt bound to permit the showing in schools of a shrewdly produced film, *Wings of Empire*, that depicted the stirring achievements of the parent Royal Air Force. Having admitted the RCAF to the premises, the board could hardly deny the other services, and before long both Navy and Army spokesmen were presenting their "educational programs" to assembled students. The senior service already had its foot in the door anyway, what with Navy Weeks being regularly set aside for extolling its role as defender of the Empire's vital sea lanes.[61] In the process much of what the Navy League of Canada had already done to arouse support for its activities was delivered to the schools. The following excerpt should suffice to indicate the tone and thrust of the forgivable hyperbole:

WE PAY TRIBUTE TO THESE MEN OF THE NAVY
— for the story of their marvellous bravery and the wondrous success which has crowned their efforts can never be told or written in any language.[62]

When it came to the establishment of air cadet squadrons, some parents took a jaundiced view. Since the coveted blue uniforms had to be purchased — army cadets received free khaki issue — they complained that only the sons of the affluent could afford to enrol in the air cadets, a situation that created an unwelcome class distinction in the ranks of secondary school students.[63] Some officials readily agreed. At a time when unity on the home front was considered vital, the organization of what amounted to elite units was not greeted warmly in certain quarters. Furthermore, the program was challenged as much too costly and often inexpedient simply because of the difficulty in finding properly qualified instructors. And when, in the fall of 1941, Ottawa urged an expansion of squadrons, the Toronto board dragged its feet for a time. The board also called, unsuccessfully as it turned out, for the creation of a much less divisive common course that would permit the teaching of air cadet work and military work to all cadets.[64] Meanwhile, high school graduates who had enlisted in the army or navy might well have been angered by the snob appeal of the air force. After all, it was implicitly reinforced by no less a person than the minister of national defence for air, who claimed "High school graduates are more suitable and more generally required in the RCAF than in most other branches of H.M. Forces."[65]

Comments on class distinctions and related dangers were a reminder of those prewar criticisms of the cadet system that still occasionally surfaced in educational and community circles. Although the program was predictably supported by the Canadian Legion and "Silver Cross Women" and not so predictably by some leading church figures in Toronto, it was vocally opposed by other groups. These included the Fellowship for a Christian Social Order, the League for Social Reconstruction, the Society of Friends and other pacifist bodies, and a number of leading trade unions in the city.[66] If, they asked, the war was being fought to preserve democracy and the rights of the individual — themes that engaged the attention of those who wrote for the schools[67] — then why imperil those goals by prematurely subjecting Ontario's youth to the corrosive effects of militarization in a formal cadet program?

At about the same time a Baptist publication, whatever its stand on that program, was concerned about the effects of war upon the youngster's emotional well-being, subjected as he was to constant allusions in movies, newsreels, and radio programs to the reality of death and the tragedies of war. Its editor also addressed the questions of unalloyed pacifism and the so-called just war against tyranny, and urged Sunday school teachers to ventilate them in their classes in the hope their young charges might be acquainted with the compelling issues of the moment.[68] But a good many youngsters did not require this kind of sermonizing. They had already been confronted with stark reality and compelling issues when they had lost fathers, uncles, brothers, or even their own teachers and older schoolmates in battle zones or training accidents.

Meanwhile the same people who challenged the need for the mobilization of youth in a cadet corps protested other unwholesome developments in wartime. One such occurred in Toronto. With very little discussion its board of education forwarded to the local police, who had requested them, the names and addresses of parents born in countries outside the British Empire. And the protesters were not mollified by the reminder that the request came in the harrowing summer of 1940, when it was deemed so important to maintain a close surveillance of potentially dangerous aliens.[69] One trustee, who seemed anxious to take advantage of a wartime emergency to campaign against the changing ethnic composition of the city, went so far as to discourage any move to welcome non–Anglo-Saxon refugees.[70] Nor was Toronto unique in this respect. A resolution of the Brantford Board of Education went even further and urged that "none but citizens born under the British Flag [should] have the franchise or be elected to any governmental body ... and that an effort be made to introduce the petition in Great Britain and to all nations of the British Empire."[71] The fate of the petition is unknown, but what is eminently plain is the way latent xenophobia was brought to the surface of Ontario society during critical stages of the war.

Clearly students could be caught in the crossfire. In Hamilton, Jehovah's Witnesses objected on religious grounds when the local board decided to follow a Queen's Park directive and require all students to salute the flag and sing the national anthem at morning assemblies. (Toronto authorities, it seems, were content with the anthem only.) When the Witnesses' children refused to do so, reactions were mixed. One board member convinced himself that the sect was more "pacifistic than disloyal" and warned that "drastic action against them would convert the pupil or the parents into martyrs." But his colleagues and some local politicians were not so perceptive, tolerant, or sensitive, and insisted on treating the "offenders" as police cases.[72] In all, some dozen students were suspended for failing to observe the regulations, a move that ultimately brought a parental suit against the board. The board's policy was eventually struck down by an appeals court in 1945, but not before children in one sector of the community had learned how an inflexible patriotism seasoned with religious prejudice could sour what passed for a free society in wartime.

Earlier, in 1940, a troubled Toronto teenager came home with the news that during a class on democracy his teacher had made disparaging remarks about communists. When his mother brought the matter to the board's attention, she was assured that after a full investigation it could in no way be substantiated, a response she may have greeted with scepticism.[73] Those to whom communism posed a greater threat than fascism would have welcomed the teacher's criticisms warmly, especially at a time when the Soviet Union was still committed to its "unholy alliance" with Nazi Germany. And even after the USSR was added to the list of Hitler's victims in the summer of 1941, some of those voices could still be heard. Conversely, communist youth groups that had spoken out against the war before Russia was forced into it were soon bombarding students with urgent appeals for an all-out drive against the common enemy. The appeals came complete with criticisms of the supposedly lacklustre response of the Toronto board to the crisis that had enveloped the world. "What can be done to break down this apathy?" asked the Toronto District Young Communist League. It had a ready answer:

> First, discussion groups should point out that the Eastern Front is holding nine tenths of the Nazi Army, that our future depends on how much help we give to our Russian allies, and whether we open other fronts to relieve this pressure on them.... The brave soldiers of the Red Army are grappling with the Nazi hordes, holding them up and smashing them mercilessly. That powerful line before Leningrad and Moscow is the line which is preventing

Hitler from marching his troops down the streets of
Toronto, and planting his blood-streaking swastika
on your school flag pole.[74]

The call for a Second Front punctuated many a political meeting, school
gathering, and church service before it was achieved on D-Day in 1944,
though it rankled in some student quarters that insufficient recognition
seemed to be given to the part that Britain and Canada had played while
the USSR remained out of the fight.

Even so, material prepared by both the school and the church for
their respective readers tended to gloss over ideological misgivings and
acclaim the achievements of the stout Russian ally. Thus *Boys of Canada*,
the joint United Church and Baptist magazine, began to run war stories
dealing with the heroism of Russian Boy Scouts (the recognizable
affiliation would make it more meaningful for juvenile Canadian
readers) or the plight of Soviet civilians trapped in a beleaguered city.[75]
Before the war ended a day was set aside, in Toronto schools at least, to
commemorate the crucial Red Army victory at Stalingrad, and a growing volume of supplies was being dispatched under the auspices of the
Canadian Aid to Russia Fund. Suitably impressed schoolchildren were
subsequently shown photographs of gaunt but grateful young Stalin-
graders wearing the clothing they had personally helped to collect.[76]
Even a small rural school in Halton County managed as early as 1942 to
earmark for Russian Relief about a third of the modest funds it raised
from a salvage drive.[77]

Just as the West's allies were being applauded, other religious
writers were telling youngsters that a clear distinction ought to be be
drawn between the supposedly hapless German people and the
"impious" Nazis who had brought down so much destruction on the
world. Some essays went so far as to suggest that the democracies bore
their own heavy responsibility for what had unfolded after 1939 and
must make a greater effort in future to be their brother's keeper and to
fight racism wherever it arose. One magazine featured a column, "What
the War Has Taught Us," which received this contribution: "Had
people in general practised Christian ethics with half the zeal displayed
by the Germans in embracing Nazi ideology, there may never have
been a Second World War!"[78]

For the benefit of young readers, several writers feelingly addressed the question of anti-Semitism in general and the Nazi persecution of the Jews in particular, Hitler's first and last victims. Before the
most gruesome of the death camps were overrun by Allied armies, the
Teachers' Quarterly had urged the discussion of "the oppression of the
Jewish people in Europe in our own day":

> Let the class feel the indignity and the ostracism and
> the fear of brutality. Unless they can be made to feel
> such injustices and brought to care themselves for
> fair play for all, they will not be much interested in
> whether God cares for oppressed people or not.

The writer ended on the hopeful note that "God's sympathy for the Jews can be seen in the Allied cause,"[79] a point of view not necessarily shared by its political and military leadership. Another contributor, a non-Jew doubtless aware of pre-war restrictions on Jewish immigration to Canada, wrote a poem in blank verse, "We are the Jewish Children." He addressed it to "Protestant Boys" in the hope they might gain a better understanding of those who had come "to this new land out of ancient homes of blood and persecution and pain," and who carried in their veins the "blood of the ... mighty men of thought and action by which our people have blessed the world."[80]

On a related theme, stories and articles were published that sympathetically treated the Japanese Canadians rounded up on the West Coast and placed in camps in the far interior. But others also claimed that "blind race prejudice" was not the rule everywhere in British Columbia and that mainstream children often went out of their way to ease the lot of these "second-generation Japanese."[81] Young readers of church magazines were treated as well to discourses on the need to create a more democratic world in every sphere, one founded on principles of social and economic as well as political justice. A whisper of the once potent Social Gospel was heard as a young correspondent recounted what a concerned soldier had poured out:

> I'd like to fight for a just cause and a new world, but
> when I take my gun, I see the young fellows ... being
> beaten by the police [in the thirties] — their only
> crime being hunger — and I find my gun heavy. To
> bring such a world into being we must start, not
> after the war, but *now*.[82]

The British notion of fair play, made so much of at the war's outset, was in some circles being transformed from a facile slogan into a force for inspiring the social, economic, and moral betterment of humanity.

While juvenile readers were being encouraged to mull over questions affecting the long-term future, those in charge of the schools, like the community at large, began to plan for the celebration of victory, a much more manageable immediate goal. The first steps were taken in Toronto as early as the fall of 1944, when it appeared certain that the bell would soon toll for the Axis powers. That the conflict dragged on for many more months did not, in the event, dampen the enthusiasm. As at the beginning of hostilities, so at the end, the United Kingdom was fulsomely lauded (along with her allies), and students were carefully integrated into the proceedings.

In this case, however, the schools and the churches could look forward to a festival of thanksgiving rather than simply a brave morale-boosting exercise in the midst of gloom and adversity. One proposed school service began with the understandably exultant:

> Our arms have beaten the Nazi to his knees. Our
> navies have scourged his ships from the ocean. Our
> young men have shot his planes from the skies. Our
> armies stand victorious on the soil of Germany.
> Gone ... is the brutal German soldier, the death
> camp, the hideous torture chamber, the dread
> Gestapo.

To which pupils were to respond: "We resisted evil and God gave us victory, we fought the good fight and the Lord scattered our enemies before us."[83] Then the assembled youngsters were called upon to recite "This England" from *Richard II* and lustily sing one of the war's great favourites, "There'll Always be an England." Following this, the script directed the teachers on stage to present a dramatic rendition of what Canada had contributed to the Allied triumph.

The planned closing prayer ended on a more reflective note and encapsulated the hopes of those who looked forward to a better and more sensitive world than the one that had ushered in the war. It called upon the nation to deliver itself from that "low spirit which, having known a great salvation, would return again to selfishness and pride." For some, children and adults alike, the low spirit had shown itself in the less than humane and democratic notions that had gained ominous ground in some political and educational circles at critical points of the war. For others, it may have revealed itself in the notion publicized in the *Canadian High News* in 1942 that war as the supreme character-testing device was a "very good thing." For still others, it had been the more mundane confrontation between Ottawa and Queen's Park over the role the schools should play in meeting the challenge.

But for all, or nearly all, those youngsters who had grown up in Ontario during the Second World War it would become a memorable time of unprecedented crisis when whatever passed for the normal had frequently been challenged, modified, or set aside altogether by constant appeals to the spirit, the mind, and the emotions.

NOTES

1   Toronto Board of Education Archives, Curriculum and Programme Division [hereafter TBE, CPD], file 21; Statement prepared by C.C. Goldring for *Canadian High News*, Sept. 9, 1942.
2   *The Scouter*, Oct. 1941, p. 156.
3   Archives of Ontario [hereafter AO], Government Documents ED/EM (1940), *Empire Day in the Schools of Ontario, May 23rd, 1940*.
4   TBE, CPD, file 29B, "Empire Day Talk to Central Technical School Students, May 23, 1940," pp. 2-3.
5   See Robert M. Stamp, "Empire Day in the Schools: The Training of Young Imperialists," *Journal of Canadian Studies*, 8 (Aug., 1973), pp. 32-42. It would take some years for the official term "Commonwealth" to supplant "Empire" in common usage.
6   Hamilton Education Centre [hereafter HEC], *Minutes of the Hamilton Board of Education, 1941*, p. 13.
7   *Teachers' Quarterly*, May 23, 1943, p. 61. This was a Baptist publication.
8   Neil Sutherland, *Children in English-Canadian Society: Framing the Twentieth Century Consensus* (Toronto: University of Toronto Press, 1976), pp. 192-93. For examples of the laudatory way a church magazine covered the subject, see J.R.P. Sclater, "Youth Hails the King" and "The King and Queen in the United States," *Girls of Canada* [hereafter GOC], May 21, 1939, pp. 161, 164-65; June 4, 1939, p. 180. This and the other church publications cited are housed in the Canadian Baptist Archives, McMaster Divinity College.
9   TBE, CPD, file 14, A.S. Redfern to C.C. Goldring, Nov. 19, 1938.
10   AO, Government Documents ED/EM (1943), *A Programme for Empire Day in the Schools of Ontario, May 21st, 1943*, p. 3.
11   The words were unmistakably Winston Churchill's.
12   *A Programme for Empire Day, 1943*, p. 5.
13   Interviews with former pupils of Memorial School. The Kipling revival is traced in AO, Government Documents ED/EM (1942).
14   TBE, Minutes of the Toronto Board of Education, Oct. 1, 1942, p. 155. On the varied "Flag Days," see Minutes of the Management Committee, 1940-41, Apr. 8, 1941, p. 47.
15   TBE, CPD, file 29B, "Empire Youth Sunday, May 25th, 1941."
16   *Teachers' Quarterly*, June 20, 1943, p. 89; June 27, 1943, pp. 43, 83.
17   TBE, Management Committee Minutes, 1940-41, Apr. 23, 1940, p. 45.
18   For the varied attempts in the early years of the century to promote unity of sentiment and understanding among the Empire's youth, see James G. Greenlee, *Education and Imperial Unity, 1901-1926* (New York: Garland, 1987), esp. Chap. 1.
19   Interview in Hamilton, Ont., with Professor Emeritus Harold Lang, Oct. 9, 1986. Lang served as editor of several joint Baptist and United Church youth publications in the early war years.
20   See *Boys of Canada* [hereafter BOC], Mar. 2, 1941, p. 71; Sept. 7, 1941, p. 281; Oct. 26, 1941, p. 340; and *GOC*, Apr. 7, 1940, pp. 107, 118; June 23, 1940, p. 199. For the role that juvenile literature and other literary, theatrical, and educational devices supposedly played in fashioning an Imperial "core ideology" in Britain, see John M. MacKenzie, *Propaganda and Empire: The Manipulation of British Public Opinion, 1880-1960* (Manchester: Manchester University Press, 1984).
21   See Olive Stevens, *Children Talking Politics: Political Learning in Childhood* (Oxford: Oxford University Press, 1982), pp. 1-2, and R.W. Connell, *The Child's Construction of Politics* (Manchester: Manchester University Press, 1971), p. 18.

22   Canadian Baptist Archives, McMaster Divinity College, *Story Hour: For the Little Ones*, July 6, 1941, p. 1. For other samples of the genre, see the issues for Apr. 19 and July 5, 1942 ("Remember, Lord, the men aboard my daddy's submarine").

23   *GOC*, Mar. 8, 1942, pp. 73ff., and Mar. 15, 1942, p. 82.

24   In Hamilton, which was perhaps typical, some of the early evacuees had to be housed in unused school quarters until supporters could be found and private accommodation arranged. Ruth Grieve, "The Impact of the Second World War on the Educational System of Ontario with Special Reference to the City of Hamilton" (Undergraduate research paper, McMaster University, 1978), pp. 19-20.

25   *GOC*, March 21, 1943, p. 95; May 9, 1943, p.151.

26   Ibid., June 7, 1942, pp. 182-3.

27   On this theme see three BSA theses at the University of Guelph Archives: M.S. Nelles "Planning and Managing a 50-Acre Fruit Farm" (1922), pp.15-17, T.H. Jones," Niagara Peninsula Fruit from the Grower to the Consumer" (1919), pp. 22-24, and W.S. Van Every, "Fruit Farm Organization" (1922), pp. 33-34, 35.

28   TBE, CPD, file 17 (Farm Service, 1943 to 1954), "A Brief on the Use of Secondary School Students on Farms in 1944," p.1.

29   Interview in Ancaster, Ont., with Lorna Chaffey Johnston, May 12, 1987.

30   *GOC*, June 13, 1943, p. 189.

31   Brant County Board of Education, Minutes of the Paris District High School Board, Aug. 14, 1940, pp. 76-77.

32   TBE, Toronto Board Minutes, May 31 and Oct. 31, 1940.

33   See TBE, CPD, file 36 (Department of Labour, Working Hours of Children, 1943-1951), "Some Thoughts on Student Workers, Oct. 25, 1943."

34   Ibid., F.H. Atkinson to Goldring, Oct. 15, 1945.

35   Ibid., file 33 (Truancy, General, 1943 to 1945).

36   On the introduction of compulsory religious education by George Drew's government in 1944, see Stamp, *The Schools of Ontario, 1876-1976* (Toronto: University of Toronto Press, Ontario Historical Studies Series, 1982), pp. 177-78, 181-82. For the discussion of child care, consult TBE, Toronto Board Minutes, 1942, pp. 96, 99, 279, 416.

37   *Quest*, Aug. 15, 1943, p. 519.

38   *Teachers' Quarterly*, Mar. 7, 1943, p. 72.

39   Interviews with former students of Delta Collegiate Institute. On the other hand, a church periodical loftily pointed out, "In some groups it is as important to know the big news from Washington or Chungking [China's wartime capital] as to know the newest jive tune." *Sunday School Quarterly*, Oct.-Dec. 1943, p. 5.

40   TBE, CPD, file 31, box 34. The "clean" baskets were specifically requested by Ottawa's Wartime Prices and Trade Board, mainly for the farming community.

41   Ibid., file 9 (Collections), A.G. Dixon to Principals, Sept. 11, 1941. If Brant County was typical, students who collected aluminum elsewhere were not rewarded so entertainingly. (Brant County Board of Education, Minutes of the Paris District High School Board, Mar. 5, 1941, p. 85.)

42   Halton County Board of Education, Minutes of the Milton High School Board, Jan. 12, 1940, p. 241. A special Red Cross Dance was also ruled out on the grounds there were enough school dances already. (See pp. 223, 241, 249.)

43   HEC, *Minutes of the Hamilton Board of Education, 1941*, pp. 328-29.

44   Jack Holmes, "Canadian Boys and the War," *BOC*, Mar. 14, 1943, p. 83.

45   AO, RG 2, Department of Education, Miscellaneous Records, series T, box 5, "Dear Teacher from pupil Betty Martin."

46   In a cautious Milton, for example, the program was put on a trial basis for one month before it was implemented. (Halton County Board of Education, Minutes of the Milton High School Board, Feb. 27, 1941, p. 233.)

47 The educational tug-of-war between wartime Ottawa and Queen's Park, part of a general political confrontation, is productively explored in Stamp, *The Schools of Ontario*, pp. 172-73.
48 Grieve, "The Impact of the Second World War on the Educational System," p. 13.
49 TBE, Toronto Board Minutes, 1942, Jan. 27, 1942, p. 13. See also Donald Shier, "The Magic of Camouflage," *BOC*, Jan. 23, 1941, p.28.
50 TBE, CPD, file 31, box 34.
51 Azriel L. Eisenberg, *Children and Radio Programs: A Study of More than Three Thousand Children in the New York Metropolitan Area* (New York, 1936), pp. 6, 18.
52 AO, Pamphlets, file 39, 1942, *Young Canada Listens: School Broadcasts, 1942-1943*, p. 17; TBE, Toronto Board Minutes, 1942, Sept. 8, 1942, p. 298.
53 Argyle and Sutherland Highlanders of Canada Archives, "Scotty Sent Us" (an account of the achievements of Pvt. Earl "Scotty" McAllister.) Dr. Robert Fraser, who is preparing a history of the battalion, kindly supplied this material.
54 *BOC*, Dec. 26, 1943, pp. 409-11; July 26, 1942, pp. 238-39; *GOC*, Feb. 21, 1943, p. 63.
55 TBE, Management Committee Minutes, 1940-41, App. A, pp. 91-94. See also Stamp, *The Schools of Ontario*, p. 172.
56 Halton County Board of Education, Minutes of the Milton High School Board, Sept. 26, 1940, pp. 229-30; Apr. 29, 1943, p. 250.
57 AO, Pamphlets, file 32 (1942), "The Way to War ...," pp. 1- 53.
58 TBE, Toronto Board Minutes, 1944, App. 1.
59 Ibid., Oct. 3, 1940, p. 172; Sept. 24, 1942, p. 322.
60 TBE, Management Committee Minutes, 1940-41, Mar. 25, 1941, p. 41.
61 TBE, Toronto Board Minutes, App., Feb. 27, 1940, pp. 45, 370, 382.
62 AO, RG 2, Department of Education, Miscellaneous Records, series T, box 5, Mrs. R.C. Matthews to Fellow Worker, Feb. 7, 1944.
63 TBE, Management Committee Minutes, 1940-41, June 10, 1941, p. 83.
64 Ibid., Oct. 7, 1941, p. 121.
65 Ibid., letter from C.G. Power, Mar. 24, 1941, p. 46.
66 TBE, Toronto Board Minutes, 1939, App., pp. 52-53, 63.
67   See, for example, *Democracy in Education* (n.p., n.d.), brought out by the Canadian Council of Education for Democracy.
68 *Teachers' Quarterly*, Oct.-Dec. 1943, pp. 3-4.
69 TBE, Management Committee Minutes, 1940-41, June 11, 1940, p. 76.
70 Ibid., Oct. 8, 1940, p. 103.
71 Brant County Board of Education, Minutes of the Brantford Board of Education, May 30, 1940.
72 HEC, *Minutes of the Hamilton Board of Education*, Oct. 10, 1940, p. 283; April 17, 1942, p. 191. See also Grieve, "The Impact of the Second World War on the Educational System," pp. 5-6. For a fuller treatment of the problem, see M.J. Penton, *The Jehovah's Witnesses in Canada: Champions of Freedom of Speech and Worship* (Toronto: Macmillan, 1976). In a forthcoming study, Professor William Kaplan of the Faculty of Law at the University of Ottawa deals extensively with the notorious Hamilton cases.
73 TBE, Management Committee Minutes, 1940-41, Jan. 23, 1940, p.13; Feb. 6, 1940, p. 19.
74 TBE, CPD, file 29C, "Why We Must Smash Hitler!"
75 *BOC*, Sept. 10, 1944, pp. 289-95.
76 TBE, CPD, file 9 (Collections), Mrs. T. Lyle Blogg to Goldring, Jan. 30, 1945; Management Committee Minutes, Feb. 22, 1944.
77 Halton County Board of Education, Minutes of the Board of Trustees of S.S. #14 (Freeman), Dec. 21, 1942.

78   *Quest,* May 2, 1943, pp. 274, 275; May 7, 1944, p. 297.
79   *Teachers' Quarterly,* July 4, 1943, p. 10.
80   P.R. Hayward, "We Are the Jewish Children," BOC, Feb. 11, 1945, p. 42.
81   GOC, Mar. 22, 1942, p. 93.
82   *Quest,* Apr. 25, 1943, p. 275.
83   TBE, CPD, file 50, "A School Service of Thanksgiving for Victory," pp. 3-4.

SOCIETY AND CULTURE IN RURAL AND SMALL-TOWN ONTARIO: ALICE MUNRO'S TESTIMONY ON THE LAST FORTY YEARS

John Weaver

Anyone attempting to comprehend the culture and society of Ontario from the 1940s to the 1980s will find a valuable source in the writing of Alice Munro. Her stories possess settings, fantasies, genuine voices, and feelings for common and domestic life that create evocative chronicles of rural and small-town Ontario during the last forty years. Munro offers not only a verifiable reality, but also what literary critics might call mythic insights. To ransack her works merely for the former would be crude labour, which would overlook her unique contribution, an account of feelings and emotions. The notion that common lives from the past ought to be subjects for reconstruction through statistical analysis and studies of men and women at work has been accepted only recently. To recommend now that common feelings resting on mythic insights should enter the repertoire of historical inquiry is bound to be thought of as a questionable proposal. Even granting that common emotions have a place in history, it is true that sources are rare, and seldom can they be expected to yield the same riches as a sensitive writer long interested in the province's past. Thus there are solid grounds — as if any were needed — for accepting Alice Munro as a remarkable interpreter of Ontario's cultural history, in particular small-town social structure, community values, the migration to the cities, religious culture, sexuality, and the fantasies of adolescents.

No other important Ontario writer of fiction has so forthrightly discussed the writing of history and the limitations of traditional local history. Historians and the paraphernalia of research have figured in several of her stories, where adults read history books and school children memorize dates that they will recall as adults. A lover in "Hard Luck Stories" is in charge of acquisitions at the Provincial Archives. Patrick of *Who Do You Think You Are?* is interested in history; his "astonishingly belligerent" father is not. More important, *Lives of Girls and Women* implies two poles of historical inquiry. At one pole, Munro places the historian as a collector who, at worst, reifies facts and artifacts without ordering their meaning. At the other, she places the creative soul who wants to record the concrete but also the passions. The first, represented by Uncle Craig, belongs to the tradition of the local amateur. The same tradition receives passing treatment in the portrait of the father in "Walker Brothers Cowboy" and of Blaikie Noble in "Something I've Been Meaning to Tell You." For these enthusiasts, county histories open with dinosaurs and the origin of limestone, jump to discourses on Indians, and culminate with lists of the names of the settler families.[1]

Though Uncle Craig of *Lives* impresses on young Del Jordan the importance of accuracy and of heritage, his conception of history is deficient. He sponsors Del's initial awareness of history and, in his desire to pour everything into his history, he even has a sense of common lives, but he cannot select and evaluate. Munro rejects the narrowness of a tradition that pursues certainty and precision in concrete matters but will not tackle the complex issues of community texture, of social and cultural attitudes, of the psychological compulsions that drive family and community. Even her non-amateurs seem deficient, perhaps lacking passion and the sensitivity to discern and communicate the intensity of ordinary lives. A budding professional historian, the student David in "Labor Day Dinner" cuts too solid a figure; "he is deliberate, low-voiced, never rash."[2] Del eventually finds local reconstruction "crazy, heartbreaking." Little wonder! What turns over in her mind are pieces of an independent artistic vision. When she tries to explain her own conceptions, they tumble out like fragments still mixed with the incidental and the concrete which made up Uncle Craig's form of history. Nevertheless, shapeless and confused though it is, Del's perception of what she needs to record includes sensations and emotions. "And no list could hold what I wanted, for what I wanted was every last thing, every layer of speech and thought, stroke of light on bark or walls, every smell, pothole, pain, crack, delusion, held still and held together — radiant, everlasting."[3] Hers is becoming an artist's vision, akin to an aspiration to total history. In 1971, the year *Lives of Girls and Women* was published, Uncle Craig's incomplete history of Wawanish County might well have been received more cordially by the historical academy than Del's wish.

Alice Munro shares the goals of social historians, and both have come to recognize certain themes as central to their inquiry and as frustratingly problematic: feelings, values, and motivation. The narrator of "The Stone in the Field" rediscovers a childhood mystery while reading a microfilmed newspaper at a Toronto library. Curiosity and the magnetism of the home region lure the narrator back into an on-site search and a questioning of local residents. Any hope of learning the truth evaporates:

Rural Ontario and the chronicler: Alice Munro with her Presbyterian grandparents, William and Sadie Laidlaw, on the Turnberry Township farm where she grew up. (Courtesy Alice Munro.)

> Now I no longer believe people's secrets are defined
> and communicable, or their feelings full-blown and
> easy to recognize. I don't believe so. Now, I can only
> say my father's sister scrubbed the floor with lye.[4]

Although warning that completeness must finally elude historians and other artists, Munro never abandons Del's quest. She presses boldly on to compile chronicles about common lives and, although these certainly go much further than Uncle Craig's notions about people's lives, she retains the material details of concrete history. Munro's finely honed memory has certainly documented various drives and feelings among a number of small-town character types. Several of her very best stories (for example, "The Progress of Love" and "A Queer Streak") offer astonishingly compressed cradle-to-grave profiles of common folk. Moreover, these lives are shown to have been bewitched by unpredictable turns of fate or by incidents whose meanings have been incompletely grasped by the protagonists. Therefore, Alice Munro has left ample traces of her attempt to exhume and record the truth while appreciating both the material circumstances and the accidental influences on common lives in small communities.

Munro's own comments about her work are further reason to trust her material: "Most of the incidents in *Lives of Girls and Women* are changed versions of real incidents. Some are completely invented, but the emotional reality ... [is] solidly autobiographical."[5] Munro's remark concerning what townsfolk think about her work inspires confidence too. "Sometimes they feel cheated by not having the church on the right street. Then you do, constantly, get the thing about `But I grew up there, and life wasn't this bad.' "[6] Had they reacted enthusiastically, welcoming an Ontario *roman du pays*, the reader would have had cause for scepticism. Had she scathingly condemned her roots, there would have been a different basis for rejection or caution. In fact, her ambivalence — the occasional word of praise for rural and small-town Ontario's vanishing values — appears as a struggle to portray a particular culture as fairly as anyone can who has moved away. Tracks of honest effort wind through her tales as she moves from southwestern Ontario to the cities and, in *The Progress of Love*, explores the Ottawa Valley.

Always the details ring true; it is worth noting how true by considering the similarity between her home town of Wingham and the fictitious town of Jubilee. *Lives of Girls and Women* presents a close mental mapping of the region around Wingham, Ontario. Munro's disavowal of the importance of matching physical details in fiction with those in reality, and deflects the reader's attention from the remarkable similarities between her fictional world and a corner of Huron County. She may shuffle the furniture around, but her socio-demographic and religious portraits correspond to a census-based analysis with remarkable accuracy. Lesser touchstones of authenticity fill the stories: Silverwood's ice cream, a B.A. service station, the high dark-wood booth partitions in restaurants, linoleum, hands stamped with purple ink at the dance hall, the seals on the grade thirteen examination envelopes, the Legion Hall, the Kinsmen's fairs, the *Family Herald*.

Returning to the traits of the population, consider the census information for Wingham; during the 1940s, the town barely broke above the 2,000 mark, or about 15 per cent below the turn-of-the-century enumeration. Wingham was a town in relative decline. Its high-water mark may have been attained in 1897, the year of the Jubilee. Ethnically, Wingham figures as a precise model of rural and small-town Ontario: 65 per cent English and Scottish; a quarter Irish; 10 per cent "other." Ninety-five per cent had been born in Ontario. The distribution of religious denominations, however, varied markedly from the province as a whole, in that it was overwhelmingly United Church and Presbyterian. It is quite likely that the Presbyterian strain predominated, because the post-church union holdouts made up a quarter of the population, and half of the United Church may have consisted of unionist Presbyterians. Del's father's family, nominally United Church, had been Presbyterian at the time of union. A Presbyterian outlook, so much a part of Alice Munro's explanation of rural and small-town self-denial, probably influenced the mentality of half the town.[7] If Munro's major characters stumble upon Roman Catholics with open-eyed disbelief — "a picture on the wall of Mary" is a clue to alien practices — it is because a mere 6 per cent of Wingham supposedly did "what the Pope [told] them to do".[8]

The most frequently cited level of education in Huron County in 1941 was grade seven; more girls than boys advanced to grades 12 and 13. Del of *Lives* goes on; her brother does not. This was the educational reality in the small-town schools of Ontario until the restructing of secondary education in the mid-1960s. Alice Munro may have placed the church on the wrong street; yet she sensed the town's decline, depicted the influence of religious values, and remarked upon the modest formal education of its youth. *Lives of Girls and Women* and many of her stories point out the irony that English Canadians regarded French Canadians as suffering from a rural backwardness. Small-town Ontario values inhibited risk and non-conformity. In fact, one of Munro's major contributions to an understanding of the culture of rural and small town Ontario has been her obsession with the values that have anchored people to a limited area, to conformity, and to a pride that is admirable, thwarting, and indolent.

The demographic and social traits are not the only ones that Munro depicts accurately, for she also has the geography correctly in place. For instance, the topography and man-made environment in and around fictional Jubilee resemble those of Wingham. A road much like the Flats Road of fiction runs through Lower Wingham. To the north, the terrain becomes rugged in the vicinity of Alps Creek, and like the marginal region of Jerico Valley in *Lives*, it was mistakenly cleared by land-hungry settlers. "They haven't progressed here much beyond the pioneer state. Maybe they're too lazy. Or the land isn't worth it. Or a combination of both."[9] The Maitland River becomes the Wawanash of fiction; in "The Stone in the Field" there is less disguise, for the river is "Old Father Maitland." Bluevale, south of Wingham, inspired the Blue River of *Lives*. The radio station in *Lives* sits on a rise outside the town on Highway 4. In later stories, the archetypal Ontario small town is brought up to date and, accordingly, has expanded at the margins. The Canadian Tire store occupies what used to be a vacant lot; a Petro-Car [sic] station has replaced a boarding house on the edge of town; senior citizens' housing has taken over the site of the old rink.[10]

Munro not only has a way of evoking time and place with correct details, but she often refracts them convincingly through youthful eyes, establishing a hierarchy of places as seen by a young girl in the years before Ontario was shrunk by television and expressways. In the experimental exercises of mental mapping conducted by geographers, maps drawn from memory are dominated by frequently travelled corridors. Munro's recollections have the same minute detail along familiar routes and distortions on the outer fringes. Her observations made *en route*, in other words, have recorded authentically the sights and some of the feelings they have stirred among children; they also report on features of an environment that no longer characterize rural Ontario. Usually the children of "The Progress of Love" go from Sunday school directly into church, but one morning the outsiders staying at their home whisk them away for a Sunday drive in a Chrysler car — not the farm pickup. They depart from the normally travelled paths:

> Today we spent this time driving through the country
> I had never seen before. I had never seen it, though it
> was less than twenty miles from home. Our truck went
> to the cheese factory, to church, and to town on Satur-
> day nights. The nearest thing to a drive was when it
> went to the dump. I had seen the near end of Bell's
> Lake, because that was where my father cut ice in
> winter.[11]

Extensive mental mapping occurs early in *Lives of Girls and Women*. The Flats Road receives rich treatment. Later, when Del moves into town, she acquires a precise knowledge of the town's geography. "I had," says Del, "a sense of the whole town around me." The town she describes, like most of Ontario's small towns, had matured in the late nineteenth century: Victoria Street, Khartoum Street, the Orange Lodge, the absence of a bar. The second-hand images that Del receives about the United States, Windsor, and Toronto faithfully recreate a small-town youngster's attitudes about improper, dangerous, but exciting places.[12]

On the margins of the youngster's mental map, there exists the commotion of the big cities. Uncle Benny's trip to Toronto in *Lives of Girls and Women* is a wonderful anti-saga, repeated to some degree by Sam, Edgar, and Callie in "The Moon in the Orange Street Skating Rink." Sam went to Toronto, when he was ten, and he and his father used the wrong door on the streetcar. So now Sam feels he had "to anticipate the complexities ahead so they wouldn't take him by surprise."[13] Returning to *Lives*, Bobby Sherriff's breakdown occurs in the city. Nevertheless, Fern thrills Del with reports about the fast night life of Detroit. No television sets project city streets into front rooms. Urban ways are still thought of as mysterious and treacherous in a world where a drive to the next town is an adventure. "I hoped to travel as far as Porterfield or Blue River, towns which derived their magic simply from being places we did not know and were not known in, by not being Jubilee."[14] The limited horizon and tentative spirit of exploration ring with an authoritative sense of how young eyes and minds perceive near and distant communities.

Munro is a trustworthy guide to the Jubilees of Ontario. From here onward, this supported claim must remain in mind as the discussion moves through ever more unverifiable insights: first about the realms of work; second, about social rank; third about religious identities or prejudices; fourth, about pride and denial; finally, about urges and inhibitions. No witness to history can hope to impart anything like completeness; that after all is one of Munro's major tenets. An absence of perspective too would be impossible. Alice Munro writes as a woman once steeped in the Presbyterianism of old Ontario, as someone exposed to "the scourging psalms."[15] It is from the feminine and Calvinist perspectives — tempered by later experiences — that she considers a host of fundamental social concerns, and this restricts her range.

Munro's female narrators impart only rare glimpses of male work or of recreation.[16] Occasionally men's work performs a plot function, for example, Garnet French's dead-end job at the lumberyard and the father's territory as a salesman in "Walker Brothers Cowboy." Often enough Munro conveys the drudgery of farm toil that held marginal operators and their families to a constricted routine interspersed with scheduled excursions to church and town. Her city women find creative though underpaid positions, but in the hinterlands women could exercise their enterprise only in a very few accepted roles, such as boarding-house keeper or music teacher. Her typical women in the visible workforce of the small town are school teachers, waitresses, cleaning women, casual workers in food-processing plants, bank tellers, and telephone operators. The narrator of "The Turkey Season" guts birds because she is "still too young to get a job working in a store or as a part-time waitress."[17]

A few noteworthy renegades, for so they are treated by townsfolk, stray from the norm. Del's mother sells encyclopedias, and Violet in "A Queer Streak" holds onto her wartime job with Bell Telephone. "There was some feeling that she should have stepped down when the war was over.... [It] would have been the gracious thing to do."[18] The several descriptions of unappealing and gadget-free kitchens and floor scrubbing remind the reader of women's "invisible" labour.[19] Uncle Craig's typing — his work — is oddly respected by the women, who also regard it as frivolous. They respect the line between men's work and women's work — "the clearest line drawn":

> The veranda was where they sat in the afternoons, having completed morning marathons of floor scrubbing, cucumber hoeing, potato digging, bean and tomato picking, canning, pickling, washing, starching, sprinkling, ironing, waxing, baking. They were not idle sitting there; their laps were full of work — cherries to be stoned, peas to be shelled, apples to be cored. Their hands, their old, dark, wooden-handled paring knives, moved with marvelous, almost vindictive speed.[20]

Workplaces — except in "the Turkey Season" — are not considered extensively. Neither really is social stratification, except that it intersects frequently with the religious denominations that engross Munro. In *Lives of Girls and Women* she describes the social standings without denominational adjuncts. At the apex of the town are "Mrs. Coutts, sometimes called Mrs. Lawyer Coutts, and Mrs. Best whose husband was the manager of the Bank of Commerce."[21] Del's mother, hoping to sustain independence by selling encyclopedia, tries to penetrate the charmed circle by aspiring to be an intellectual chatelaine. "My mother had hoped that her party would encourage other ladies to give parties of this sort, but it did not, or if it did we never heard of them; they continued giving bridge parties, which my mother said were silly and snobbish."[22] Her mother, in turn, had a negative reference group — the people on Flats Road. "She spoke to people here in a voice not so friendly as she used in town.... She was on the side of poor people everywhere ... but she could not bear drunkenness, no, and she could not bear sexual looseness, dirty language, haphazard lives, contented ignorance; and so she had to exclude the Flats Road people from the really oppressed and deprived people, the real poor whom she still loved."[23]

All small towns probably have had a Flats Road — designated by equally evocative names — and residents whose poverty is attributed to "haphazard lives." On these urban fringes stand the houses where "a wall would be painted and the job abandoned, the ladder left up; scars of a porch torn away were left uncovered."[24] It is probable too that, in Jubilee as elsewhere, water and sewer lines have not extended into these areas with rural tax rates, just beyond the town's boundary. Neither the village bourgeoisie nor, usually, the terribly poor overwhelm Munro's accounts of social landscapes. Most often she writes of households where money has been very tight — poverty among people who never thought of themselves as poor. What are the consequences of this commonplace poverty?

> It meant having those ugly tube lights and being proud of them. It meant continual talk of money and malicious talk about new things people had bought and whether they were paid for. It meant pride and jealousy flaring over something like the new pair of plastic curtains, imitating lace, that Flo had bought for the front window. That as well as hanging your clothes on nails behind the door and being able to hear every sound from the bathroom. It meant decorating your walls with a number of admonitions, pious and cheerful and mildly bawdy.[25]

The status or socio-economic divisions are usually reinforced by the religious denominations, which announce social views in their architecture and conceivably express the social drift of the congregation in rituals and sermons. In fact, in Munro's work there is an almost inverse relationship between social rank and the strength of evangelical faith. In Jubilee, as in most southern Ontario towns, the United Church is "the largest, most prosperous." Inside it boasts glossy golden oak pews, a splendid show of organ pipes, and stained glass windows. Owing to some complex interaction of history and social dynamics, its members have come to avoid religious extremes and to sustain a bourgeois liberalism in furnishings, liturgy, and sermons. Even seating expressed the ethos, for amidst the subdued riches the pews "were placed in a democratic fan-shaped sort of arrangement."[26] All other churches are relatively poor, but at the United Church "doctors, lawyers, merchants passed the plate."[27] In *Who Do You Think You Are?* the Milton ladies, Miss Mattie and Miss Hattie, epitomize an inherited prosperity allegedly found among established United Church families. "Their brick house, with its overstuffed comfort, their coats with collars of snug dull fur, seemed proclaimed as a Methodist house.... Everything about them seemed to say they had applied themselves to the world's work for God's sake, and God had not let them down."[28]

The United Church has been accorded a significant position in Alice Munro's rendering of Ontario, and although her depictions betray a critical bias, her commentary is authentic. The United Church, in her accounts, plays down Christian orthodoxy. Thus it is the United Church minister — thankfully — "who usually took up the slack [at funerals] in the cases of no known affiliation."[29] Rather than for doctrinal rigour, the United Church is notable for its secular activities and respectability, both of which are essential ingredients of the plot in "A Queer Streak." Violet, who attends Ottawa normal school, switches churches in the city. "She said that at the United church there was a lot more going on. There was a badminton club ... and a drama club, as well as skating parties, tobogganing, hayrides, socials."[30] It is while bobbing for apples in a church basement that she meets Trevor, the assistant minister. "The ministry then, in that church, attracted vigorous young men intent on power, not too unlike the young men who went into politics."[31] The minister's role as a public figure and his standing as the quintessence of a bourgeois consensus guide Trevor's decision to break his engagement to Violet, who trustingly reveals the queer streak in her family. She cannot have anything in her background "that would ever give rise to gossip or cause a scandal."[32]

Except for the Loyalist lakefront towns, where "there was a remnant of the old Family Compact, or some sort of military or social establishment to keep it going," the Anglicans have little prestige or money. Presbyterians "were leftovers, people who had refused to become United. They were mostly elderly."[33] Nevertheless, the residual strength of the Calvinist sect persists in the mentalities of the "Scotch" and Irish stock.

Munro's account of Baptists presents an interesting counterpoint to the less socially fluid and less evangelical denominations that claim the bulk of the town. "No person of any importance or social standing went to the Baptist church, and so somebody like Pork Childs, who delivered the coal and collected garbage for the town, could get to be a leading figure, an elder in it."[34] In the chapter "Baptizing" Del's boyfriend, Garnet French, introduces her to, among other things, Baptist rituals, and Garnet himself is shown to have gained a purpose through conversion. Yet Del is an adventurous young girl and the Baptists seem tedious. She cringes at the thought of becoming familiar with Pork Childs. It is the darker side of Garnet that interests her.[35] In a later short story, incorporated into *Who Do You Think You Are?* ("Privilege"), Munro again equates evangelicalism or fundamentalism with poverty. "Many of the Protestants had been — or their families had been — Anglicans, Presbyterians. But they had got too poor to show up at those churches, so had veered off to the Salvation Army, the Pentecostal."[36] The evangelical alternatives have been a part of Ontario towns, but — here Munro's rendition seems plausible — they have had no paramount influence on community values. That may help to explain the understanding she reveals for them in *Lives of Girls and Women,* a work that ever so tentatively dallies with the slight departures from the norm that could be magnified into shocking deviation by contrast with small town order.

"A small but unintimidated tribe," the Roman Catholics worship in modest churches, "bare and plain."[37] Their unobtrusiveness in southern Ontario towns helped define the cultural boundaries that set most of Ontario apart from the cities or fringe regions like the Ottawa Valley. Alice Munro does not explore the Roman Catholic position from within the minority. She comes to it from a vantage point on one side of a traditional discord, a discord that tried to banish inter-denominational intimacy. The father in "Walker Brothers' Cowboy" probably rejected an old sweetheart because she was Roman Catholic. Relatives who marry Roman Catholics are lost oddities in the family genealogy kept by Uncle Craig in *Lives of Girls and Women.* A house guest from outside the Ontario consensus who surfaces in "The Progress of Love" causes muted consternation by driving his host's young lads over to the nearby McAllister farm to play: the McCallister children are Catholic girls.[38] Munro treats the expressions of bigotry like an outlandish but comfortable old suit. Foolishness about "strangled nuns under convent floors, yes, fat priests and fancy women and the black old popes" float about as chatter among innocuous old folk. Munro's clearest exposition of outrageous anti-Catholic notions and their common place in small town talk of the 1940s, and beyond, appears in "Accident."

> "Of course the O'Hares being Catholics, they've got four or five more. You know, the priest came and did the business on him, even if he was stone dead."
> "Oh, oh, said Frances' mother disapprovingly. There was not much hostility to Catholics in this disapproval, really; it was a courtesy Protestants were bound to pay each other.[39]

In *Lives* Munro describes a seemingly benign Orange Lodge that does little more than organize card parties. Although "King Billy" has status as a commonly recognized cultural representation of something, that something has become a fuzzy concept now portrayed as a slightly foolish symbolic figure. King Billy wears "a cardboard crown and a raggedy purple cloak"; the nickname is borne by Violet's poor bastard father in "A Queer Streak" and by a dapple-grey horse. Perhaps Munro revises history here, for this particular story could only have happened around 1900. From the vantage point of the 1980s, an innocent and spoofing characterization has a reason: why not help to douse the Orange embers with soft ridicule? However, in 1900 the lodge which engaged seriously in exclusionary politics, was more than a farce.

Indeed, one of the implications of the religious divide encouraged by Orangeism is hinted at in "The Progress of Love." The lawyer, Bob Marks, wants to start a practice in Euphemia's town, "but there already was one Catholic lawyer."[40] In his epilogue to *The Orangeman*, Donald Akenson maintains that the Orange tradition may not have died out politically.[41] If so, Alice Munro, no apologist, writes for those who recognize bigotry and hope to combat it by ridiculing it as a silly excess of the past.

Many church events inspire Alice Munro's satirical sketches and reflections on hypocrisy. On balance, her depiction of religion betrays no anti-clerical venom; she has too fine a touch and is too able a social chronicler for that, but she certainly runs close to witty caricature. Her capacity see hypocrisy derives from an acute knowledge of several traditions of Ontario Protestantism. "The question of whether God existed or not never came up in Church. It was only a matter of what He approved of, or usually what He did not approve of."[42] Such were the sermons of the mainline denominations. Morality and current affairs were frequently served to Protestants of mid-twentieth century southern Ontario:

> My mother wanted to know what the sermon had been about.
> "Peace," said Fern. "And the United Nations. Et cetera et cetera."
> "Peace," said my mother enjoyably. "Well, is he for it or against it?"
> "He's all in favor of the United Nations."
> "I guess God is too then. What a relief. Only a short time ago He and Mr. McLaughlin were all for the war. They are a changeable pair."[43]

Since Del's mother is an atheist, her conduct is described as eccentric. Her daughter is more conventional. As a young girl Del sought religious experience and a confirmation of God. Later, as an adolescent, she attends an evangelical tent meeting and understands, with slight amused detachment, the "balmy" comfort that many derived from a fire-and-brimstone sermon. The evangelical strain tended to be an embarrassing relative of mainline Protestantism in small-town Ontario. Mr. McLaughlin, the United Church minister, is at the meeting. Consistent with her stereotype of this denomination's ministers, he keeps a "suave downcast face; it was not his kind of exhortation." [44]

Religion defines sub-communities within the town; that is to say, in themselves the denominations divide but they also confirm the divisions of social rank. Concurrently, the images of the United States help to reconstitute the community *qua* community and give it something against which to exercise its pride. In truth, America was useful in defining what southern Ontario towns were not — not rich, not lively, not chaotic, not "cultured," not even gauche. Godless and decadent, American civilization affronted, enticed, and informed. Defending the Lord's Day meant opposing Sunday sports and newspapers, but American Sunday editions from Detroit and New York were snapped up at local drug stores, which were allowed to open on Sunday. Relatively poor and self-consciously pious, the towns of southern Ontario concocted a sense of identity that required American excesses. For Munro, windfalls originate in the States and when they invade poor Ontario homes, they incite ingratitude. In "The Progress of Love," Euphemia's mother burns her inheritance from Seattle, though not necessarily because it comes from the States. Yet it is significant that the source of the legacy, a disreputable father, ended his days in the benighted republic.[45] In *Lives of Girls and Women*, Americans — Uncle Bill Morrison and his young wife Nile — appear ludicrously affluent and generous, thus affronting local self-esteem. Their big car comes "nosing along between the snowbanks almost silently, like an impudent fish."[46] From this car, a vehicle of revelation, Del suddenly sees the town's shabbiness. The saving grace in these confrontations between rich outsiders and local inadequacies is the former's alleged lack of taste and dignity. Niles' high heels are comic and her green finger nails are "perfect artificiality."[47] Aunt Iris's gifts in "Chaddeleys and Flemings" are too loud.[48] If asked for an appraisal of the United States, many small-town residents would agree with Del's mother: "Many bad, and crazy, as well as restless and ambitious people went there eventually."[49] Nevertheless, the high culture of the great American cities reaches into small town Ontario; and Del becomes a culturally attuned and knowledge-hungry adolescent: what she "really wanted to do on Saturday afternoons was stay home and listen to the Metropolitan Opera."[50]

Although Munro shares the endeavours of cultural and social historians who want to understand common acts and attitudes, she does more than describe work and domestic situations, social ranking, denominational and community divisions, and such cultural phenomena as Ontario's two-faced glances across the border. Rather, she pushes boldly on to apply her insight to the psychological aspects of life in Ontario's small communities. For this ambitious enterprise she makes use of female narrators, usually ones who have forsaken countryside or village — physically anyway. These deserters have advanced — or at least moved on — to Toronto, Vancouver, and Ottawa. By focusing here on rural and small town life, we do not need to follow the narrators into their adult and urban lives. Although her narrators are women who have gone out into a wider world and shaken off some of the small town manners and mannerisms, Munro also deals extensively with the people who stayed behind. Outsiders and eccentrics, alien fortune seekers and seducers, perverts and fools walk and drive her streets, but they do not preoccupy her. She resists the temptation to dwell upon the colourful or outrageous, preferring instead the more universal characters who either accept the standards of the community or who, even though they move away, never quite overcome their early conditioning.

In *Lives of Girls and Women*, Del's mother urges her to leave. "Do you intend to live in Jubilee all your life? Do you want to be the wife of a lumberyard worker? Do you want to join the Baptist Ladies Aid?"[51] Del's answer is an emphatic no, and soon her mother has no worries, as the university catalogues replace Del's romance with Garnet French: "He was fading in the clear light of my future."[52] In retrospect, the "clear light" registers irony, because Munro depicts the spiritual or emotional gains and losses of the great post-war migration from small towns to metropolitan centres ambiguously with occasional dollops of nostalgia. "We drove through country we did not know we loved.... Tall elm trees, separate, each plainly showing its shape, doomed but we did not know that either."[53] For every sentimental passage, one can find another of hard doubt somewhere in her stories. "The Stone in the Field" is unrelenting and concludes without a scrap of nostalgia: "Mount Hebron is cut down for gravel, and the life buried here is one you have to think twice about regretting."[54] It is one thing for the striver (deserter, traitor) to mull over these critical thoughts. It is another for the uninitiated to sneer at the hard lives. Richard, the affluent Vancouverite in "Connections," jeopardizes his marriage by treating his wife's roots as "a low-level obscenity." "Richard always said the name of my native town as if it were a clot of something unpleasant, which he had to get out of his mouth in a hurry."[55]

Munro occasionally flays urban encroachment; she has excoriated the sprawl that consumes rural land and small towns in her two most overdrawn, black and white, short stories. In "The Shining Houses," the smart boys, real estate operators, dispossess a charming old lady, using the pretext of "betterment for the community."[56] Gordon, the transparently spoiled neurologist in "Prue" rattles about vacuously in a new house whose existence insults the efforts and values of old Ontario.

> His house is new, built on a hillside north of the city, where there used to be picturesque, unprofitable farms. Now there are one-of-a-kind, architect designed, very expensive houses on half-acre lots. Prue, describing Gordon's house, will say, "Do you know there are four bathrooms? So that if four people want to have baths at the same time there's no problem."[57]

As a small-town product, Munro resents people without a sense of history who have no understanding of the community they either insult as a backwater or invade with outside ambitions and wealth. Nevertheless, as a renegade she herself cannot condemn them with an insider's passion. Consequently, in the "The Progress of Love," the narrator initially resents the hippie commune that occupies her parents' farm in the mid- or late 1960s. The members shun the electrical service that her family "finally" installed. "What makes you think you can come here and mock my father and mother and their life and their poverty?"[58] But she reconsiders, possibly because of the circumstances of her own development — as a divorcee she has even dated a Catholic separated from his wife:

> I knew they weren't trying to mock or imitate my
> parent's life. They had displaced that life, hardly know-
> ing it existed. They had set up in its place these beliefs
> and customs of their own, which I hoped would fail
> them.[59]

The commune does collapse. The house sells for ten times its purchase price. Skylights and carriage lamps are among the improvements made by a young couple from Ottawa. "I've been told I'd never recognize it." We know it is not just the house that has been changed several times, but the rural ways that introduced this story:

> My father was so polite, even in the family. He took
> time to ask me how I was. Country manners. Even if
> somebody phones up to tell you your house is burning
> down, they ask first how you are.[60]

Elsewhere, too, Munro writes of the allegedly vanishing values both critically and appreciatively. The manners and conduct — cleanliness, courtesy, and abstinence — taught by Aunt Ena to her children in "Jesse and Meribeth" made them feel superior "in spite of, or perhaps because of, relative poverty." According to the narrator, "nobody has a good word nowadays for such narrowness and proud caution and thread-bare decency." The voice here is honest, for she continues by remarking on a very human dualism. She herself has circumvented the strict rules but generally "accept[s] that even a superiority based on such hard notions [is] better than no superiority at all."[61]

Munro offers plausible insights into the mentality of local people who have stayed. She records practical decisions to adhere to the basic values of the community, for example to insure against failing. She also recognizes cultural habits at work in the inertia of people's lives, habits that seem traceable to socio-economic and cultural sources. She lists the "hard-set traditions, proud poverty, and monotony of farm life" that carried over into the farm service communities.[62] In other words, the very material circumstances of life helped fashion a culture of moorings, but there is more — tradition. Del's father and brother in *Lives of Girls and Women* slide into a routine that brings regression. This pair is gripped by the apparent contentment with getting by. Did the failure of the fox farm trap them in a struggle to retain what was left? Described but not developed, these men have less revelatory significance than many other characters whom Munro marshals for depictions of the old Ontario values which nurtured roots.

Some of Munro's characters are more explicit about the practice of self-denial. "They like people turning down things." Del's cousin turns down a scholarship. "Why was this such an admirable thing to have done?"[63] There is, Munro plausibly suggests, a perverse pride in not being overtly prideful, in not being disrespectful of the community's ways. Family, community, and upbringing are understood to mean specific codes of self-denying but self-assured behaviour, absorbed at the family dinner table and in Sunday school. Pride sometimes meant outrageous insolence in order to maintain class distinctions, but its more likely and subtle expression in small-town Ontario included an egalitarian assault on haughtiness. One should not "snivel," "kowtow," or "high-hat." This very spirit implies a sense of superiority and concurrently supports the local consensus; it may be thought of as parochial and self-deceptive and even as loyalty.[64] Throughout her stories, Alice Munro implies that there is a bond between hard lives and pride.

Moving on, flaunting personality, or innovating within the community insulted local pride. Leaving was an act that rebuked the grinding effort of honest folk and snubbed the wisdom of one's forbears. Del's father treats her politely but remotely at the time of her grade thirteen examinations, and she wonders why. "He approved of me and he was in some way offended by me. Did he think my ambitiousness showed a want of pride?"[65] Frances in "Accident" spent four years at the conservatory, enough time to shed her small-town instincts, and actually to believe her affair with Ted could remain a secret. The possibility is raised that she always was at odds with the community outlook. Too brazen! She did not fit in. She has the "outsider's quick movements, preoccupied look, high-pitched, urgent voice, the outsider's innocent way of supposing herself unobserved." "Don't you think you're any genius," she has been told.[66] Are Del and Frances victims of a resentment that girls can pursue education almost legitimately or of the small-town preference for self-denial? There is no one answer, but Munro is preoccupied with the mentality behind self-denial.

The narrator's father in "The Stone in the Field" arrives at certain insights about his own resemblance to a stone anchored in the field. He goes one step further by suggesting that self-knowledge and an understanding that one is tied down do not guarantee a means of escape. Because he used a wheelbarrow to feed the horses instead of honouring the tradition of carrying pails, the narrator's father was beaten for laziness. "Any change of any kind was a bad thing. Efficiency was just laziness, to them." The daughter observes, "You ran away." "I didn't run far," he retorts. The father is perplexed by the lack of courage in the community — his own lack too. Their ancestors had the courage to emigrate, but somehow it "got burnt out of them."[67] It must be said that some decendants of Huron Tract settlers did move on; they migrated to western Canada. But Munro's obsession — a crucial contribution to understanding Ontario culture — is with the psychology of the persisters, not with that of the transients.

The father has identified the magnetism of static value systems and guessed at or reflected upon their roots. "Their religion did them in, and their upbringing." In his historical novel, *The Orangeman*, Donald Akenson contends that the patriotism and political culture of Ontario were coloured by Irish Protestantism.[68] Conceivably, Scottish and Irish Protestantism engendered even deeper mental outlooks, which conditioned daily conduct at home, at work, and among neighbours. Self-denial could be one of these outlooks. Munro's many references to religion, including canny details about church architecture and social hierarchy, bear witness to the imprint of Ontario Protestantism. How does she see this religious contribution to culture affecting people's lives? Older folk repress their impulses. The grandmother in "Winter Wind" may have wanted to run off with her old beau when they were both in their fifties. "Where could they have run to? Besides, they were Presbyterians. No one ever accused them of misbehaving."[69] Instead, the grandmother prefers an enduring self-denying love. Commitments are made for a lifetime and alternatives not mentioned. "We must never speak of this again."[70] It is conceivable that these attitudes, associated with a Presbyterian outlook, were what David the history student has in mind. "David says that everybody born in this country before the Second War was to all intents and purposes brought up in the nineteenth century, and that their thinking is archaic."[71]

Slightly more adventurous characters depart, but it is not at all clear that they spring entirely free of old values. Frances Makkavala journeys in several dimensions and the greatest possible distances from southern Ontario towns, short of living outside the province. She takes up with a "foreigner," a married man with a family, never again prays in the United Church, and moves to Ottawa. However, she retains a moral sense that prevents her from thinking too much about the accident that changed (she cannot even say "improved") her life. It was "too ugly to think about."[72] The community had instilled a sense of natural right that shapes her in spite of her will. Perhaps, like Munro, she is properly confused. Upbringing and the contradictory belief that "we are more than products of our upbringing"[73] struggle for ascendancy in Munro's central characters, although — and there is no occasion to dwell on it here — accidents or caprice have decisive functions in many stories. The influence of a religious element in upbringing can neither be extirpated nor starved out. "Purged from the rolls" may describe an official status for many Protestant Ontarians in the secularism of current times. Nevertheless, the moral precepts, scriptural literature, calendar, and ethnocentric Protestant sense of order remain part of the indelible upbringing that identifies Munro's generation.

Whereas Frances departs, Evangeline Steuer in "Jesse and Meribeth" returns and soon affronts community conventions. She buys the local paper for her husband to run and generally loses her function, getting things mixed up. "It was one thing to be a smoking, drinking, profane, and glamorous bachelor girl, and quite another thing to be a smoking, drinking, profane, and no longer glamorous expectant mother." The town can tolerate the doctor's affluent daughter only if she plays an accepted role or fits a stereotype, but she is too free-wheeling. Consequently Evangeline is an exemplar of wholly wrong values, those that mock self-denial. She illustrates "how money made you shameless, leisure made you useless, self-indulgence marked you out for some showy disaster."[74]

The introspection and turmoil caused by flights from the rural and small-town ethos obviously have psychological dimensions resembling if not representing the archetypal conflicts between inner urges and social pressures. These are conflicts that Freudians assign to the ego. Indeed, the restraining ethos of self-denial has the function of the Freudian superego, of the inhibitions that society and conscience impose on the desires of the id. But Munro's stories also include drives, and the cravings and wishes, even the fantasies, of her narrators should not be neglected as elements in a portrait of life in Ontario's small towns, regardless of how resistant these intangibles are to conventional historical inquiry. Adolescent urges, some powered as much by boredom and the will to excite envy as by sex, propel girls into encounters with worldly and threatening men; it cannot be readily confirmed that these "probable fictions" were commonplace. Neverthelesss, their presence in this body of fiction ought to provoke thought about sexuality and risk taking in Ontario society.

A fascination with men who exemplify exciting possibilities and outside experiences, men who are attractive because they are different, are considered in the title story from *Lives of Girls and Women*, "Wild Swans" in *Who Do You Think You Are?*, "The Turkey Season," and "Jesse and Meribeth." These sordid encounters may be meant to be didactic, but besides exposing dangers and circulating warnings they really do emphasize that irrational risk taking can counteract all that seems oppressive about small-town and rural life, especially to impressionable adolescents. The rural and small-town youths loitering around the theatre (today, the video shop and arcade), the cafe, and the poolroom or waving at passing cars, are trying to make something happen. Among the limited opportunities for amusement are the occasional organized events for a few males at the ball diamonds and arenas mentioned by Munro. Hampered by their size and codes of proper conduct, small towns have institutionalized monotony, challenging youths to fantasize, do the forbidden, and take risks — usually with cars, booze, and the opposite sex.

After taking their sexual education from a book that Del's friend Naomi discovered in a trunk, smothered with moth-balled blankets, Del and Naomi begin to tease the boyfriend of a boarder at Del's house. Art Chamberlain, the carnal radio announcer, takes advantage of the game, squeezing and jabbing Del, who places herself in hazardous and even provocative situations. Finally, he takes Del for an unromantic ride and a climactic walk in the country. An expression of raw common desire — "Evil would never be grand, with him" — his exploitative manner suggests guiltless possibilities.[75] Del yields to these and to the adventure of taking a chance. Later, because "curiosity could carry things quite a long way," she takes off her clothes for Jerry Storey.[76] Rose in *Who Do You Think You Are?* permits intimacies with a stranger on the train, even though she is offended by his repulsive advances. "Curiosity. More constant, more imperious, than any lust. A lust in itself, that will make you draw back and wait, wait too long, risk almost anything, just to see what will happen. *To see what will happen.*"[77] The narrator in "The Turkey Season" likewise confesses to an irrational urge. "I can still feel the pull of a man like that, of his promising and refusing. I would still like to know things. Never mind facts. Never mind theories."[78] Jessie of "Jesse and Meribeth" — a girl with an active imagination — invents a fantasy to make her best friend envious and it almost becomes self-fulfilling, leading to her voluntary entrapment in the summerhouse by the experienced Mr. Cryderman. In this tense episode, the desires and rationalizations of the would-be seducer are played off against the desires and self-restraint of Jessie. Her pride wins out, but she nearly waits too long "to see what would happen." Pride and curiosity contend often and with different outcomes in common lives.

In postwar Ontario, the urban features of the province's culture and society have been dynamic, pronounced, and much celebrated. Besides overwhelming the old rural Ontario, they have threatened to obscure its brief and distinctive history by emphasizing urban workers, city building, and multiculturalism. The time has nearly passed when anthropological field-work investigations of traditional Ontario rural and village values and outlooks would be feasible. The neglect is understandable and, set beside a vision of earnest academic inquiry staffed with teams of social scientists descending upon Jubilee, not to be entirely lamented. Moreover, it is unlikely that conventional historical writing could convey the emotional richness found in Alice Munro's Ontario lives. For those reasons her work is a cultural resource for Ontario. Readers enjoy the stories. Critics can praise their style. And all who have a regard for Ontario's past must celebrate the accomplishments of Alice Munro as a chronicler of deep feelings and changes. Del has supplanted Uncle Craig as the historian of Wawanish County.

NOTES

I wish to thank Laurel Braswell-Means for initiating my interest in Alice Munro's small towns, Joan Weaver for widening my understanding of Munro's people, and Violet Croydon for preparing the manuscript — with toleration and humour. This article is dedicated to the memory of Bob Fazackerley, who returned and worked for his part of rural Ontario.

1   Alice Munro, "Hard-Luck Stories," *The Moons of Jupiter* (Markham: Penguin, 1982), p. 184; *Who Do You Think You Are?* (New York: Signet, 1978), p. 87; *Lives of Girls and Women* (New York: Signet, 1974), pp. 24-27; "Walker Brothers Cowboy," *Dance of the Happy Shades; Stories by Alice Munro,* (Toronto: McGraw-Hill Ryerson, 1968), p. 3; "Something I've Been Meaning to Tell You," *Something I've Been Meaning to Tell You.* (New York: Signet, 1974), pp. 1-2.

2   "Labor Day Dinner," *The Moons of Jupiter*, p. 139.

3   *Lives of Girls and Women*, p. 210.

4   *The Moons of Jupiter*, p. 35.

5   J.R. (Tim) Struthers, "The Real Material: An Interview with Alice Munro," *Probable Fictions: Alice Munro's Narrative Acts* (Downsview: ECW Press, 1983), p. 27.

6   *Probable Fictions*, p. 33.

7   For the statistical information in Wingham see Canada, Dominion Bureau of Statistics, *Eighth Census of Canada, 1941*, Vol. 2, tables 10, 32, 38, 43, 58.

8   *Lives of Girls and Women*, p. 187.

9   *Lives of Girls and Women*, p. 184

10 For a map of the Wingham area, see Canada, Department of Energy, Mines and Resources, Surveys and Mapping Branch, Wingham 40 P/14 (1: 50,000). The physical changes in small-town Ontario cited here appear in "The Moon in the Orange Street Skating Rink," *The Progress of Love* (Toronto: McClelland and Stewart, 1986), pp. 133, 135, 159.

11 Concerning mental mapping, see Roger Downs and David Stea, *Maps in Minds: Reflections on Cognitive Mapping* (New York: Harper and Row, 1977). "The Progress of Love," *The Progress of Love*, p. 18.

12 *Lives of Girls and Women*, p. 59.

13 "The Moon in the Orange Street Skating Rink," *The Progress of Love*, p. 153.

14 *Lives of Girls and Women*, p. 57.

15 "A Queer Streak," *The Progress of Love*, p. 216.
16 "The Moon in the Orange Street Skating Rink," *The Progress of Love*, p. 140.
17 "The Turkey Season," *The Moon of Jupiter*, p. 60.
18 "A Queer Streak," *The Progress of Love*, p. 235.
19 See for example the references to the kitchen floor in *Who Do You Think You Are?*, pp. 14, 15, 17; *Lives of Girls and Women*, p. 191; "The Stone in the Field," *The Moons of Jupiter*, p. 26.
20 *Lives of Girls and Women*, p. 27-28.
21 *Lives of Girls and Women*, p. 60.
22 *Lives of Girls and Women*, p. 61.
23 *Lives of Girls and Women*, p. 7.
24 *Lives of Girls and Women*, p. 5.
25 *Who Do You Think You Are?*, pp. 69-70.
26 *Lives of Girls and Women*, p. 78.
27 *Lives of Girls and Women*, p. 79.
28 *Who Do You Think You Are?*, p. 200.
29 "Fits", *The Progress of Love*, p. 122.
30 "A Queer Streak," *The Progress of Love*, p. 215.
31 "A Queer Streak," *The Progress of Love*, p. 216.
32 "A Queer Streak," *The Progress of Love*, p. 230.
33 *Lives of Girls and Women*, p. 79.
34 *Lives of Girls and Women*, p. 79. Also see p. 180.
35 *Lives of Girls and Women*, pp. 181-83.
36 *Who Do You Think You Are?*, p. 24.
37 *Lives of Girls and Women*, p. 78.
38 "The Progress of Love," *The Progress of Love*, p. 19.
39 "Accident," *The Moons of Jupiter*, p. 93.
40 "The Progress of Love", *The Progress of Love*, p. 25.
41 Don Akenson, *The Orangeman: The Life and Times of Ogle Gowan* (Toronto: James Lorimer, 1986), p. 315.
42 *Lives of Girls and Women*, p. 81.
43 *Lives of Girls and Women*, p. 85.
44 *Lives of Girls and Women*, p. 177.
45 "The Progress of Love," *The Progress of Love*, p. 26.
46 *Lives of Girls and Women*, p. 68.
47 *Lives of Girls and Women*, p. 61.
48 "Chadderleys and Flemings," *The Moons of Jupiter*, p. 3.
49 *Lives of Girls and Women*, p. 18.
50 *Lives of Girls and Women*, p. 152.
51 *Lives of Girls and Women*, p. 183.
52 *Lives of Girls and Women*, p. 192.
53 *Lives of Girls and Women*, p. 57.
54 "The Stone in the Field," *The Moons of Jupiter*, p. 35.
55 "Chadderleys and Flemings," *The Moons of Jupiter*, p. 12.
56 "The Shining Houses," *Dance of the Happy Shades*, pp. 27-29.
57 "Prue", *The Moons of Jupiter*, p. 131.
58 "The Progress of Love", *The Progress of Love*, p. 24.
59 *Ibid.*
60 "The Progress of Love," *The Progress of Love*, p. 3. Country manners also are mentioned in *Lives of Girls and Women*, p. 7.
61 "Jesse and Meribeth," *The Progress of Love*, p. 168.
63 *Lives of Girls and Women*, p. 32.
64 Pride is a frequently mentioned quality in Alice Munro's stories. See for example, "Chadderleys and Flemings," *The Moons of Jupiter*, p. 9.

65 *Lives of Girls and Women*, p. 191.
66 "Accident," *The Moons of Jupiter*, pp. 80-81.
67 "The Stone in the Field", *The Moons of Jupiter*, p. 30.
68 Akenson, *The Orangeman*, p. 314.
69 "Winter Wind", *Something I've Been Meaning to Tell You*, p. 160.
70 *Ibid.*
71 "Labor Day Dinner," *The Moons of Jupiter*, p. 157.
72 "Accident," *The Moons of Jupiter*, p. 109.
73 "Labor Day Dinner," *The Moons of Jupiter*, p. 157.
74 "Jesse and Meribeth," *The Progress of Love*, p. 171.
75 *Lives of Girls and Women*, p. 139.
76 *Lives of Girls and Women*, p. 169.
77 *Who Do You Think You Are?* p. 63.
78 "The Turkey Season," *The Moons of Jupiter*, p. 74.

The Editors

Roger Hall is a member of the Department of History at the University of Western Ontario.

William Westfall is chair of the Department of History at Atkinson College, York University.

Laurel Sefton MacDowell teaches History at Erindale College, University of Toronto.

The Contributors

Elizabeth Arthur is Professor Emeritus of Canadian History at Lakehead University in Thunder Bay.

Paul Craven teaches at York University. He is the author of *"An Impartial Umpire": Industrial Relations and the Canadian State, 1900-11* and a number of articles on the history of Canadian labour law and the railway industry in the nineteenth-century.

Ben Forster teaches in the Department of History at the University of Western Ontario. He is author of *A Conjunction of Interests: Business, Politics, and Tariffs 1825-1879* as well as of a number of articles dealing with business and politics in late nineteenth-century Canada.

Gunter Gad is an Associate Professor in the Department of Geography, University of Toronto. His research interests embrace both the contemporary dynamics of office location in Metropolitan Toronto and the long-term transformation of the central business district.

Deryck Holdsworth is an Associate Professor in the Department of Geography, Pennsylvania State University, and also co-editor of Volume III of the *Historical Atlas of Canada*. He is broadly interested in the historical geography of the industrial city.

Richard A. Jarrell took his Ph.D. in the history and philosophy of science and technology at the University of Toronto. He is an Associate Professor of Science Studies at Atkinson College, York University.

Charles Johnston is Professor of History at McMaster University. He is author of *E.C. Drury: Agrarian Idealist*.

Gerald Killan is Professor of History at King's College, University of Western Ontario, and a former president of the Ontario Historical Society.

Douglas McCalla is Chairman of the History Department at Trent University. He is the author of *The Upper Canada Trade, 1834-1872* and the editor of *Perspectives on Canadian Economic History.*

James Naylor has recently completed a doctoral dissertation at York University on class conflict in the industrial cities of southern Ontario during and after the First World War.

Peter Oliver is a member of the Department of History at York University.

Paul Romney is author of *Mr Attorney: The Attorney General for Ontario in Court, Cabinet, and Legislature, 1791-1899* and several articles on nineteenth-century social, political, and legal history. He lives in Baltimore.

Abraham Rotstein is Professor of Economics at the University of Toronto and teaches Canadian economic history.

Carolyn Strange is a doctoral candidate in history at Rutgers University. She is currently a visiting junior fellow at the Centre of Criminology at the University of Toronto.

Gerald Tulchinsky is a member of the History Department at Queen's University. He is doing research on Canadian Jewish history.

George Warecki is a doctoral candidate at McMaster University, currently preparing a dissertation on wilderness preservation in Ontario.

John Weaver is Professor of History at McMaster University and editor of the *Urban History Review.* Having lived in St. Mary's, Hagersville, Muskoka Falls, Sharbot Lake, Madoc, and Ancaster, he claims familiarity with small-town Ontario.

Ian Wilson is Archivist of Ontario.

J. David Wood is Professor of Geography at Atkinson College, York University, and author of *Perspectives on Landscape and Settlement in Nineteenth Century Ontario.* He is continuing his research into nineteenth-century agricultural frontiers.